SANCTIFYING MISANDRY

Sanctifying Misandry

Goddess Ideology and the Fall of Man

KATHERINE K. YOUNG and
PAUL NATHANSON

McGill-Queen's University Press
Montreal & Kingston • London • Ithaca

© McGill-Queen's University Press 2010

ISBN 978-0-7735-3615-9

Legal deposit first quarter 2010
Bibliothèque nationale du Québec

Printed in Canada on acid-free paper that is 100% ancient forest
free (100% post-consumer recycled), processed chlorine free

This book has been published with the help of a grant from the
Canadian Federation for the Humanities and Social Sciences,
through the Aid to Scholarly Publications Programme, using funds
provided by the Social Sciences and Humanities Research Council of
Canada.

McGill-Queen's University Press acknowledges the support of the
Canada Council for the Arts for our publishing program. We also
acknowledge the financial support of the Government of Canada
through the Book Publishing Industry Development Program
(BPIDP) for our publishing activities.

Library and Archives Canada Cataloguing in Publication

Young, Katherine K., 1944–
    Sanctifying misandry : goddess ideology and the Fall of Man /
Katherine K. Young and Paul Nathanson.

Includes bibliographical references and index.
ISBN 978-0-7735-3615-9

    1. Goddess religion. 2. Fall of man. 3. Sin, Original. 4. Sex role
– Religious aspects. 5. Misandry. I. Nathanson, Paul, 1947–
II. Title.

BL473.5.Y66 2010   202'.114   C2009-904566-4

Typeset by Jay Tee Graphics Ltd. in 10.5/13 Sabon

Contents

APPENDIX

Acknowledgments

We want to thank the Canadian Federation for the Humanities for generously supporting the publication of this book. Thanks also to Monique David for reading and commenting on the manuscript, Maureen Garvie for editing it, and Jenna Preston for helping us in many other ways.

The Fall of Man

We have already written two volumes of a trilogy on misandry. The sexist counterpart of misogyny, misandry refers to the hatred of men in secular forms – cinematic stereotypes, journalistic excesses, legal manoeuvres, and so on. Still in the works is the third volume of that trilogy. Meanwhile, however, we have found it necessary to write this fourth and more specialized book on misandry in the specific context of religion. Before introducing this book, here is a brief introduction to our earlier work on misandry.

In the trilogy's first volume, *Spreading Misandry: The Teaching of Contempt for Men in Popular Culture*,[1] we showed how the entertainment, advertising, and even news industries have come to depict men. During the 1980s and 1990s, misandric stereotypes of men became pervasive in American popular culture. The male characters of popular movies and television shows, for instance, are usually either inadequate or evil – or both. (Exempted from ridicule or attack, sometimes, are characters who represent minority men or male feminists; they are, in effect, honorary women.) This was not the only gender pattern, but it was – and still is – a very common one. It is true that misogyny coexisted with misandry to some extent, but the two phenomena were different in one important way. Women monitored popular culture very carefully for signs of misogyny, which made it increasingly unlikely to surface in the first place. Hardly anyone watched for signs of misandry, which therefore remained "politically correct." Negative stereotypes of men (along with positive stereotypes of women), we concluded, are symptoms of a much deeper and more pervasive problem. And we identified the source of that problem as ideology in general and the ideological version of feminism[2] in particular.

We explained in our first volume that both forms of sexism, misogyny and misandry, refer to *culturally propagated worldviews*, not merely to transient personal emotions such as anger. Both forms of hatred have moral implications, therefore, not merely psychological ones. And both forms of hatred find expression not only in secular terms but also in religious terms. In the present volume we discuss the relation between secular and religious expressions of misandry. More specifically, we discuss the intimate relation between hostility toward "patriarchal" culture in general and hostility toward "patriarchal" religions in particular – that is, in the West, toward Christianity and Judaism.

Slightly more familiar than the word "misandry" is the word "ideology." We explained that word, too, in our first volume. For non-academics, the latter means nothing more than a system of ideas (probably because "idea" sounds like "ideology"). Any philosophy or worldview, therefore, could be an ideology. We use this word in a much more disciplined way, though not that of most academics. Modern political and philosophical movements on both the political left (deriving from the Enlightenment through Marxism) and the political right (deriving from Romanticism) share characteristic features that differentiate them from other political and philosophical movements. Characteristic features of ideology[3] in this sense include the following: essentialism (proclaiming that "we" are innately good); dualism (proclaiming that "they" are innately evil); hierarchy (drawing the conclusion that "we" are innately better than "they" are); collectivism (succumbing to "identity politics"); utopianism (creating an ideal society now instead of waiting for divine intervention); revolutionism (advocating radical change, not incremental reform); selective cynicism (attributing evil motives to "them"); consequentialism (arguing that even an evil means can justify a good end); and quasi-religiosity (adopting religious means such as rituals, special texts, special times, and special places for primarily secular ends). With this in mind, in that first volume, we identified ideological feminism as very problematic.

The trilogy's second volume, *Legalizing Misandry: From Public Shame to Systemic Discrimination against Men*,[4] discussed the ways in which society has used law to institutionalize misandry – often in the very name of "gender equality" (which is probably why feminists often refer instead to "women's equality," even though there can be no such thing as either that or "men's equality"). Before heading into the various legal minefields – divorce, custody, domestic violence, sexual harassment, and so on – we examined the journalistic aspect of popular culture. And we found that journalists, no less than filmmakers and advertising firms, have presented men as a truly sinister class – one that presumably deserves public denunciation on a routine basis and even legalizes hostility on an institutional basis. Whether public acceptance of their negative stereotypes came before or after the legalization of misandry is another matter. The two phenomena are so closely linked that it makes no difference for practical purposes.

Transcending Misandry: From Ideological Feminism to Intersexual Dialogue begins with a cross-cultural and historical – but not feminist – study of men. It concludes with a discussion of dialogue between men and women. Our notion of intersexual dialogue originated in that of interreligious dialogue, but it differs in at least two ways. First, it is more formal (and more disciplined) than the casual conversations that usually go on in church or synagogue basements. Second, it is less formal (and less bureaucratic) than the ecumenical projects of ecclesiastical institutions. We hope that other conflicting groups will find our method helpful.

Our premise in this new book is that the religious wing of ideological feminism has tried to rewrite the biblical story of redemption. It begins in the paradisal Garden of Eden, continuing with the sin of our primeval parents, exile from paradise, history as we know it but with the promise of redemption, and an eventual return to paradise. Christians refer to the part about sin as the "Fall of Man." And they understand the word "man" in its generic sense as a reference to all men and all women. Some feminists now, though, refer to "man" in its literal sense as a reference to *men*. In other words, the suffering that we have experienced throughout history is due to an "original sin" of our primeval *male* ancestors.

Who are these feminists, these religious counterparts of ideological feminists? We call them "goddess ideologues" (partly to distinguish them from those who advocate gender-inclusive forms of goddess religion). Rejecting the supposedly male god of Christianity or Judaism, they invoke a great goddess. She is now returning to save the world, they say, after being banished by the gods of men approximately ten thousand years ago.

Neopagan movements were flourishing during the 1980s and 1990s. Some tried to reform traditional religions, but others rebelled against them. Some were egalitarian, but others were not. Some welcomed both men and women, but others welcomed only women. Some celebrated both gods and goddesses, but others celebrated only a great goddess. Our goal here is to show that some expressions of the latter have tried not merely to spread, condone, and legalize misandry but to *sanctify* it – give it a metaphysical or even divine mandate – in connection with goddess religion.[5] The result has been goddess *ideology*,[6] a religious expression of ideological feminism.

Finally, a few words about us. Katherine Young is James McGill Professor in the Faculty of Religious Studies at McGill University. Paul Nathanson is a senior researcher there. We have worked together at McGill for many years on research projects. Young specializes in Eastern religions and gender; Nathanson specializes in Western religions, secularity, and gender. Underlying all of our collaborative work is an interest in several problems that afflict modern democracies: extreme individualism (which focuses exclusively on personal rights); extreme collectivism (which focuses exclusively on the group rights of ethnic, linguistic, religious, sexual, or other minorities); the relation of both to society as a whole; the rhetoric of rights and its relation to the culture of entitlement; the moral implications of political ideologies; the shift from political ideologies as personal worldviews of the few to political ideologies as civil religions of the state; and, ultimately, the possibility of "dialogue" between conflicting groups.

The difference between religious studies and theology will be obvious to many readers but not to all. We discuss only the observable features of religion. It could be that the existence of Christianity is due ultimately to divine will. Not being theologians, we refrain from speculation on that topic. Being academics, our job is to explain historical events and to discern historical patterns. In this case, doing so would mean discussing the various forms of Christianity as they emerged and developed in specific historical contexts – that is, in connection with social, economic, political, intellectual, artistic, and other cultural forces.

We use words accordingly. Like scholars in both religious studies and anthropology, we use the words that apply broadly to many religious traditions. We use "myth," for instance, to describe a very ancient and very widespread oral or literary genre. More specifically, we use it to describe one form (among several) of the narrative genre. From our point of view, myths are stories about the human condition. More specifically, they are stories about collective identity (which might involve collective origin, destiny, purpose, meaning, belonging, and so forth). Communities transmit these stories from one generation to another, often in the context of ritual. Most myths use symbolic language, because they are about profound truths, ordinary language being inadequate to express truths that emerge in connection with universal paradoxes or existential mysteries.

In both theological and common parlance, however, the word "myth" has a highly pejorative connotation. In this sense, a "myth" refers to a proposition. More specifically, it refers to one form of proposition: a false one. From this point of view, a myth is some primitive or childish explanation for a natural phenomenon, an explanation that modern science has superseded. Sometimes, in fact, the word takes on distinctly sinister connotations. Cultural commentators, for instance, often use "myth" as a euphemism for "lie" – that is, a false claim that advertisers or politicians foster in order to mislead the public.

Why is there such a gulf between the popular and scholarly usages of "myth"? Why does it refer to ignorance or deception in one case but not the other? Consider the etymology. The ancient Greeks used *mythos* when referring to stories of their gods and goddesses. The early Christians, however, believed that these myths were false. Not only did they have other stories about the divine-human encounter but they also had other words for them: first the Greek word *evangelion* (good news), later the Germanic word *godspel* (gospel), and so on. During the Enlightenment, philosophers and scientists went one step further. They believed that both the Greek myths *and* the Christian gospels were false. As a result, the word "myth" is now synonymous for many people with "illusion" or even "lie" – that is, the very opposite of truth.

Why, then, would scholars insist on using "myth" in something like its original sense? No one today believes that the Greek "myths" reveal ultimate or absolute truth in any metaphysical sense (although many people acknowledge their psychological insight). In fact, not everyone did so even during the later phases of ancient Greek civilization. Many people today, on the other hand, believe that the Christian "gospels" do indeed reveal ultimate or absolute truth in the metaphysical sense.

The word "myth" is more likely to be useful for our purpose in this book, at any rate, than prescriptive ones such as "scripture" (or very general ones such as "story"). Unlike theologians, scholars need words that describe but do not prescribe. By describing all stories that have a similar cultural function as "myths," in other words, they leave the theological evaluation of those stories to religious believers. Christians can acknowledge that the gospels are myths (as examples of a literary genre), for instance, but also believe that they are scriptural (as uniquely revealed repositories of ultimate truth); the two words are not mutually exclusive. In this book, we make no truth claims about Christian or Jewish theology. We make claims only about the ways in which goddess ideology uses Christian or Jewish theology.

The word "god" poses a similar problem. Religious people would prefer us to write "God," not "god." And we do, when the context makes it clear that we are referring to a name or the functional equivalent of a name – that is, what Christians or members of other religious communities call the object of their devotion. For generic references, however, we use the word without a capital letter. Otherwise, we would be adding piety to scholarship. Those two things do not mix.

SANCTIFYING MISANDRY

Pop Goes the Goddess

In *The Chalice and the Blade*,[1] Riane Eisler popularizes the notion of a primeval feminist utopia. In the beginning, she claims, was a golden age of women. Under the benevolent aegis of a great goddess, women lived with men in an egalitarian society. Eisler does not describe it as a matriarchy, which (as the functional equivalent of a patriarchy) would undermine her claim that this was an egalitarian society. Instead, she calls it a "gylanic" one. But because her word begins with "gy," part of the Greek word for woman, she clearly implies that women were more important than men. What she means is that this was a *gynocentric* society; it revolved around women. Nonetheless, she claims, men flourished just as women did: "It makes eminent sense that the earliest depiction of divine power in human form should have been female rather than male ... It further seems logical that women would not be seen as subservient in societies that conceptualized the powers governing the universe in female form – and that 'effeminate' qualities such as caring, compassion, and nonviolence would be highly valued in these societies. What does not make sense is to conclude that societies in which men did not dominate women were societies in which women dominated men."[2]

We see a fundamental contradiction here, because Eisler describes a world in which women really do dominate men. She never resolves this contradiction. In fact, she never acknowledges it. Her ultimate goal in any case is not to theorize or reminisce about a primeval paradise, one that men destroyed in the process of establishing their brutal patriarchal societies, but to announce glad tidings: the dawn in our time of a new golden age. She describes this age too as egalitarian. Once again, though, she makes it clear that the new order will be a "gylanic" one. It will rely primarily on the long-suppressed ways of women. Both women and men will flourish, to be sure, along with the earth itself. But men, as such, will have little to contribute except for their cooperation with women (and, by implication, repentance for their evil ways).

Writing almost twenty years later, Dan Brown refers explicitly to Eisler's book as one of those that inspired him to write *The Da Vinci Code*.[3] He is probably not someone who worries about controversy; the controversy that has surrounded his novel, in any case, certainly did not prevent it from becoming an immediate best-seller and eventually a Hollywood movie. Here is the plot.

Paris. After midnight. Someone has murdered Jacques Saunière, a curator at the Louvre. Because the murderer has left written evidence in some kind of code, the police call on Robert Langdon. In town on business, he is well known as a Harvard professor of "symbology" (presumably what academics call "semiotics" or "semeiology"). French "cryptologist" Sophie Neveu soon joins him at the crime scene. But Langdon is really a suspect, as it turns out, and Neveu is the victim's granddaughter. Sensing police corruption, the two escape together and try to solve the mystery themselves. This leads them to one symbolic clue after another, some of them based on the secret writings and esoteric iconography of Leonardo da Vinci. But it becomes clear that much more is involved than murder. Even Langdon and Neveu, therefore, must consult another expert.

Leigh Teabing is a Briton who lives just outside of Paris. As he explains in several lectures disguised as dialogue, Saunière belonged to the Priory of Sion, a secret society that originated in 1099 and has counted luminaries such as Leonardo, Victor Hugo, and Isaac Newton among its grand masters. Closely associated with it were the Knights Templar, moreover, until the church accused them of heinous crimes and murderously suppressed them. The Priory's mandate is both to preserve an underground religion, based on the teachings of Jesus but long persecuted by Christians (not only for denying Jesus's divinity but also for honouring women and glorifying sex) and to preserve the bloodline of France's Merovingian dynasty (which began when Jesus and Mary Magdalene married and fled to France with their daughter).

Members of this Priory must therefore guard two secret treasures. One is the Holy Grail. This is not merely the chalice that Jesus used at the Last Supper, as folklore would have it. It is the body of Magdalene: carrier of the *sangréal*, *sang réal*, or royal blood of Jesus. The other secret treasure is a stash of documents proving Magdalene's identity as well as the church's corruption of scripture in order to hide the pagan origin of Christianity as a fertility cult and thus preserve its own power. The Priory's most specific enemies are sinister members of another secret organization. The church created this one: Opus Dei. When not busy mortifying their own flesh or molesting children, these pious ascetics are busy murdering those, such as Saunière, who might reveal the truth.

In other words, all of Christian history since the days of Constantine has been a titanic conspiracy to cover up the true meaning of the true church – which is to say, the one that Jesus and Magdalene founded, the one that only suppressed texts such as the non-canonical gospels[4] found at Nag Hammadi describe faithfully. The church did so in order to hide evidence that Jesus and his early followers had revived an ancient goddess religion that the patriarchal Isrealites had displaced. In the end, readers learn that Neveu is not only a rightful heir to the throne of France (and presumably that of Judaea, or Israel, as well) but also a blood descendant of Jesus and Mary!

Both attempts to popularize goddess theory – those of Eisler and Brown – have been astonishingly successful. Ashley Montagu hailed *Chalice* with quaint hyperbole as "the most important book since Darwin's *The Origin of Species*" (and with good reason, as we will show, considering the reputation that he earned for writing *The Natural Superiority of Women*).[5] Isabel Allende welcomed it as "one of those magnificent key books that can transform us." No wonder it has been reprinted more than thirty times and been translated into more than twenty languages. A quick search on Google produces a list of 31,200 references for *Chalice* and 64,800 for Eisler herself. Like *The Da Vinci Code*, in short, *Chalice* is an eminently mainstream work. Consequently, it says as much about the people who celebrate it – and about our society – as it does about the person who wrote it.

As for *Code*, Ron Howard, one of Hollywood's most successful mainstream directors, wasted no time in adapting it for the big screen. It became a "major motion picture" starring Tom Hanks,[6] although it was not as popular as the novel.

If Brown had written a similar book about some ancient Jewish conspiracy to horde a vast fortune and control the world (and some authors have indeed written books of that kind, though seldom disguised as novels),[7] protesters would have called it anti-Semitic, picketers would have rallied in front of bookstores selling it, and lawyers would have prosecuted the author under "hate laws." (Actually, *Code* does have a vaguely anti-Semitic subtext, which we will discuss in a moment.) The fact is that many Americans (and a much higher number in more secular countries) believe that Christians – especially conservative Catholics and evangelical Protestants – are legitimate targets of prejudice, presumably, partly because those Christians have promoted their own forms of prejudice. As if two wrongs make a right.

What provoked controversy over *Code* was its promotion of hostility toward religion, especially Roman Catholicism. The Catholic Church has long been attacked, especially by Protestants, as the powerful and sinister institution par excellence. Something else about *Code* did not provoke much controversy, however, because few people noticed it. The symbolic status of the Catholic Church has shifted recently. The focus has shifted from its alleged preoccupation with power for its own sake to its alleged conspiracy against women. More specifically, say its adversaries, the Catholic Church has tried to erase evidence that women were once powerful among the earliest Christians. Some feminists, in fact, claim that the church has concealed evidence of an ancient gender war.[8]

Catholic critics have focused heavily on Brown's portrayal of Mary Magdalene as the wife of Jesus and mother of his children. We will return to her in chapter 5. Of primary interest for the time being is Brown's more general portrayal of the conflict over gender. And very few of the angry Catholic critics, if any at all, have recognized the importance of that topic[9] except as a minor aspect of the attack on their religion. We suggest, though, that the attack on religion is merely one aspect of the attack on "patriarchy."

Code's vast popularity at a particular moment – in 2003, the world was still awash with the residue of millennial fever – should surprise no one. But nothing about it was actually new, certainly not the conspiracy theory of history, for instance, or the ideological mentality that underlies every conspiracy theory of history and this one in particular,[10] or the ways in which both can function within religion. Moreover, these phenomena show no sign of disappearing soon. To study them is therefore to study a truly significant though profoundly disturbing phenomenon that emerged in the late twentieth century.

Brown relies on two main types of source. One type includes various conspiracy theories of the nineteenth and twentieth centuries in Europe. These rely, in turn, on a heady combo of nationalism, reworked folklore, and pseudo-science. The other type includes various academic and popular attempts during the past thirty years to rewrite world history as a titanic conspiracy of men against women. These rely ostensibly on archaeology and archetypal psychology but in fact on a mélange of neo-Romanticism, religion, and ideological feminism.

From biblical or even pre-biblical religion, Brown takes the notion of a primeval paradise, or lost golden age. But he sees it from the perspective of ideological feminism. In the beginning, as it were, men and women lived together in harmony not only with each other but also with the natural order by worshipping the "sacred feminine" (known as a great goddess). They valued peace, equality, and pleasure – especially sexual pleasure. But everything changed when men rebelled for some unexplained reason (which implies that it is something innate in men) against this paradisal order. According to Brown, this happened much later – in the fourth century, when Constantine made Christianity the Roman Empire's official religion – than it did according to most goddess ideologues. Under Constantine, he says, Christianity was transformed for political reasons from a life-affirming and neopagan fertility cult into a death-oriented and ascetic patriarchal religion. The church drove followers of both the old pagan religion and early Christianity underground and persecuted those who could not hide. Men reigned supreme, in other words, over a world of evil and suffering.

But some people preserved the memory of paradise. According to some modern goddess devotees, these people were female practitioners of the "old religion" (that of a great goddess), whom the church persecuted as witches. According to Brown and his other sources, these people were and are members of the Priory. For hundreds of years they have hidden their secret lore but also propagated it clandestinely through symbols hidden in the songs of troubadours, paintings by Leonardo and other famous artists, operas by Wagner, and even movies by Disney. The story ends at the "end of days," of course, once more in paradise.

In some modern forms of goddess religion, paradise means a utopia for women under the aegis once more of their great goddess. Sophie Neveu's first name, by the way, refers to *sophia*, Greek for "wisdom." Some Christian feminists in our time use that word – often as a name – for either the supposedly female Holy Spirit or a supposedly female aspect of God. (We discuss what we call Sophianity in chapter 5.) Brown, however, uses that word in the context of a restored Merovingian monarchy!

Although Brown's book is a work of fiction, he includes a preliminary page called "Fact" (which he has amplified in an interview).[11] He singles out two "facts" in particular. First, he says, the Priory of Sion was founded in 1099 and "discovered" in 1975 by archivists at the Bibliothèque Nationale in Paris. Second, Opus Dei was founded by the Roman Catholic Church and has become notorious due to "reports of brainwashing, coercion, and a dangerous practice known as 'corporal mortification.'"[12]

Brown implies, although he does not actually say, that his portrayals of these organizations and their goals (as distinct from the characters representing them, which he has invented for narrative purposes) are factual. Opus Dei is indeed a real organization. Founded in 1928, it describes its goal as fostering intense spirituality among lay people. The "Priory" too is – or was – a real organization. It was founded in 1956, not 1099, by four Frenchmen with nationalistic goals. One of them, Pierre Plantard, spent six months in jail for fraud and embezzlement.[13] Worse, he indulged in both anti-Semitic and anti-clerical ranting, both of which were common (though not always combined in one person) at that time.[14]

Of most importance here, for reasons that we will make clear, is Brown's belief that Christianity as we know it, especially Catholicism, requires the faithful to think of Jesus as a divine figure and *not* an earthly one. Ecclesiastical authorities, he opines, "needed to convince the world that the mortal prophet Jesus was a divine being. Therefore, any gospels that described earthly aspects of Jesus's life had to be omitted from the Bible."[15] Actually, there was a struggle over that topic. But Brown, like his sources, has failed to notice the outcome, which calls his own theory into question.

In the second century, Marcion wanted to omit those earthly aspects. He saw the Old Testament god as nothing more than a primitive and tribal demiurge, creator of an evil material world that trapped the spirit. Given this dualistic premise that he absorbed from gnosticism, the prevalent philosophy of his time, it is no wonder that Marcion wanted to discard the Old Testament as scripture. By eliminating the material dimension of Christ – his physical ancestry, cultural identity, and historical context – the church could have turned him into an entirely immaterial and therefore otherworldly saviour.

But, as we say, the church rejected this point of view. It disagreed with Marcion, charged him with heresy, and retained the Old Testament. That was partly because the Old Testament contained "prophecies" or "prefigurations" that the church could use to support New Testament claims about Jesus. But it was also because the church rejected the whole idea of an entirely otherwordly Jesus. On the contrary, it insisted on an *incarnational* theology that linked (especially through sacraments) the material and the immaterial, the physical and the spiritual, the immanent and the transcendent (links that no one, to our knowledge, has made on websites devoted to critiques of *Code*). The whole point was that a divine Christ had entered the material world, taken human form as Jesus of Nazareth, and then sacrificed his own mortal existence in order to save others from sin.

How could Christ be both human and divine, both mortal and immortal, both material and immaterial? This paradox lies at the very heart of Christian faith. It is a paradox that every Christian church (except for the Unitarian one) has always maintained as doctrine and even enshrined in creeds. It is a paradox that makes possible the eucharist, in fact, which Christians claim to experience as the sacred (a spiritual or immaterial reality) through the profane (food and drink). It is a paradox, moreover, that most Christian churches (except for some Protestant ones and, briefly, Orthodox ones) have celebrated in countless paintings, sculptures, and other works of representational art – which is to say, expressions that place a high value on the body and its senses as vehicles that convey meaning.

Even though some Christian churches encourage believers to practice various forms of asceticism, moreover, not one encourages them to do so by denying the physical life and suffering of Jesus. In any case, the canonical gospels make no attempt whatsoever to erase the earthly Jesus. He was born to a woman (in a stable, according to some witnesses). He attended weddings and drank wine with his friends. He argued about sacred law with his colleagues. And, most significantly, he died on a cross. If that was not an earthly life, what would be? Incarnational theology – this includes not only the birth of Jesus (narrowly, the incarnation) but also his life, death, and physical resurrection – is not a minor adjustment in Christianity; it has always been a defining feature and *sine qua non* of Christianity. To the extent that feminist ideologues in general and goddess ideologues in particular attack Christianity for ignoring the material world – its fragility, beauty, and sensuality – they are mistaken.

Like his ideological allies, Brown would have us assume that pre-Christian pagan religions were superior to Christianity: not only more "natural" and more "feminine but also more peaceful, more harmonious, and more egalitarian. But as we argue in chapter 1, most early states, which included goddesses in their pantheons, were anything but peaceful, harmonious, and egalitarian. They produced not only agriculture, after all, but also class hierarchies. Some of these societies practised human sacrifice, moreover, and many practised slavery. But wait: what about even earlier societies, Paleolithic ones? We know almost nothing about those. Scholars generally assume that they were peaceful, because we lack incontrovertible evidence of military activities. Small bands wandering around in search of food did have lots of space to move away from rival groups instead of fighting with them. Moreover, they left behind no stone fortifications. But they did leave behind stone arrowheads, which could have been used for both hunting and warfare. And if they built fortifications of wood instead of stone, these would have rotted and disappeared long ago without leaving a trace.

Brown's endorsement of goddess religion in its ideological form (and feminism in its ideological form) could not be more obvious in the way that he describes the male origin of sin: "The days of the goddess were over," he writes. "The pendulum had swung. Mother Earth had become a *man's* world, and the gods of destruction and war were taking their toll. The male ego had spent two millennia running unchecked by its female counterpart. The Priory of Sion believed that it was this obliteration of the sacred feminine in modern life that had caused what the Hopi Amerindians called *koyanis-quatsi* – 'life out of balance' – an unstable situation marked by testosterone-fueled wars, a plethora of misogynistic societies, and a growing disrespect for Mother Earth."

Moreover, Brown's endorsement of goddess religion in its ideological form (and therefore of feminism in its ideological form) is equally obvious in the way that he describes the female origin of salvation. Referring to a great goddess, he writes, "[H]er story is being told in art, music, and books. More so every day. The pendulum is swinging [again]. We are starting to sense the dangers of our history ... and of our destructive paths. We are beginning to sense the need to restore the sacred feminine."[16]

We have already referred to an anti-Semitic subtext in Brown's novel. This is not too surprising. One Priory founder, as we have already noted, was explicitly anti-Semitic. And some feminist ideologues are implicitly anti-Semitic.[17] This deserves a few words here. Brown would have readers accept the premise that patriarchy began with Constantine – that is, more than three hundred years after Jesus. This allows the novelist to escape the charge of explicit anti-Semitism. But anti-Judaism, at least, is implicit in his claims about Jesus. If Jesus was the "first feminist,"[18] after all, then the Jews who have rejected him – which is to say, most Jews of his time and all Jews ever since – have rejected his "feminism" as well. This means that Judaism, unlike early Christianity and the Christian underground (represented in this book by the Priory), both was and is mired in spiritual bankruptcy and patriarchal evil.

Actually, there is some truth to the idea that Jews began the process of "repressing the sacred feminine." Everything that scholars know about the ancient Israelites indicates that this process began among them centuries before Jesus. Although there was a general shift to masculine symbols throughout the ancient Near East, the change in ancient Israel probably had as much to do with its creation of a distinct religious and national identity based on monotheism – that is, with separating from the identities of their polytheistic ancestors and neighbours – as it did with attitudes toward women. But this process was exacerbated in another context: increasing suspicion of the material world, including the body and sex – what St Paul called "flesh" (*sarx*) as opposed to "spirit" (*pneuma*) – which originated in the dualistic world of Persia and became prevalent throughout the Hellenistic world. And this dualism probably had more to do with the failure of those polytheistic cultures to provide satisfying answers to suffering than with any perverse hostility toward the body and sex (let alone toward women).

To accept Brown's version of history, we must first believe that men either produced or corrupted almost all textual evidence of Jesus (and, by implication, of ancient Israel) in order to promote a conspiracy against women. Brown believes that the Christian gospels are inherently untrustworthy (except, of course, for stories that might support the claim that Jesus, unlike other Jews, was a proto-feminist) and the other gospels – such as the gnostic ones that Brown cites and Elaine Pagels[19] has analyzed in great detail – were inherently trustworthy.

But Christians can defend their own scriptural canon; our task here is to point out an inherent contradiction in attacks on the canonical gospels. The non-canonical gospels, being the products of gnosticism or gnostic forms of Christianity, foster the very dualism – mind versus body, spirit versus flesh, asceticism versus sensuality – that would have been far *more* hostile to both sexual activity and women than anything that the church preserved. As Richard Abanes points out, the Gospel of Phillip (which Brown mentions) says that sexual relations, even within marriage, defile women. Why? Because all matter and everything to do with it, including the body and its sexual proclivities, were inherently evil according to the gnostic worldview. But feminists generally acknowledge that the canonical gospels represented a step forward for women from their allegedly degraded status in Judaism, even though later Christianity represented a step backward. Christian feminists point out that the canonical Jesus included women among his followers, for instance, and even that they present a woman – Magdalene – as first to see the risen Jesus.[20]

At one point, Brown informs readers that "the Church burned at the stake an astounding *five million* women."[21] That figure is indeed astounding. In fact, it is almost certainly false. But why stop at five million? Some feminist ideologues claim the church burned or hanged nine million women as witches (a topic that we discuss in chapter 2). The fact is that we do not know how many people were burned or hanged as witches. We do know that, for several hundred years, the church convicted both men and women of witchcraft. And we do know that this situation changed dramatically after the Black Death, when they began to convict mainly women. Even then the church did not incite crazed and screaming mobs of vigilantes to butcher women (and some men). It tried them in courts (a courtesy, as it were, that it did not extend at the same time to *communities* of heretics such as the Cathars or of infidels such as the Jews) after neighbours (often women) had accused them.[22] We have many court records of those witch trials, not all of which resulted in conviction, but many other records could have been lost. Over the three hundred years of witch-hunting at its height, say non-ideological historians, between thirty thousand and a hundred thousand people were killed as witches all over Europe, in both Catholic and Protestant countries.

Given the title of his book, it is hardly surprising that Brown makes a considerable effort to show that Leonardo – no one would ever have called him "Da Vinci" – was a grand master of the Priory and that we should interpret his work in terms of ideological feminism. At one point, for instance, Robert presents Sophie with evidence from Leonardo's *Last Supper*. In this painting, no chalice – that is, no cup – appears. Clearly, says Robert, this indicates that Leonardo wanted viewers to see a *symbol* of the chalice. And that symbol, he suggests, is one of the apostles. Why would an apostle symbolize the chalice? Because he is really a woman: Magdalene, who supposedly carried the blood of Jesus in her womb. How does he know that the apostle in question, John, is really a woman? Because he is slender and beardless. In short, he does not look like a grown man. But as Bruce Boucher and many others have pointed out, John was traditionally painted that way, not as a woman but as a boy: "St. John was invariably represented as a beautiful young man whose special affinity with Jews was expressed by his being seated at Jesus' right."[23]

Finally, it is worth noting that Brown explicitly (but possibly without understanding) endorses what academics call postmodernism. In one passage, someone says that "history is always written by the winners. When two cultures clash, the loser is obliterated, and the winner writes the history books – books which glorify their own cause and disparage the conquered foe. As Napoleon once said, 'What is history but a fable agreed upon? ... By its very nature, history is always a one-sided account."[24] Postmodernist historical relativism sounds very ironic in a book that glorifies those who believe that their own version of history is absolute truth. It sounds very disturbing, moreover, in view of the fact that Nazi war criminals used the same argument to defend themselves at Nuremberg. To be fair, the character who speaks these lines, Teabing, turns out to be a villain. But his cause, saving the world from patriarchal Christianity, remains glorious at the end of the novel. Our point here (and elsewhere),[25] though, is that Brown promotes this relativistic approach to history in precisely the way that feminist (and other) ideologues do: as a disingenuous and cynical method of clearing the way (deconstructing points of view that they dislike) so that they can move in with their own ideologies (which reject relativism and rely on their own truth claims).

What is going on? As we have already suggested, the massive and enduring popularity of both *Chalice* and *Code*[26] indicates a world-view that is not merely profoundly gynocentric but also profoundly misandric. In addition, as we have already suggested, the ideological version of goddess religion, goddess ideology, is directly related to ideological feminism.

In the following chapters, we discuss the recent rise of goddess ideology.[27] It uses metaphysical language, either within or beyond traditional religious communities, to promote femaleness and its innate superiority to maleness – which is to say, ideological feminism (as distinct from egalitarian feminism). This book is about the ways in which ideological feminists sanctify misandry (the sexist counterpart of misogyny).

Of interest to us in this context are not only the theories of goddess ideology that have emerged in academic circles but also the goddess "texts" that have emerged in popular culture – mainly in novels, movies, television shows, and "documentaries." We are by no means the first to take popular culture seriously within an academic context. Feminists of all schools have been doing precisely the same thing for at least thirty years. So have semioticians of various schools. Irrelevant in this context are aesthetic appraisals of popular culture; equally irrelevant are the conscious – that is, commercial – motives of those who produce and market these artifacts. Very relevant, on the other hand, are their semiotic qualities: what these artifacts can tell us about the unstated assumptions of the culture that produces them and about the subconscious hopes and fears of the people who consume them. Just as feminists found that portrayals of women in movies or sitcoms said something about common perceptions of women and could have damaging effects on real girls and women, we have found that negative portrayals of men say something about common perceptions of men and can have damaging effects on real boys and men.

Our point here is not to show that goddess symbolism prevails in popular culture but that it *occurs* in popular culture. And what *occurs* in popular culture, by definition, *is* popular – that is, widespread. Those who produce popular culture for profit, in other words, deliberately avoid themes that are likely to baffle consumers such as viewers or readers and thus fail to generate revenue. Instead, they select ones that are likely to confirm whatever passes for conventional wisdom. In this case, we suggest, the presence of goddess ideology in popular culture testifies to the status of ideological feminism as conventional wisdom.

This book provides several case studies, along with *Code* and *Chalice*, to illustrate our thesis about goddess ideology and its misandric fallout. The structural focus of three chapters in our book, moreover, is a set of "documentary" films: *The Goddess Remembered*; *The Burning Times*, and *Behind the Veil*. Each presents a highly popularized, tendentious, and distorted version of history, not a scholarly one.

But novels, movies, and television series are not the only venues of popular culture. Goddess ideology can attract considerable interest among those who gravitate toward New Age spirituality in one or more of its many versions: psychotherapeutic, medical, environmentalist, feminist, and so on. An obvious movement of this kind relies on the "Gaia hypothesis."[28] This amorphous and fluid movement supports a variety of "alternative" approaches to religion, including neopaganism. Within that context, goddess ideology overlaps with goddess religion – that is, Wicca, a modern goddess religion that claims to be the fastest-growing religion. Although some forms of Wicca rely on both gods and goddesses, "Dianic" Wicca relies exclusively on a great goddess and therefore is gynocentric at best and ideological at worst.

Even within mainstream religions, however, masculine imagery remains problematic. Some feminist Christians and Jews continue, therefore, to demand not only the repudiation of "sexist" language (such as the generic use of "he" in prayers) but also the addition of feminine symbolism (such as references to the maternal aspects of God). As we will show, they sometimes end up trying to introduce various aspects of goddess religion as supplements to Christianity and Judaism. One example is what we call Sophianity, an attempt to meld goddess worship and mainstream Protestantism.

Finally, both goddess religion and goddess ideology are *de rigueur* among those who study women and religion. We discuss the latter in connection with Mary Daly. Whatever her current status as a "role model" for young women or her current influence on

Christian churches, Daly remains an icon for ideological feminists as the founding mother of feminist religious theory. No historical survey course on feminism can ignore her and her colleagues.

These case studies clearly presuppose widespread public interest not only in goddess religion but also in goddess ideology (and therefore in ideological feminism as well). Our research builds on that of Cynthia Eller, who has already written an exhaustive discussion of goddess movements during the 1990s[29] (without, however, focusing heavily on their specifically misandric fallout).

Our book is about the recent past, not the present or future. We discuss goddess ideology during the 1980s and 1990s in connection with the rise of ideological feminism – that is, as the religious (or at least ostensibly religious) wing of ideological feminism. Goddess ideology is a kind of frontierland – more precisely, a no man's land – between ideological feminism and mainstream religion. With that in mind, we discuss the origins of some ideas that became fundamental to both goddess ideology and ideological feminism. Even though the baby boomers produced both movements, the next generation has appropriated much of the worldview that informs them, consciously or subconsciously, as conventional wisdom. Not being fortune tellers, we cannot predict the future of goddess ideology (or of ideological feminism, for that matter). Since the late 1990s, some traditional religious communities have cracked down on both goddess religion and goddess ideology (though not necessarily on ideological feminism itself, which opposes tradition just as fiercely but less directly). As we say, though, this book is primarily about ideas that arose during the 1980s and 1990s. Those twenty years marked an expansive turning point in the history of feminism, including the separation of ideological feminism, let alone goddess ideology, from egalitarian feminism.

PART ONE

From Goddesses to Witches (and Back): Rewriting the Bible

INTRODUCTION

How did things come to be as they are? Why do the innocent suffer? Why do the evil prosper? Who or what is responsible for this state of affairs? And where will it all end? These questions about the human condition, about ultimate origin and destiny, are fundamental and universal. All societies, therefore, must be able to provide satisfying answers. These answers are what anthropologists classify as myths. Of interest here are the myths and secular myths that feminists have created to explain the condition of women in what they classify as patriarchal societies. Of particular interest are the myths of those feminists whom we classify as goddess ideologues, who are trying not only to re-establish an ancient goddess religion but also, in doing so, to establish the conspiracy theory of history. Like all myths, theirs purport to reveal the hidden cause of everything that is wrong with the world. And our hypothesis, which directly or indirectly informs every chapter of this book, is that the myth of goddess ideology follows closely the mythic paradigm of biblical religion. The latter has become deeply embedded by now in patterns of thought common to both religious and secular people in our society. Before discussing the myth of goddess ideology in chapters 1 through 3, we must pause for a very brief discussion of its matrix in Western thought.

The most basic biblical paradigm of all is a drama in three acts; some of our most influential stories to this day rely on it.[1] Act 1 begins in paradise, the Garden of Eden as described in Genesis. Adam and Eve live in a golden age, knowing nothing except peace and harmony. This happy state of affairs could go on forever, but something goes wrong. In Act 2, our primeval ancestors disobey God by eating forbidden fruit. After this lapse from innocence and consequent fall from divine grace – that is, after they have succumbed to what most Christians call Original Sin – God expels them from the bliss of eternity in paradise. In other words, they enter the chaos of history as we have known it ever since in everyday life. This is the realm of suffering, confusion, conflict, and injustice. Worse, this lamentable state culminates with a catastrophe of cosmic proportions as described in Revelation – for Christians, the Bible's concluding book. And yet the story does not end in catastrophe. In Act 3, God intervenes to inaugurate a new golden age in a new or restored paradise. The faithful remnant, having learned from the experience of history, returns to a state of eternal bliss – what Jews call the Messianic Era and Christians the Kingdom of God.

According to the biblical version, all three of the earthly creatures involved – the man, the woman, and the serpent – are guilty. And God punishes all three. Even within the biblical tradition, though, people have interpreted this drama in several ways. Post-biblical commentaries have often ignored its complexity. According to one of these later traditions, sin originated with Eve for being the first to eat the forbidden fruit and, by implication, extended to her female descendants. This version emerged in the inter-testamental period (from the fourth century BC to the second century AD),[2] a time of increasing polarization (due to the increasing influence of a dualistic worldview that originated in Persia and came to prevail in the Hellenistic world of both Jews and Christians): mind versus body, spirit versus flesh, immateriality versus materiality, otherworldly preoccupations versus worldly ones, perfection versus corruption, asceticism versus hedonism, maleness versus femaleness. In their efforts to cope with external forces beyond their control, men projected their stress and fear onto women and began to look on them with mounting suspicion. One result was sexual segregation, confining women to the private realm. The mentality that generated this aberration from the biblical worldview found its way into apocryphal works of non-canonical or semi-canonical status such as Ecclesiasticus. Unfortunately, the same attitude found its way also into canonical works attributed to St Paul, such as the first letter to Timothy.

According to the most recent version of this archetypal human drama, the myth of goddess ideology and its secular equivalents, our primeval ancestors live peacefully and harmoniously in paradise under the benign aegis of a great goddess. But something goes wrong. Men secretly conspire to take control. Rebelling against the primeval order, they set up their gods (and some goddesses) in place of the great goddess and create patriarchal societies – which is to say, everything that is wrong with the world to this day. After accomplishing their goal, moreover, men hide their collective guilt and project it onto women. This is the conspiracy theory of history. Like so many Jews and Christians over the centuries, however, goddess ideologues and their secular counterparts can already see the dawn of a new golden age – this one, of course, for women. Men per se need not apply (unless, in the view of some feminists, they convert to feminism).

I

Paradise Lost:
A Golden Age for Women

The symbolism of paradise fulfills a primordial and fundamental human need to imagine how things ought to be in relation to how they are. For this reason, it has inspired the collective imagination of our own society, among many others, for millennia. As the archetypal paradise in the Western imagination, Eden has always been a metaphor that describes the ideal world. Two paradoxical features of this biblical way of thinking about paradise are of particular importance here.

First, Eden exists paradoxically in a time beyond time. It provides a kind of prologue to scripture and therefore to the sacred history that it records. As the ultimate goal not only of Israel and the church but also of individual Jews and Christians, moreover, Eden provides a kind of epilogue to scripture and sacred history. For orthodox Jews, returning to Eden after death is the soul's ultimate destiny, and something similar is true for Christians. Jews and Christians believe not only in the immortality of every individual soul, though, but also in the eschatological redemption of God's holy community. Whether on the individual level or the collective, paradise means a return in some sense to the paradise from which God banished our primeval ancestors at the dawn of time. Westerners use either rural or urban imagery to represent paradise, but the latter merely expands on the former. Standing in the heart of the Heavenly City, after all, is the Edenic Tree of Life.[1] The point is that both the Garden and the Heavenly City exist in eternity, not in time; we cannot find them within the present world order as described by historians. We can, however, experience brief glimpses of them in sacred time and sacred space. On Shabbat, for instance, Orthodox

Jews abolish time and enter eternity. They experience not only the primeval paradise but also the eschatological one, not only nostalgia for a lost world but also a foretaste of the world to come.

A second paradox involves the problem that underlies all of history. As Jews and Christians have told the story, evil originated within Eden. From this we can conclude either that Eden was not all that it was cracked up to be or that Adam and Eve were unable to understand what made it so special. Religious interpreters of the story have agreed in assuming the latter, but they have not always agreed on precisely why their primeval ancestors failed to understand what it meant to live in paradise.

In this chapter, then, we will discuss Act 1 of this drama in connection with (1) three popular documentaries about an alleged golden age in the remote past, (2) the possibility that our remote ancestors worshipped a goddess of the kind that these films describe, (3) the possibility the golden age was one for women, and (4) the possibility that it was a golden age for anyone.

In *The Goddess Remembered*,[2] an NFB documentary directed by Donna Read, viewers meet a group of goddess devotees, including some who have become famous as her advocates. The group's discussion about the revival of goddess worship, however, is part of a larger one. Clearly intended to edify and inspire as well as inform, the film amounts to a kind of cinematic pilgrimage from modern times to the remote past and back again. Most religious traditions identify pilgrimages closely with myths. And so it is in this case.

Almost immediately, it becomes clear that the story is a creation myth, not merely a history lesson. Characteristically, it begins long, long ago – *in illo tempore*, as Mircea Eliade would have said – when the world was young and innocent, before the patriarchal world came into being. "The spiritual journey of Earth's people began with the idea of the Goddess, universally called The Great Mother ... [and] creation stories centred on a goddess. The reverence our ancestors once felt ... [for] the primal power of the female ... [was] reflected in those dimly lit times of the prehistoric ages, when the power to give and nurture was supreme."[3]

Accompanied by reverent music that corresponds cinematically with visual and verbal cues, the narrator goes on to describe a paradise in which women gave birth, provided sustenance through their knowledge of plants, and healed others with their medicinal skills.

She does not describe these activities as merely useful or even admirable, by the way, but as "magical."[4] Not many viewers would be surprised, therefore, when told that these activities of ordinary women inspired thousands of female figurines – that is, devotional objects from prehistoric sites.

Suddenly, through the "magic" of montage, viewers return to the present. *Plus ça change, plus c'est la même chose.* A contemporary woman, Jean Bolen, describes her own ecstatic experience of giving birth. Doing so, she observes, ended her medical career – which is to say, her exile in the world of men – by putting her "in touch with the Women's Movement" and with every woman who had ever given birth. Remembering women's experiences at the "deepest ritual level" of labour and delivery links her to the women of all times and all places.[5] Remembering this exclusively female experience evokes nostalgia for a lost paradise in which giving birth was glorified to the point that everyone worshipped women.

Off in Malta, viewers learn, are "the oldest known remains of a goddess-worshipping culture."[6] In dulcet tones the narrator describes a Maltese temple as "the place of healing, the place of community," the place where "the sick found comfort." It was the place also of direct contact with the goddess – direct, that is, for the priestesses who officiated there and proclaimed the oracles. Though long abandoned, the "monumental" site continues to evoke mystery and, by implication, holiness among the seekers of today. "And I really found, and I felt it, that the people at that time lived happily," opines the guide to one of these shrines built "long before the civilization of Egypt. They were living peacefully."[7] Of Crete, another site of goddess temples, viewers learn that its ancient culture excelled in the arts, the sciences, and technology but "unlike other civilizations of its time ... lived in cooperation and harmony."[8] The message is very clear: this great goddess presided over a primeval paradise associated not only with "connectedness" to the natural order but with achievement in the cultural order as well. In other words, it was a "civilization" just like the "patriarchal" ones of Egypt, say, or Greece – but better!

And not only better, according to the narrator, but older. Long before the arrival of gods, those celestial parvenus, the great goddess generated everything worth generating. This supposedly establishes her primacy and, presumably, that of women as well: "Ancient texts record that the goddess known as Au Sept was the oldest of the old. She from whom all becoming came forth."[9] For the sake of expediency, the film makes an implicit connection between the two – as if antiquity per se could be a criterion of value. Following this logic, the narrator would have to admit that the hundred thousand years preceding goddess worship would have produced a religion still more admirable.

Carefully selecting the most edifying epithets by which goddesses were known, and carefully avoiding the fact that gods were often known by very similar ones, the narrator continues: "The ancient Hebrews called her Hokhma, she who knows all. The Chinese called her Quan Yin. She was known by many names. Eye of Heaven, Guardian of the Justice and Truth of the Universe, she who gave the unalterable laws of life, she who insisted upon truth and kindness. It was she who designed the stylus so that words could be recorded. She who invented numbers so that sheaves could be measured."[10]

Now consider *Behind the Veil,* another documentary, directed by Margaret Westcott.[11] As the narrator describes a peaceful and prosperous paradise created by women, viewers see sunlight glinting merrily on the surface of crystal streams and sea birds floating effortlessly over foamy shores of Ireland. This soft and verdant world, presumably one of natural harmony, is the cinematic equivalent of "sugar and spice and everything nice." Meanwhile, the narrator talks about the great goddess whose spirit inhabited this place: "She lived in the wild places, the brooks, the forests, in the hillsides, and the mounds. The earth, Her dwelling place, is the womb for all life."[12] Because Ireland had no towns or cities at the time, of course, it should surprise no one that religious imagery was rural.

In the background, musicians playing lutes or recorders try to recreate the sweet melodies and simple rhythms of northern folk tradition – supposedly evoking a half-remembered golden age. Over all this, the narration continues. It is all very sotto voce, very beguiling, very seductive.

The Burning Times,[13] again directed by Donna Read, won an award for the Best International Documentary Special at the Fourteenth Annual National Cable Ace Awards. Like *Goddess*, it begins with a reminder of a lost golden age. In the beginning was a great goddess, presumably, who presided over a society in which everyone honoured women and lived in harmony with nature. As the film opens, viewers see a spring near the city of Bath in England.

The narrator observes that "for thousands of years, this spring was sacred to the ancient tribes of Britain." We then see a shrine to the Celtic goddess Sulis, which the Romans rededicated to their goddess Minerva. It is striking that men and maleness are virtually absent from this paradise of women, especially in view of the fact that women often complain nowadays about their own erasure from myth, religious symbolism, and history.

But did our remote ancestors worship a great goddess of the kind that these films describe? To answer that question, we must discuss four basic claims: that a great goddess was (a) the *primeval* object of worship (that of our remotest ancestors); (b) the *supreme* object of worship (without serious rivals, especially from gods); (c) the *universal* object of worship (as a single essence that takes on slightly various forms according to time and place); and (d) the *primordial* object of worship (which continues today, whether overtly or covertly, as it was in the remote past).

First, consider the notion that a goddess was the primeval object of worship. This is not a new idea in the late twentieth century. Nor was it the creation of early feminists. Johann Jakob Bachofen, a Swiss anthropologist of the nineteenth century, was the first to take this point of view. He argued that human history revolved around women – that is, mothers. In other words, motherhood was the ultimate source of all morality and religion.[14] Among the many influenced by him was Friedrich Engels. According to this matriarchal theory, human history has evolved in four stages: a "wild" stage ("hetairism") of communistic and polyamorous communities that worshipped a proto-Aphrodite; a tamer stage of matriarchal and agricultural communities that worshipped a proto-Demeter; a transitional phase that saw the emergence of patriarchy and the worship of a proto-Dionysos; and the now-familiar patriarchal, or Apollonian, stage that eradicated all trace of matriarchy – what Bachofen called Mutterrecht.[15] However, for Bachofen, the important thing was not origin but evolution. He associated the rise of patriarchy with the rise of civilization in all its glory. For second-wave feminists such as Marija Gimbutas and Riane Eisler, on the contrary, the important thing is not evolution – which they consider regressive rather than progressive – but origin.

In *The Creation of Patriarchy*,[16] historian Gerda Lerner writes that "in the *earliest* known phases of religious worship, the female force was recognised as awesome, powerful, transcendent."[17] Else-where, she writes of surviving evidence of goddess veneration in cave paintings and sculptures from the Neolithic period. "We can understand why men and women might have chosen this as their *first* form of religious expression," she says.[18] Veneration of this mother goddess, presumably, had become pervasive during this period in both Europe and the Near East.[19]

Because the historical evidence for Lerner's theory is weak, she substitutes another type: she relies on psychoanalytical theories, in fact, rather than archaeological evidence from Palaeolithic hunting and gathering societies or even anthropological evidence from con-temporary hunting and gathering societies. Of primary import-ance to her is "the psychological bond between mother and child. We owe our insights into the complexities and importance of that bond largely to modern psychoanalytic accounts ... The life-giving mother truly had power over life and death. No wonder that men and women, observing this dramatic and mysterious power of the female, turned to the veneration of Mother-Goddesses."[20]

That is an interesting idea but hardly convincing enough to say, in effect, that "in the beginning was the great goddess." Because Lerner addresses the public at large, not only her academic col-leagues, taking this approach is a deft move. After all, how many people really care about the strict application of historical meth-ods? For many readers, what is nothing more than a psychoanal-ytical hypothesis[21] assumes the status of historical fact.

Lerner indulges in hopelessly anachronistic arguments to estab-lish the supremacy of a great goddess. She refers, for instance, to goddesses from ancient states – Sumer, Babylon, Phoenicia, Canaan, Greece, and so on. On the other hand, she implies that she is still discussing the alleged great goddess of Neolithic times – in other words, of a period even before the cultural upheaval that accompanied the rise of these states. Furthermore, even she men-tions that people had demoted these goddesses; after the emergence of states, they had turned the goddesses into wives and daughters of supreme gods and thus relegated them to minor cults. Yet she main-tains also that the "awesome, powerful, transcendent" nature of the prehistoric great goddess remained intact.

Like "patriarchal" monotheists, ironically, archaeologist Marija Gimbutas refuses to recognize any deity other than a great goddess.

In *The Language of the Goddess*[22] she refers to evidence of ancient belief in a parthenogenic creator: a goddess who creates from her own substance. Gimbutas actually denies evidence for an ancient belief in the marriage between an earth mother and a sky father. (By implication, our primeval ancestors had no idea that reproduction required both men and women. According to anthropologists, though, the people of some primal societies realize that sexual intercourse between men and women is necessary but also *insufficient* for reproduction.)[23]

Even Gimbutas, nonetheless, must acknowledge the widespread presence of male symbols. In fact, she illustrates them in her book. She begins a section on female imagery with a quotation from William Irwin Thompson: "The natural rhythm of the male is a phallic one of rise and fall ... The myths would, therefore, quite naturally tell stories in which the male is the climactic, tragic figure of flourish *and vanish*."[24] This concept could explain her subsequent denial of the maleness in female imagery. "Phallic cult articles ... do not represent a male god but rather a vivifying and fructifying force of nature appearing as an aspect of life column symbolism; or they are fused with the divine female body and subsumed to the power of the Goddess."[25]

Another comment is even more striking: "This female figurine has a phallic head whose lower part may be shaped like testicles ... Although the male element is attached, these figurines remain essentially female. They do not represent a fusion of two sexes but rather an enhancement of the female with the mysterious life force inherent in the phallus. The Goddess figurine creates a base from which the phallus, understood as a cosmic pillar, rises. It comes from her womb in the same way that stalagmites and stalactites grow from her womb in the cave."[26]

Elsewhere, Gimbutas writes that from the "body of the sacrificed bull, new life emerges in an epiphany of the Goddess as flower, tree, column of watery substance, bee, or butterfly."[27] This contradicts common sense. Bulls are male by definition, after all, not female. On what basis can she use the sacrifice of a bull rather than a cow or some other female animal as an example of *goddess* worship? Wishful thinking. In effect, Gimbutas solves what she considers the problem of female imagery by refusing to take seriously its obvious reference to maleness. And obvious it is in at least some cases. At

Grotte Chauvet, the recently discovered cave near Marseilles, are pictures of horses with appendages that could not possibly be identified as anything other than, well, penises.[28]

But wait. Gimbutas becomes even more ingenious when it comes to bull and bison imagery in the following period, the Neolithic. Bull heads were prominent in Neolithic art, she suggests, because of "the extraordinary likeness of the female uterus and fallopian tubes to the head and horns of a bull."[29] She refers to an "explanation" given by Dorothy Cameron in *Symbols of Birth and Death in the Neolithic Era*.[30] Cameron claims that people would have noticed the shape of the fallopian tubes when birds of prey ate the flesh of exposed bodies; because the body lay flat, the fallopian tubes would have turned upward instead of downward and thus resemble the head of a bull with its upward-turned horns!

This speculation is tendentious to say the least. Turned the other way, after all, we could say just as easily – no, more easily – that the artifact resembled something far more familiar: an erect penis with scrotum. As it happens, that is exactly what a virtually identical design represents on a piece of sculpture by Armand Vaillancourt. Standing at the entrance to an office building, *Erotisme 1983–88* includes a nude male with the appropriate genital equipment clearly represented[31] by a design that only a feminist ideologue could interpret as the uterus of a half-eaten female corpse. It is highly doubtful, moreover, that our ancient ancestors would have observed the minuscule fallopian tubes and even more doubtful that vultures would have eaten just the right amount to expose the fallopian tubes and uterus so that someone would see them all together. Finally, it is extremely doubtful that anyone would have known that these tubes were connected with reproduction. After all, no one had seen the human egg before modern times.[32] Nevertheless, Gimbutas concludes with confidence that "it has become clear that the prominence of the bull in this symbolic system comes not from that animal's strength and muscularity as it does in that of the patriarchal Indo-Europeans but rather from the accidental similarity between its head and the female reproductive organs."[33]

In her cross-cultural study of 150 tribal societies documented by anthropologists,[34] Peggy Sanday tries to establish correlations of this kind. She observes one between the sexual symbolism in creation stories and gender roles in everyday life. Moreover, she identifies a correlation between sexual symbolism and systems of food production.[35] Sanday concludes that male symbols are characteristic of societies that prefer hunting big animals; that female symbols are characteristic of societies that prefer fishing and gathering; and that both female *and* male symbols are characteristic of societies that prefer hunting of *both* kinds. Societies that have no preference often combine hunting for big animals with hunting for small ones and fishing and gathering.[36]

If the correlations found in these contemporary hunting and gathering societies are legitimate clues to those found in prehistoric ones, and we have no reason to reject the possibility outright (because several fundamental features are common to both), then we should examine economies very carefully when discussing sexual symbolism. According to Gimbutas, subsistence during the Palaeolithic period in "Old Europe" (before the Indo-Europeans began migrating there in approximately 4500 BC)[37] required people to hunt waterfowl and small animals, to fish, and to gather plants. This might correspond, as Sanday suggests, to female symbolism. Gimbutas argues, in fact, that a bird goddess was one of the earliest forms of the great goddess and continued as such from the Palaeolithic into the Neolithic period. Another early form might have been a fish goddess.[38]

But does the evidence include only female symbols? Both female and male symbols, according to Sanday, would correlate just as well with the kind of economy that Gimbutas describes. Besides, does the evidence indicate only one type of economy throughout Europe? The fact is that people also hunted big game animals such as bison in regions such as Lascaux. Hunting these massive creatures would correlate, according to Sanday, with either male symbols or both male and female ones. In short, both sexual symbols and methods of food production probably varied from one part of Europe to another. Some regions might have produced mainly female or both female and male symbols, and other regions – those that supported the hunting of big animals – might have produced primarily male or both male and female symbols. We have no reason to assume, in short, that goddess worship was the earliest phase of religion.[39]

Now, was this great goddess merely part of a larger pantheon that included both other goddesses and gods, or was she supreme – that is, did she reign over the entire pantheon? Feminists have taken one of two positions. The extreme position is that she was without any rivals. The moderate one is that she was without any *important* rivals or consorts. The former is more ambitious, of course, and harder to argue. Ironically, advocates often describe their great goddess as the perfect counterpart and therefore the ultimate rival of the cosmic gods familiar in "patriarchal" forms of monotheism. If Astarte, Inanna, Isis, and Brigid were merely local goddesses, after all, it would be impossible to claim a status for any of them comparable to that of the cosmic gods. If they were local manifestations of a universal and supreme goddess, on the other hand, the competition between "women's goddesses" and "men's gods" would have been more evenly matched.

Early written records make it clear that ancient Near Eastern civilizations worshipped both gods and goddesses.[40] This was certainly true, according to Tikva Frymer-Kensky, in Sumer: "The presence of both gods and goddesses in the ancient Sumerian pantheon provided a divine counterpart for society and meant, moreover, that the cosmos was shared by male and female powers each of whom had an impact on events and processes. Every aspect of Sumerian religio-philosophical thinking assumed this basic cosmological premise, and culture, nature, and society were all perceived along gender lines. The male-female division of the animal (and human) world was projected onto the cosmic sphere and permeated philosophical reflection."[41] According to Frymer-Kensky, "Goddess worship was not a separate religion, and goddesses as well as gods were an integral part of Sumerian religion and thought. The stories about goddesses do not come from any separatist women's cult and are neither female fantasies nor women's mythmaking. They are mainstream literature, the high culture of ancient Sumer."[42]

But Gimbutas tries to argue for the supremacy of this great goddess. Failing to produce a convincing case, she resorts to plan B: trying to show merely that female symbols were more important than male ones. Even trivializing obviously male symbols, however, proves harder than she might have imagined, which makes her try to get away with blatantly anachronistic theories. Here is an example.

Although Gimbutas warns against using speculative titles such as fertility goddess or mother goddess,[43] she herself uses an equally speculative title. She refers in one passage to "the absolute rule" of this great goddess. In another, she opines that these "life-givers and death-wielders [were] 'queens' and as such they remained in individual creeds for a very long time in spite of their official dethrone-ment."[44] For Gimbutas, these "queens" were mere remnants by the time of states.[45] In other words, they originated before states. But how can this be? It makes no sense to talk about queens, whether mortal or divine, before there were states, monarchies, over which they could have ruled. Neolithic Europe had towns, trade, and pos-sibly a rudimentary form of writing, but it did not have states or collections of states. Consequently, it could not have had earthly monarchs, let alone divine ones. No wonder Gimbutas turns to Greek texts by Herodotus and Hesychius (who lived after the for-mation of states) and even to a Latin one by Lucius Apuleius (who lived at the height of the Roman Empire!) to find goddesses who were worshipped as heavenly queens and supreme deities.[46]

The whole idea of one supreme deity, in fact, might represent a kind of monotheism that was itself a product of state formation.[47] One important aim of these new states, after all, was the unification of heterogeneous populations. To the extent that many deities repre-sented many racial, religious, or linguistic interest groups, any one deity that absorbed the others would have helped unite the people of a new state – one that relied on kingship rather than kinship.[48]

Next, was this great goddess universal? Was she the same every-where, in other words, no matter what her name was? It would be ahistorical to say that she was.[49] That would mean either denying or trivializing historical evidence of distinctive cultures and circum-stances.[50] According to Mary Lefkowitz,[51] it would mean succumb-ing to reductionism – actually, two forms of reductionism. First, it would reduce all representations of women to a single pattern, thereby eliminating the many differences within and among tradi-tions. Second, it would reduce all of womankind to a genital iden-tity. The first reduction relies on the second. For what could women in wildly different societies have in common except for the most rudimentary biological characteristics?

Feminists usually reject ahistorical positions on principle, ironi-cally, for overlooking the specific conditions that affect the lives of women at particular times and places. Many of them make an exception, nevertheless, when it comes to ancient goddesses. They embrace with delight the idea that ancient goddess cults focused on a universal goddess.[52]

Finally, was this great goddess primordial? Advocates of this posi-tion mean that her cult was (and still is) the ultimate form of religion.

Unlike the word "primeval," which refers only to the remote past, "primordial" refers to the entire continuum of time. The primeval refers to whatever existed "in the beginning"; the primordial refers in addition to whatever links the remote past, the present, and the remote future. It refers more specifically to whatever is fundamental, essential, or pure – and by implication to whatever is unchanging or eternal. Advocates of a great goddess claim for her primordiality in both senses. To paraphrase what some consider the notoriously "patriarchal" *Book of Common Prayer*, she "was in the beginning, is now, and ever shall be, world without end."

Sam Gill is among those who question the motivation of promoters of the idea of "Mother Earth" as a primordial goddess. In a study of North American Indian religions,[53] he discredits the notion. Despite its appearance in traditional sources, he argues, feminine symbols represented neither a great goddess nor even major goddesses. Only in modern times, he argues, has belief in the latter emerged in connection with popular legends.

Belief in "Mother Earth" as a goddess common to Amerindian religions, says Gill, originated with a casual remark by Tecumseh. In 1810 the Shawnee leader said that "the earth is my mother and on her bosom I will repose."[54] Although he said this merely because he wanted to sit on the ground during negotiations with white people rather than sit in their strange chairs, the statement made a profound impression on many scholars. In 1893, E.B. Tylor quoted it in his influential *Primitive Culture*.[55] Eventually, Tecumsah's remark had a profound impact on the very people being studied. The Shawnee proclaimed "Mother Earth" as the central deity of Amerindians and even as a female creator dwelling in the sky, her life cycle coinciding with the evolution and destruction of the earth.[56] Gill says that her acceptance "as a major figure gives a primordial and spiritual foundation to the story, culture, morality, and values of Native Americans especially when considered over against Americans of European ancestry."[57]

The same thing happened in connection with Smohalla, the Wanapum leader of a millenarian movement. Protesting the introduction of agriculture, he asked: "Shall I tear my mother's bosom"? James Mooney reported these words in his famous book on the ghost-dance religion generated by the Sioux outbreak of 1890.[58] Interpreting the reference as to some earth goddess, both scholarly and tribal authorities popularized this statement.[59]

Gill shows that "scholarly" accounts have contributed to the pervasive assumption among scholars of a supreme goddess. The same thing happened in connection with a primordial goddess. Religion per se, some came to believe, originated with the worship of an earth goddess.[60] After quoting the Smohalla statement, Eliade wrote that these "relics of the old worship of the Earth-Mother ... come to us from very distant ages. The emotion that we feel when we hear them is our response to what they evoke with their wonderful freshness and spontaneity – the primordial image of the Earth-Mother. It is an image that we find everywhere in the world, in countless forms and varieties."[61] As Gill concludes, scholars often begin their research with preconceived ideas about a primordial mother goddess.

In *The Religions of the American Indians*, for example, Ake Hulkrantz identifies as birth goddesses some female figurines of Palaeolithic hunters from Europe and Siberia. He then identifies these with the mistress of animals known to Siberian hunters today. Finally, he associates all female figurines – including Amerindian ones – with one great deity, universal and eternal, explaining all transformations as hers! From what Gill has discovered, it seems clear that there never has been a single primeval goddess, much less a supreme, universal, and primordial one.

Did the alleged goddess preside over not merely a golden age but over a golden age specifically for women? In other words, did the cosmic power of this goddess once correspond to that of ordinary women in everyday life? And, more important for feminists, could it do so once again? Many feminists make a direct link, in fact, between what they call "theafocal" and "matrifocal" societies. The writers under discussion here have chosen their words carefully, rejecting the popular word "matriarchal." In this section, we (a) define "theafocal" as well as "matrifocal" and (b) discuss the theory of female primacy.

The word "matriarchy" refers to *rule* by mothers – that is, by women. Because we have no evidence of a matriarchy, either in the remote past or at any time since then, many academics reject the word.[62] Anthropologists usually refer more specifically, therefore, to "matrilocal" societies (in which husbands move away from home to live with the families of their wives) or "matrilineal" ones (in which property passes through the female line). The word "matri-

focal" refers to societies that focus primarily on the needs and interests of mothers – which is to say, of women – but some academics
use this word in ways that add up to something very much like
matriarchy. The same is true of words such as "matristic."

By "theafocal" cultures, we refer to those that focus primarily on
the worship of goddesses (as distinct from "theofocal" ones that
focus primarily on the worship of gods). The importance of establishing a link between theafocal societies and matrifocal ones is
obvious to many goddess ideologues. If earlier societies associated
goddess worship with power for women, after all, then fostering the
former now would be one way of attaining the latter.

The academics under discussion here, at any rate, would have us
believe that the power of women reflected the omnipotence of a
great goddess. It was presumably women, not men, who had the
real power in those halcyon days. As mothers, women had sole
power over life and death in prehistoric times. The implication is
that men had less important functions and, as a result, less power.
But did they?

As for the primacy of women, feminist ideologues have come up
with several theories. Each purports to show that women were
equal or even superior to men during this alleged golden age. For
Gerda Lerner, it all boils down to the primary role of women in
reproduction. She correctly challenges the simplistic conclusion of
biological determinists that men's "greater physical strength, their
ability to run faster and lift heavier weights, and their greater
aggressiveness"[63] gave them categorical supremacy. She begins by
observing that these biological qualities contributed to gender roles
based on what was functional and ensured the survival of the species in early times, but then she argues that men made virtually no
contribution at all to early societies!

Forced to acknowledge at least some degree of complementarity
due to the genetic role of men in reproduction and their functional
role in providing resources while women nursed the young, Lerner
nevertheless asserts that the most basic dyad was that between
mother and child; fathers were useful accessories at best. But she
ignores the fact – a surprising one, given the current preoccupation
with mothers, especially single mothers, and general disinterest in
fathers – that men bond not only with their mates[64] but also with
their biological children, protecting them and providing for them.

David Geary and Mark Flinn make these points in connection with the evolution of human parenting and family life,[65] arguing that some female primates remain with their own birth groups but other female primates (including female chimps, bonobos, gorillas, and humans) do not. Evolution therefore suggests that humans have inherited their predilection for patrilocality from closely related species.

In addition, Geary and Flinn point out that the behaviour of male humans is closer to that of male gorillas than to that of any other primate. Male gorillas have harems but also form long-term relationships with female gorillas and participate in parenting. The authors surmise that knowing who their offspring are has made these males willing to invest heavily in parenting. They suggest that the Australopithecines (hominids who lived some four million years ago) had the same strategy, because polygyny was most common in later hominid societies and accompanied by male parental investment. Gradually, male dominance gave way to pair bonding due to evolutionary changes, some of which had already occurred in primates: greater similarity in the size of males and females (which meant that males found it harder to dominate females); a longer developmental period for offspring (which made protection and provision more important); concealed ovulation (which reduced mating competition between males); and nonreproductive sexuality (which kept males sexually interested and involved). Females found these changes advantageous for their offspring and therefore themselves as well. By remaining loyal to their own males, which established paternity, they reduced the urge of those males to dominate harems and therefore increased their own influence over those males. Even with "co-wives," therefore, pair bonding with males was a successful strategy for females.[66]

But Lerner is entirely preoccupied with the primacy of mothers. At one point, she observes that the "infant's survival depended on the quality of maternal care,"[67] as if the quality of paternal care was not only of a different kind (which was true) but also irrelevant (which was not). According to her, "the first sexual division of labour, by which men did the big-game hunting and children and women ... food gathering, seems to derive from biological sex differences. These biological sex differences are not differences in the size and endurance of men and women but solely reproductive differences, specifically women's ability to nurse babies."[68] She adds here that women and children hunted small animals in areas without large game.

Like Lerner, Eisler, the consummate popularizer, attributes the importance of goddesses and matrilineality to women's reproductive capacity.

It of course makes eminent sense that the earliest depiction of divine power in human form should have been female rather than male. When our ancestors began to ask the eternal questions (Where do we come from before we are born? Where do we go after we die?), they must have noted that life emerges from the body of a woman. It would have been natural for them to image the universe as an all-giving Mother from whose womb all life emerges and to which, like the cycles of vegetation, it returns after death to be a gain reborn. It also makes sense that societies with this image of the powers that govern the universe would make a very different social structure from societies that worship a divine Father who wields a thunderbolt and/or sword. It further seems logical that women would not be seen as subservient in societies that conceptualized the powers governing the universe in female form – and that "effeminate" qualities such as caring, compassion, and nonviolence would be highly valued in these societies.[69]

Lerner's argument is based on a premise that virtually all feminists now take for granted: that women can do everything that men can do but also that men cannot do everything that women can do. In effect, men are superfluous. Apart from allowing mothers time to suckle their babies, Lerner opines, the only significant role of men in history has been to oppress women. But is it true that men had no distinctive function at all in these societies?

Even evidence provided by Lerner herself from the ancient Near East suggests otherwise. A Sumerian myth, for example, explicitly indicates that neither men nor women were considered autonomous, that both women and men were believed necessary for reproduction. In settling disputes, for instance, Ninmah realizes than Enki must contribute the sperm, and he realizes that she must gestate the new life.[70]

Preoccupied with female primacy, Lerner writes that the "ego formation of the individual male, which must have taken place within a context of fear, awe, and possibly dread of the female, must have led men to create social institutions to bolster their egos, strengthen their self-confidence, and validate their sense of worth."[71] Because men contributed only due to neuroticism, in other words, they were tainted *ab initio*.

But what of Lerner's motivation? It is clearly other than scholarly. To say the least, she uses scholarship in the service of political advocacy. Her aim is to convince readers that men have been irrelevant biologically, economically, and in every other way throughout history. Men might indeed have envied the dramatic role played by women in childbirth; even so, the quality of paternal care was related to survival, sexual attraction, and affection. Otherwise, there would have been separate and autonomous societies for men and women, each sex needing the other only for reproductive purposes. Besides, men's reactions to female biology might have involved emotions other than either envy or fear. They might have felt relief that they were not subject to the discomfort of periodic menstruation, morning sickness during pregnancy, the horrendous pain of labour, and the likelihood of dying in childbirth.

Throughout the Palaeolithic and into the Neolithic – which is to say, throughout most of human history – men had obvious and necessary functions: reproductive, economic, and others as well. This accounts for the historical and cross-cultural roles of men as providers, protectors, and progenitors.[72] Lerner's attempts at psychohistory notwithstanding, ego formation of the individual boy must have occurred in a context that allowed him a somewhat positive sense of masculine identity.

Additional questions arise in connection with the idea that primeval women enjoyed more power than modern women do (or have until very recently). Were women powerful hunters? Some people would like to think so.[73] But men in general were biologically equipped to do some things better than women in general. Hunting big game involved tracking animals, sometimes for great distances, and this required not only physical mobility but also spatial orientation and memory. Hunting these animals (or even big fish) involved throwing spears and carrying the carcasses home, moreover, which required considerable upper-body strength. The fact that most men had these qualities to a greater extent than most women meant that societies chose them as a class to provide animal protein along with hides, bones, and other resources. At any rate, they were free of the limitations on mobility that resulted from pregnancy and lactation. Consequently, many hunting and fishing societies selected men for these functions (although women, too, contributed by hunting for smaller animals or birds, fishing, and gathering plants).

After the domestication of animals, these advantages remained institutionalized as gender roles. Even after the development of agriculture, men remained economically important. Pushing a massive iron plough, after all, required much more upper-body strength than pushing a wooden hoe. Only by acknowledging these biological differences and recognizing the lack of anthropological evidence for hunting or plough agriculture as normative functions of women (despite exceptions in hard times)[74] can we account for cross-cultural similarities in the definition of gender when it comes to food production. We can easily either overestimate *or* underestimate the importance of male size, strength, and mobility.[75]

Barbara Ehrenreich, for instance, probably underestimates it. She observes that it "is tempting to discern, in myths connecting the goddess to the hunt and the menstruating woman to the hunting animal, a time when real women played a central role in the realms of both economies and religion: in the economy, as participants in the hunt; in religion, as beings whose bodies had the seemingly divine gift of bleeding without dying, and doing so regularly, in tune with the most salient of the night skies."[76] Women were powerful, she suggests, partly because their periods synchronized in groups. As predatory hunters, they personified goddesses. In her opinion, the link was direct and positive.

Hunting, she explains, was an innovation that occurred late in the evolutionary scheme of things. Before that, human beings banded together to defend themselves against wild animals and scavenge for their meat. Later, they banded together for the offence. The entire group now hunted, she writes: men, women, and children. How did the latter do so? By dancing, making a lot of noise, and driving the animals into traps (over cliffs, into cul-de-sacs, or bogs) where they died or could be killed with stones, spears, and clubs. So women, like men, were hunters. For evidence, Ehrenreich points to analogies in hunting and gathering societies. The !K'ung, for example, see one between a girl's first menstruation and a boy's first kill. And Ehrenreich points to the fact that Amerindians included women and children in their group hunts.[77] But Ehrenreich's reconstruction of history raises more questions than it answers. She observes that women and children were more fearful than men because they were left unprotected during the hunt.[78] Does this not imply that men were acknowledged as better or stronger hunters? In any case, her position presents several problems.

First, the !Kung refer to a woman's first kill metaphorically, analogically, not literally. In fact, it is well established[79] that women are *not* routinely big game hunters in hunting and gathering societies – including that of the !Kung.[80] Second, the analogy between a girl's menstruation and her first kill might be due to a morphological similarity between vaginal bleeding and the bleeding wound of an animal. Third, the link between menstrual bleeding among women and ritual bleeding among men might not have originated in connection with the blood of either prey animals or predatory ones. Instead, it might have originated in connection with the envy that men felt because women went through a natural rite of passage – unlike the arduous and dangerous cultural one that boys went through before entering manhood – or because women could apparently produce life. (Lerner identifies the problem as "fear" and "possibly dread," as we have already noted. We identify it as envy. But both might be involved.) Fourth, the idea of a predatory goddess need not have originated in the power of hunting women at the dawn of human history, for which we have no evidence. It might have originated among adolescent boys who feared being shamed by girls and women for failing to kill an animal during initiation. Hunting, especially for big game, was a very intimidating prospect. Boys had to measure up if they were to be accepted as men; girls and women were the cheerleaders. Boys might have elaborated on this fear, as men, by creating the myth of a predatory goddess. Women would be like predators, in other words, willing to eat those who failed to become real men with the courage to kill on behalf of the community.

It is true that early anthropologists, being men, had no access to female informants and therefore did not hear about some ways in which women contributed to food production. It is true, moreover, that women could have participated in some forms of hunting. For instance, they could have made some weapons, sighted game animals, and either set snares or helped men drive these animals over cliffs. Nonetheless, as we say, women did not routinely become big-game hunters. On the contrary, that was the primary distinction between women and men. Otherwise, why would rites of passage from boyhood to manhood so often have involved killing big-game animals?[81]

And finally, we doubt that women really were routinely engaged in direct struggles with wild animals, especially big ones. What if they were pregnant, nursing, or taking care of young children? And what about the smell of menstrual blood, which would have attracted animals? Most women, at any rate, would surely have stayed on the sidelines.

But did women not invent horticulture and therefore overtake men as the most important producers of food? Lerner writes that horticulture flourished at a time "when matrilineal, matrilocal systems abound[ed] ... [and] group survival [demanded] the demographic equalization of men and women."[82] If earlier hunting and gathering societies were so egalitarian, as Ehrenreich points out, why the sudden demand for this "demographic equalization" of men and women? And if they had not been so egalitarian, if women had dominated, why argue that their importance increased? Neither Gimbutas nor Lerner can provide us with adequate answers to these questions.

From the perspective of Lerner, Gimbutas, and Eisler, the primacy of women was due to matrilineality. But any specific evidence of that in Neolithic religion, including its myths and rituals, would have to come from later texts. After all, no one recorded the meanings attached to artifacts from those preliterate societies. Knowledge of folklore, moreover, would have to come either from ancient written texts or from modern ethnographies of contemporary societies. Both sources present the temptation of anachronism: reading the culture of a later period into that of an earlier one. The fact that Gimbutas includes Minoan culture, that of a state, makes her data for the earlier period highly suspect.

We must sort out the relation between matrilineality and the Neolithic innovation of horticulture. Here is the feminist syllogism: horticultural societies are matrilineal; Neolithic societies were horticultural; ergo, horticultural societies of the Neolithic must have been matrilineal. But archaeological evidence does not support this theory, and anthropological evidence indirectly refutes it.

The link between matrilineality and horticulture, at least in the modern period, is much weaker than anthropologists might have expected. According to one study, only 25 per cent of the horticultural societies examined were also matrilineal. According to a related study, only 56 per cent of the matrilineal societies examined were also horticultural.[83] Obviously there is no direct correlation between matrilineality and horticulture in contemporary societies. Why should anyone believe that it was otherwise during the Neolithic? In any case, the study indicates that the first two premises of Lerner's syllogism are false.

Even in those horticultural societies that are matrilineal, women are not necessarily dominant; husbands, but usually brothers, control women in many of these societies.[84] Besides, not all Neolithic societies were horticultural. Even in horticultural ones, moreover, women did not necessarily dominate the economy; horticulture often coexisted with hunting or pastoralism,[85] after all, either of which might have been equally or more important than horticulture.

Thus, despite the claim for matrilineality as the norm in early horticultural societies, presumably because women controlled the economy, patrilineality is actually more common in the ones described by anthropologists. Trying to establish a global evolutionary model based on prehistoric European and ancient Near Eastern evidence is risky, to say the least.[86]

Although Gimbutas claims that the societies of Neolithic Europe were matrilineal,[87] she still pays lip service to the idea that social egalitarianism prevailed: "A balanced, nonpatriarchal and nonmatriarchal social system is reflected by religion, mythologies, and folklore, by studies of the social structure of Old European and Minoan cultures."[88] She offers inadequate documentation from the Neolithic, however, to prove her point. In fact, her statement is immediately preceded by one claiming precisely the reverse: "The Goddess-centered art with its striking absence of images of warfare and male domination reflects a social order in which women as heads of clans or queen-priestesses played a central part."[89] Because monarchs first appeared in early *states*, of course, there could have been no queens – or kings, for that matter – in these Neolithic societies.[90]

Fast forward, now, to the present. It is to serve needs of modern women, after all, that feminists such as Lerner and Gimbutas are so intent on proving the existence of early matrilineal societies. According to Lerner, "we can assert that female subordination is not universal, even though we have no proof for the existence of a matriarchal society. But women, like men, have a deep need for a coherent system of explanation that not only tells us what is and why it got to be as it is but allows for an alternate vision of the future."[91] At issue, in other words, is the impact of archaeology on modern women. That is the political subtext underlying these discussions of matrilineality. But suppose that its prevalence in ancient times could be proven? Was it really the ideal form of social organization even then? Maybe not.

Feminists who celebrate the autonomy or even superiority of women seldom consider that matrilineality often presents a problem for women: it can include some form of male dominance. To Lerner's credit, she does observe that in "most matrilineal societies, it is a male relative, usually the woman's brother or uncle who controls economic and family decisions."[92] Even so, she assumes that matrilineality reflects the power of women. It is true that women in matrilineal societies have some real power, because property passes from one generation to the next through their line. And when subsistence is based substantially on horticulture, women might have considerable power over the production of food as well.

This positive correlation between the economic participation of women and their social or political status is important for anyone considering the ways in which we could change our own societies. But Gimbutas and Lerner take an approach that is historically unprecedented: ignoring the mechanisms by which women bond with men in the interest of survival or group well-being. Because they prefer to think of conflict between men and women – one sex having power over the other – they seldom think about *solidarity* between women and men. Underlying at least some arguments based on this approach, therefore, is a vision of *two* societies, one of men and the other of women and children.

Also very often ignored is the fact that matrilineal societies pose particular problems for men. David Schneider and Kathleen Gough point out that the conflict between a man's position as both brother in the clan of his sister and biological father in that of his wife has generated what scholars have called the "matrilineal puzzle."[93] A.R. Radcliffe-Brown and Daryll Forde discuss the tensions inherent in this kind of social structure:

The ways in which domestic authority is divided between a man and the head of his wife's kinship group are surprisingly varied. In some cases there is a formal allocation of rights and privileges between father and mother's brother in return for service and payments. In other cases the balance is less well defined, and every marriage produces what can only be described as a constant pull-father-pull-mother's brother, in which the personality, wealth, and social status of the two individuals or their respective kinsmen give the advantage to one side or the other ... the dominant principle of Ashanti kinship is the rule of matrilineal descent ... The chief problem of kinship relations among them is to adjust the jural and moral claims and bonds arising out of marriage and fatherhood to those imposed by matrilineal kinship. Conflict between these rival claims and bonds is inherent in their kinship system.[94]

Men face additional problems in matrilocal and matrilineal societies. The anthropological record shows that biological fathers are often marginalized. "In matrilineal descent groups," write Schneider and Gough, "the emotional interest of the father in his own children constitutes a source of strain."[95] Karla Poewe points out that "while in matriliny different fathers do not necessarily matter or are incidental, in patriliny mothers always matter."[96] It could be argued that men have a legitimate reason for preferring patrilineality, therefore, because this system gives both mothers *and* fathers a stake in their biological children. "Many men ... complain bitterly" in the former "that they and their kin are forgotten by their sons and daughters, who are said to remember only their mother's people."[97] Women, on the other hand, have at least some status in both systems. Why must we assume, then, as many feminists do, that the primary or even sole purpose of patrilineality has always been to subjugate women? It could have been to solve some real and pressing problems of men *and thus of society as a whole.* As we have already observed, men need encouragement to bond with both women and children. The result was a masculine identity that revolved around a distinctive, necessary, and publicly valued contribution to society: protecting women and children.

Finally, did the alleged goddess preside over a golden age for anyone? A golden age, by definition, involves peace and happiness, and so it is for the feminist versions that we are discussing here. But unlike their ancient mythical counterparts, these versions supposedly rely on modern historical analysis. They give the impression of scientific accuracy, therefore, and thus of legitimacy. Who would be impressed nowadays, after all, by claims without demonstrable facts? In this section, we discuss the rhetoric of peace and the rhetoric of happiness.

Promoters of a great goddess usually describe her as peaceful.[98] Gimbutas writes that the civilization that flourished in "Old Europe between 6500 and 3500 BC and in Crete until 1450 BC enjoyed a long period of uninterrupted peaceful living which produced artistic expressions of graceful beauty and refinement, demonstrating a higher quality of life than many androcratic, classed societies."[99] Apart from anything else, the word "civilization" in this context is noteworthy. Gimbutas recognizes that its usage is debatable and makes an effort to explain it.[100] In her view, scholars have unfairly reserved the word for androcentric cultures. That being the case, why not redefine it to fit gynocentric ones? Her stated aim is to elevate the status of gynocentric small-scale societies, ones that others might consider more primitive than the androcentric ones that overtook it. She must believe that a word can mean whatever she wants it to mean. But that is not the only problem.

Derived from the Latin *civilis*, which means "citizen," "civilization" has a technical definition. In anthropological parlance, it refers specifically to large-scale societies characterized by complex forms of social organization, burgeoning cities, advanced technologies, and usually literacy as well. These societies relied on agrarian or trading economies in the ancient world and rely on industrial economies today.[101]

In popular parlance, though, the word "civilization" has powerful but ambiguous emotional connotations. On the positive side, "civilized" people are supposedly not only materially or technologically but also morally or spiritually superior to those who are "uncivilized." Because this is patently absurd, scholars have made an effort to correct what postmodernists now attack as "ethnocentrism." On the negative side, "civilization" is supposedly degenerate and contemptible.[102] Our industrial civilization clearly has problems; no wonder that the Romantics pined nostalgically for the rustic simplicity and moral purity supposedly known to their parents and grandparents, and neo-Romantics for that of their remote ancestors. This denunciation of civilization (and corresponding glorification of wilderness) is nothing new. It was not new in the nineteenth century, when poets and painters celebrated the vanishing British pastoral landscape or American frontier. It was not new in the eighteenth century, when Rousseau eulogized the "noble savages." Or in the sixteenth century, when urban and elite Europeans were glad to receive reports of a New World and hope for a new beginning there. Some of those who emigrated found what they were looking for – a bucolic garden – and embraced it as an antidote to the decadence, corruption, and tyranny of "civilization" in the Old World. Others found a "howling wilderness" to be feared, endured, and, if possible, tamed.[103]

By referring to the Neolithic world as a gynocentric "civilization," Gimbutas acknowledges only positive aspects of the word "civilization." Playing a trick on her readers, she wants women to cash in on the prestige associated with the inherent benefits of civilization but not to pay the price of acknowledging its inherent problems. To have her cake and eat it too, she makes an expedient distinction between good civilizations and bad ones. Gynocentric ones are good and androcentric ones bad. In other words, she claims all the good aspects of civilization for women and assigns the bad ones to men. This ploy, based on both dualism ("they" are evil) and essentialism ("we" are good), amounts to nothing more than academic opportunism.

Back, once again, to the notion of primeval peace. To substantiate her claim, Gimbutas relies primarily on an argument from silence. She points out, for example, that archaeologists have found no weapons at Palaeolithic and Neolithic sites in Europe. Elsewhere, she does admit that archaeologists have found weapons there. She just denies that early people used these for *war*. But how can anyone know that? The same weapons that killed animals could easily have killed other people. And if early warriors simply hurled rocks or stones at each other, these would be impossible to identify as weapons. Their slingshots would have decayed and disintegrated. Similarly, Gimbutas points out that no signs of fortification from these periods have been found, yet this might just mean that they built fortifications of wood, which again decayed and disintegrated long ago.

Actually, archaeologists do not have to rely completely on arguments from silence. They have found several depictions of what might have represented violence: human bodies that might have been felled by spears. Some of these are ambiguous, and what might be spears entering the bodies might also be "life forces" emanating from them. But one depiction recently discovered at Grotte Chauvet, a cave near Marseilles, clearly shows a spear puncturing one body. Jean Clottes has pointed out that this body lies prostrate on the ground like that of a dead animal. Archaeologists could interpret even this picture in several ways, of course. It might have represented a mythical being, a sacrificial ritual, a murder, a casualty of war, and so on. What all of these interpretations have in common, though, is an act of violence. Archaeologists have dated the picture to either 19,000 or 27,000 BP (before present). Both dates are well within the "golden age" that was characterized allegedly by caring and sharing and loving and everything else now associated with a matriarchy under the aegis of a great goddess.[104]

These cultures, at least the Palaeolithic ones, probably were more peaceful than many that followed them, to be sure, but we say so for more substantial reasons than the mere paucity of evidence to the contrary. Unlike ancient horticultural societies, most ancient hunting and gathering ones – which were nomadic – probably did not need to institutionalize warfare; they could have solved conflicts or avoided them more easily simply by moving on.[105] Another reason is sheer logic: raiding arose only when people stored their resources – grain, say, or domesticated animals – and thus made it profitable for other people to raid them. When people settled on fertile land or near water to grow crops, they made it profitable for other people to push them out or at least steal their resources.

Matrilineality itself, in the contemporary cultures studied by anthropologists, often produces warlike mentalities instead of peaceful ones. Matrilineality often correlates with raiding or warfare, as it does among the Nayar in Kerala. Moreover, sacrificial systems frequently correlate with violence, as they did in most Neolithic societies. Sacrifice, whether animal or human, is not exactly a peaceful act. Even Gimbutas furnishes evidence of this: "Womblike caves ... were sanctuaries. At Scaloria in ... southeastern Italy ... one hundred and thirty-seven skeletons, most of which were in a mass burial and had traces of peculiar cuts at the base of their skulls, were found ... Perhaps Death and Regeneration Mysteries were celebrated here ... In the analogous [sic] vagina-uterus-shaped cave of Koutala on the Cycladic island of Serifos ... a stalagmite appears in

the form of a female figure. In front of it were the remains of offerings Neolithic dishes, animal bones, and charred material."[106]

Closely related to the rhetoric of primeval peace is that of primeval happiness. According to Gimbutas, it is "a fact that these people
lived in times much happier than our own."[107] A "fact"? These people endured predation by wild animals that we no longer have to
fear and famines that we can now prevent, given the will, through
foreign aid. But they did not always endure; they experienced rates
of both infant mortality and maternal mortality that we would now
consider shockingly high, for instance, and an average lifespan of
only thirty years.[108] We have a word to describe the mentality of
those who dismiss these facts in order to bask in the false but
beguiling glow of nostalgic sentiment: romanticism. Scholarship, it
is not.

Like suffering, happiness is a subjective experience, a state of
mind. It is not an objective reality that we can measure reliably.
Statements about happiness in earlier times are notorious not only
for their subjectivity but also for their political connotations. Just as
some conservatives believe that people were happier in the immediate past (before the 1960s), after all, some feminists believe that people were happier in the remote past (before patriarchy). We can
know something about the material conditions under which people
lived, to be sure, but we can know little or nothing about their subjective *experience* of those conditions. This is true even when written
records are available, because those people who were most satisfied
with existing conditions were the ones who produced and preserved
records (except, to some extent, for the ancient Israelites).[109]

We can make inferences about levels of happiness but only on the
basis of our own notions of what happiness is in the first place.
These notions might or might not coincide with those of our ancestors. The solution is not relativism; we all do have preferences of
one kind or another. But surely we should try to separate these preferences from scholarly analysis and not imagine that the evaluation
itself is an objective statement of fact or that it reveals more about
"them" than it does about "us."

Consider the implicit claim that we can legitimately evaluate even
ancient societies according to a hierarchy of happiness. Surely
peaceful societies were happier, after all, than warlike ones. And if
we define "happiness" as the absence of war, that might be correct.

But is that an adequate definition? If it were, then we would have to say that the Western world was happier under the Roman Empire than at almost any time before or since. The *pax romana* effectively meant the end of war for millions of people. Trade and commerce flourished, for generations, as did the arts and sciences. Being pragmatic and opportunistic, the Romans were quite content to let conquered nations retain their languages, their customs, their deities, and even their (puppet) kings or queens. Moreover, some Roman administrators actually believed (as did the British in their time) that they had a moral responsibility to improve the living conditions of those they conquered. Their legal system and engineering feats really did improve life in many ways.

Nevertheless, the result was not necessarily anything that we would call "happiness." Subject peoples resented Roman taxation and Roman dominance, even though they could become Roman citizens. Moreover, the Romans themselves succumbed to anomie brought on among the upper classes by indolence, idleness, self-indulgence, and sheer boredom (an important but often overlooked problem in human history). Maybe the Jews were foolish for rebelling against Rome, because their refusal to cooperate meant that the Romans eventually made life miserable for them. But the point here is merely that the absence of war in itself does not generate happiness. Like suffering, happiness is an extremely complex state and depends on a wide range of both subjective and objective factors.

If human beings can be happy, and if human beings are finite, then it follows that the ability of human beings to experience happiness must be finite. Happiness is at least partly the result of necessary choices, either individually or collectively made. No one can "have it all." Elizabeth Gleick has observed in connection with feminist utopianism that "perhaps the problem is not feminism but the relatively recent notion that 'happiness' is within our grasp, that we can all have everything we want, when we want it, without making sacrifices. This is a point not only our mothers, but our fathers, too, would probably like to make."[110]

Selecting one way of life, no matter how desirable, always means rejecting another one that might be desirable in some quite different way. Stable states in the ancient world usually provided protection to agriculturalists, but this does not necessarily mean that they were happier. It might mean merely that they did not have to worry about the dangers of constant warfare that were common to many small-scale Neolithic societies.

Besides, the comparison can work both ways. Consider warlike pastoral societies. Ancient pastoralists were free from backbreaking work in the fields from sunrise to sunset. And, constantly on the move with their herds or flocks, they were relatively free from dependence on the weather. At the very least, they were free to move around. From their point of view, freedom might have seemed worth the price of war. Whether we share that point of view or not, we can hardly deny it as a logical conclusion from the fact that human existence precludes perfection and therefore demands choices. Some pastoral peoples eventually chose agriculture, and others did not. But even those who did – the Hebrews being an obvious example – sometimes remained ambivalent after losing much that was of value in the process. In short, every choice has a price.[111]

Even if we were able to make truly objective statements about happiness, however, the argument would still be flawed. Ancient agriculture, no less than pastoralism, presented inherent problems as well as benefits. For one thing, more efficient modes of food production often led to population explosions. This meant that people needed more complex forms of social, economic, and political organization. Many thousands of people could not live as simply and freely as a few dozen. And this in turn led to the development of hierarchy and all the problems (along with the benefits) associated with it.

Moreover, cultivating the soil inevitably placed a high value on land. The more successful a society, the more land it required. More land required more labour, so there were two solutions: having many children or recruiting slaves. Limiting the population might have been one way of solving the problem of scarce resources, but this was seldom the first choice. Finding more land must have been a more attractive solution. This presented no major problem at first. But settled communities eventually found themselves competing directly for land and access to water with other settled communities, as we have already observed, and therefore raiding or conquering each other.

Also, raising crops never involves a state of perfect equilibrium with the natural environment. Being human always means living within both nature and culture, but cultivation is, by definition, an attempt to exploit and control it. And nature itself is neither stable nor harmonious. It involves conflict, after all, because most animals kill and eat each other. This means that a sense of mystical "oneness" with nature, though possible now and then as a temporarily altered state of consciousness (often by means of ritual or meditation), is inherently limited by the constraints that human existence imposes. At any rate, the effects of cultivation – modification and even disruption of the natural environment – were insignificant at first. But the long-term results of new technologies were not less real for being initially less apparent. When these succeeded on a large scale – which was necessary in order to support the increased population – the effect sometimes became very problematic.

People often imagine that the harmful effects of exploiting nature are entirely modern problems due to the use of high technology. In fact, the ancients knew very well about problems such as soil erosion and soil exhaustion. The currently arid "Fertile Crescent," for example, really was fertile at one time. But by the Roman period, deforestation – partly due to grazing, but also partly due to cultivation – and poor agricultural practices were already turning this region into the desert that it has remained ever since.

Even if the problems inherent in agriculture took a longer time to show up in the case of horticulture, that is no reason to ignore them. Why pretend that horticulture was more characteristic, normative, or definitive than technologically more sophisticated agriculture? The two phenomena were closely related; the latter continued the former, although the tools made possible with the discovery of iron smelting made the process much more efficient. But agricultural problems were inherent even in horticulture, which also involved changing nature to suit human needs. This is very important because of claims that goddess-worshipping horticultural societies were inherently superior to later god-worshipping agricultural ones. Our point here is to oppose the idea that these were utopias. Each technological development that solved some problems also created new ones. Generally speaking, though, people preferred to solve problems despite the new ones created in doing so.

Was the Neolithic a golden age of egalitarian harmony under the aegis of a great goddess, one that later ages eclipsed? If we can consider the past four or five millennia recent history (and we can), then we have a clear answer. Even if it took a thousand years in some places for horticultural villages to become agricultural states and come into conflict with other agricultural states, that transition was nevertheless a passing phase in the larger context of cultivation (let alone human evolution and development). To give that particular phase normative value would make no sense.

Tendentious claims about a great goddess are extremely problematic, then, for several reasons. For one thing, they rely on contradictory evidence. Furthermore, anthropological studies challenge their allegedly universal applicability. Because the claims rely on beliefs about the essential nature of men and women, we must take these problems seriously. Scholarship around a great goddess purports to be verifiable in archaeological and historical terms, but experts in these very fields disagree. Underlying these problems, moreover, is a much more serious one: political claims that depend ultimately on beliefs, not data. There is nothing wrong with beliefs in themselves, but there *is* something wrong when academics conflate them with scholarship. That happens when they bring in carefully selected evidence to "prove" what are essentially religious, political, or therapeutic and thus inherently unverifiable claims.

We explain the half-truths mentioned so far as the result of research projects at prestigious universities. Lerner, for instance, is a well-established academic who has written numerous books. She is Robinson-Edwards professor of history at the University of Wisconsin and a past president of the Organization of American Historians. In *The Creation of Patriarchy*, she writes that her historical reconstruction is based on the archaeological records of ancient Near Eastern civilizations. Many academics see her book as sound historical scholarship. She sees it as something more than mere historical scholarship, however, observing that "revolutionary ideas can be generated only when the oppressed have an alternative to the symbol and meaning systems of those who dominate them."[112] She observes also that the "system of patriarchy is a historic construct; it has a beginning; it will have an end."[113] There is no question about her intention of bringing about that end by rewriting history. The only question is whether she does so within the constraints imposed by archaeological and textual evidence – that is, by scholarship.

Marija Gimbutas, who died in 1994, was a professor of European archaeology at the University of California at Los Angeles. Developing the new discipline of "archaeomythology," she wrote more than twenty books and two hundred articles on "Old Europe." In

The Language of the Goddess and *The Civilization of the Goddess*, she presented what she considered facts, not mere theory. Gimbutas stated with supreme self-confidence that she was "not interested in theory. The materials speak for themselves."[114] In other words, she relied on the traditional assumption of scholarly objectivity – an assumption, by the way, that many feminists have attacked as a pernicious illusion fostered by "the male model." Nonetheless, other feminists make even more dramatic claims on Gimbutas's behalf. Eva Keuls contributes the following remark to the book jacket of *Civilization*: "This work, the fruit of decades of research, yields insights that totally upset traditional concepts of the forces that have shaped human history ... Gimbutas is destined to go down in history as a scholar who has profoundly affected the way we think about ourselves and where we come from."[115] (Keuls, a professor of classics at University of Minnesota, wrote *The Reign of the Phallus: Sexual Politics in Ancient Athens*.)

Lerner, who knows the tests of historical scholarship, chooses a different way to admire Gimbutas. On the same book jacket she observes that this "bold and imaginative reconstruction of earliest religious symbols based on dominance of the Great Goddess offers an alternative to androcentric explanatory systems. It can never be proven, but that it *might* have been is enough to challenge, inspire, and fascinate. An important work."[116]

The books of Lerner and Gimbutas are crossovers between academic and trade books, popular among educated but not necessarily academic readers. Publishers have been well aware since the 1980s that books about women and goddesses, both fiction and non-fiction, sell very well. Not surprisingly, Gimbutas's book has come out in a glossy coffee-table edition.[117] We have already discussed Eisler's massively popular *Chalice and the Blade*.

Some authors have capitalized not only on feminism but also on the New Age vogue. Barbara G. Walker, whose academic background consists of a B.A. from the University of Pennsylvania, has brought out a new book almost every year. Because one of her books has the word "encyclopedia" in the title and another the word "dictionary," each is found in the reference sections of countless university libraries. Here is one passage from the *Woman's Encyclopedia of Myths and Secrets*:

Few words are so revealing of Western sexual prejudice as the word Goddess, in contrast to the word God. Modern connotations vastly differ from those of the ancients to whom the Goddess was a full-fledged cosmic parent figure who created the universe and its laws, ruler of Nature, Fate, Time, Eternity, Truth, Wisdom, Justice, Love, Birth, Death, etc.

Male writers through the centuries broke the Goddess figure down into innumerable "goddesses," using different titles or names she received from different peoples at different times. If such a system had been applied to the usual concept of God, there would now be a multitude of separate "gods" with names like Almighty, Yahweh, Lord, Holy Ghost, Sun of Righteousness, Christ, Creator, Lawgiver, Jehovah, Providence, Allah, Saviour, Redeemer ... ad infinitum, each one assigned a particular function in the world pantheon ... The names and titles of the Goddess were ever more minutely classified, and some were even masculinized, humanized, or diabolized. Yet such classification tends to disintegrate under deeper study that reveals the same archetypal characteristics in nearly all the "goddesses."[118]

Walker's analogy is false, although it seems convincing enough at first. The masculine names and titles that she lists all originated in a single but fragmented religious tradition. Other differences aside, Jews, Christians, and Muslims have always acknowledged that they worship the same god and that this god has many functions. They have never acknowledged – except, possibly, for a few avant-garde theologians in our time – a similar kinship between their own God and the Hindu Vishnu, say, or the Zoroastrian Ahura Mazda. It is true, therefore, that *insiders* such as theologians acknowledge the existence of only one god and consider the others either false gods or forms of the one. But outsiders such as historians have always acknowledged the existence of many. From that point of view, it is not only possible but also desirable and even necessary to fragment "God" – that is, to classify gods according to function, period, place of origin, and so forth. For scholars, it would be not only anachronistic but also irresponsible to trivialize the historical experiences and unique insights of such different peoples by arguing that their gods are just interchangeable manifestations of a great god who is "awesome, powerful and transcendent."[119]

By the 1990s, some scholars were becoming sceptical of theories around a great goddess. In 1991, one of us (Katherine Young) published a long article, "Goddesses, Feminists, and Scholars," which is the seminal source for this book.[120] The article included sections on the great goddess as the first form of religious expression, the great goddess and monotheism, and the great goddess in matrilineal societies. It challenged the prevalent theories – those of Lerner, Gimbutis, Walker, Naomi Goldenberg, and others – by examining in detail the anthropological and archaeological evidence for those theories. Young concluded:

> Thus, it cannot be argued that a goddess is "the earliest known phase of religious worship" or the "primordial form as the source of all." Moreover, if the evidence varies even within Europe, it cannot be argued that the "Great Goddess" is universally an aspect of the Palaeolithic period . . . In any case, we have found several discrepancies between the data and the interpretations. We also have found that the comparative analysis has been sys-tematically ignored. In an age of mature scholarship and on such an important topic, it is curious that we must ponder the motives of well-known scholars in the field when they claim that "The Goddess" is primordial.[121]

Young drew attention to the parallel between a new myth of par-adise and the biblical one, moreover, and to the fact that the claim of a primordial great goddess attracts women who are so critical of patriarchal myths: "While omnipotence, supremacy, and partheno-genesis mirror the patriarchal concept of a supreme deity, it is hardly coincidental – but highly ironic – that these terms also reflect current feminist interest in power, superiority, and reproductive autonomy."[122] In addition, Young criticizes female academics for self-consciously selecting or deselecting evidence in order to pro-mote their feminist goals. In other words, they replaced scholarship with "engaged scholarship." Doing so had been common since the rise of intellectual fashions such as deconstruction and postmodern-ism that legitimate bias by arguing that everyone is biased anyway. Engaged scholarship is therapeutic for women, some of them argue, because it reveals how women have been oppressed by patriarchy.

In a 1992 article, "The Twilight of the Goddess," Mary Lefko-witz took issue with the practice:

> These technicians of the psyche do not abandon the pretence to historical knowledge. Along with a spiritual claim and a psycho-logical claim, they are making a historical claim. Virtually all the

authors of books and manuals on the Goddess and her modern cults, whether they are writing for worshippers in California or in England, are confident that they are correctly reconstructing the rites and the beliefs of a lost ancient religion. They argue that the Goddess, and more generally a religion that reflected the power held by women in ancient societies, preceded the male dominated religions described in all the familiar mythologies. They insist, in sum, on myth *and* history. Where historical claims are made, however, historians have a right to ask a few questions. Was there ever such a Goddess? And was there ever such a woman centered archaic religion?[123]

By 2000, Cynthia Eller had focused her interest in goddess religion on its emergence in prehistory. In *The Myth of Matriarchal Prehistory: Why an Invented Past Won't Give Women a Future*, she expands on Young's "Goddesses, Feminists, and Scholars" and provides useful additional archaeological and anthropological evidence against the premise of a women's utopia in the remote past. Eller focuses on Western data. Unlike Young, though, she does not draw attention to the biblical parallels. We will return to Eller in chapter 7.

Although we focus on a period between the 1970s and the 1990s, we should add that academics are still writing books to challenge the theory that a supreme goddess reigned over a matrilineal utopia. Consider *Goddesses and the Divine Feminine* (2005) by Rosemary Ruether:

Although I am very sympathetic to the need for a redemptive alternative to the systems of violence that threaten humanity and the earth, I find myself skeptical of a great deal of this explanatory line. We cannot know with much certainty what the cultures were like before written history in the ancient Near East or elsewhere. I find it likely that preagricultural gatherer societies were more egalitarian, in the sense of having little class hierarchy, but gender arrangements may have varied. At best, perhaps some had parallel spheres for men and women, where both were more or less equally valued.

I doubt the existence of female-dominated societies in which the relations between men and women, humans and nature, were totally harmonious. I suspect that some of the tensions from which later hierarchy developed were present earlier in nascent form. The growing ability to accumulate and concentrate wealth allowed these nascent tensions to become explicit.

The powerful goddesses we find during the second and first millennia BCE in societies in Mesopotamia, Palestine, Egypt, and Greece – such as Inanna/Ishtar, Anat, Isis, and Demeter – do not strike me as survivals of some original, pro-woman, great goddess who goes back to Paleolithic times. Kingly and queenly gods and goddesses, I believe, were inventions reflecting the same process by which urban society, social hierarchy, and literacy were developing sometime in the fourth to third millennia BCE.[124]

To conclude, some academics have used not only their expertise in history and archaeology but also their ideological points of view to reinterpret the data on gender, both human and divine, from prehistoric Europe and the ancient Near East. Wanting to improve the lives of women, they consciously or unconsciously gravitate toward a gynocentric view of history – which is to say, one that would provide women with a glorious past: a once-and-future golden age under the benevolent aegis of a great goddess. We suggest that political motivation has fostered their selective use of evidence and over-determined interpretations of data. Moreover, we suggest this motivation has both contributed to and drawn from the therapeutic or ideological fantasies of many feminists. Lerner, Gimbutas, and Eisler were writing, after all, during a conflicted era in the history of feminism.

In the late 1980s and early 1990s, many second-wave feminists continued to believe that women were simply the *equals* of men, taking their inspiration not only from the liberalism of Betty Friedan but also from that of Martin Luther King's civil rights movement. But other second-wave feminists began to believe that women were the *superiors* of men, taking their inspiration not only from one tendency of first-wave feminism but also from Malcolm X's Black Power movement. They sometimes paid lip service in public to sexual equality, because egalitarianism was the political lingua franca, but they nonetheless believed in sexual hierarchy. The historians and archeologists among them found what they wanted: female statues to indicate societies that valued fertility but no weapons of war to indicate societies that valued war. With all this in mind, they postulated a golden age of women in the remote past. But, as some critical feminists now realize, they conveniently ignored contrary evidence or made claims based on lack of evidence.

Some feminists have based their reconstructions on several fundamental but questionable claims. First, they claim, our primeval ancestors worshipped only goddesses or a supreme goddess; if they worshipped any gods at all, these were minor players in prehistory. Second, they claim, women were more powerful than men. Third, they claim, the lack of war made this world a veritable paradise on earth. The claims are false, however, because they rest on half-truths: they are partly true but also partly untrue. We discovered the untrue halves by revisiting the data, noting scholarly debates, suggesting alternative explanations, and testing claims against both historical and cross-cultural patterns.

It is true, for instance, that female symbols were probably more common in both prehistoric (and contemporary small-scale societies) than in the pantheons of large-scale societies – those of the world religions, which emerged after state formation. But this does not mean that the former were exclusively or even dominantly female. Anthropological evidence shows that some small-scale societies worship primarily gods, others primarily goddesses, and still others both gods and goddesses. It shows that gender symbols correlated, moreover, with the type of economy and the size of animals hunted. And it shows that these societies have various social structures, some matrilocal or matrilineal, others patrilocal, and still others combining these in various ways. To the degree that there is continuity between prehistoric or early historic societies and contemporary small-scale ones, these patterns are worth considering carefully. What archeological evidence we have, in fact, actually supports anthropological evidence.

It is true, moreover, that we have no evidence for war in Paleolithic societies. War probably originated in connection with raiding, which became desirable and feasible only after the domestication of plants and animals. And earlier wooden fortifications, if any, would have disappeared long ago. But this state of affairs says nothing about the status of either women or goddess worship. Divine queens (or kings, for that matter) were possible only after the rise of states that were led by their mortal counterparts.

Lerner, Gimbutas, and Eisler have presented carefully selected empirical data to create and support their academic theories. These theories in turn spawned utopian fantasies of dominant women and great goddesses. We can explain the growth of goddess ideology in connection with a hermeneutical circle that appeals not only to academics (such as Lerner and Gimbutas) but also to popularizers (such as Eisler and Walker).

Given the fact that feminism originated as a product of contemporary Western culture, it is hardly surprising that the feminist paradise is a new version of the biblical Eden. It is very surprising, however, that those who represent one of the most secular segments in Western societies – that is, academics – have exploited scholarship to create, or recreate, a myth. But this is the age of "engaged scholarship," much of which is ideologically driven.

Back now to *Goddess Remembered*. Obviously if this film is accurate, men's spirituality was marginalized in the old religion just as it is in the new – that is, in goddess ideology. Not once in the entire film does anyone consider that what might have seemed like a paradise to women might have seemed like something very different to men. Not once does anyone suggest that men, like women, developed a unique form of spirituality that could have been valued by society as a whole, let alone by men themselves. Not once does anyone suggest that men, like women, could have developed uniquely valuable qualities of any kind, let alone spiritual ones. Evidently there was no room in paradise for masculine spirituality. In the "egalitarian" societies imagined by this branch of feminism, men were free to exist as the "equals" of women as long as they acknowledged the supremacy of women.

This worldview – as distinct from the one that produces objective scholarship on women or some political activities on behalf of women – is explicitly gynocentric and therefore ignores the needs and problems of men. Gynocentrism is a form of essentialism – as distinct from scholarship or political activity on behalf of women – to the extent that it focuses on the innate virtues of women. But this worldview is explicitly misandric too, because it not only ignores the needs and problems of men but also attacks men. Misandry is a form of dualism to the extent that it focuses on the *innate vices* of men. In this moral or even ontological hierarchy, women are at the top and men at the bottom. (The same is true, at least theoretically, of androcentrism as a form of essentialism and misogyny as a form of dualism. But misandry is now publicly acceptable – accepted as "politically correct," embedded in popular culture, institutionalized in law – and misogyny is not.) Along with all the academic problems that we have discussed, then, is this moral one. Although ideologically oriented academics usually pay lip service to an egalitarian worldview, they actually promote a profoundly hierarchical one. In the one that we have been discussing, women are neither subordinate nor equal but superior to men.

In the next chapter, we focus on Act 2 of the new ideological myth, "the Fall" and its aftermath. According to goddess ideology (and its overtly secular counterpart, ideological feminism), men are not merely irrelevant but also collectively guilty of a primeval (but enduring) conspiracy against women and therefore are the ultimate source of all evil.

2

The Fall of Man
A Dark Age for Women

In Act 2 of the biblical myth about human origin and destiny, a serpent tempts the prototypical humans. They fall from the state of grace – that is, divine favour – and enter one of sinfulness.[1] Because of the Fall, God expels Adam and Eve from the paradisal world of Eden into the temporal world of conflict and chaos. According to the biblical version of this story, as we observed in the previous chapter, all three actors in this drama are guilty: Adam, Eve, and the serpent. Therefore, God punishes all three. According to some post-biblical versions, however, most of the guilt belongs to Eve and her female descendants. But according to the most recent interpretation, that of goddess ideologues and indirectly many of their secular counterparts, all of the guilt belongs to men.[2] Unlike the biblical story, in which Eve tempts Adam, the reverse is not true in this new version. Men do not tempt women. Instead, they conspire against women, take control from women, and oppress women. In other words, advocates believe, women bear no responsibility at all for what goes wrong.

Partly as a result of the pleasure of nostalgic reverie for a lost paradise, goddess ideologues focus most of their attention on Act 1. Act 2 is much more confusing, due to the emergence of patriarchal evil. Just as the goddess-ideological version of Act 1 has less to do with reality than with wishful thinking, so does Act 2. The golden age of women ends prematurely when the gods and their male thugs replace the great goddess and her female "healers" and "nurturers." This dualistic stage in the reconstruction of history relies no less than the earlier stage on a selective and tendentious sifting of the evidence.

In a way, this rewriting of Act 2 – of the Fall – relies more heavily on Freud's psychoanalytical version than either act does on the original biblical story. For Freud, a "primal crime" at the dawn of human history brought neuroticism into the psyche. Who committed this primal crime? Sons, he says, who murdered their father in order to usurp his power and have incestuous relations with his wives. Even though many feminists despise Freud – they loathe his theory of penis envy, for instance, and attack him for ignoring the possibility that many fathers really do molest their daughters – they seldom attack this theory about men. Consciously or subconsciously, many have adapted it to suit their own purposes (and therefore, through Freud, adapted the biblical paradigm as well). For them, the "primal crime" that brought suffering into history was perpetrated by men who controlled, bullied, raped, and even tried to exterminate women in order to usurp female power. This primal crime, say goddess ideologues, led directly to the patriarchal system – a malevolent social order that fosters brutality, suffering, confusion, conflict, misogyny, and evil – that has prevailed ever since gods replaced goddesses in the remote past.

Like both the biblical myth and its Freudian versions, that of goddess ideology is really about the present as much as, even more than, the past. The story of a primal crime symbolically represents what ideologues believe is the primary feature of everyday life today, the primary problem to be solved now. Unlike the Freudian version, this one has a distinctly metaphysical dimension. The word "patriarchy" in this context refers to more than an oppressive social or political system: it refers ultimately to an ontological and cosmic state. As we have already said, it is the equivalent of what Christians call Original Sin. It is the equivalent, also, of what Jews call Exile (*galut*) – which refers not merely to a demographic diaspora but also, and more importantly, to a state of alienation from God. Unlike the biblical version, however, that of goddess ideology has revolutionary political implications. Goddess ideologues do not believe that merely reforming the existing system can solve the problems that "patriarchy" entails.

Of great importance for those who promote this theory are two transitions: from an age of powerful women to one of powerful men and from an age of peace to one of war. Implicitly and even explicitly, goddess ideologues claim that women are somehow egalitarian even when dominant (which makes no sense) and therefore are innately good. Similarly, they claim, men are somehow violent even when not dominant (which is the only explanation for their rebellion) and therefore innately evil. But the main point is that men brought in the new order, either by rebelling from within or by invading from without, as the result of a universal conspiracy against women. First, they conspired to steal the power of women. Ever since, they have conspired to cover up what they did. But this theory poses a very serious question, one that feminists have never answered adequately: if the old order was so egalitarian and peaceful, why did local men want to rebel against it,[3] or foreign men want to destroy it? Many conquering societies, after all, have adopted or at least adapted what they considered the superior cultures of conquered societies. Among the more obvious examples would be Rome, which adopted much of Greek culture after invading its homeland.

Before proceeding, it is worth noting that academics have proposed several other explanations, some of them very fanciful. According to Elizabeth Davis, who popularized academic theories about female superiority, men were marginal figures in a matriarchal society, functionless outcasts who satisfied their sexual needs by indulging in pederasty. Innately brutal and removed from the moralizing influence of women, they rebelled and seized power for themselves. Their diet played a decisive role in the success of this rebellion. Eaters of meat have unusually large sexual organs, she opines, which "might have proved irresistible to women."[4] Josephine Schreier has come up with an even more *outré* theory. The men of matriarchal societies naturally identified themselves with powerful women, she claims, imitating them in childbirth and wearing their clothing during public rituals. Flattered by this, women elevated men to positions of power and even kingship. Then, these ungrateful men used their authority to take over.[5] But these two theories are of no use to feminists. Unwittingly, both Davis and Schreier make men look clever as well as evil. Even worse, they make women look stupid as well as good. In any case, as theories they are not only too silly but also too general according to the standards of scholars.

All three of the "documentary" films that we discussed in chapter 1 – *The Goddess Remembered*,[6] *Behind the Veil*,[7] and *The Burning Times*[8] – present goddess-ideological and therefore gynocentric versions of the transition from paradise to patriarchy. All three films blame every one of our problems on men. *Goddess* focuses directly on a transition in ancient Europe and the Near East along with its aftermath, which it describes in terms of militarism, sexism, and racism. The other two films focus on additional aspects of the aftermath. According to *Veil*, Christianity marginalized a primordial women's religion either by forcing it underground or by hiding its remnants in the "subaltern" tradition of Catholic nuns. According to *Burning*, Christianity tried to annihilate this underground women's religion by annihilating women as witches.

In this chapter, we focus on each of these three films in turn. In each case, we show how the film portrays the transition and its aftermath, pointing out that feminists have used the same arguments and demonstrating that those arguments are inadequate. We conclude with a brief discussion of how modern people retell this story in secular terms.

Goddess begins with an attack on "progress." No one wants to do away with penicillin or refrigeration; what some want to do away with are the bad by-products – acid rain, say, or nuclear weapons – of the same cultural forces that produced those good things. And some feminists identify those cultural forces explicitly with men. After this overture, the narrator introduces the main theme: "By 1500 B.C., volcanoes, earthquakes and armed invasions had buried the last great goddess culture ... All over the Western world, waves of conquerors descended on the peaceful goddess-worshipping cultures. And at Delphi, too, the gentle temple became a male-dominated hive of exploitation, with the gentle voice of the priestesses buried under layers of hierarchy."[9] At this point, Carol Christ speaks up: "And I think the transition had a lot to do with the rise of warfare in the Middle East, which ... became a significant factor in some places around 3000 B.C. and was a strong factor in the Middle East by 2000 B.C. just about everywhere."[10] Whatever went wrong, in other words, it began with them, not us. The narrator sums it all up:

History books call it the Dawn of Western *Civilization*, the golden age of Greece. For the man, it was the beginning. For the woman, it was the end. The Greeks announced that history would now begin, and proceeded to obliterate or pervert the 25,000 years that had gone before ... The violent and

erotic became linked as they never had been before. Man, said
men, had always been the natural master of the earth. He was
now also the procreator. Athena sprang fully armed from the
brow of Zeus. Eve was born from Adam's rib. Female inferiority forever was proclaimed by the book of Genesis. It is not
to be imagined that women accepted the subordinate status
peaceably. There were pockets of female resistance that gave
rise to legends of Amazons. But the male soon asserted his
total domination, and so it has been for 3,500 years.[11]

Ominous music provides the background for a commentary by
Carol Christ: "So I think that what we've had ever since the rise of
militarism in societies [are] ... warrior cults. They're really celebrating war. They're antagonistic to natural death, but they're creating
massive death in warfare all the time."[12] Actually, almost every living
religious tradition, each the product of a society in which men dominate, has acknowledged that war is a major problem. Some have
condoned killing only under specific circumstances, and others –
Jainism, for instance – have rejected killing in most circumstances.

Unwittingly, Charlene Spretnak introduces an idea that might yet
– in spite of her own efforts and those of her allies – make the future
better than either the present or the past: "I don't think you can
understand patriarchy unless you look at the fact that fear is at the
core."[13] This is true – but fear of precisely what? Women, no less
than men, will need courage to take this question seriously. The film
links women explicitly with nature and thus with whatever is
primordial, traditional, good, healthy, and useful. It links men
with modern technology and thus with whatever is supposedly
unhealthy and dangerous. By now our polluted "patriarchal" society has "long forgotten the spirit of the earth goddess."[14] But the
underlying cause of all our woe, according to Goddess, had nothing
to do with passive forgetting.

Just as men actively prohibited goddess worship in the name of
their gods, viewers learn, just as men actively undermined reverence
for the earth in the name of industrial exploitation, so they actively
displaced the primacy of women as "nurturers" with that of men as
conquerors and destroyers. After Louisa Teish, an Amerindian, tells
viewers that the European settlers on the frontier considered her
people savages, Starhawk adds this: "You know, sexism and racism
do go together. They are two sides of the same thing."[15]

Having looked at the story in popular culture, we turn now to the same story in elite culture – that is, academic culture. Like every golden age, say some academic feminists, that of women ended prematurely. Gerda Lerner describes its demise and that of its reigning goddess in the two passages that follow:

> Sometime during the agricultural revolution relatively egalitarian societies with a sexual division of labor based on biological necessity gave way to more highly structured societies in which both private property and the exchange of women based on incest taboos and exogamy were common. The earlier societies were often matrilineal and matrilocal, while the later surviving societies were predominantly patrilineal and patrilocal. Nowhere is there any evidence of a reverse process, going from patriliny to matriliny. The more complex societies featured a division of labor no longer based only on biological distinctions, but also on hierarchy and the power of some men over other men and all women. A number of scholars have concluded that the shift here described coincides with the formation of the archaic state. It is with this period then that theoretical speculation must end, and historical inquiry begin.[16]

> My thesis is that, just as the development of plow agriculture, coinciding with increasing militarism, brought major changes in kinship and in gender relations, so did the development of strong kingships and of archaic states bring changes in religious beliefs and symbols. The observable pattern is: first, the demotion of the Mother Goddess figure and the ascendance and later dominance of her male consort/son; then his merging with a storm-god into a male Creator-God, who heads the pantheon of gods and goddesses. Wherever such changes occur, the power of creation and of fertility is transferred from the Goddess to the God ... [These changes are accompanied by changes in symbols] from (1) the vulva of the goddess to the seed of man; (2) from the tree of life to the tree of knowledge; (3) from the celebration of the Sacred Marriage to the Biblical covenants.[17]

As older traditions declined, Lerner continues, the notion of creation changed from being "merely the acting out of the mystic force of female fertility to being a conscious act of creation, often involv-

ing god-figures of both sexes"[18] such as a son or brother who mates
with the mother goddess and must die before his rebirth. With the
development of writing and the elaboration of symbol systems
came a major change. No longer did people consider creation, or
creativity, an exclusively female domain that only female symbols,
such as mother goddesses, could represent. From then on, they considered creation and creativity as domains of men and used male
symbols – the gods of wind, air, and thunder – to represent them.
This change correlates with the establishment of archaic states in
the Near East, says Lerner, beginning in the third millennium BC.
Absolute kings ruled these states[19] and defended or expanded them
with the help of (male) military leaders. The process ended with the
rise to supremacy of national gods such as Marduk in Babylonia
and Ashur in Assyria. At the same time, goddesses became their
wives or daughters and proliferated in forms that remained vital in
popular religion. Generally speaking, though, gods replaced goddesses as major cosmic forces. Not surprisingly, therefore, priests
replaced priestesses.

Did this supposedly sinister scenario take place also beyond the
ancient Near East, as Lerner claims? In a word, yes.[20] Similar sce-
narios occurred in Japan, Arabia, China, and Africa. But did they
take place everywhere? The answer is no. Generally speaking, the
formation of states correlates with the advent of patrilineality
(where it had not previously existed) and the prevalence of either
gods or gods and goddesses and, eventually, supreme gods.[21] But
the process by which these things came about was hardly uniform.
Various kinds of transition took place. Four of them are worth
noting here.

In some regions, it is true, the transition was from matrilineality
and goddess worship to patrilineality and supreme-god worship
(often after an interim stage that featured the sacred marriage of a
god and goddess). Goddesses became marginal in the sense that
their creative functions no longer dominated creation myths and
were no longer central to definitions of political power; they entered
popular culture as specialists linked with sickness, death, fertility,
and magic. The process took from a few generations to complete to
a few centuries. In other areas, no such developments took place.
Instead, the transition was from many equal gods to one supreme
god. Archaeological evidence in these regions indicates a preference
for gods, not goddesses. The switch among these peoples was there-

fore not from goddesses to gods but from many gods to one god. In yet other regions, the transition was from a *deus otiosus*, a supreme but nominal god, to a supreme and active god. And in still others, several gods vied with each other for supremacy.

This takes us to the next ostensibly academic argument: that men conspired and perpetrated these seismic shifts. There are many feminist versions of the conspiracy theory, ranging from the conceivable to the fanciful. All of them are hostile to men. The bottom line in each theory is that men managed to remove goddesses and women from power in various ways: by exploiting their reproductive capacity, by overthrowing them violently, or even by flattering them.

Lerner argues that men conspired to make women into their tribal resources and later, with the rise of private property,[22] into their possessions:

> Women's *biological vulnerability* in childbirth led tribes to procure more women from other groups and ... this tendency toward the theft of women led to constant intertribal warfare. In the process, a warrior culture emerged. Another consequence of this theft of women is that the conquered women were protected by the men who had conquered them or by the entire conquering tribe. In the process, women were thought of as possessions, as things; they became reified while men became the reifiers because they conquered and protected. Women's reproductive capacity is first recognized as a tribal resource, then, as ruling elites develop, it is acquired as the property of a particular kin group. This occurs with the development of agriculture.[23]

There is something to what Lerner says. The need for communal survival would surely have placed a high value on the reproductive capacity of women.[24] It is true that every community considered women among its resources in connection with reproduction and some forms of food production. Without enough women to renew the population and ensure communal survival, moreover, an obvious solution would have been to replace the exchange of women between communities with raiding other communities for women. This did mean that women were *like* communal possessions in some ways. And it is true that raiding could have set up a cycle of relation: endemic warfare. But Lerner's theory creates as many problems as it solves.

Gynocentric (and misandric) to the core, she makes raiding for women and therefore the oppression of women central to human history. But human societies have always structured reproduction. Patrilocal or patrilineal societies, at any rate, have always exchanged women in the context of marriage; we have no reason to assume that stealing women was always and everywhere the norm. Lerner argues not only that early societies saw their own women primarily as resources to be exploited and those of other communities as property to steal (as if they did not also consider their own men as resources to be exploited and those of other communities as enemies to be killed) but also that warfare originated primarily with raiding for women (as if it did not have many other causes). Her whole theory is therefore reductive, to say the least.[25]

She ignores the fact that death in childbirth was nothing new for women at the time of state formation. It had always been a danger. She ignores the possibility or even the probability, moreover, that societies had always structured reproduction in one way or another. After all, they had to bring men and women together in reliable ways and on an enduring basis for the sake of future generations. Even very early societies probably guarded against incest by insisting on exogamy – marrying people from other bands. At first, men might well have sought wives from other villages.[26] This haphazard practice might have developed into an orderly exchange of sisters between bands. They must have recognized the strategic importance of having female relatives in other bands. For one thing, linked bands were more likely to combine their efforts at hunting. In addition, women with ties to both bands could act as mediators between them in disputes. We can trace all of these things, in fact, to the proto-human period of *Homo erectus* or even *Homo habilis*.[27] In short, early humans recognized the value of finding wives from beyond the local community long before the establishment of states and their systematic efforts to control the reproductive capacity of women.

Lerner opines that the status and power of women declined in early Near Eastern city states because men decided to take control over female reproductive capacity. Only this can explain the notion of exchanging or stealing women, she believes, thus turning them into things, or "reifying" them. But she assumes that men did so to increase the population, forgetting that the population of this region had already increased dramatically just *before* the emergence of city states.[28] And local resources, mainly land and water, were not unlimited; people might well have tried to *check* the population, not to increase it still further.

As well, it was during the Neolithic, just before the formation of states and their "patriarchal" institutions, that the notion of private property originated in connection with the domestication of plants and animals, "By about 7000 B.C." Robina Quale writes, "the pattern of separate sleeping huts and storage huts had changed to one of a single, separate sleeping and storage facility for each family. Clearly a sense of mine-and-thine was being inculcated."[29] By that time, stockpiling important resources had already become both desirable and possible. Because people could steal herds and grain, they had to claim them as property. If they linked private property with women, then, they probably began doing so during the Neolithic period – the alleged golden age of women![30]

Lerner succumbs, unfortunately, to extreme reductionism. Even though she mentions several other theories, giving the appearance of judiciously assessing each, she fails to take any of them seriously. She manages to make the exploitation of female reproductive capacity the origin of all evil, including capitalism (by arguing that women were the original form of private property) and slavery (by arguing that the exploitation of female labour in reproduction provided the model for the exploitation of male labour), and war (by the very act of raiding). In short, she says, women were the archetypal victims and men the archetypal victimizers. Even though feminists such as Lerner generally repudiate this victim/victimizer model in order to claim that women are actors, or "agents," in history, they find it expedient to use that way of thinking in their own explanations for the rise of patriarchal social structures.

Feminists evidently assume that ancient gods and goddesses, like men and women, were opposites. But were they? Not necessarily: ancient Near Eastern goddesses, for instance, were sometimes very warlike. Tivka Frymer-Kensky refers to the bellicose characteristics of Sumer's Inanna (Babylon's Ishtar). She had a distinctly masculine profile. For one thing, she bestowed political power on the king by bringing him military victories.[31] She remained his lover and protector but only as long as he succeeded in battle.[32] In hymns to her, written by a priestess and princess of Sargon, she is a "strong and ferocious warrior, devastator of the land, one whose rage is not tempered."[33] According to

Frymer-Kensky, she represented "sheer force, rage, and might, with a physical power, that exists in a somewhat uneasy relationship to the orderly world of the hierarchical pantheon.[34]

Ideological feminists evidently assume, moreover, that powerful ancient goddesses represented powerful women. But did they? With the latent power and autonomy of women in mind, Lerner notes that Ishtar was "mistress of the battlefield, more powerful than kings, more powerful than other gods."[35] At issue for Lerner is the "empowerment" of women.

"My point here," she writes, "is that men and women offering such prayers when in distress must have thought of women, just as they thought of men, as capable of metaphysical power."[36] When discussing the power of women, she is willing to appropriate martial goddesses. When discussing the pacifism of women, on the other hand, she is very careful to do nothing of the kind.[37] The association of goddesses with war is not entirely surprising in view of their association with birth and, by extension, with rebirth (and thus their ability to rescue warriors from death in battle). In the rush to glorify the maternal aspects of goddesses, feminists often forget this aspect or relegate it to a footnote.

But Innana's close ties with the king did not give her authority over the gods; moreover, it did not make her a role model for ordinary women. She was not a domestic goddess. In myths, she does not bear children, nor does she spin, dye, or weave. In a way she is more like a role model for men! Tikva Frymer-Kensky writes, "Inanna was the very spirit of battle. Warfare, the 'festival of manhood,' was 'Inanna's dance,' a theme that continued throughout Mesopotamian history. Iconographically, she holds a bow, the classic weapon of war and the standard symbol of manliness."[38] By the Babylonian period, Inanna-Ishtar had become a divine anomaly, a masculine personality with a female form: "Ishtar was the 'manly' goddess, the exception that proved the rule about females."[39]

And Inanna-Ishtar was not the only goddess of this kind. Consider Anat, a Canaanite goddess. According to Susanne Heine, Anat "fights, wades in the blood of her opponents," is "sated with her killing; the heads she has cut off reach up to her waist ... She is filled with joy as she plunges her knees in the blood of heroes."[40] There were others: Athena and Minerva in the West, Kali and Durga in the East, and so forth.[41] Here is one description of Candamari, a local version of Kali: "The goddess adorns herself with pieces of human corpses, uses oozings from corpses for cosmetics, bathes in rivers of wine or blood, sports in cremation grounds, and uses human skulls as drinking vessels ... devotees gather at her temple and undertake forms of ascetic self-torture. They burn incense on their heads, drink their own blood, and offer their own flesh into the sacrificial fire."[42]

The *Devi-mahatmya* describes Kali as a warrior. In this passage, she springs from the head of Durga. "She is black, wears a garland of human heads and a tiger skin, and wields a skull-topped staff. She is gaunt, with sunken eyes, gaping mouth, and lolling tongue. She roars loudly and leaps into the battle, where she tears demons apart with her hands and crushes them in her jaws. She grasps the two demon generals and in one furious blow decapitates them with her sword ... Kali defeats the demon by sucking the blood from his body."[43]

How does Marija Gimbutas explain the takeover by men? According to her and her supporters, men took over in the context of an invasion. In his foreword to Gimbutas's *Language of the Goddess*, Joseph Campbell points with approval to the opposition that he sees in her account: "manipulated" systems (which she associates with men) versus natural and peaceful ones (which she associates with women):

In contrast to the mythologies of the cattle-herding Indo-European tribes that, wave upon wave, from the fourth millennium BC, overran the territories of Old Europe and whose male-dominated pantheons reflected the social ideals, laws, and political aims of the ethnic units to which they appertained, the iconography of the Great-Goddess arose in reflection and veneration of the laws of Nature. Gimbutas's lexicon of the pictorial script of that primordial attempt on humanity's part to understand and live in harmony with the beauty and wonder of Creation adumbrates in archetypal symbolic terms a philosophy of human life that is in every aspect contrary to the manipulated systems that in the West have prevailed in historic times.

One cannot but feel that in the appearance of this volume at just this turn of the century there is an evident relevance to the universally recognized need in our time for a general transfor-

mation of consciousness. The message here is of an actual age
of harmony and peace in accord with the creative energies of
nature which for a spell of some four thousand prehistoric years
anteceded the five thousand of what James Joyce has termed the
"nightmare" (of contending tribal and national interests) from
which it is now certainly time for this planet to wake.[44]

Consider this carefully in view of what Gimbutas writes. In the
introduction to one of her books, she traces the decline of prehistoric Europe's worldview to invasions by Indo-Europeans between
4300 and 2800 BC, "changing it from gylanic (i.e., egalitarian) to
androcratic and from matrilineal to patrilineal ... We are still living
under the sway of that aggressive male invasion and only beginning
to discover our long alienation from our authentic European Heritage – gylanic, nonviolent, earth-centered culture."[45] Riane Eisler
invented the word "gylanic," a tendentious combination of abbre-
viations for *gyne* (woman) and *andros* (man),[46] to indicate sexual
equality.[47] Gimbutas's use of the word here is disingenuous, though,
because sexual equality is not what she has in mind. In fact, she
refers in many places to the female-dominated society of a once and
future paradise. "Our authentic European heritage," she said in one
interview, "was a nonviolent, earth-avowing culture where the ruling was in the women's hands."[48] Presumably, it was that series of
invasions by Indo-Europeans from the Russian steppes that put an
end to this supposedly idyllic state.[49]
Other scholarly theories about the Indo-Europeans abound.
The point here is that the theories have provoked heated debate.
Because Gimbutas does not acknowledge such debates, she relies
on ideology. This is why she not only argues for an Indo-European
invasion but also attributes it to the evil of men. For her, as for her
supporters, men are *collectively guilty* for having engaged in "the
ultimate hubris, symbolic matricide, by setting up an all-mascu-
line theology":[50]

Parthenogenetic goddesses creating from themselves without the
help of male insemination gradually changed into brides, wives,
and daughters and were eroticized, linked with the principle of
sexual love, as a response to a patriarchal and patrilinear [*sic*]
system ... Furthermore, Zeus had to "seduce" (with a nod toward
historical accuracy, we might prefer the term "rape") hundreds

of other goddesses and nymphs to establish himself ... [Later] the Killer-Regeneratrix, the overseer of cyclic life energy, the personification of winter, and Mother of the Dead, was turned into a witch of might and magic. In the period of the Great Inquisition, she was considered to be a disciple of Satan.[51]

Eisler largely recapitulates the version of the theory that Gimbutas made famous:

The title *The Chalice and the Blade* derives from this cataclysmic turning point during the prehistory of Western civilization, when the direction of our cultural evolution was quite literally turned around. At this pivotal branching, the cultural evolution of societies that worshiped the life-generating and nurturing powers of the universe – in our time still symbolized by the ancient chalice or grail – was interrupted. There now appeared on the prehistoric horizon invaders from the peripheral areas of our globe who ushered in a very different form of social organization. As the University of California archaeologist Marija Gimbutas writes, these were people who worshiped "the lethal power of the blade" – the power to take rather than give life that is the ultimate power to establish and enforce domination.[52]

Eisler specifically points the finger at barbarian invaders – the Hittites, Dorians, Assyrians, Hebrews, and so on – who waged wars of conquest in the Fertile Crescent. These invaders were "divinely inspired and therefore "utterly destroying the men, women, and children of every city."[53] She calls this development "a great social shift to technologies of destruction."[54]

Of greatest importance to Gimbutas is one fact: that the Indo-Europeans glorified war and warriors. She does pay lip service to the possibility that their invasions might have originated because of ecological change: the Indo-European homelands were becoming arid, making pastoralism difficult. At the same time, the domestication of horses made long-distance travel possible. These factors, she admits, created the possibility of moving on in search of better lands. So far, so good. But she ignores the Indo-European struggle for survival as a motivating factor for migration – even for invading and raiding – which might make these patterns seem not quite as morally reprehensible. Instead, she highlights other factors: the male-oriented social structure, male-dominated pantheon, and war-like behaviour. According to Gimbutas, we can attribute the loss of paradise directly to the invasion of (male-dominated) Indo-European tribes. Never mind that most pastoral societies worship dual-sex or male-dominated pantheons and practice patrilineality, facts that anthropologists attribute to the special connection between big animals and the men who herd them.

Given these problems with the theories of Lerner and Gimbutas, we still must ask: Why *did* matriarchy and goddess worship collapse? Why *did* patriarchy and god worship replace it? Contrary to Lerner's view, the setting from which androcentrism emerged – the Neolithic world – often involved intense competition and sporadic conflict, not peace and harmony.[55] This is what led to warrior cultures. Because men were the raiders (but also the defenders), and because raiding created new wealth, the economic status of men increased directly. That of women either decreased or increased only indirectly in connection with the success of fathers, husbands, or other related men. The waning of horticulture (which involved wooden hoes that women could push as well as men) and the advent of plough agriculture (which involved iron ploughs that men could push more easily than women) meant that women in the new economic and political order of proto-states lost not only their role as fundamental contributors to the food supply but also their opportunity to control its surplus through trade. Some women continued to work in the fields, it is true, but their contribution was less valued than it had been. Consequently, elite women were precisely those who did not have to work in the fields. Moreover, patrilineality meant that inheritance followed the male line, not the female one. Accordingly, elite women became economically dependent on men. Access to valuable resources was sometimes more difficult for them, in other words, than for men. In short, the new states not only marginalized women economically but also subordinated them politically.

Tribal norms were breaking down with the advent of chiefdoms and kingdoms. In their initial phases, these early states – proto-states – encouraged extreme forms of domination among elite men.[56] This was a period of radical individualism[57] and experimentation. Rulers symbolized their power by placing themselves beyond all constraints. Most men and women suffered, not surprisingly, from the ruthless power of these despots – not only from those of their own societies but also from those of invading ones. (When foreigners captured women, for instance, they raped and enslaved them; when foreigners captured men, they raped them first and then either enslaved or slaughtered them.)

But were these problems due solely or even primarily to the malice of chiefs and early kings (let alone to the inscrutable lust for power of men in general)? The problems that emerged for women had at least as much to do with fallout from the advent of agriculture. This included the continuing need for more land and easier access to water, the storage of surplus crops (which made raiding attractive), the growth of hierarchy due to specialization, the rise of individualism at the elite level (which fostered imitation at lower levels), and the advent of private property. Besides, men had faced real problems in matrilineal societies, which forced them to invest in the children of their sisters instead of in their own.

The rise of highly stratified states presented most men with another problem. We refer to fragmentation of the functional value attached to male bodies. The human body per se, whether male or female, confers identity and even high status to the extent that it contributes directly to communal survival. The male body had always done so in connection with fatherhood. But its other functions had begun to change. Hunting had given way to horticulture, pastoralism, and warfare. With the rise of states, however, began a process – several processes, actually, including the emergence of cities, literacy, warfare, trade, and social stratification – that gradually eroded the status (and recently even the identity) that the male body had once conferred.

These early states still relied on male bodies for reproduction. They still relied on male bodies for food production too, but the transition from hunting to agriculture meant that this function no longer conferred high status (although elite men continued to hunt for sport and thus retained its symbolic status in vestigial form.) Elite men owned arable land, to be sure, but the men who actually ploughed the fields were nothing more than serfs on noble estates or peasants. These early states relied on male bodies for warfare as well, but the need for a high level of organization meant that this function could no longer confer high status on all participants. Elite men – kings and their noble retainers – were leaders and generals, but most men by far were merely their cannon fodder. Worse, from this point of view, the bodies of middle-class men – traders, artisans, scribes, priests, and so on – had no functional importance whatsoever and therefore conferred neither high status nor even identity. To ensure their loyalty and subservience, political or religious leaders conferred some status on them and thus distinguished them not only from both upper-class and lower-class men but also from women. The carrier of status was culture (education), not nature (maleness). Middle-class men lived in the public sphere and had exclusive access to professions and crafts that required extensive training. Middle-class and elite women, on the other hand, did not. They lived in the private sphere and earned status precisely for *not* having to enter the public sphere, let alone to work in the fields alongside male and female peasants or serfs.

In short, technological and economic shifts were ultimately responsible for producing androcentric social, political, and religious worldviews. Over the past few centuries, and especially over the past few decades, similar shifts have made the male body increasingly obsolete. As a result, men with the highest status are precisely those who do *not* have to demonstrate physical prowess at anything distinctively male; instead, they can devote themselves to sedentary professions, the arts, leisure – or the organization, administration, and command of armies in wartime. Men with the lowest status, on the other hand, must still live by the sweat of their brows – that is, by the brute strength of their male bodies. These men are from the classes that contribute to society as agricultural laborers, industrial workers – unless machines replace them – and cannon-fodder for conscript armies.[58]

That androcentrism created major problems for *women* is the other part of this story, of course, and feminist historians are recovering that story from obscurity. Our point is not to trivialize the problems of women in androcentric societies but to point out three things. First, androcentric institutions did not originate in conspiracies of men against women. Second, they have not permanently solved the problems of men in any case (fatherhood being the one and only function of the male body that still confers identity on men, although even that could easily disappear due to biotechnological developments). Third, gynocentric replacements are likely to be just as problematic as androcentric ones.

We have already noted that the domestication of plants and animals made stockpiling both possible and desirable, and that this in turn made raiding both possible and desirable in horticultural or pastoral societies. Why then, as Gimbutas argues, should violence be characteristic of the Indo-Europeans in particular? They became warlike, we suggest, for the same reason that other groups did: economic or physical survival. They raided because of famine and because of a dramatic technological innovation: domestication of the horse. In any case, there is no scholarly consensus over where the Indo-Europeans came from, whether they invaded or merely migrated in waves, and whether they were all pastoralists and warriors.[59]

In her conclusion, Gimbutas observes that some female symbols have lived on underground: "They could have disappeared only with the *total extermination of the female population.*"[60] She implies that men made systematic though unsuccessful attempts to murder women on a colossal scale as part of their plot to take over the world from women. And she goes further. She believes that men are collectively guilty for having attempted a kind of sexual *genocide*, the deliberate extermination of women:

> The dethronement of this truly formidable goddess whose legacy was carried on by wise women, prophetesses, and healers who were the best and bravest minds of the time, is marked by blood and is the greatest shame of the Christian Church. The witch hunt of the fifteenth to eighteenth centuries is a most satanic event in European history in the name of Christ. The murder of women accused as witches escalated to more than eight million ... This was the beginning of the dangerous convulsions of androcratic rule which 460 years later reached the peak in Stalin's East Europe with the torture and murder of fifty million women, children, and men.
>
> The Old European culture was the matrix of much later beliefs and practices. Memories of a long-lasting gynocentric past could not be erased, and it is not surprising that the feminine principle plays a formidable role in the subconscious dream and fantasy world. It remains (in Jungian terminology) "the repository of human experience" and a "depth structure." To an archeologist it is an extensively documented historical reality.[61]

This is a perfect illustration of what we call the "selective cynicism" of so many political movements.[62] Gimbutas uses Stalin to represent all men. Why should we grant Stalin greater historical importance than Moses, Jesus, Francis of Assisi, the Buddha, Mahatma Gandhi, or Martin Luther King? In representing a distinctively human openness to change, in fact, the latter are much *more* important than the former. In evolutionary terms, the human race is in its infancy. We came down from the trees only yesterday, as it were. Recorded history itself represents nothing more than a nanosecond in the larger scheme of things, and so it should not seem remarkable that many people, including women, continue to live, anachronistically, more as biological organisms than enculturated beings. Truly remarkable, on the other hand, is that some people – including men – have already intuited that culture provides us with the flexibility to make choices. They have taught us that we can use moral or legal codes to resolve conflict, for example, and even to overcome brutality with compassion. History gives us no excuse for cynicism. True, not everyone supports the radical pacifism of Jesus, Buddha, Gandhi, or King; they find good reasons to support the traditions of a just war. The point here is only that Stalin does not represent all men or even most men.

Despite the initial loss of life and the consolidation of androcentrism, the new states must have seemed attractive to people in general – including women. States must have met at least some fundamental needs. Otherwise, the experiment would not have been repeated so many times and in so many places. The needs included greater security, a steady food supply, surplus food that could support specialization, trade, and creativity, luxury goods, and so forth. Moreover, states made possible economic and social reorganization. With economies based on agriculture and trade, which produced more surplus food than small-scale societies did, populations began to grow very quickly. This meant that many more people needed food and that many more people lived together. The informal mechanisms that worked well for small bands were no longer effective for large societies. But there was a price for efficiency and prosperity: more extreme hierarchy than found in Neolithic societies. This developed because of more surplus goods, greater individualism – those who led raids and military expeditions could control the surplus wealth and become chiefs or kings – and less accountability to the ethos of sharing that characterized small-scale societies.

These early states solved some problems but exacerbated others. They were often extremely fragile structures, for instance, and collapsed with the slightest shocks due to drought or the disruption of trade routes. When the Chou dynasty in China was disintegrating, therefore, Confucius advocated a return to the stability of a state but one that would be governed by benevolence rather than brutality. For him, the ideal man was the *ch`un tzu*, the gentleman, not the warlord. Confucius's vision of society might not appeal to everyone now (although we should not confuse it with the one that the Han dynasty implemented later on in his name),[63] but it was a very attractive and peaceful one for its time.[64] And we could cite other examples. Despite their initial fragility, in any case, many states became stable.

In some of them, the economic position of women gradually improved. In *Daughters of Isis*,[65] Joyce Tyldesley argues that Egyptian women of the dynastic period had more opportunities than the women of any period before the nineteenth century AD in Europe and America. Because they owned property, Egyptian women were active in commercial life. They could work outside the home, many industries being open to them, or represent their husbands in commercial activities. They were prominent participants in cultic activities at temples, often as priestesses, especially when the deity was a goddess. They could testify in court. They could marry the men they chose, close personal relationships between husbands and wives being among the most touching aspects of Egyptian life as represented by the artifacts that they left behind. Or women could live alone, not under the protection of men. A few women actually seized control of the country and ruled directly as pharaohs instead of indirectly as regents or consorts.

This is not to say that Egyptian women were "liberated" in the modern sense; Egypt was a profoundly conservative society. On the other hand, it was conservative in ways that placed no fewer constraints on men than on women. Both women and men expected to live according to traditional patterns. For both women and men, that involved getting married and having children. (Both women and men were, in fact, emotionally attached to their families.) In addition, both women and men did precisely the same jobs as their parents and grandparents and great-grandparents had done for centuries. First and foremost, however, women did what only women could do: give birth to and nurse their infants. What amazes modern historians is the degree of freedom that women enjoyed in a society that assumed that their most important function was to produce and care for children.

The stereotype of ancient Egypt as a society based on brutal tyranny (originating, of course, in Exodus) is false. Apart from anything else, slavery was uncommon until the New Kingdom's imperial age (that is, after approximately 1,500 years of recorded history). Even then, the entire economy did not rely on slavery (as it did in Greece and Rome). Brutality was an uncommon experience, moreover, even among the peasant and labouring classes. Nevertheless, it was a hierarchical and male-dominated society. What we can learn from Egypt and its neighbours, both in the Near East itself and in the Greco-Roman world, is the surprising degree of variation possible within societies of this kind and the surprising fact that women sometimes fared better in conservative societies such as Egypt than in philosophically experimental ones such as Greece.[66]

Early civilizations, no matter how conservative in theory, did change. By the rabbinic period, Jews had mandatory marriage contracts in order to protect the economic interests of women in case of divorce.[67] Hindu widows received economic support for life (although laws made that support minimal). Muslim women too had marriage contracts and inheritance rights.[68] Seen from the perspective of modern societies, Islam granted women little freedom; seen from that of pre-Islamic Arabia, however, Islam was a step in the right direction for women. Many states came to regulate the number of marriages for ordinary men,[69] varying from one to four[70] but sometimes more. By the laissez-faire standards of many chiefdoms and early states, regulation of any kind was revolutionary. Some states relied on moral or legal systems that frowned on premarital or extramarital relationships for anyone, although many tolerated a double standard that favoured men.

The new states gradually solved political problems by replacing the ideal of ruthless power with that of noblesse oblige. The ideal of the omnipotent king gave way, therefore, to that of the *just* king or the *wise* king.[71] Religious leaders criticized the capture of women to define the status of warriors or to punish their enemies. And they expressed this transition ritually. Many traditions replaced human sacrifice, common though by no means universal in horticultural societies and early states, first by animal sacrifice and then by symbolic re-enactments or by substitutes (effigies, fruits, flowers, and so on). They abolished infanticide, at least in theory, as well as many other practices that we now find deplorable.[72]

States eventually limited the power not merely of rulers but even, in some cases, of the gods. Consider the case of ancient Israel, where people took over some of the functions that they had formerly assigned to God. But the corollary of more human power was more human responsibility. Bound to God through covenants, people did what God had done. In the biblical tradition, according to Frymer-Kensky,

> Humanity serves as the pivot around which the world, and God's power, revolve. Israel develops additional explanations of history in which human beings have an even greater role: they are not only the fulcrum of action; they are the initiator of change in the universe. God's absolute power is not arbitrary: it is called into play in reaction to human behavior. Human beings have a direct impact on the environment: ultimately, the well-being of the earth and the people of Israel or their destruction is a result of human action ... Divine dominance means divine conditionality, as humankind becomes the reason for and instigator of divine action ... Underlying penitential prayer is an understanding that God does not determine the condition of nature unilaterally. God's control over nature is reactive, and depends ultimately on the action of Israel.[73]

The historical record is certainly uneven. Religions such as Buddhism and Jainism, originating as attempts to reform the sacrificial rituals of Vedic religion, proclaimed the principle of *ahimsa* (non-injury). By the classical period, from the fourth century BC to the fourth century AD, so did Hinduism, for everyone except the *kshatriya* class (warriors). This group had to protect its state, although it now heeded the notion of a just war. And very similar things happened elsewhere. The religion of ancient Israel was clearly a series of attempts, no matter how faltering, to diminish brutality and tyranny. Both rabbinic Judaism and Christianity represent further moves in the same direction. Jesus advised his followers to love not only their neighbours[74] but also their enemies[75] and even to "turn the other cheek" when attacked.[76] No wonder an early disciple proclaimed that God is love.[77] At that very time, the early rabbis were saying much the same thing. Hillel, the most famous of all, urged his disciples to love and pursue peace,[78] and Simeon ben Gamaliel assured his disciples that the cosmic order is founded on three principles: truth, justice, and peace.[79] Several rabbis proclaimed that destroying even one life is the same as destroying the world in God's eyes, and saving even one life is the same as saving the world.[80]

These traditions had come to understand history at least partially as the process of extending compassion into more and more areas of life. Sure, you can focus attention on the darkest events in history, but you can focus attention also on the brightest ones. Again, why grant Stalin greater historical importance than Gandhi? The best approach, we argue, is to examine the archaeological, historical, and anthropological records very carefully for details of changes and then to choose the most appropriate explanations for these, taking account of cross-cultural data.

The conspiracy theory of history relies on either inadequate scholarship or politically motivated mythmaking – or both – in the name of scholarship. It draws a spurious dichotomy between the Neolithic period and those that followed it (including our own). No evidence indicates the existence of a prehistoric golden age of women, whether promoters call it "matrilineal," "matrifocal," "gylanic," or whatever. Even if it had been a golden age for women, though, the society described by Gimbutas and Lerner was hardly an egalitarian one – not unless egalitarianism means that everyone is equal but that women are somehow more equal than men. Nothing, therefore, indicates that the alleged memory of an ancient paradise on earth would actually serve us as well as the vision of a future one. And if goddesses and women were as powerful as the feminists discussed here claim, we must conclude that men had good reason for rebelling (although, in doing so, they replaced one set of problems with another). Ironically, their reason for doing so – marginalization – would have been precisely the same as that of the women who are rebelling in our own time. If there is another round, though, modern men will have even better reasons for rebelling than their distant ancestors. For one thing, modern men have the advantage of hindsight. Besides, the exclusion of men from "women's spirituality" is now far more complete than it was, allegedly, at the dawn of history. Our remote ancestors created societies that, though androcentric, varied considerably. Many allowed both gods and goddesses, for instance, along with imagery that appealed to both men and women. And all valued the contributions of both men and women.

Veil tells the same basic story as *Goddess* but focuses attention more specifically on the fate of goddess worship under Christianity. Viewers learn that for centuries, especially in Celtic Ireland, goddess worship had a benign influence on the new religion. After a reassertion of patriarchal authority from Rome, the church forced it into an underground existence. With the rise of modern feminism, however, goddess religion is emerging once more as the true and primordial religion. To make sure that no one misses the subtext, according to which men are collectively guilty for everything that is wrong with the world, the narrator concludes by noting: "Two thousand years of patriarchy have brought us spiritual confusion and to the brink of physical destruction."[81]

We have already examined the conspiracy theory of history, so there is no point in challenging every detail of the "history" that *Veil* presents. It is enough to note that this film, like *Goddess*, selects factoids that allow only one interpretation. Like *Goddess*, moreover, it presents them very carefully in cinematic terms to reinforce that interpretation.

The film begins by introducing viewers to the primeval paradise of women and their great goddess. This one is in pre-Christian Ireland. But wait – here come the men with their patriarchy! Suddenly, sinister shadows fall across the rocky landscape. Suddenly, music turns into something more like noise: the clashing dissonance of percussion or brass instruments. Cinematic unity continues, however, because of the narrator. Her voice falls to a tender hush in solemn reverence for brave women who fell in the struggle for peace and harmony but then rises stirringly in righteous indignation over the tyranny of men that overcame them.

Veil is frankly and consistently polemical. Like *Goddess*, it makes not even the faintest attempt to present more than one point of view. Several techniques ensure that viewers get the right message. The historical narrative, for example, strategically frames a prologue and an epilogue that consist of interviews with contemporary nuns. This gives the impression of objective journalism. The nuns are real people who speak for themselves just as they would if being interviewed for, say, a segment of *60 Minutes*. They discuss their original reasons for entering the convent and their current thoughts on women in the church.

Although the nuns express dissatisfaction with Christianity, they do so in appropriately theological or quasi-theological terms. To this extent the film is a documentary; it documents the thoughts and feelings of people in a particular time, place, and situation. Nevertheless, *Veil* intends to provide far more than documentation or observation. The frame clearly refers in some way, after all, to what it frames; the former sets the tone for the latter and how viewers perceive it. As a result, viewers connect objective interviews with a highly subjective reconstruction of history. This technique provides an aura of legitimacy. Viewers connect the religion of modern Christian nuns, moreover, with that of ancient pagan priestesses. They get the impression, in other words, that these nuns consciously or subconsciously represent modern devotees of the great goddess. The nuns supposedly understand Christianity as if they were newly converted Celts.

Veil does not rely only on "subtle" cinematic techniques of this kind. Its polemical approach appears explicitly in the script from the narrator's first words: "Through the ages, society has cast women in a role."[82] The opening lines of any film are always significant by virtue of the mere fact that they *are* the first. Directors choose them to set the tone for what follows. And this director is no exception. It is true, of course, that "society has cast women in a role." But though *Veil* is not about men, intellectual honesty alone should have prevented the implication that society has stereotyped only women and denied choices only to women. Every society has denied choices to most men and stereotyped them. In fact, every society has expected men to do precisely what their fathers and grandfathers did for generations beyond memory. For most men by far, that has meant backbreaking labour in the fields. In the society of feudal Europe, even male nobles had only two choices: the chalice or the sword – that is, being either clerics (some of whom had to renounce material goods and all of whom had to renounce sexual activity) or knights (who had to risk their lives in battle). In other societies, both men and women have had more than one role.[83]

From the beginning, therefore, critical observers should be able to see that *Veil* has nothing to do with intellectual honesty, which would mean admitting the complexity and ambiguity of history. Like *Goddess*, it has a simple message that viewers can reduce to the following: universal happiness prevailed under a Celtic goddess, supposedly, before the nasty Christians under St Patrick invaded paradise and tried to destroy it. But women preserved enough of the old religion, suitably disguised, to provide their modern daughters with hope for a future return to paradise. *Veil* sums up this message, this *kerygma*, in a cinematic goulash of half-truths, lies, and fantasies.[84]

According to one rhetorical segment of narration, "it is only the men the church sanctions to stand at the altar, only the men who have the right to consecrate the bread and wine of the Eucharist, only the men who have any power to ascend to the hierarchy."[85] Yes, but for Catholicism, like most traditional forms of religion, no realm is beyond its scope. And this includes the natural order. For Catholics, nature is not merely the way that things are but also the way that things should be. It reveals not merely the activities of cells and proteins but the venue of holiness and salvation. God, they believe, had a reason for creating both men and women. Put differently, God created both men and women for distinctive purposes.

Although Catholic theologians have held that priesthood is a calling reserved for (some) men, they have held also that some callings are reserved, not by default but by design, for women. Motherhood is one of these. Catholics define motherhood not in purely biological, psychological, sociological, or economic terms but primarily in ontological and metaphysical terms. Motherhood is a divine calling, not just a job. It is a source of divine grace, not just a reproductive necessity. Another divine calling for women is monastic life. The narrator notes, in fact, that "among those who have chosen religious life in the Catholic Church, there are more than twice as many women as men."[86] But if Catholicism serves the needs of women so poorly and the needs of men so richly, how can we explain the anomaly of so many more women than men choosing monastic life? One obvious explanation is that, given the need for priests, many men who would otherwise have become monks (male monastics whose female counterparts are nuns) decide instead to become parish priests (who have no female counterparts).

Later on in *Veil*, the narrator says that "tradition dictates priests be men. Women just don't resemble Christ. A theologian replies: 'By that reasoning, all priests should be bearded Jewish fishermen.'"[87] This glib rejoinder trivializes the discussion. Superficially, men clearly "resemble" the earthly man, Jesus of Nazareth, more

closely than women do. Of interest to theologians in a tradition
that acknowledges divine will behind the creation of two sexes,
however, is that they do so ontologically and teleologically, not just
physically, ethnically, or professionally. Besides, the same tradition
says that both men and women are created in the image of God and
thus "resemble" the divine saviour, the Christ, in whom "there is
neither Jew nor Greek ... neither slave nor free ... neither male nor
female."[88] That Catholic theologians would attach importance to
distinctions of this kind might seem preposterous to outsiders and
self-serving or even heretical to some insiders, but no understanding
of the controversy is possible unless we take seriously both sides on
their own terms.

Any historian could find other examples in *Veil* of oversimplifi-
cation.[89] The trouble is that only a very few viewers are likely to
be historians; the director almost certainly did not aim her film
at them. She aimed it, on the contrary, precisely at viewers who
are either unable or unwilling to question what the film tells them.
Given no access to more information or to other opinions, how are
they to think for themselves or make up their own minds? The production team had no intention of allowing any such possibility. It
expected viewers to agree with the narrator. *Veil* is what could be
called indoctrination or even propaganda, in short, because its aim
is to convince and convert, not to teach – that is, encourage viewers
to ask questions of their own and think clearly for themselves.

Some statements in this film – not many, but some – are actually
false. "By the time of Christ's birth, the Goddess based religions
were almost erased and God as male was the predominant faith."[90]
Actually, Rome was crammed with temples dedicated to the many
goddesses of Greece, Rome, Egypt, and other civilizations. Their
power was declining, it is true, but so was that of the many gods.
Spreading rapidly throughout the empire, though, were several
"mystery religions." These included the Eleusinian mysteries (based
on the myth of two goddesses, Demeter and Persephone); the mysteries of Isis and Osiris, Cybele and Attis, Aphrodite and Adonis
(based on the myth, in each case, of a fertility goddess coupling
with a god); and the Orphic mysteries (based on the myth of a fertility goddess who must live in the underworld, temporarily, due to
the stupidity of a god).

In another false statement, the narrator claims that "there is no
written record of precisely who was present at the Last Supper."[91]

She tries to argue that the women who followed Jesus "became his most loyal and ardent disciples" – not *among* the most loyal and ardent, mind you, but *the* most loyal and ardent. Actually, there is a written record of who was present at the Last Supper: "When it was evening, he sat at the table with the twelve disciples."[92] Were women there as well? The text itself gives us no reason to believe that anyone was there beyond the twelve disciples. And if other New Testament passages are reliable enough to prove that Jesus welcomed the presence of women, as *Veil*'s narrator claims, why should this one be unreliable – in need of supplementation – because it fails to prove the presence of women?

Sometimes *Veil* falsifies its own statements by adding contradictory ones elsewhere. At one point, the narrator observes that simplicity was for St Brigid "the way to spirituality." One day, she received a shipment of "glittering, shining vestments, sent ... directly from Rome. Ornate symbols of male priestly power. Brigid had them given away to the poor. She would not allow her faith or her followers to adopt ostentatious accessories."[93] Yet a few minutes later, the narrator praises a monastery, founded by the nun Scholastica, for establishing the mediaeval textile industry! Women "brought weaving to a fine art. The ornate needlework of the medieval nuns was an expression of their spirituality. They wove elaborate vestments."[94] Ornate vestments represent sinfulness when men use them, apparently, but spirituality, artistry, and industriousness when women do so.

Still other statements represent nothing more substantial than wish-fulfillment. According to the narrator, "most of the early Roman Christians were women, and it is [sic] in their homes [that] Christianity flourished. On the sites of these early meeting places now stand mighty churches in honour of the many who were martyred."[95] Actually, we have no idea of how many Christians there were in the early period, let alone how many were either women or martyrs. Some evidence does indicate that many converts from the upper class were women. Written accounts indicate that influential women, including members of the imperial family, increasingly found Christianity attractive as the old order collapsed around them. The men of this class might or might not have found Christianity attractive, but they had one practical reason for not converting: survival. For one thing, converting would have made it impossible for them to function in public life as magistrates of the state. Refusing to acknowledge the imperial cult, in fact, would have made them enemies of the state and thus candidates for "suicide." In any case, there is no reason at all to assume that most converts from the lower classes and the slave population were women. And most of the early converts were probably drawn from those classes, which had no major stake in the existing order.[96] The underlying claim of *Veil*, at any rate, is that Christianity owes not merely as much to women as it does to men but more. So much for the egalitarianism of women's spirituality. If Christianity was (and is) an evil religion of men, moreover, why argue that women were its primary supporters in the early period?

The most egregious example of wish-fulfilling but truth-distorting fantasy involves *Veil*'s exploitation of Jesus as a prototypical feminist. Notorious in his own time as in ours for not fitting conveniently into any category, Jesus has been "appropriated" by one ideology after another. If both guerillas[97] and pacifists,[98] both socialists[99] and capitalists,[100] both American slaves and Nazi "Aryans"[101] could claim him as a prototype, why not feminists? Katharina von Kellenbach, herself a feminist, has written extensively about one of the problems that feminist appropriation creates. To rescue Jesus from the attack on patriarchal religion, Christian feminists routinely present him as un-Jewish or even anti-Jewish.[102] Not only did he respect women, feminists often say or imply, but he was unique in doing so. In fact, they often suggest, this was one of the main reasons for his rebellion against the supposedly misogynist religion – even the misogynist God – of his Jewish compatriots. Because *Veil* is a feminist ode to nuns, brides of Christ, we can hardly exaggerate the importance of this matter. If Jesus was not a feminist, after all, they would have no legitimate reason for remaining nuns or even Christians.

Well, Jesus was indeed innovative in some ways – but not more so than some other Jewish teachers of his time or even earlier. For historians, the rise of rabbinic (or Pharisaic) Judaism – a historical process that was well underway at that same time – was a religious revolution no less radical in its way than the parallel rise of early Christianity. Jesus wanted everyone to be his follower, sure, but the rabbis wanted everyone to follow them. As it happened, the message of Jesus appealed more to marginal Jews than to other Jews (Jesus himself being from what was then a backwoods region). But his rabbinic adversaries were just as intent on converting the entire community to their form of religion (and were eventually successful among those who refused to join the followers of Jesus). Among Jesus's followers were women. As someone who questioned all established customs and institutions – which is to say, those that supported other Jewish groups – Jesus did not feel bound by the belief that men and women should have different spheres of activity. We have no evidence that he sought out women, but when he did encounter them, he did not make a point of distinguishing them from men. This demonstrates universalism, perhaps, but not feminism.

And his universalism rested firmly on eschatological expectations. Jesus believed that the temporal world was coming to an end, very soon, to be replaced by the eternal Kingdom of God. In that case, *all* distinctions – including those of class, ethnicity, and sex – were irrelevant. Other Jews, those who were coalescing around the rabbinic movement, did not support this eschatological perspective. Like Jesus, they believed in the coming of a new world order – what they called the Messianic Age. Unlike Jesus, however, they were by no means certain that its advent was imminent or even that it would mean more than getting rid of the Romans. Most believed that the social order, though not necessarily the political order, was going to endure in the immediate future. One of their primary tasks, therefore, was to maintain some form of social order while waiting for the Messianic Age (which is what Jews have been doing ever since). They understood gender as a way of enhancing the experience of everyday life *within* the realm of time, or history (as distinct from eternity). Like all other human societies before and since, differing only in degree, theirs was a gendered society. Feminists can argue convincingly that this particular gender system was inadequate from the perspective of modern women, surely, but they cannot argue convincingly that the rabbis were misogynists merely for using gender as one of their organizing principles – or that Jesus was a feminist merely for discarding gender (although he did not quite do that either).

Besides, it is a mistake to assume that the innovations of Jesus were all of the "liberal" variety that appeals to many modern feminists. In forbidding divorce, for instance, he was far more restrictive than the majority of rabbis, who continued to permit divorce and even to legislate protection for divorced women. Removing Jesus from his Jewish context, in short, means presenting Judaism as the obsolete predecessor of Christianity, its antithesis, the ultimate source of misogyny and evil. This adds up to the latest version of Christian anti-Judaism (and thus to a form of anti-Semitism).

To illustrate Jewish brutality, for example, the narrator points out that "women were stoned to death for adulteress behavior."[103] Actually, stoning had become extremely rare by the time of Jesus. Although the Pharisees (rabbis) kept capital punishment technically on the books, they were extremely reluctant to use it for any crime, let alone this one. According to no less an exalted figure than Rabbi Akiba, who lived only one or two generations after Jesus, "a court which has pronounced a sentence of death, should taste nothing at all that day."[104] The rabbis insisted on a very high standard of proof in capital cases, including adultery cases – so high, in fact, that the effect was to abolish capital punishment despite scriptural requirements. Besides, scripture mandated the same punishment for men as for women. Consider the following passage: "If a man commits adultery with the wife of his neighbor, both the adulterer and the adulteress shall be put to death."[105] This passage does not describe the method of execution, but it was undoubtedly death by stoning.[106]

Another half-truth concludes *Veil*'s commentary on scripture. The narrator claims that "it is to a woman the risen Christ first appears."[107] Well, maybe so and maybe not. On this matter, the New Testament is ambiguous. The gospel of Mark, which scholars consider the earliest, offers no information at all on the risen Christ; it ends at the empty tomb. The other gospels do include stories of the risen Christ. According to the gospel of John, probably the latest one, Mary Magdalene is the first to see the risen Jesus as she waits outside the empty tomb for Simon Peter and another disciple, "the one whom Jesus loved."[108] According to Matthew,[109] Magdalene and "the other Mary" see an angel at the tomb. Knowing that they are looking for Jesus, the angel tells them that "he is not here." Later, Jesus himself appears to them before he does to the other disciples. According to the gospel of Luke,[110] on the other hand, Magdalene is among the women who see two angels at the tomb – but again, not Jesus himself. Later, Jesus appears first to several male disciples on the road to Emmaus. Paul's account of the resurrection in I Corinthians, which probably predates any of the gospels, notes that the risen Jesus appeared to Cephas and "the twelve." It includes no reference to Mary Magdalene or any other woman.[111] We will have much more to say about Magdalene in chapter 5.

Veil does not exactly attack religion or even the Christian religion. It supports religion, including Christianity, to the extent that
it conforms to, or is conducive to, feminist notions of "women's
spirituality." The film glorifies female spiritual luminaries and
ecclesiastical leaders – Druid priestesses, St Brigid, Abbess Hilde-
garde, and so forth – as traditional and pietistic hagiographies do.
The following eulogy of St Brigid, for example, is supposed to
edify the faithful – these would be feminists but not necessarily
Christians – or to attract converts, not to stimulate intellectual
inquiry.

But Brigid, aware of the need beyond her own community, travelled across her island. From the Druid she had learned things
she knew could ease people's lives, and she set out to share her
knowledge with her people. Brigid's sense of justice was unerr-
ing. People would often ask her to mediate in disputes and she
always settled things fairly. She is know[n] for land reforms
which protected the rights of women and poor farmers. Brigid
loved animals and with her Druidic skills she cured them when
they seemed hopelessly sick, Her advice on growing crops has
over time earned her the title of patron saint of agriculture.
She was a legend in her own time as well. Wherever Brigid had
been, she left behind people who were better off for knowing
her. The Goddess Brigid and the new Brigid had much in common. They tell of her miracles, simple stories of simple acts.[112]

This account is symbolic, not historical. Viewers learn of Brigid
only what later generations wanted to remember of her. Did she
ever feel confused? Did she ever lose her temper? Did she ever make
mistakes? Did she have any flaws at all? If not, of course, she
wouldn't have been human. The aim of *Veil*, though, is not to show
that women are human – which would mean, after all, that women
are flawed just as men are – but to show that women are, well, goddesses. *Veil* vilifies male spiritual luminaries and ecclesiastical leaders, by contrast, just as the most traditional and pietistic passion
plays – such as the one that villagers still perform every ten years at
Oberamergau – once vilified Jews. It is not as if no man ever
became famous for precisely the kind of thing that the film praises
Brigid for. According to legend, after all, St Francis conversed with
the animals. What does that represent if not closeness to nature? He

gave away to the poor all his possessions, even the clothes on his back. What does that represent if not the simple way of life? Pointing this out, however, would have diminished the apparent gulf between "male religion" and "female religion" and thus a presumably innate difference between men and women.

The whole point of *Veil* is that only women have been truly religious, whether as devotees of a goddess or as disciples of Jesus, the allegedly proto-feminist Prince of Peace. Had it been otherwise, the film would have condemned the nuns as dupes of patriarchy. Instead of treating them with condescension or even contempt, the film treats them with respect and admiration. Even though it acknowledges one shadow in the otherwise luminous history of nuns – "cruel nuns, who seemed to delight in making students miserable" – the narrator quickly adds that "there is, maybe, some excuse."[113] For one thing, families sometimes placed even unwilling children in convents or monasteries. Moreover, convents, like all other bureaucracies, bred pettiness and meanness. But the real cause of surly nuns, according to *Veil*, was the evil of men! *Men* imposed rules intended specifically "to inflict suffering rather than ease pain."[114] Never mind that the rules for monks were no different in this respect from the rules for nuns. *Veil* assures viewers that very few nuns simply enjoyed humiliating or degrading other people; it implies that only monks or priests were like that. Women, apparently, cannot be evil. If they seem that way, it is because men somehow force them to be that way. To make sure that viewers get the message, *Veil* tells them that by blaming Eve for the expulsion from Eden, men "provided the setting for the victimization of women, and ultimately for patriarchy to avoid confronting the true nature of evil."[115] In the context of *Veil*, viewers connect "the true nature of evil" with something inherent in these men – that is, something innate in maleness.

It is not hard to see why *Veil* treats the nuns with so much respect. Unlike many other women, they choose celibacy. As one of them, Sarah, explains, "We give up the use of sex; we don't give up our sex ... We remain women and don't want to not be women. We want to be women completely and fully, and what happens ... is that all of the energies, our physical energies that are not used in ... an act of sex are transformed, purified ... and give us more energy to love."[116] Feminist viewers probably conclude, at some level of consciousness, that they might well envy the nuns, for unlike most women, they are free from any emotional or physiological need for contact with men.

Now consider together *Veil*'s two primary messages: only women are capable of true love, and only by rejecting sexual contact with men can women know true freedom. In that case, the ultimate role models for women would be lesbians – that is, women who not only reject sexual contact with men (providing them with the one source, allegedly, of true freedom) but also enjoy it with other women (providing them with the one source, allegedly, of true love). It is unnecessary to ask whether the nuns in this film are lesbians, and some of them explicitly affirm their love for male friends. As Sue Seeker puts it, "I need the love of males as well as females to keep my commitment honest ... and to make me a whole person."[117] There is no reason to read into the celibacy of these women anything more than what they actually say. What the film *implies*, however, is another matter. At issue here is not lesbianism itself but lesbianism as a political choice based on hostility toward men.

Veil's ultimate aim is to promote not only the idea of female autonomy (which is foolish in any case, because humans are social animals and therefore always interdependent, never autonomous) but that of female superiority. The narrator makes this very clear in one passage: "There was a time in earth's ancient history," she intones, "when religions were linked to earth itself, to nature. The life giving nurturing powers of women were revered, women were goddesses. The fertility of the earth and women held a power respected and worshipped."[118] Commenting on the spiral motif in pre-Christian art, she makes the same point once more while ignoring the parallel Hindu and Buddhist notion of *samsara*: "Birth, life, death, rebirth. It is women who represented this continuation of life, it is woman they worshipped and this is her symbol."[119] That really says it all. Men worshipped women, and women presumably worshipped themselves! For the feminists who produced this film, women deserve more than to be treated with respect as the equals of men: they deserve to be worshipped as a unique source of natural and even cosmic power that is inaccessible to men. This message is what lies "behind the veil" in *Behind the Veil* just as it does in *Goddess*.

Like *Goddess* and *Veil*, *The Burning Times* is based on the conspiracy theory of history. Like *Veil*, it comments on the fate of goddesses under Christianity, but it is about a relatively recent rerun of the conflict between men's dominant religion and women's underground religion: the witch craze that swept through western and central Europe from the fifteenth century to the early eighteenth. After a very brief prologue on the lost golden age of women, *Burning* cuts immediately to the chase. Viewers learn that men caused the transition from good religion to bad – not this or that group of men, by the way, but men in general. They directed their nefarious plans specifically against women in order to reassert control over them. Men claimed that women who had embodied goodness (as healers and visionaries) really embodied evil (as secret followers of Satan). Men had already turned the pagan festival of Samhain (honouring the "ancestors and life") into Halloween (honouring the "night and death").

Burning presents a political explanation for the witch craze. This phenomenon – more than Confucian foot-binding, Hindu *sati* (the act of a wife burning herself on the funeral pyre of her husband), and Islamic *purdah* (veiling in public) – symbolizes for many feminists all that is wrong not only with men in general but also with Western men in particular. They not only controlled and exploited women, *Burning* says, but also tortured and killed them on a massive scale during a particularly dark period. This is not news to historians, of course, who have heavily documented the witch hunts. Unfortunately, those who produced this film decided not to rely exclusively on historical documentation, deciding instead on an overtly political interpretation and a highly manipulative presentation. Although their assessment is a foregone conclusion, their spin reveals much about the deep structures of their thinking on a very troubling topic.

Burning discusses the historical context of these witch hunts. For many reasons, the film says, this was a time of upheaval. Rulers confiscated peasant land, for instance, and laid charges of witchcraft against those who resisted. Neither priests nor physicians, moreover, could offer a cure for the Black Death. When people turned instead to rural women and their folk remedies (even after they too failed to find a cure), the church charged its rivals with being witches. The proportion of women increased, to be sure, at least partly due to the slaughter of men during incessant warfare. When women seemed too independent and threatening, as a result, rulers prevented them from inheriting property and targeted them as potential witches. Moreover, conflict raged between Protestants and Catholics. When the former resorted to anti-clericalism, the latter diverted attention by focusing attention on witches (although the film refrains from mentioning that Protestant countries accused and executed at least as many as Catholic ones did). The rise of capitalism, it continues, was a factor. After all, witch hunts became a profitable business. Not to be ignored, finally, is the invention of printing in Europe. Anyone who could read the *Malleus maleficarum* could find information on how to deal with witches. And a literate middle class was growing at this very time.

Burning blames the witch hunts not only on male officials but once again, on men as a class. These episodes occurred, viewers learn, simply because men wanted to destroy the alleged powers of women: their ability to heal or care for the sick; their role in reproduction as midwives, abortionists, and providers of birth control; their contribution to fertility in the form of magic, ensuring plentiful crops and herds; their harmony with and celebration of nature; their experience of altered states of consciousness; and their prophetic, visionary, and mystical roles. Although the film seems to consider a variety of causes, in other words, it actually reduces all of them to a single underlying one: misogyny.[120] More specifically, they claim, men wanted to control women in general (by intimidating them with accusations of witchcraft) but also reproduction in particular (by banning midwives and everything else associated with female power). In connection with the latter, *Burning* attacks not only (male) physicians but also (male) scientists. Viewers learn of Francis Bacon, a "father" of the scientific method, who suggested that officials establish procedures "to tease or torture the secrets out of mother earth."[121] The not-so-subtle reference is to rape.

One interesting claim in *Burning* is that men reacted to independent women by attacking their religion. These forms of female power were all related, says the film, to pre-Christian (that is, pagan and shamanic) traditions in the West and to similar ones in Africa, South America, and so on. For obvious reasons, the church had always wanted to destroy (or at least to domesticate and control) its pagan rival, which survived in the countryside, and used inquisitions to do so. This allegedly explains the glorification of Mary as a counterpart of pagan goddesses and the incorporation of local goddess shrines into the cults of Christian saints, architecturally baptized by building huge cathedrals on these sites. Viewers do not learn that the cult of Mary only became massively popular seven hundred years after the arrival of Christianity in western and northern Europe.

Burning is clearly correct in pointing to the burning of witches as a major problem in European history. But the problem is complex, and the film's historiography is primitive. *Burning* has at least three basic flaws: dubious presuppositions, selective evidence, and inadequate explanations. Beginning with the first flaw, feminist interpretations of the witch hunts have two dubious underlying presuppositions. One involves a link between folk religion and "women's religion." The other involves several dichotomies: between goddess religion and Christianity, between folk religion and elite religion, and between "women's religion" and "men's religion."

First, consider the link between folk religion and women's religion. *Burning* presupposes that these are synonyms. Although this might have been largely true during the later witch hunts, it was untrue of earlier ones – which casts doubt on the idea of direct continuity between either period of witch hunting and some primeval goddess religion. Using both historical and anthropological studies, Carlo Ginzburg[122] suggests that European folk religion consisted of at least two archaic strata, sometimes overlapping. One originated in the Celtic and Roman religions, which had survived in the folk religion of Romania and other isolated parts of Europe. The other, an even more archaic one, originated in Siberian shamanism. As a result, this folk religion involved widespread beliefs in animal metamorphoses, nocturnal gatherings, night flying, and ritualized journeys to the land of the dead. Ginzburg pays particular attention to folk religion in Friuli, a culturally marginal region of the Italian Alps. As late as the sixteenth and seventeenth centuries, he claims, its folk religion contained precisely these features, and in fact the same thing is often true even today.

Ginzburg agrees with the goddess ideologues (and, ironically, with the mediaeval church as well) that this folk religion was largely one of women, a goddess religion. But he shows that the dominance of women in folk culture was a relatively recent phenomenon. It had once been a religion of both women and men. Many people believed that women, in a state of ecstasy, died temporarily and flew by night to a realm of the dead. There they asked beneficent goddesses for favours such as prosperity, wealth, and

knowledge.[123] The pattern for men, he says, was somewhat different. He deduces that from descriptions of folk religion still practised in marginal regions of Europe (not only in Friuli but also in
parts of eastern Europe and Iceland).[124]

In Friuli, for example, men and women called themselves *benan-*
danti. The women were involved primarily in processions of the
dead. The men were involved primarily in battles against both male
and female witches to ensure the fertility of the fields.[125] But both
left their bodies, travelling invisibly in spirit, and both might have
consumed the hallucinogenic mushroom *Amanita muscaria*. This
complementarity between men and women did not last. Women
maintained the folk subculture in those marginal regions where it
persisted. Ginzburg suggests that men conformed to the official religion of public life, Christianity, and left the folkways to women. In
some places the folk religion was partially absorbed by Christianity; in others it remained as a subculture[126] and came to be associated, fatefully, with heresy.

Back now to *Burning*. The film assumes a totally dichotomous
relation, in moral terms, between goddess religion and Christianity.
This in turn has two corollaries. One is that Christianity, being male
dominated, was (and is) totally malevolent. This claim is fairly easy
to challenge. We do not defend mass persecutions, but we do point
out the obvious fact that Christianity, like all other religious traditions, has motivated people to act both malevolently and benevo-
lently. The other corollary is that goddess religion, being female
dominated, was (and is) totally benevolent. This claim is harder to
challenge, because we have so little historical evidence. At the very
least, though, we can observe a distinct tendency to romanticize the
behaviour of people who lived five hundred years ago in a world
very different from our own (although the same tendency can be
observed in recent approaches to any group classified as oppressed).

Substituting common sense for hard evidence, at any rate, we
have no compelling reason to believe that every peasant who
claimed magical powers actually used them in ways that we would
now consider benevolent. Nor is there any compelling reason to
believe that the peasants of today are immune to such common
human failings as envy, greed, anger, spite, malice, and so on. Their
ancestors probably turned to "wise women" for many reasons, not
only for "fertility," "healing," and "harmony with nature" (whatever that means). To put it bluntly, we have no reason whatsoever

to assume that all "witches" were, in the narrator's words, "leaders, counselors, visionaries and healers"[127] or even, as Margo Adler puts it later on, women "at the edge of social change."[128] At least some of them might have been up to whatever mischief their peasant clients were willing to pay for.

Burning assumes in addition a totally dichotomous relation between folk religion and elite religion. The folk religion of late medieval and early modern Europe was almost certainly like so many other folk religions in at least one very important way: syncretism. In other words, it probably consisted of elements from many sources – including Christianity. These people (like many of their spiritual descendants in modern Africa, say, or Latin America) maintained what modern scholars have classified as pre-Christian traditions, but this does not mean that they considered themselves non-Christians. Just because the church suspected them of being heretics, for that matter, does not mean that they considered themselves heretics. Actually, the film's narrator does admit that "many European healers who were burned relied on Christian faith when performing their cures." But she goes on immediately to trivialize this, because "their healing arts were rooted in the traditions of their ancestors.[129] The implication is that secular (non-Christian or anti-Christian) viewers should dismiss the importance of Christian faith (even though the "healers" themselves did not). But Ginzburg agrees with *Burning* on one point: that the church was correct in identifying the folk religion as a rival one. No matter how distorted, ecclesiastical records do represent something more than the misogynistic imaginings of paranoid clerics.

Besides, as scholars such as Melford Spiro pointed out long ago, even elite religions are often highly syncretistic. If Buddhist monks in modern Burma can participate in the animistic beliefs and rituals of local folk religion,[130] surely Christian monks or priests in late medieval and early modern Europe could have participated in the pagan beliefs and practices of local folk religion. In short, the sharp division between folk and elite religion, fundamental to so much of the recent work on witches in Europe, is extremely dubious. Whatever fantasies the witch hunters of long ago projected onto their victims, it must be said that many scholars of our own time are projecting their own fantasies – neat dichotomies between pagan and Christian, folk and elite, female and male – onto those very same people.

Again, the film assumes a totally dichotomous relation between women's religion (represented by those who worship goddesses) and men's religion (represented by those who worship gods in general and Christ in particular). According to Starhawk, a "modern witch," the shamanic tradition, presumably led by women, emphasized "traditions of developing within yourself altered states of consciousness without using drugs, without, you know, using chemicals – but through meditation and through very simple methods, like chanting, like singing together."[131] Evidently, Starhawk either does not know or does not care that meditation, chanting, and singing are all well-known techniques in Judaism, Christianity, Islam, Hinduism, Buddhism, and other religions that *Burning* associates with men – all of which insist on the goal of a highly developed inner, spiritual life. In addition, she either does not know or does not care that early European folk religion involved the use of hallucinogenic mushrooms.

Later on, Margo Adler opines sweetly that pagans, those who maintained the women's goddess religion, "made their rituals and their celebrations as things that were important because they were part of life experience. They helped the crops grow, they helped the animals come in, they helped talk about the relationship of the moon and stars and the planets. And they really did not have a lot to do with belief. They are [*sic*] based on action, experience, celebration, custom."[132] The implication is that men care only about meaningless abstract doctrines, while women care about the really important things.

Actually, Adler is wrong on three counts. For one thing, she is wrong about the place of belief in religion. Traditions appealing to both men and women – in fact, all religions – are based on beliefs about the cosmos and how humans fit into it. But some religions, including Christianity, make these beliefs explicit. Others either do not, or they attach less importance to their verbal articulation.

Besides, Adler is wrong about the non-rational aspect of religion. Traditions appealing to both men and women – in fact, once again, all religions – find expression in symbolic, mythic, intuitive, and artistic ways (although when it comes to the mythic and intuitive, that has been less true of Protestantism than of other religions).

Finally, she is wrong about the practical aspect of religion. Traditions appealing to both men and women – yes, once again, all religions – make every effort to affect the conduct of everyday life.

Christianity, at any rate, can hardly be accused of indifference toward the way people live. Indeed, its early critique of Judaism was based precisely on the allegation that Jews cared more about ritual than about ethics. So, for that matter, was the Protestant critique of Catholicism. We could say much more about all this, but it is enough to point out here that Christianity – allegedly suitable only for men – is an extremely rich and flexible tradition (although these very qualities have made it susceptible to some horrifying possibilities). That, more than any political factor, accounts for its survival. In short, Adler's dichotomy is not merely simplistic but false.

But suppose that most of the medieval "leaders, counsellors, visionaries, and healers" really were women. That would make nonsense of the claim, whether implicit or explicit, that this religion was superior to "elite religion" or "men's religion." If inequality contaminated the latter in the form of male supremacy, after all, why would it not contaminate the former in the form of female supremacy? Toward the end of *Burning*, Starhawk inadvertently makes the contradiction and its double standard very clear: "When women get in touch with our own power from within, we find we do have the ability to do many, many things. And that kind of power is not competitive, it is not hierarchical. If I've the ability to do something, it doesn't mean you don't."[133] No, not if "you" happen to be another woman. Would Starhawk say that men have the same "power" as women? Not likely.

But was the European folk religion – that is, women's religion – really entirely benevolent? Ginzburg points out that it was both benevolent *and* malevolent, depending on circumstance or perspective. At first, even the peasants did not always consider it benign. They blamed local problems on both male and female witches who, as enemies of fertility, caused battles.[134] The peasants were ambivalent, therefore, about both women *and men*. In addition, Ginzburg observes, the protagonists of these ecstatic cults

present themselves as beneficent figures, possessors of an extraordinary power. But in the eyes of the surrounding community this power was inherently ambiguous, apt to be transformed into its opposite. The belief that the "protagonists" could, out of negligence, bring back illnesses instead of prosperity from their nocturnal journeys, highlights a symbolic ambivalence that probably also characterizes the diurnal behaviour of these figures. They attracted resentment and hostility with their claim that they could identify the witches in the neighbourhood; [they] practised blackmail vis-à-vis the peasants, threatening to unleash storms.[135]

No wonder the witches were so marginal. People associated them with the dead, the dead with both positive and negative experiences, and these experiences in turn with any marginal group – including heretics such as Protestants or Catholics, infidels such as Jews, and even lepers.

Having discussed the dubious presuppositions of *Burning*, let us now consider its selective use of evidence. Because these films focus on the history of women alone – ignoring that of other groups such as Jews and Christian heretics, who faced persecution in virtually the *same ways* both before and during the witch craze – they do a serious injustice to historical complexity. Of extreme importance here is the remarkable overlap between accusations made against witches and those made against other groups. Both witches and Jews faced charges of using human blood for ritual purposes. As early as the thirteenth century, for instance, officials accused witches of using human blood, especially that of Jews and children, for magical purposes.[136] But no one saw Jews as victims. On the contrary, officials accused Jews of the same thing. "In 1401 the townspeople of Freiburg, petitioning for the expulsion of the Jews, affirmed that their danger to the community extended far beyond an occasional child murder, for they dry the blood they thus secure, grind it to a powder, and scatter it in the fields early in the morning when there is a heavy dew on the ground ... then in three or four weeks a plague descends on men and cattle, within a radius of half a mile, so that Christians suffer severely while the sly Jews remain safely indoors."[137] According to one French account, a Jew tried to poison the wells of Christians with ground human heart. A supplier for the Jews foiled their plot by substituting a pig's heart, however, which Jews supposedly would not touch. Given the link between Jews or other outsiders and witches, it would not be too surprising to find inquisitors taking unfounded legends about Jews and applying them to witches. In any case, both Jews and witches were tried and executed for practising ritual murder.

People saw clear links, in short, between the alleged sorcery of Jews and that of witches; moreover, they saw clear links between sorcery and heresy. In many ways, to judge from both theology and folklore, Jews and witches (along with heretics, lepers, and other threatening groups) were interchangeable in the collective imagination. All were accused of carnality, unnatural sexuality, infanticide, cannibalism, desecration of the host, blasphemy, and other nefarious liturgical practices. Europe was pervaded by an ethos that included belief in magic, whether pagan, heretical, Jewish, or Christian. The target of hostility could change easily, therefore, depending on the vulnerability of particular groups and the urgency of particular circumstances.

The witch hunts, in short, were part of a much larger phenomenon. They represented one kind of persecution. Most victims of the witch hunts in particular were women. But most victims of persecution in general were not. To understand the witch craze, it is true, it is necessary to understand the specific ways in which people perceived women. Negative perceptions blotted out positive ones. But to understand the larger *persecution* craze, it is necessary to understand in addition the specific – and almost identical – ways in which people perceived other groups. Negative perceptions governed, because positive ones had never existed.

We turn now to the film's inadequate explanation for the witch hunts. One flaw concerns not the events themselves but their interpretations. Some female experts on "women's history" attack male scholars for refusing to take seriously the fact that most of the accused witches, at least between the fifteenth century and the seventeenth, were women – to admit that misogyny is the one truly significant factor in history. Anne Llewellyn Barstow indulges in this kind of academic terrorism. Agree with us, she implies, or you are a bad scholar. But any good scholar, male or female, would be reluctant to reduce the complexity and ambiguity of history to one neat, consistent pattern. Not only would that obscure the truth, which is always much messier than people would like, but it would put them out of business. In fact, at least some male scholars – and not only the most recent among them, the ones most likely to have been influenced by feminists – have indeed noted that gender was a factor in the witch hunts. The only question is how this factor related to others.

When it comes to explaining historical events, many feminists see gender as one factor among many, albeit the most important one. Theoretically, they are prepared to acknowledge that they can explain many historical events more fully in connection with additional factors such as religion, class, or race. Other feminists see gender as the only significant factor and therefore the *fulcrum* of history – which is to say that women are the pivot around which all of human history revolves.

But even if we could study history exclusively in terms of gender, even if we could reduce history effectively to the story of relations between men and women, misogyny would still be an inadequate explanation. *Burning* acknowledges several possible causes of the witch hunts, to be sure, but it takes only misogyny seriously. Literary evidence notwithstanding, it is by no means self-evident that all or even most men have ever hated women. What does seem self-evident is that most or even all men have been ambivalent about women. The fact is that, at one time or another – paradoxically, often at the same time – men feel both anger and love for women, both fear and respect, both envy and admiration. Moreover, the same is true in reverse. Most or all women have been ambivalent about men. The same is true of the way *all* people feel about their parents, children, relatives, friends, and communities. Ambivalence is a universal feature of the human condition, largely because ambiguity is a universal feature of reality itself (or, at least, of the ways in which finite beings perceive the world). The witch hunts surely do represent a period when misogyny took hold. At issue for historians of the witch craze, however, is not why misogyny exists but why it swept away all other attitudes toward women – who included wives, sisters, daughters, even mothers – at a particular time and place. That is a task for historians, not for political activists masquerading as scholars.

Misogyny was probably not the only factor in the witch hunts and possibly not even the most important one. However, some feminists are not satisfied with that position. They must argue that misogyny is central to any understanding of the witch craze and, by extension, to any understanding of European or even world history. To do so, they must argue that the persecution of witches was essentially unlike (or more significant than) the persecution of any other group, that the persecution of women was not merely evil but the ultimate and primordial paradigm of evil. At this point, historiography turns into something other than scholarship. To move beyond that point, historians must first consider why the secular and ecclesiastical authorities began persecuting other groups even earlier and then consider why they suddenly added women to the list of persecuted groups.

Although misogyny was partly responsible for the persecution of witches, it was not responsible for the persecution of other groups at the same time and even earlier. It seems unlikely, to say the least, that there was no relation between one form of persecution and others in the same society at the same time. What caused this zeal for persecution? The answer is surprisingly and, at first glance, deceptively simple: intense collective stress.

In *Entertaining Satan*,[138] a study of the witches in early New England, John Demos detects patterns that he ascribes to periods of stress. For him, witchcraft was no meandering sideshow; it was deeply rooted in the larger history of that society. He argues that once the ethos of witchcraft had been created and transported to New England, along with other forms of occultism, it tended to become manifest in distinctive circumstances. If so, then the witchcraft trials revealed something important about "emotions, drives, unconscious pressures and conflicts"[139] in the larger society of New England.

According to Demos, periods of intense social conflict – divisions in the church, disputes over property control, Indian wars, and so on – were not themselves notable for witch hunts. The periods notable for witch hunts followed.[140] The events provided scapegoats, thus relieving tension that lingered from earlier conflicts, which had consumed so much energy that no one at the time had considered the possibility of finding scapegoats. Because people believed that these earlier conflicts had been expressions of divine wrath, they gave themselves over both individually and collectively to soul-searching. This gave rise, in turn, to gossip and finger-pointing. New Englanders saw God's will in epidemics (influenza),[141] natural disasters (famines, fires, and earthquakes), and other unusual phenomena (comets, eclipses, droughts, and so on). It was real stress, in short, that gave rise to extreme anxiety and ambivalence in New England. And if this was the case in New England, it was probably the case earlier in Europe as well. After all, most of those who lived in New England had migrated from Europe in the immediate past. So what, or who, were the sources of this stress?

On the eve of the witch craze in Europe, some sources were old and others new, some were external and others internal, some were real and others imagined. Europe was a tinderbox about to be ignited. What lit the fuse that brought medieval civilization to an end? What lit the flames that consumed so many in what amounted to collective hysteria? Of paramount importance to both clergy and laity alike was not *what* had caused this sudden catastrophe but *who*. The answer in a nutshell: heretics (usually, from the sixteenth century, either Protestants or Catholics), infidels (in the absence of Muslims, almost always Jews), and women (almost always socially and economically marginal ones). An additional factor, though, was the longstanding tendency toward dualism in Christianity (a topic that we will discuss in due course).

One source of external pressures was the encroachment of Islam. The Muslims had entered southern France in the early Middle Ages, reaching Tours by 732. Christians pushed them back into Spain, but Muslims remained there (at least in Andalusia) until the late fifteenth century. In western Europe, therefore, it was a draw between Islam and Christendom. In eastern Europe, it was touch and go.

From the very beginning, Islam was a military threat to Christians. In fact, Islam was firmly in control of the Holy Land itself within a generation of Muhammad's death. Later on, as Joshua Trachtenberg has pointed out, Europeans were horrified by a rumour "that the Jews had conspired with the Moors of Spain to destroy the Church of the Holy Sepulchre in Jerusalem in 1010." That year Europe experienced "a series of floods, pestilence, and famine, with an eclipse thrown in, which were interpreted as divine punishment for the destruction of the church."[142] It was this sort of thing that provoked the crusades. But not even they could hold onto any Islamic territory for more than a few generations. When the witch craze broke out, moreover, Islam was on the march again, this time with the Turks, not the Arabs, representing Islam.

Other sources of stress in Europe were purely internal. By the late Middle Ages, the church confronted one heretical group after another: Cathars (or Albigensians), Waldenses, Luciferians, Hussites, Adamites, and so on. Most or all faced the accusation (as the witches did later) of worshipping the Devil as a goat, a cat, or some other animal.[143] These disputes over orthodoxy and heresy were not purely theological. Given the close relation between religion and the established order in those primitive European states, heresy could become a major factor in political fragmentation and social chaos. And the role of clerics was as important as that of monarchs in supporting the state. The church's insistence on doctrinal unity was closely linked, in fact, with the quest for political unity.[144]

It was in this context that after the early thirteenth century people made a fateful link between heresy (heterodox beliefs) and sorcery (conjuring magic), both of which could involve witchcraft. Given this link, it is not surprising to find that women faced exactly the same charges and punishments as all other alien and threatening groups, ones that might well resort to black magic in an effort to subvert the Christian order. Everyone believed in magic, the only question being whether the magic in question was good or bad. Ecclesiastics distinguished in effect between "our" magic and "their" magic. They associated the former with God, church, and state, the latter with Satan and heretics – including people who practised folk religion.

Still other sources of stress were external in one sense but internal in another. Jews had been living within this region since Roman times but as resident aliens and infidels for much of the time. Unlike Muslims, Jews posed a threat that was neither military nor political. Like the Muslims, however, they posed a threat that was both theological and psychological. Given the origin of Christianity as a Jewish sect, this threat was far more disturbing to Christians than that of Islam. At issue, ultimately, was not the belief that contemporary Jews were somehow guilty for the death of Jesus; it was the mere fact that Jews continued to exist as a separate community within Christendom – which is to say, as witnesses in daily life to the triumph of Christianity – without seeing the need for salvation through Christ. This called into question the basic premise of Christianity. If Jews were right, it must have seemed that Christians had no foundation for their own faith. During the course of daily life, moreover, Christians could ignore Muslims beyond Christendom but not Jews within Christendom. Although Jews were socially and politically isolated from the larger community, they were economically integrated with it. Rulers, in particular, depended on them.

In view of all these stresses, it makes sense to challenge the notion that Europeans of this period were "paranoid." According to Rosemary Ruether, only paranoia could explain why they turned so savagely against women, aliens, and non-conformists.[145] By definition, "paranoia" refers to neurotic fear based on delusion. But the sources of stress just mentioned were surely not delusional. Modern observers can argue that the church and its androcentric society did not deserve to survive these threats, but they cannot argue convincingly that these threats were non-existent. Those who believed in a pervasive conspiracy of witches were ruthless, yes, but (given the knowledge available to them) they were neither stupid nor sinister – not more stupid or more sinister than their descendants three hundred years later, at any rate, who believed that a pervasive conspiracy of "satanic ritual abuse" was rampant.[146] That late twentieth century phenomenon is worth exploring, albeit briefly. People had always accused men of ordinary sex crimes much more often than women. When it came to this new craze, however, the sex differential was less obvious. Yet almost as soon as suspicion began to fall on women too, a reaction set in. Suddenly people began to question the whole idea of "repressed memory."[147] The hysteria over "satanic ritual abuse" began to subside relatively soon, after a few years rather than a few centuries – but not before governments changed laws to accommodate new theories and before courts had destroyed thousands of families.[148]

Back now to the witch craze. At issue here is not whether Europeans had good reasons for feeling threatened but what they did as a result. The church established inquisitions during the twelfth century to prosecute heretics.[149] In theory, these tribunals did not attack Jews or Muslims (if any of the latter happened to be passing through Christian countries) per se.[150] They were infidels, not heretics. By definition, infidels were those without faith – that is, without the true faith (Christianity). Unless rulers banished them altogether, a constant temptation to rulers who owed them money, they gave infidels the legal right to practise their own religions within the restrictions imposed by law.[151] But the inquisitions did attack Christian heretics, who were another matter entirely.[152]

Things were more complicated in Spain, home of the most durable and effective inquisition. Ferdinand and Isabella banished all Jewish and Moorish infidels in the late fifteenth century, but many Jews stayed on as *conversos*. So many of them stayed, in fact, that the crown eventually considered them impossible to assimilate. The Church suspected, with good reason, that many of these "new Christians" continued to practise the old religion in secret. These were the crypto-Jews, or *marranos*. (Anthropologists have discovered their descendants still living in remote villages.[153]) The Spanish Inquisition could not go after Jews and Moors per se, because they did not officially or openly exist per se. But it could go after those suspected, justly or unjustly, of heresy – that is, of lapsing from Christianity into their old Jewish or Islamic ways. By definition, heretics were Christians who had lapsed into "error" and therefore fell within the church's jurisdiction. Of greatest importance in this discussion is that the category included not only *marranos* but also those who maintained the pre-Christian folk religion with its rituals and forms of magic.

Now for the catastrophe itself. Anxiety had been building up gradually but steadily for centuries. It became intolerable, very suddenly, due to an event that no one could have foreseen or controlled: the Black Death. This was the medieval version of what we call "the Bomb," or "nuclear winter," but with one big difference. Unlike us, our ancestors not only feared the ultimate nightmare but actually experienced it. The first outbreak of bubonic plague occurred in 1347. Within months, it killed between one-third and one-half of the population of Europe.[154] Using original documents of the period, Johannes Nohl portrays the effects on European society.

The plague struck people quickly, beginning with an inexplicable pain. According to some descriptions, large boils appeared on the thighs or upper arms. Once infected, people were stricken with high fevers. They vomited blood for about three days before expiring. The plague was highly contagious, being transmitted by anything (such as clothing or food) and anyone (no matter how rich or holy). Entire households, including the animals, were wiped out overnight. Not surprisingly, few dared to enter infected households. Corpses rotted. Trying to escape the path of death, people died along the roadsides. Trying to absolve them of their sins, priests were struck down as well. Proper burials were impossible, so the stench of decaying bodies was horrendous. Farm animals roamed about uncared for. Relatives abandoned each other. Many resorted to suicide. "Nothing was to be heard save the wailing of the dying, the lamenting of the relations, and the tolling of the bell for those about to be buried, and the mournful call: `Bring out your dead!'"[155] Towns emptied. Fields lay abandoned. Trade came to a standstill. And then there were the locusts. Even survivors, therefore, had to cope with famine. Many reacted with a combination of hedonism (eat, drink, and be merry, for tomorrow you die) and immorality (take what you can, and Devil take the hindmost).

According to the paradigm suggested by Demos, plague was a disaster of precisely the kind that would eventually generate a collective fit of "soul-searching." During outbreaks, of course, the most urgent need was for protection, although the Christian sacraments provided access to neither supernatural prevention nor magical cure. After (or between) outbreaks, on the other hand, the most urgent need was for an explanation. Christian theology was unable to provide a reason for the plague that seemed satisfying to most people. How could the church explain what was happening?

> The priests pushed and crowded round the sick beds and endeavoured to prove the efficiency of their appeals to the saints, intercessions and relics, their consecrated candles, masses, endowment vows, sacrifices and other pious means of robbery. If a physician attained a good cure, it was attributed to the intercession of the saints, the vows or the prayers of the priests. If the cure was a failure, the physicians were rendered responsible for the death of the patient, and the lack of trust in God and the saints was stated to be the cause of death, which was regarded as a punishment of God, for which the relations had to do penance by an excess of masses for the repose of the soul.[156]

One answer was logical but almost as terrifying as the plague itself: those who suffered and died deserved to do so. That people would blame themselves for a plague might seem strange to most of us. Given the logic of monotheism, however, many must have seen no alternative. If God was in control, nothing could happen without divine approval. And if God was just, no one could suffer except the sinful. (This, by the way, was how Jews explained their own suffering: exile from Judaea under the Romans, for example, and later from Spain under Ferdinand and Isabella.) At first, theologians understood the plague as the wrath of God in punishment for the sins of individuals, even sins as innocuous to our way of thinking as wearing fashionably long-pointed shoes.[157] Throughout the region, flagellates went from village to village torturing their own bodies in a penitential ritual known as the "dance of death." Far from being an attempt to glorify death, this was a desperate attempt to appease Lord Death.

As indicated in the Book of Job, the existence of innocent suffering has long been a problem in monotheistic traditions. In the biblical story, Job is a good man. Satan wants to test him. And God agrees, knowing that Job will not abandon his faith. Job remains loyal after terrible tribulations, but he does demand an explanation. The response from God is twofold. From the midst of a mighty whirlwind, he reminds Job that no mortal can understand the deepest mysteries of a divinely created cosmos. This in itself might or might not satisfy Job. What does satisfy him is the mere presence of God. Theodicy (the attempt to justify a benevolent deity in a malevolent world) has been transformed into theophany (the direct and overwhelming experience of holiness).

During the plague, some Christians found the account of this experience more satisfying than any explanation, but most people, like Job's so-called friends in the biblical story, were not spiritual virtuosi. They still wanted an explanation, something or someone to blame. And there were several candidates.

Some blamed the church. "Boccaccio reports that processions instituted by the Church and all humble supplications to God were of no avail. Was it ecclesiastical corruption that had so aroused the wrath of God?"[158] Everyone knew that church notables consulted the stars, indulged in magical practices, used amulets or charms, and even performed occult rituals to banish the plague into marble columns.[159] The hagiographies of contemporaneous saints abound in tales of these activities.

Others blamed God directly. Listen to one passage from the miracle play by Theophil: "O thou thoroughly wicked God, if I could but lay hands on Thee! Truly I would tear Thee to pieces. I deny Thee, deny Thy faith and Thy power. I will go to the Orient, turn Mussulman, and live according to the law of Mahomet. He is a fool who puts his confidence in Thee!'"[160]

Still others blamed sinister cosmic forces. Even though it made no sense in terms of monotheism, the dualistic belief in an anti-God made sense to those who suffered for no obvious reason. Many, including both leaders and the led, came to believe that two forces governed the cosmos, not one: God and Satan.[161] The two were engaged in a cosmic struggle that would end only with the total victory of one over the other.[162] In a world marked by repeated outbreaks of the plague, it must have seemed beyond dispute that Satan's agents were rampant on earth – that is, either already in charge or very nearly so. One logical response might have been to worship Satan instead of God. Another would have been to defend God and community against those who did – which is to say, those who served Satan by subverting the Christian order. We do not know how many people chose the former and actually became witches. We do know that many chose the latter and became persecutors of infidels and heretics.

Given this perspective, it is not surprising that some people blamed the Black Death on the most obviously alien infidels in their midst: Jews. According to Nohl, the social chaos produced by the plague was particularly catastrophic for Jews.[163] "On one Sunday in Strasbourg, nearly two hundred Jews were burned alive in 1349 for causing the plague. On their way to execution the inhuman crowd had even torn their clothes from their backs."[164] Similar fates were experienced by the Jews in Germany, Austria, Italy, Spain.[165] Rumours about Jews poisoning the wells or practising cannibalism provoked either persecutions or pogroms.

Trachtenberg traces the origin of the accusation of cannibalism to agents of Antiochus IV, a Syrian king who had profaned the Jerusalem temple. These agents tried to justify him by spreading the rumour that Jewish priests had been sacrificing Greeks and eating them.[166] In the twelfth century, this story reappeared. Even before that, however, several other versions had surfaced. According to one, Jews crucified and sacrificed Christians at either Easter or Passover, thus mocking Christ's followers.

These collective fantasies emerged in the context of medieval magic, which made use of poisonous potions – supposedly made from human blood, entrails, or fat – and even influenced early modern medicine. But Trachtenberg places the ultimate blame on early and medieval theology, which relied partially on anti-Jewish slander.[167] No wonder that the crusaders, intending to destroy Muslim infidels in the Holy Land, began by destroying Jewish infidels at home. No wonder that alleged victims of the Jews, such as St Hugh of Lincoln, became martyrs with tombs that served as pilgrimage sites. The passions unleashed among Christians, Trachtenberg notes, "were not again confined through many centuries ... Minorities were hounded and decimated, not least among them the Jews."[168]

One factor that led to the expulsion of the Jews from Spain in 1492, though by no means the only one,[169] was a widespread belief that they were in the habit of eating Christians and drinking their blood for ritual purposes. Some people believed that Jews preferred eating Christian heads or hearts,[170] parts of the body that many cannibalistic societies prefer.

And nothing had changed by the time of the great witch craze. The blame game had set off a chain reaction. Its epicentre was in the western Alps. People had already identified this region with plots by marginal groups. It was there, in 1348, that the Jews had allegedly plotted against Christendom. By about 1380, regional inquisitions were holding heresy trials. The targets were artisans, traders, peasants – any people who might have linked up with the Waldenses, Cathars, or even the folk religion.[171]

But in this region of the Alps (unlike Friuli, further south), most practitioners of the folk religion were women. Maybe peasant women had not bothered to upgrade from folk religion to official religion. More men might have conformed to Christianity, because that was the required religion of public life. If so, the church might have had reasonable grounds for suspecting more women than men of nonconformity. The peasants too might have had reasonable grounds for doing so. They believed that there were both good and bad witches, each category including both men and women. But because most participants in the folk religion were women, the peasants might have associated more women than men with bad witches. And witches could bring back illness instead of prosperity, presumably, from their nocturnal journeys.[172] The peasants might well have considered it self-evident that these bad witches, usually women, were responsible for the plague. For quite different reasons, therefore, both peasants and clerics might have agreed on one belief: that women were more likely than men to be involved in this particular kind of subversive activity.

We suggest an interesting but controversial analogy between human sacrifice in ancient times and the persecutions of witches, heretics, or Jews in the late medieval period. The trials, tortures, and executions were not only public events but also highly ritualized ones (as were all trials, tortures, and executions). Even though procedures varied from one time and place to another, villagers knew exactly what to expect. In cases of witchcraft, for example, the authorities stripped their victims (to eliminate spells in their clothing); shaved their heads (because hair is power and, when braided, conceals fate); required them to walk backwards (so that inquisitors could avoid the evil eye); tortured them (to induce confessions) as trained priests fed both the questions and the answers to them; and finally either hanged them or first hanged and then burned them at the stake. This ritualized context, accompanied by magical thinking, was very similar to that of human sacrifice in earlier societies.

Human sacrifice was common in chiefdoms and early states.[173] As the latter stabilized, however, new religious movements introduced radical changes. Usually, they replaced the sacrifice of humans with the sacrifice of substitutes: first animals, then fruit and grain, and finally prayer or some other spiritual discipline (a "sacrifice of the heart"). This is what happened when the Israelites settled in Canaan near one or two societies that still practised human sacrifice, which explains the biblical polemic against it. The evolution was somewhat more complicated in the case of Christianity, which brought to consciousness once again the notion of human sacrifice. It was very different from notions of human sacrifice that had been prevalent earlier in the Near East, nonetheless, because Christ was not a hapless victim; he willingly offered himself as a sacrificial victim. As a unique event, moreover, it could never be repeated in time (even though it could be re-experienced in eternity at every eucharist).

The eucharist allows at least Catholic and Eastern Orthodox Christians to participate in that unique and final human sacrifice. At the communion rail, they consume not merely bread and wine but also the flesh and the blood of Christ.[174] This explains the difference between Jewish and Christian interpretations of a story in the Book of Genesis. What Christians call the "sacrifice of Isaac" relies on the belief that Isaac's abortive sacrifice prefigured the effective sacrifice of Christ. What Jews call the "binding of Isaac," on the other hand, relies on precisely the opposite belief: that God neither requires nor wants human sacrifice of any kind. Christians do not refer to human sacrifice, of course. For them, after all, Christ is more than human (even though in strictly theological terms he is paradoxically both fully divine and fully human). At every eucharist, therefore, they re-experience the sacrifice of Christ and not merely that of an ordinary man named Jesus.

Even though ritual displacement has obviously worked most of the time, does it always work? Does it work under extreme pressure? Did it work during and just after the Black Death? Or did many people feel the need, once again, for a ritual that looked more like the real thing? If so, there was a major problem: that sort of thing would have been unthinkable in a Christian context. Apart from anything else, it would have contradicted fundamental theological convictions and rendered the eucharist obsolete. In desperation, nevertheless, people might have tried to legitimate the "sacrifice" of witches by associating them with the Devil rather than God. The victims were executed, technically speaking, not sacrificed. But, once again, why would so many of these particular sacrificial victims have been women? Because among the rivals of Christianity – and thus, according to the church, among both enemies of Christ and "supporters of Satan" – were followers of a rival religion, a women's religion, what feminists now call "goddess religion."

This theory is not too far-fetched in view of the fact that Christians had long accused Jews of practising human sacrifice – what Christians called "ritual murder" and Jews called the "blood libel" (because Christians accused them more precisely of killing Christian infants at Passover and using the blood to bake unleavened bread). In fact, officials of the state, acting on advice from officials of the church, periodically burned Jews at the stake for allegedly doing that very thing. This might well have been the ultimate expression of human desperation in the wake of widespread death, destruction, and moral decay. From testimonies taken under torture and interpreted by inquisitors, a paradigm of witchcraft emerged. It then spread with itinerant preachers and, thanks to the invention of printing, witch-hunting manuals. The atmosphere in which persecution of all kinds thrived continued for several centuries. This was due to a continuing sense of threat from repeated outbreaks of the plague, the pressure of Islam on the march, the Renaissance, the Reformation, the development of science, the outbreak of peasant rebellions, natural disasters, astrological predictions, and so on.

Ecclesiastical hostility toward women might have coincided with the widespread belief, probably well founded, that the services offered by peasant women included both contraception and abortion. Even worse was the suspicion, probably well founded, that they were still offering these services in the midst of a demographic catastrophe. Among the most urgent needs of survivors, after all, was to replenish the population. It must have seemed obvious to everyone that procreation was not only desirable for theological reasons but also necessary for purely practical ones. At the very least, the authorities could discourage contraception and abortion.

One way of doing that was to supervise reproduction more carefully than ever before. Physicians, who had less to do with mysterious folklore than did midwives, might have seemed more trustworthy from this point of view. Because midwives had been a necessary part of daily life for centuries, it would have been hard to ban them suddenly without some explanation. As it happened, there did seem to be one. Midwives used their pagan magic to mediate between life and death, so the church had long suspected these women of practising infanticide. And that suspicion led in turn to the even more sinister one of witchcraft.[175]

It is at least possible that a real need for repopulation in the wake of catastrophic plagues, rather than the pure malevolence of misogyny, linked the crackdown on midwives to the roughly simultaneous crackdowns on infanticide and witchcraft.[176] In that prescientific age, remember, it still made sense to ask not *what* had caused a catastrophe but *who*. People suspected midwives and peasant women because of their alleged involvement in both abortion and infanticide. Whatever else was wrong with abortion and infanticide, after all, they were obvious threats to the survival of depopulated communities.

In this same marginal area of the Alps, inquisitors heard testimonies from practitioners of a female-dominated folk religion. Informing these testimonies were ecclesiastical obsessions with heretical conspiracies. The resulting image was that of a sinister sect that focused on a parody of the Sabbath. Inquisitors reported

> male and female witches [who] met at night, generally in solitary places, in fields or on mountains. Sometimes, having anointed their bodies, they flew, arriving astride poles or broomsticks; sometimes they arrived on the backs of animals, or transformed into animals themselves. Those who came for the first time, had to renounce their Christian faith, desecrate the sacrament and offer homage to the Devil, who was present in human or (most often) animal or semi-animal form. There would follow banquets, dancing, sexual orgies. Before returning home, the female and male witches received evil ointments made from children's fat and other ingredients. These are the basic features that recur in most descriptions of the [witch's] Sabbath.[177]

This sort of thing spread like wildfire from one region to another because of an itinerant preacher by the name of Bernardino. In the early fifteenth century he began to preach against female witches.

Bernardino himself was propagating a cult focused on devotion to the name of Jesus and had attracted the surveillance of church authorities for possible heresy. The pope recalled him to Rome in 1427. After prevailing against all heresy charges, Bernardino began once more to preach against witches, this time in Rome itself. But not everyone agreed; even then, some people thought that witchcraft existed only in the imagination. When Bernardino questioned these scoffers, some admitted that they knew witches (or of witches).

After that, everyone took Bernardino and his sermons more seriously. In fact, suggests Ginzberg, many of the questions used later by inquisitors were probably based on his sermons. And some of these sermons, no doubt, entered the *Malleus maleficarum*. This was a handbook, an encyclopaedia of misogyny, published expressly for inquisitors in 1486 and distributed throughout western Europe. The effect of this book was to unify or solidify the notion of witchcraft. At one time ecclesiastics had understood it as an illusion, a fantasy, the punishment for which had been nothing more than penance or expulsion from the parish. But as they came to suspect that folk religion might be the venue of real witchcraft, and as social stress increased, they began to understand the witches' "sabbath" as a real event and thus a real crime, one that involved worship of the Devil or service to the goddess Diana. The punishment was now much more severe: hanging (in England and New England) or burning.

Given the nature of symbolic language, a human propensity for blaming scapegoats to relieve stress, and historical trauma, it is not surprising that the climate of persecution spread like wildfire. Anything could set off a witch hunt or some other form of persecution: a peasant rebellion, a bad harvest, a cold winter, a petty crime, a mere insult. And the result, usually after a brief lull, could be a collective frenzy, a craze, a panic, an epidemic of killing.[178] Once the phenomenon of witch hunting became firmly established throughout the countryside, almost any source of social stress could provoke the persecution of almost any target. During these crises, no one was safe: not men, not young women, not children, not even the rich (although they usually took steps to defuse dangerous situations before mobs threatened them). Demos points out that the magistrates and other authorities were often sceptical. They worried, moreover, about ruptures in public order.[179] Nevertheless, situations frequently got out of control. Once the tumour had developed, to use a medical metaphor, it quickly metastasized.

Because the plague returned periodically – there was an outbreak every ten to twenty years – it helped to perpetuate the belief in witchcraft. Men sacrificed bulls. Peasants ploughed furrows around villages to create magical barriers against evil forces.[180] Old women sold amulets for protection against pestilence.[181] Prophecies and omens, such as comets and earthquakes, abounded. Sometimes disaster really did strike, which solidified the popular beliefs. Magic, prophecy, and witchcraft all increased, partly because neither physicians nor priests could control the plague. Nohl writes:

> The plague not only depopulates and kills, it gnaws the moral stamina and frequently destroys it entirely; thus the sudden demoralisation of Roman society from the period of Mark Antony may be explained by the Oriental plague as 600 years before the epidemic, which was really of the nature of yellow fever, coincided too exactly with the decay of the best period of antiquity not to be regarded as its cause. In such epidemics the best were invariably carried off and the survivors deteriorated morally. Times of plague are always those in which the bestial and diabolical side of human nature gains the upper hand. Nor is it necessary to be superstitious or even pious to look upon great plagues as a conflict of the terrestrial forces with the development of mankind.[182]

The Black Death was the final blow to medieval civilization. The result was profound devastation, demoralization, and destabilization. Fifteenth-century art represents this very dramatically. Among the more popular motifs in woodcuts were "Knight, Death, and the Devil" and the "Four Horsemen of the Apocalypse" (one of whom represents the plague). In this atmosphere, artists glorified the gruesome, the grotesque, the macabre. For the first time, tomb sculptures depicted worms eating their way through rotting flesh; the unmistakable focus was on physical decomposition, not spiritual rebirth. No wonder that the narrator of *Burning* attacks Christianity as a religion of death and ridicules priests who "declared that the end of the world was at hand."[183] But these priests were unlike the evangelists who stand on street corners today. At that time the apocalypse seemed to

have already begun. In the midst of massive and inexplicable devastation, it must have seemed self-evident to anyone with common
sense that the end of a world, let alone the collapse of a worldview,
was indeed at hand. Christianity was not a religion of death, but it
was also not a religion of vaccination.

Finally, consider what happened in the aftermath of catastrophe.
No one should be surprised that this pathological and even lethal
mentality persisted as late as the seventeenth century, when the balance between tradition – by that time, many educated people called
this "superstition" – and science still held. In hindsight, it is clear
that one civilization was ending and another beginning, and the
process was very painful. This was partly because the sources of
stress that we have already discussed, ones that had provided fertile
soil for the witch hunts, did not go away. On the contrary, they continued to generate chaos of one kind or another for approximately
three hundred years.

By 1453, the Muslims had taken Constantinople, which had been
the capital of an Eastern Roman Empire for almost exactly one
thousand years. Despite the Venetian navy (and sometimes in cooperation with it),[184] the Ottoman Turks continued advancing until
well into the seventeenth century. At the peak of their power, their
sway extended into the heart of Europe. They held Budapest for
almost 150 years after 1541. It was only in 1683, at the gates of
Vienna, that they finally retreated. The legacy of this conflict is still
evident in religious conflicts of the Balkan countries and Cyprus.
But the point here is that, throughout the period under discussion,
Europeans experienced Islam as an aggressive and alien civilization
that posed a mortal threat to their own.

Internal sources of stress, moreover, continued to generate anxiety. For one thing, there was the Hundred Year's War – really a
series of battles that erupted periodically between England and
France. And although the church had been coping with heretical
groups for many centuries, suddenly, in the sixteenth century, one
of them succeeded. The church could neither assimilate Protestantism as yet another reform movement (as it had, say, the Franciscans) nor exterminate its practitioners by conquest (as it had, say,
the Albigensians). The Protestant Reformation led, in turn, to the
Catholic Counter-Reformation. For the next few centuries, therefore, much of Europe became sharply polarized theologically, politically, and militarily. This confirmed the ancient belief that religious

deviance was tantamount to political treason. In other words, heretics were still enemies not only of the church but also of the state.[185]

In elite circles, the Renaissance revived pagan traditions – the traditions of Greece and Rome, not the folk traditions of local peasants – possibly due to loss of faith in Christianity and a growing secularism that directed its attention to the revival of classical art and literature. The rich decorated their palaces with openly pagan nymphs and sprites. They enjoyed poems and paintings about pagan gods and goddesses. But the pagan influence was not merely decorative or allegorical. Inquisitors worried even more about its effect on sophisticated scholars than they did about its effect on worldly courts. They did not accuse Galileo of worshipping pagan gods, to be sure, but they did accuse him of promoting scientific methods that derived ultimately from pagan philosophers and therefore of challenging Christian doctrines in the most direct way possible.

Another continuing source of stress was both external and internal. By the sixteenth century, rulers were forcing Jews to live in ghettos.[186] And the political position of Jews became increasingly anomalous with the rise of nation states. During the medieval period, Jews had lived in isolated but self-governing communities. In the early modern period, however, rulers were less willing to tolerate the existence of what amounted to states within states. They wanted more control over all their subjects, Christians and Jews alike. Generally speaking, tension increased.[187] Especially in the fifteenth and sixteenth centuries, rulers persecuted Jews and expelled them sporadically. The only consolation for Jews might have been that things would have been much worse had Christians not been so busy tormenting other groups as well.

The witch hunts, according to Thea Jensen in *Burning*, constituted nothing less than a "women's holocaust."[188] Because no one knows the exact number of those executed, viewers learn, an estimate will have to do. But, they could ask, which estimate? Or, as postmodernists like to ask, whose estimate? "The high number that people use," viewers learn, "is nine million over three hundred or more years."[189] Neither the word "holocaust" nor the figure of "nine million" is likely to have been coincidental. "Holocaust" now refers primarily to the Jewish loss of "six million" (another multiple of three) under Nazi rule. The use of the word should not trouble anyone.[190] No matter what the actual number of people killed, after all, it was surely a very high number. Although some

Jews are troubled by any analogy at all with their own tragedy, others recognize that Jews are not alone in being victims of mass murder. It is hardly illogical, therefore, to consider events of this magnitude holocausts.[191] What should trouble everyone, though, is the fact that this film tries to *upstage* the Jewish tragedy for political purposes, to exploit the suffering of Jews in order to score political points for the suffering of women.

Burning claims not merely that women have suffered just as Jews have suffered, but that women have suffered *more* than Jews and even that female suffering is the paradigm of *all* suffering. "Many suffered," intones the narrator of *Burning*, "but women suffered most of all."[192]

The analogy between Jewish and female holocausts is explicit in the film, so we must take it seriously. Estimates for Jewish victims of the Nazis vary, according to historians (as distinct from those who deny that the Nazis resorted to mass murder at all), from five to six million. Most Jews would agree that the latter is a symbolic, but not unreasonable, number. Estimates for female victims of the witch hunts, however, vary wildly. Even a feminist "historian" considers nine million extremely exaggerated. Anne Barstow notes:

> Because many records are lost and those which survive are often vague about numbers, gender, and sentencing, we will never know how many persons were accused, were executed, were women or men. But enough is known to detect trends in these records. My estimate of total executions (perhaps 100,000 throughout Europe, 1300–1700) and gender breakdown (80 percent of those accused and 85 percent of those executed were female) are based on recent regional archival studies as well as on sixteenth- and seventeenth-century estimates ... The current trend among some feminist groups to claim 3,000,000, 6,000,000, or even 10,000,000 female victims is sheer fantasy.[193]

Of course anyone with moral sensitivity would be horrified at the thought of 100,000 victims. And it would make no moral difference whatsoever even if the number were closer to 10,000 or even 1,000, for that matter. But it would make a *historical* difference (which should be of interest to those who take pride in having founded the academic discipline of "women's history"). And the difference between 9,000,000 and 100,000 would make an enormous historical difference – so enormous, in fact, that it calls into question the scholarly and even moral credibility of those who propose "the high number" without evidence to substantiate it.

If we call the witch craze a "women's holocaust," in any case, we should at least be honest enough to call World War I a "men's holocaust."[194] The reason for slaughter was different in each case, to be sure. The late medieval or early modern state officially punished women but unofficially sacrificed them. The modern state officially required young men to sacrifice themselves on the national "altar" (although it contradicted that quasi-Christian symbolism by resorting to military conscription and glorifying mothers who "gave" or "sacrificed" their sons). But in both cases, the state was defending society in ways that sacrificed people according to their sex. And in both cases, it tortured and killed people primarily because they happened to have been born into one sex or the other. All those required by law to fight and die for their countries (though not, of course, all who ended up dying anyway) had at least one thing in common: as soldiers sent into combat, by legal definition, they were all males.

In a way that would surprise or even shock feminists, especially those of the "women's history" school, the notion of a "women's holocaust" could actually promote reconciliation between men and women if it were set alongside the notion of a "men's holocaust." The effect would be to focus attention on at least some parallels between the suffering of women and men.

But reconciliation between women and men is unlikely in the near future. In fact, the rhetorical temperature is rising, not falling. The cost of male evil, according to some feminists, is a world rapidly spinning out of control and approaching its cataclysmic end. After 1945 and until very recently, people imagined doom primarily in terms of a nuclear apocalypse. Today, they imagine it more often in terms of an environmental disaster due to a deadly combination of industrial pollution and technological tinkering.

One feminist, Elizabeth Davis, describes this phase of the cosmic drama:

> The era of the cult of masculinity is now approaching its end. Its last days will be illumined by the flare-up of such a comprehensive violence and despair as the world has never seen. People of good will seek help on all sides for their declining society, but in vain. Any social reform imposed on our sick society has only

value as a bondage for a gaping and putrefying wound. Only a
complete destruction of society can heal this fatal disease. Only
the fall of the three-thousand-year-old beast of male materialism
will save humankind.[195]

Davis has lifted references to the "complete destruction of society," the "beast" representing evil, and the need to "save humankind" straight out of the apocalyptic tradition. Ironically, the
notion of an apocalypse, a cataclysmic end to history and the creation of a new world order – an eternal one not subject to the vicissitudes of history – comes directly from "patriarchal" Judaism
(represented by the Book of Daniel) and Christianity (represented
by the Book of Revelation).[196] More than a few feminists make the
same point. Carefully noting that the coming apocalypse is due
entirely to men, for example, Mary Daly (the subject of chapter 5)
looks to the immediate future as "a period of extreme danger for
women and for our sister the earth and her other creatures, all of
whom are targeted by the maniacal fathers, sons, and holy ghosts
for extinction by nuclear holocaust, or, failing that, by chemical
contamination, by escalated ordinary violence, by man made
hunger and disease that proliferate in a climate of deception and
mind rot."[197]

Given the conspiracy theory of history, it should come as no surprise that popular culture continues to make use of it – even though
many Westerners are no longer familiar with the biblical version.
This must be what Toni Morrison had in mind when she wrote *Paradise*.[198] The story takes place in Ruby, Oklahoma, an all-black
town settled by ex-slaves after the Civil War. At the heart of town,
both literally and metaphorically, is the oven used for baking bread.
On the outskirts of town is a convent. Ruby's marginal and victimized women find refuge there, taken in by the dying nun Consolata
(who, as a holy woman, clearly represents a goddess). One woman
has run away from her abusive husband, another has threatened the
men in town with her aggressive sexuality, and so on. Finally, local
men attack the convent and murder the women hiding there. After
that primal crime, notes reviewer Lisa Schwarzbaum, the men cannot figure out how to behave in paradise. "Twisted by ignorance,
by pride, and even by religion as Morrison sets them up to be, how

could they? The Oven itself becomes a burden. Home to life-affirming bread baking, of course, but also associated in our minds with
Holocaust-scale destruction, it beckons and glowers and makes for
added guilt."[199]

The dualism of this book is not only between black and white but
also – primarily – between men and women. Even Schwarzbaum,
who has written an otherwise favourable review of Morrison's
novel, is disconcerted by "something in the setup, the unrelenting
struggle of good, victimized women hurting at the hands of nar-
row-minded, victimizing men, the unsubtle sermons about the dangers of black folks repeating white folks worst ways."[200] But not
all reviewers consider sexism a significant problem. One reviewer
notes it but quickly dismisses it. "It is a mistake common to both
Morrison's admirers and critics," writes Paul Gray, "to understand
her fiction too quickly. The violent act that begins and ends *Paradise*, the assault of the men of Ruby on the women in the Convent,
cannot be described simply as a feminist parable, as some early
reviewers have already dubbed it."[201] It would be hard to imagine
anyone turning a blind eye to a framing device of this kind in
any book presenting *women* as archetypally evil beings. "These
people, particularly the men," continues Gray, "are fascinating
mixtures of virtues and vices: proud, independent, argumentative,
close-minded."[202] Sure they are. And so are all sexists and racists.

The problem, witch hunting, is not merely a matter of fiction –
not even in a modern and ostensibly secular society. Consider the
moral panic that broke out in the 1980s over "satanic ritual abuse"
and "recovered memory syndrome" (which we discuss in *Legalizing Misandry*).[203] It began with rumours that one teacher at California's McMartin Preschool had sexually molested one child. Before
long, children there and at many similar institutions were reporting
the most bizarre sexual orgies. Some children told the authorities
that their own parents had been involved. And adults believed
them: not only their parents but also lawyers, judges, psychologists,
journalists, and eventually legislators. Word was out. Members of
satanic cults – mainly men – were apparently raping, ritually sacrificing, and even eating children in suburban basements all over the
country. Meanwhile, thousands of therapists were using hypnosis
and drugs to establish that their patients – mainly women – had
been raped as children by their fathers. Many of these patients

sought emotional relief by going to court. And millions of respectable people believed them, too: friends, lawyers, therapists, judges,
legislators, journalists, and even some of the accused fathers.

Eventually, this phenomenon – at times it seemed like mass hysteria – came to an end for two main reasons. Very few lawyers produced hard evidence to support claims of "repressed memories,"
for one thing, and no lawyer produced any hard evidence at all to
support claims of "satanic ritual" atrocities. Moreover, psychologists began to question the two theories that had generated both
forms of panic: the notion that children never confuse reality with
fantasy (even when asked leading questions) and the notion that
adults repress horrific memories (even though no one had repressed
horrific memories of events such as the Nazi death camps). These
modern witch hunts are over, but their legacies live on. Thousands
of families were ruthlessly torn apart.

In addition, society itself was affected. States and provinces
changed their laws and their rules of evidence in order to facilitate
convictions despite lack of evidence. Schools and social-welfare
bureaucracies changed their policies in order to separate children
"at risk" from their suspected families. Less obvious to most people
was the effect on men who might have become teachers, daycare
workers, scout leaders, and so on. Many decided that the risk of
falling under suspicion, no matter how innocent or beneficial their
interactions with children, was too great. Finally, society itself has
suffered by the resulting polarization between men and women.
This polarization had many causes, of course, but this turned it into
a dramatic public spectacle that will probably linger in the collective memory for a long time.

3

Paradise Regained:
A New Golden Age for Women

Act 3 of the biblical drama is about returning from exile to paradise, from sin to grace, on both the personal and the collective levels. Part of the story takes place within time, or history: after
expulsion from Eden but before inauguration of the Messianic Age
or coming in fullness of the Kingdom of God[1] (which amount to
much the same thing). For Jews, scripture concludes with an affirmation of hope in collective return to the Promised Land.[2] But tradition indicates that this will consist of more than a mere return
from political exile and the resumption of business as usual in the
ancestral homeland. The new world order will feature conditions so
unlike those known to us in everyday life – the conflict and chaos of
history – that they compare only to those of paradise lost.

In effect, therefore, entering the Messianic Age means returning
not only to the Promised Land but also to Eden. For Christians,
scripture concludes with an affirmation of hope in Christ's return to
inaugurate the Kingdom of God,[3] which implies a return to paradise. The Book of Revelation, which concludes the New Testament,
makes this motif explicit by noting that the heavenly Jerusalem will
contain within it Eden's Tree of Life.[4] It all amounts not only to the
notion that history is moving toward a goal but also to the notion
that this goal is a *return*. In spite of all the historical tribulations
caused by the Fall, Christians expect to regain the original state of
peace and harmony after the end of history and therefore to enjoy a
new golden age – which is to say, a return to paradise. Similarly,
goddess ideologues expect to enjoy a new golden age – which is to
say, a society that celebrates or even divinizes women. But these
goddess ideologues (and some evangelical Christians) expect the

new golden age to dawn in the very near future. And one obvious sign, they observe, is a direct or indirect return to goddess worship.

In this chapter, we discuss (1) the goddess in one of our three films, (2) the goddess as a popular religious movement, and (3) the goddess in popular culture.

The Goddess Remembered captures in testimonials the desire of women to restore their lost golden age. Jean Bolen tells viewers that she left Protestantism behind and, through Artemis, discovered the mountains, the wilderness, the stars, "feeling one with nature," and so on.[5] Mary Tallmountain tells viewers that she left Roman Catholicism behind after discovering in the Virgin Mary the Mother – that is, the "woman behind this thing."[6] Elena Featherstone "shares" her story of rediscovering the corn goddess of her Amerindian ancestors. No matter what separates them, all have one thing in common: rejection of what Louisa Teish calls "the great bearded white man in the sky."[7] As she puts it, "You couldn't say nothing to the dude. He didn't answer prayers, you know."[8] Obviously, celebrating goddesses sometimes involves trivializing and even falsifying gods (which reverses the process that celebrated gods by trivializing and even falsifying goddesses).

Using the New Age talk that remains *de rigueur* in some circles, Bolen sums it all up: "I have a sense of the goddess as life force, as affiliation, as that which links us all at a deep level to be one with each other and one with Nature. And in that we are all connected with Gaia or Mother Earth."[9] After deploring the horrors of our economic system, Charlene Spretnak makes the same point: "But we feel very much that the kind of connectedness women's spirituality and goddess spirituality teaches about the earth is missing in politics today."[10] And again: "When we look at those statues [from goddess cultures] that are half human and half bird, or half woman, half some other animal, [we recognize] our embeddedness in Nature, our connectedness as a species – we don't stand apart from Nature."[11]

This is a big word, "connectedness." From our point of view, though, these women feel "connected" to everything and everyone *except men*. The irony here is that they have built their goddess theories on a foundation that male scholars laid in fields such as archaeology, history, and religious studies over the past century. Shekinah Mountain Water even gives credit to Robert Graves, author of *The White Goddess*,[12] for introducing her to the holy mysteries of femaleness.[13]

It is not enough to pore over archaeological texts or even to visit ancient ruins. Authenticity for modern goddess ideologues requires not only the claim to antiquity but also the claim to unbroken *continuity* with antiquity – preferably in connection with "transgressive" or "subversive" activities, which supply the frisson of romantic glamour. With this in mind, viewers learn about allegedly underground goddess cults: "In every culture, links to earlier beliefs are revealed through customs, myths and celebrations. The dance around the May Pole" – an odd example because the pole could well be a phallic symbol – "is done all over the world. At the great basilica in Mexico City today, they honor the Virgin Mary. They still dance where once there was a temple to the goddess Tonansin. They used to bring her rounded cakes of corn just before the rains were due ... Shamans and healers in Mexico are still mostly women, carrying on thousands of years of tradition."[14]

Next, viewers see some English religious sites that are currently in use: Salisbury Hill, Avebury, and Stonehenge. "Local villagers still cut back the grass on this chalk hill so that the great Celtic goddess, Rhiannon, can face the sky."[15] The dubious implication is that they do so as worshippers of Rhiannon. Cults of this kind in Europe and America, nevertheless, are small at best. "But in Africa," says the narrator, "the goddess is still worshipped. Afrekete, Yemanje, Oya, Mawulisa, Oshune, dark reservoirs of strength and female power."[16] If all goddess cults were manifestations of a single religion, of course, it would make sense for Western goddess ideologues to claim kinship with African cults and thus direct and unbroken continuity with the past. No wonder that the cinematographer has matched shots of a temple site in England with what would otherwise have to be considered incongruous: a modern hymn to the Babylonian goddess Inanna!

At the very beginning, viewers hear that their ancient ancestors were "small, peaceful groups formed around mothers."[17] Later, the narrator solemnly declares that the "sharing bond between mother and child was at the centre of clan life. They roamed long distances learning the secrets of the Earth, drawing nourishment and medicine from the plants, the trees and roots. Vulva-shaped openings in the earth have been found colored with red ocher, a symbol of life's blood. For the female was often honored in prehistoric art. The miracle of birth and sustenance offered by her body. The bleeding that came and went with the changings of the moon. She was magical, like the goddess Earth."[18] Evidently, fatherhood was irrelevant. So much for equality on the home front. How about the religious front?

Listen to Spretnak describe life among the insiders: "We don't structure women's spirituality groups hierarchically. It's simply women in a neighbourhood who might meet once a month with the full moon or the new moon to celebrate things that are happening in their lives, the lives of their children or their families, or to mark the passages of the sun, the moon, the earth, to celebrate the earth's holy days, the solstices, the equinoxes. And it's our creativity, it's our expression of who we are and what we feel and how we relate to the earth and to the people we love."[19] Words such as "we" and "our" leave no doubt that men need not apply for membership. (A few of these communities tolerate men in as sympathetic observers; some Wiccan communities allow men as full members).

There is nothing inherently wrong with excluding one sex from religious groups. There is something wrong, however, with doing so because of hostility. Describing the healthy, happy, wholesome world of women, Spretnak cannot resist the opportunity to attack that of men. "They" are hierarchical, she says, but "we" are egalitarian – even though she unwittingly reveals her own hierarchical way of thinking in the very act of saying so. Merlin Stone is equally blind to the main contradiction in her own thought: "And the need for dominance. Well, that's it; that's the whole concept of hierarchy and the whole concept of some people are better, or some types of people are better. And any kind of oppression, whether it's sexist or racist or ethnic or economic or any kind of concept that there is that kind of built-in hierarchy, I think is something that, as we get deeper and deeper into feminist spirituality, we find ourselves trying to question and to break down."[20]

But *Goddess* is nothing if not dramatic testimony to the notion that one human type *is* better than another, that – polite disclaimers notwithstanding – women *are* better than men. Obviously, Stone and her friends are not trying quite hard enough to question or break down the concept of hierarchy. Elsewhere, Spretnak discusses the elation that women experience when studying the artifacts of goddess cultures: "You say, yes, this is the female, this is in myself as well."[21]

All the same, viewers learn on several occasions that ancient goddess cultures were "egalitarian." The narrator states that as a fact, as if it were self-evident to all historians and archaeologists. As we have already said, though, that is anything but self-evident. Spretnak expects viewers to believe that a society can be both "matrifocal" and "egalitarian" at the same time. Even though the "female has a place of honour and respect," she argues, "[that] doesn't mean domination ... there was not a putting down of men in order to elevate women. It was just a natural reverence for the bountiful powers of Mother Earth and the bountiful powers of the female."[22] Just? What exactly did men have that evoked an *equivalent* form of "natural reverence" and thus made egalitarianism possible in the first place? She never tells viewers, possibly because the question never occurs to her.

To give the film due credit, no one shrinks from saying what others would consider dangerous: the solution for women is a revolution, not merely a reformation.[23] "Women have always gathered together," the narrator whispers with excitement. "And tonight, in San Francisco, historians, theologians, environmentalists and political activists meet and talk about their revolution. The history and mythology of women, ignored and distorted through centuries of patriarchy, is being rediscovered."[24] Unlike the revolutions of men, viewers hear, the revolution of women will be peaceful! Of course, there is no *need* for women to use violence; the pen (or a modern equivalent such as the talk show, the court house, or the legislative assembly) really is mightier than the sword (a topic that we discuss much more fully in *Legalizing Misandry*).[25]

The women in *Goddess* use overtly religious language. "A growing number of people," says the narrator, referring not to people in general but to women, "are looking to the past through women's spirituality to find new visions for the future. They remember the eternal rhythms; they draw strength from the creation of their own goddesses."[26] Precisely what she means by these very traditional words "spirituality," "visions," "eternal rhythms," "creation," and "goddesses" is hard to say. It really makes no difference. By a process of linguistic inflation, evident for decades in liberal churches, formerly technical words of this kind can lend an aura of ultimacy to almost anything that the speakers consider valuable or important. Most churches would draw the line at "goddesses," to be sure, but many of them do find ways of asserting the various female aspects of God – even while acknowledging, with traditional theologians, that God is neither male nor female (and that gendered attributes, whether masculine or feminine, are theological concessions to the human need for anthropomorphic descriptions of God).

It is not important to know whether the women in *Goddess* actually believe that they are worshipping supernatural beings. It is enough to observe that they believe in what amounts to worshipping themselves: "It helps me a lot to remember that I am an ancestress of tomorrow. And that what I say and do today, 5,000 years from now may be coded into the symbolism of what they believe then," says one.[27] Future women will regard what she now says, in other words, as scripture – that is, as divine revelation. "If you think that way," she concludes, "no tiny act is meaningless. Everything becomes very, very important."[28]

Even after the narrator has duly noted all of this, or possibly because she has done so, her final words are startling. "There are many ways to pay homage to the wonders of creation, to discover the fullness of what it means to be human. There are things to be remembered. For 25,000 years, our ancestors found power in union and cooperation. If we listen to the echoes, they have much to say."[29]

By this time, after an hour of glorifying and congratulating themselves as women whose innate spirituality has sustained the great goddess for thousands of years, it must be clear to viewers that "the fullness of what it means to be human" refers specifically and uniquely to femaleness. Being female, in other words, means being fully human. Being male, by implication, means being less than fully human.

If this is what women hear in "echoes" from the remote past, then the likelihood of a truly egalitarian society in the future must be very faint. On the basis of common sense alone, it should be obvious that "union" or even "cooperation" between men and women would be possible only if we value and honour the distinctive qualities and contributions of both sexes.

According to this film, it is now payback time. Women's spirituality will marginalize men's spirituality, it implies, just as men's spirituality marginalized women's spirituality. Not once in the entire film does anyone consider that what might have seemed like a golden age to women (assuming that there was a golden age in the first place) might have seemed like something less to men. Not once does anyone suggest that men, like women, developed a distinctive form of spirituality that both they and women could have valued. Not once does anyone suggest that men, like women, could have developed distinctively valuable qualities of any kind, let alone spiritual ones. Viewers must conclude that there was no room in paradise for men's spirituality or even for men as such. In these "egalitarian" societies, goddess ideologues imagine, men were free to exist as the "equals" of women as long as they acknowledged the *supremacy* of women.

Given all this gynocentrism, it would hardly be surprising if men finally got fed up and either rebelled or welcomed invading men who did it for them (just as many Christians in seventh-century North Africa, dominated for generations by Christians in Constantinople, welcomed the invading Muslims). Given a circumstance that the film itself describes, a society that valued only femaleness, the wonder would be not that men rebelled against the system (assuming its existence) but that it took them thousands of years to reach that point.

So far, we have discussed this cosmic drama in three acts as a theory. But it is not merely a theory: it is a movement, albeit a highly eclectic one. Cynthia Eller, a specialist in religious studies, calls it "feminist spirituality." By "spirituality," she refers to the experiential but not the institutionalized aspects of religion. Unfortunately, she works with not one, not two, but three incompatible descriptions of this movement. First, she says, "Spiritual feminists ... are women who say they are spiritual feminists."[30] Second, she says that the "primary characteristic of feminist spirituality is variety."[31] And third, she says more helpfully that "it is possible to sketch the movement in terms of the few things that are matters of general (if not total) agreement."[32] These things amount to five characteristic features: "valuing women's empowerment, practicing ritual and/or magic, revering nature, using the feminine or gender as a primary mode of religious analysis, and espousing the revisionist version of Western history favored by the movement."[33] For Eller, those who endorse at least three of these five characteristic features are spiritual feminists. We will suggest another label for them.

Eller's academic methods rely on the phenomenology (or anthropology) of religion: starting, empathically, with the insider's perspective and temporarily bracketing out her own outsider's perspective; analyzing the movement's popular literature; being a participant-observer of rituals, courses, workshops, and retreats; and interviewing women both to confirm other sources and to document first-hand experiences. She finds that the "sociological profile of the feminist spirituality movement is summed up like this: white, of middle-class origins, fairly well educated (beyond high school), of Jewish or Christian background usually, though not always, having a significant amount of religious training), in their thirties or forties, and disproportionately lesbian."[34]

At least three cultural sources contributed in the late 1960s to this new movement. One source was second-wave feminism, which focused heavily on consciousness-raising groups and their critiques of patriarchy. One radical "collective" of this kind was WITCH: Women's International Terrorist Conspiracy from Hell. Its manifesto identified all women as witches (but, of course, in a good way), called for revolution to destroy patriarchy, promoted women's power and independence, viewed the historic witches as martyrs, and urged modern women to form covens. But even though the witch had emerged as a symbol, notes Eller, it was "a symbol without a practice."[35] This was still mainly a political movement.

Although political feminism was enough for some women, it was not enough for women such as Zsuzsanna Budapest. After escaping the Hungarian revolution and migrating to America, Budapest became a feminist activist. In Los Angeles, she organized women to protest rape and other problems. But she came to realize that political revolution alone would not bring about significant change. Only a spiritual revolution, she believed, could do that. And she was in a good position to lead one. After all, she claimed to have inherited the necessary knowledge. Her mother in Hungary had practised witchcraft in the woods with other witches and had gone into trances that left her speaking ancient Egyptian (which supported her claim to being a reincarnated priestess of Hathor). Budapest included these sources in her *Holy Book of Women's Mysteries*,[36] which she published in 1979. Possibly to imitate the covens of WITCH, she created the Susan B. Anthony Coven Number One of what she saw as a religious movement. She focused on Dianic witchcraft, named after the Roman queen of heaven who was associated with the moon, hunting, and the renewal of animals, and had female priestesses.

A second source of the new movement was closely related to Budapest's feminist witchcraft. This was what Eller calls "goddess spirituality," which had many subdivisions. Some women interested in witchcraft as a religion turned to neopaganism, a movement that originated in Britain during the 1960s and has by now become familiar to most people as Wicca.[37] According to Eller, it "was small, and feminists entered in numbers large enough to make a real impact ... they ... swaggered in, ready to rearrange the furniture."[38]

Not surprisingly, many old-timers were unhappy about this invasion. "The first point of conflict was that feminists by and large had no interest in sharing their circles with men, and precious little interest in worshiping a god of any sort ... they often were impatient with the measured pageantry and role-playing that characterized some ... rituals or ... the encyclopedic lists of greater and lesser divinities and spirits. They wanted to worship a goddess – a big one, bigger than the god of patriarchy – and they wanted to worship themselves through her."[39] More "traditional" neopagans were unimpressed. From their point of view, both polytheism and gender duality were inherent in paganism – including witchcraft. They not only tolerated but also needed men and gods. A second point of conflict was the neopagan emphasis on secrecy. This emphasis existed, says Eller, "partly out of fear of persecution, but also out of a love of the concept of hidden lore, or mystical truths that could only be revealed to the initiated few. Feminist witches, in contrast, tended to be more evangelical, wanting to get the good word out to their sisters. Far from insisting on long periods of training and gradual initiation into higher mysteries, feminist witches hearkened back to a phrase from the WITCH manifesto: You are a Witch by being female."[40]

Yet another point of conflict was what the newcomers perceived as sexism. This, says Eller, was "a rude surprise to feminists who thought they had left all that behind in established religions."[41] One neopagan, Starhawk, became very influential. Budapest had introduced her to feminist witchcraft in the early 1970s, but Starhawk rejected feminist separatism. She allowed men to participate, although her movement remained profoundly gynocentric.[42] She began by combining neopagan witchcraft with feminist witchcraft. Over the years, she has written books on ancient goddesses, women's spirituality, ecology, and the problems of contemporary society. Of great interest to us, Starhawk contributed to three films for the National Film Board of Canada – the films that we have been analyzing here, two of which involved collaboration with

Donna Read. In 2003, she and Read made *Signs out of Time*,[43] a documentary film about Marija Gimbutas. Starhawk now focuses much of her attention on ecology and "earth activist training," calling her approach "engaged spirituality" – which is to say, politicized spirituality.

Other women turned instead either to dead ancient religions or to living Eastern ones that had been transplanted to the West and popularized – what academics called "new religious movements" and journalists called "new religions" or "alternative religions." Feminists were interested in these for three reasons. First, they featured goddesses:[44] ancient Greek religion, for instance, or Hinduism (especially via theosophy). Second, they featured female spiritual guides; consider Hindu Tantric ones, say, or Taoist ones. Third, they featured experiential techniques such as personal experience, meditation, magic, and ritual. Gradually, experimentation within these old and new religious movements evolved into the New Age movements that became popular in the 1970s.

Common to all[45] was a preoccupation with the self and its relation to both the natural order and cosmic energies of one kind or another. Seekers experimented with spiritual techniques such as "channeling" and holistic healing (which focuses not only on the physical dimension of health but also on the emotional, mental, and spiritual ones). They moved from one movement to another under that broad umbrella, often improvizing on whatever they found while using the rhetoric of tolerance and inclusion.

Meanwhile, both the reaction against traditional Western religions and the "marketplace" approach to ideas led to fluctuating belief systems, rudimentary organizations, and a profound disregard for authority – especially that of institutionalized Christianity. Both feminists and spiritual feminists liked this "transgressive" or "subversive" mentality, of course, because they identified authority with men and patriarchy. Every woman, at least in theory, could be a feminist leader, a spiritual teacher – even a goddess. Spiritual feminists also liked New Age myths of a golden age. They saw the latter romantically as the precedent for a new one in which spiritual values would replace material ones and where nature, science, philosophy, and art would work together in creating utopia. But they valued the language of science too, because of the legitimacy that it conferred.

Still other women chose to stay within Christianity or Judaism. By retrieving, reinterpreting, and emphasizing whatever feminine imagery they could find in Judaism or Christianity, they hoped for extensive reforms to suit the needs of women (a topic that we discuss in the next chapter). But some of them found that these traditions were inherently androcentric and thus of no use to women. They left, therefore, to find truly gynocentric alternatives.

A third source of the new movement was what we would call, very broadly, psychotherapy. We refer to psychotherapeutic movements that promoted self-actualization of one kind or another, not merely curing neuroses. Many Wiccans were especially attracted to the psychology of Carl Jung, even though many feminists rejected Jung's belief in the need to unite characteristics that were either distinctively feminine or distinctively masculine. Jung argued that the human mind was inherently polytheistic and found evidence for his claim in both folklore and dreams, both of which reveal universal and archetypal symbols. These reflect psychological processes. For Jung, the great task – what he called "individuation" – was to recognize, integrate, and then internalize these archetypes to achieve a balanced self. Even though we can never have perfectly objective answers to religious questions, said Jung, we can nonetheless experience religion subjectively. Doing so can promote psychological development, moreover, if practised in the right ways and at the right times. Ultimately, in theological terms, Jung acknowledged radical immanence. Wiccans recognized their own worldview in Jung's use of Eastern or ancient pagan lore and his insistence on experiential religion. Many Wiccans, in fact, became Jungian analysts. So did some spiritual feminists. Both have encouraged people to choose deities, myths, and rituals for which they feel spiritual or psychological affinities.

Some women were attracted to other psychotherapeutic movements. Examples include Abraham Maslow's "human potential" movement[46] and "transpersonal psychology" (which drew not only on the work of Jung but also on that of William James) – that seek altered states of consciousness within a transcendental dimension. These movements encourage people to cultivate ultimate or "peak" experiences of "unitive consciousness." They encourage the belief that science can integrate body, mind, emotion, and spirit. And they use the overtly religious language of ecstasy, awe, transcendence, immanence, mysticism, and so forth, but in contexts that are otherwise secular (such as "wholism," Rolfing,[47] EST,[48] and primal therapy)[49] or secularized (such as yoga and transcendental meditation).[50] But not all of these therapeutic movements are quasi-religious. Consider "object relations," a branch of psychology that places the mother-child relationship at the centre of psychic being (and, not coincidentally, attacks Freudians for being patriarchal and misogynistic).

These three sources – feminism, goddess spirituality, and psychotherapy – have all come together in what Eller calls feminist spirituality but we call goddess ideology. We do so because feminist spirituality corresponds almost exactly to what we have described elsewhere as ideology. It is a religious version, as it were, of ideological feminism (as distinct from egalitarian feminism).

In our prologue, we discussed two massively and enduringly popular books: *The Chalice and the Blade* by Riane Eisler and *The Da Vinci Code* by Dan Brown. Here are a few more examples of the fallout from goddess ideology in popular culture.

By 1995, observes Suna Chang of *Entertainment Weekly*, the great goddess had clearly arrived in Hollywood and was ready for her close-up. In production were *Buffy, the Vampire Slayer* and *Sabrina, the Teenage Witch*. At the planning stage were a cartoon spinoff of *Sabrina*, a remake of the movie *Bell, Book and Candle*, a film version of the play *Into the Woods*, a film version of the sitcom *Bewitched*, and a live-action adaptation of *The Lion, the Witch, and the Wardrobe*. "Sure, this all has great entertainment value," says Phyllis Curott, a Wiccan, "but witch-craft is cutting-edge feminism." According to Alice Hoffman, author of *Practical Magic*,[51] the "current coven is a modernization of the witch. They're fun to watch, but they also deal with issues like abuse and love." And, writes Chang, "without saying the M-word (well, okay, *millennium*), the timing appears to be right."[52]After all, Wiccans take public relations very seriously. Camel had to withdraw its cigarette ad because it featured a bubbling cauldron and three women smoking in front of their voodoo doll. Some Wiccans protested the appearance of an evil witch, moreover, in *Buffy, the Vampire Slayer*. To avoid these problems, Hollywood moguls now hire consultants from covens.

Even mainstream religious groups are taking the divine female very seriously. Some Reconstructionists, the most liberal of all Jews, have revised their prayer book (which was itself a radically rewritten version of the traditional one) with this in mind. In *Kol*

Haneshamah, therefore, they have not merely used gender-inclusive language in references to people (as have Reform and Conservative Jews) but have applied the same principle in references to the deity. In some cases, they leave the Hebrew in its traditional form but alter the English translation with gender inclusivity in mind. Some innovations are relatively uncontroversial. During the *amidah*, for instance, Jews have traditionally prayed to the "God of our fathers, God of Abraham, God of Isaac, and God of Jacob." Reconstructionist Jews now pray to the "God of our ancestors, the God of Sarah, God of Rebekah, God of Rachel, and God of Leah." Similarly, the transition from *elohim* (the usual word for God) to *shekhinah* (a female aspect of the deity) would not seem very jarring in traditional circles, because Jews and especially Jewish mystics have recognized the latter for at least two thousand years. Elsewhere, however, *Kol* is more controversial. One well-known traditional hymn, for example, retains the original Hebrew words *avinu malkeinu* but allows worshippers to translate them either as "Our God, our Father" or as "Our Mother, our Queen." To begin blessings, Reconstructionist Jews may now say *barukh at* (the feminine form of "you") instead of *barukh attah* (the masculine form). In its most controversial innovation of all, *Kol* allows worshippers to substitute *ha'elah hakedoshah* (the holy Goddess) for *ha'el hakadosh* (the holy God). Liberal Christians have made very similar liturgical choices.[53] Some Protestant ministers refer to a divine "She" (not even "He or She"). And some Presbyterians have considered references to God as "Sophia" (which we discuss in chapter 4).

All of this amounts to a surprisingly pervasive, though often camouflaged, new worldview. Like every other worldview, it has its founders, rituals, beliefs, political implications, and so on. This one is saturated with feminist politics and psychology.

> Because feminists are creating a new worldview ... their role is functionally equivalent to that of religious founders. And when feminists systematically explore their new worldview, they do so as the functional equivalents of theologians which is why feminists "revisioning" or "re-imagining" (as in the "Goddess" and "Sophia" movements) have been called "thealogy" (*thea* referring to goddess, *theo* to God). But ... the new feminist religion is religious only on the surface. Lurking beneath it is an implicitly secular value system related to feminist politics and psychology.

In [Rita] Gross's words, "Goddess religion surely could be use-ful for feminists working for social change, for the psycholog-ical empowerment that comes with saying 'Goddess' is one source for regenerating the energy needed to continue working for economic, political, or social justice issues. And without ongoing psychological and spiritual renewal, social activists usually burn out or become embittered and ineffective."[54]

Some feminists admit the secular aspect of goddess cults, as Rita Gross does in the preceding passage. At other times, in reaction to criticism or trivialization, they hotly deny it. But goddess ideology can have religious surface structures (such as prayers or rituals) and secular deep structures (political goals).

So far, we have discussed goddess mythology in connection with its meaning for women. Occasionally, we have referred to its mean-ing for men. That requires more attention. The clear message for men is that the new order will have no room for them *as such*. Men, it implies, are innately irrelevant at best and innately evil at worst. Even though a few Western men have converted to feminism, and even though some men have become Wiccans (who refer to both gods and goddesses), not many are flocking to goddess shrines. This should come as no surprise. The social and political vision that fem-inists advocate as a "return to the goddess" can lead only to pro-found alienation among men.

One episode of a popular television series presented its own ver-sion of restoring the lost golden age of women. *Northern Expo-sure*[55] attracted most of its viewers from an intellectually sophisti-cated elite, but it held its own in the prime-time schedule for six years during the 1990s. It was, in short, a mainstream production. Here is the episode's plot.

An old-timer, aided by a series of flashbacks, tells Joel Fleischman and other inhabitants of Cicely, Alaska, about their town's early history in the late nineteenth century. "In the beginning," it is inhabited primarily by men, miners given over completely to booz-ing, whoring, and fighting. They represent raw nature. Wolves rear one of them, in fact, and he literally wallows in the muddy swamp that passes for a street. But a woman challenges the rules. She enters the saloon and begins to sing "Nearer My God, to Thee." (Accord-ing to some witnesses of the *Titanic* disaster, its orchestra played that hymn just before the ship that represented "male" technology sank beneath the waves).

Along come two women from the outside world, though, and everything changes. Cicely (from whom the town eventually derives its name) and Roslyn are everything that the men are not. In other words, they are fully human. Cicely refers condescendingly to the uncouth, uneducated, and unrefined men as "savage beasts" to be soothed. Picking one of them out of the mud, she observes that he is thwarting the process of evolution itself. In short order, benign female leadership civilizes the town. Roslyn seizes leadership after knocking out a drunken miner for "abusing" his power.

The men, overawed by the beauty and sensitivity of Cicely, nonetheless confer leadership on the two women. Before anyone can say "feminization" – and someone *does* say it – Roslyn and Cicely begin teaching the men how to read and pray. Pretty soon they establish a theatre. There the inhabitants find spiritual nourishment in *tableaux vivants*, poetry readings, and dance performances à la Isadora Duncan. In academic parlance, culture supplements nature – elite culture, that is, which Americans since frontier days have associated stereotypically with women. Or, to put it another way, female nature (everything progressive and benevolent) replaces male nature (everything primitive and barbaric) as the dominant force in town.

Like so many television shows set in the past, this one has nothing whatever to do with history and everything to do with what its producers consider the interests of contemporary viewers and consumers (whether they know it or not). This one defines their interests very precisely according to a specific way of thinking: that of goddess ideology. Roslyn specifically aims to restore the "matriarchal, pagan society" in which everyone once lived peacefully and harmoniously, "a community," as Cicely puts it, "where all are equal, all are valued."

Everyone? Well, everyone who matters. Men, clearly, do not. They can make no distinctive contribution of their own, at any rate, to this community. At best they can learn enough from women to become acceptable inhabitants. At worst they can continue in their evil ways and thus place themselves beyond redemption. Roslyn supervises the town's defence against a man who, after a woman refuses his overtures, intends to take revenge on everyone.

When Cicely confesses that she would like to meet a man, Roslyn advises her to forget such a silly dream. Although men need women, she observes, women *do not need men*. Using psycho-analytical insights from feminists such as Nancy Chodorow[56] or even Mary Daly,[57] Roslyn acknowledges that men, who to achieve adulthood must stop identifying with their mothers, need women to replace the primary source of gratification. But because women continue to identify with their mothers – that is, with women – they have no comparable need to replace the primary source of theirs. Loving men is too hard for women and hardly worthwhile in the first place. It seldom works. "Fortunately," she says, "there are alternatives." Roslyn is not just another strong and intelligent woman: she is a combination of the archetypal earth mother and the archetypal wise woman (formerly reviled by men, presumably, as the archetypal witch or hag).

In fact, Roslyn is nothing less than an incarnation of the great goddess as understood by the feminist ideologues and "thealo-gians" of our own time. In the end, a (male) sniper kills Cicely. Stricken by grief, Roslyn withdraws from the town but ends up fighting and dying in the Spanish Civil War. This event recapitulates the lamentable but, to goddess ideologues, temporary eclipse of matriarchy by patriarchy. The clear implication, of course, is that modern residents of Cicely, on hearing this tale, will complete the work that these feminist pioneers began almost a century earlier.

Now consider Theodore Roszak's science-fiction novel, *The Memoirs of Elizabeth Frankenstein*. Nina Auerbach's glowing review says it all. Roszak's "Lady Caroline and Elizabeth are goddess worshippers, but not in the sanctimonious contemporary way; they are acolytes of an erotic female faith that has joined spirit and body, women and nature, since prehistory. The violation and dispersion of these 'cunning women' by the rapacious science of Victor [Frankenstein] engenders a harrowing parable of lost female union ... Mr. Roszak's allegory of male science violating female nature sounds schematic in synopsis, but it's a great read."[58] In Roszak's version of Mary Shelley's story, both Lady Caroline and Elizabeth are worshippers of a primordial goddess. In other words, they participate in an underground religion of women that has continued from prehistoric times. Not for them the dichotomy between mind or spirit and body (although the dichotomy between male and female is another matter). Not for them the sinister science that motivates Victor to create his monster.

Another novel, Jean Auel's massively popular *The Clan of the Cave Bear*, which lasted for seventeen weeks on the *New York Times* list of best-sellers,[59] perfectly exemplifies the mythic paradigm of goddess ideology. Auel projects the institutionalization of rape back onto the poor old Neanderthals, about whose social and cultural world we actually know almost nothing. Not that their evolutionary successors fare any better. Says Ayla, Auel's heroine, "Men and their needs! Clan men, men of the Others, they're all alike."[60] Though living among the Neanderthals, Ayla is a *modern* woman, not only in the biological sense but also, anachronistically, in a cultural sense. In this novel and its two sequels, Ayla progresses from victimization (rape in particular and female subordination in general) to heroism (risking her life to save a child and hunting better than the men) to virtual divinization (on account of her ability to heal).

The goddess takes a somewhat different form in *Medea: A Modern Retelling*,[61] by Christa Wolf. The novelist's aim is to rehabilitate Medea, who has infamously entered popular consciousness (to the extent that any character from ancient Greek drama can still enter popular consciousness) as a vengeful, matricidal priestess. Medea uses her black arts to help Jason and his Argonauts mow down enemy warriors, butchers her own younger brother, throws what remains of him into the sea, murders princess Glauce out of revenge for seducing Jason, and stabs her own young sons. "If one goes back far enough," according to Rita Much in her review, "one finds that Medea's name actually means 'Wise One' and that she was famous in goddess-worshipping cultures for her magic, which she used to heal the sick. Like all goddesses during the patriarchal takeover of Europe by Indo-European invaders who worshiped male sky-gods, her role was radically rewritten and invariably debased."[62] So it was all merely a misunderstanding.

Wolf finds support for this position from none other than Margaret Atwood, who offers a warm introduction. Lest anyone misunderstand the novel, Atwood makes it clear that Wolf focuses on the power of men and the hideous lies on which they build it. For Atwood, the book is "ingenious, brilliant and necessary." Wolf feels justified in writing a monumental vindication, at any rate, not only of Medea herself but of the maligned great goddess as well. Her Medea is utterly innocent. Moreover, she is "a radical feminist victim of a 2,500-year-old male conspiracy and smear campaign."[63]

To substantiate all this, Wolf relies on a goulash of standard conspiracy theory and popular psychology. Far from being murderously jealous of Glauce, for example, Medea feels compassion for her as the victim of "recovered memory syndrome." Glauce's fits are due to repressed memories of her sister's ritual sacrifice by Creon. What about Medea's unfortunate sons? Far from murdering them, she prays to Hera for their protection from Creon. His evil male advisor, however, incites the crowd to kill them. And so on.

This novel is largely an excuse to attack men as patriarchs (as if many feminists believe that women still need an excuse). For Wolf, "patriarchy" originated in nothing less than the primordial lust of men for power and violence. Unlike Atwood, though, reviewer Rita Much is not convinced; she finds the book melodramatic rather than tragic. Her additional comments are worth quoting here, because Wolf's book is characteristic of almost everything written these days about goddesses:

> This Medea seems to me to be a sadly diminished figure, the perfectly innocent victim of egregious misrepresentation rather than of extremes of passion, romantic love, the thirst for revenge and her hunger for justice. Instead of a force to be reckoned with, Medea occasionally comes across as sanctimonious.
>
> The great lengths Wolf goes to in order to sanitize her reputation borders on the ridiculous. When [Medea] runs off with Jason, for example, she has her mother's blessing, and before the couple arrive in Corinth they visit Odysseus's old flame, the witch Circe, who explains to Medea that female wickedness is solely the consequence of association with men who are "Great, dreadful children." Medea's dragon-slaying magical powers are reduced to forms of alternative medicine, like massage and art therapy (she even talks in a New Age way about the inner child, and her efforts to help Glauce involve a makeover and useful wardrobe tips). And Jason is little more than a sniveling brownnoser, hardly worthy of the regard of a granddaughter of the sun god Helios and priestess to Hecate, goddess of the underworld.

Though Euripedes goes a long way in making Medea sympathetic and in clarifying her motives, I'm still waiting for the version of the myth that presents her heinous acts as somehow logical and inevitable, as a last effort on her part to remain who she was, at the expense of those who made her who she was. We may not like to admit it, but women do kill their children.[64]

Something similar emerges from feminist takes on *Medea* as a play. In a letter to the *New York Times*, Sara Jasper Cook takes exception to Vincent Canby's review.[65] "The wrecked family connection is, I think, central to Medea's tragedy," Canby writes. "Not so different from the archetypal Oedipus (by way of Aeschylus or Freud), she experiences metaphorically what women have always experienced, at least until recently. Falling in love (or even just getting married), a woman puts aside her love for her father and brothers, her culture, her history, and leaves her family for a foreign one, sometimes far away. In giving life to her lover's children, she transfers her loyalty completely. There is no going back." Her lover's children? Are they not also her children? And how does any of this explain Medea's murder of her own children?

Here is Cook's answer: "Paradoxically, Medea is now entirely vulnerable, dependent on Jason, just like ordinary women following society's mandates. What recourse is there for such a woman, if she is strong enough, when her man decides to move on? Only to take his children away from him, one way or another." Only? Never mind that they are also *her* children; since when is murder the "only" recourse in any situation except physical self-defence? Cook has tried not only to explain Medea's behaviour but also to *legitimate* it.

In doing so, moreover, she does a grave injustice to any standard of morality and also to women. From her perspective, a woman's children are nothing more than pawns in a power struggle. At issue here is not only the difference between Greek and Israelite worldviews – consider the biblical story in which a mother prefers to give up her child rather than let Solomon take a sword and divide it between her and another woman – but also the difference between those who allow ideology to override common sense (let alone common decency) and those who do not. *Medea* is a tragedy primarily because of a flaw in its central character – and, by implication, in everyone – not because of some flaw in this or that social order.

Mary Lefkowitz has offered some specific explanations for the popularity of the goddess movement. For one thing, she observes, goddesses have come into fashion as manifestations of New Age consciousness. "In this instance, American feminism has combined with American spiritualism. New Ages always look to old ages and the older the better; and the New Agers in America have found in the Goddess their customary enjoyments, that is, the archaic and the esoteric."[66] The half-understood notion of "pluralism," adds Lefkowitz, has convinced many people to search for religious truth as if they were filling their trays at a spiritual cafeteria. "They have ... found in the Goddess," she writes, "another opportunity for what might politely be called syncretism, but is really a kind of pseudo-mystical mixing and matching of symbols and ideas that have nothing in common with each other except the contemporary use to which they may be put."[67] Was there, she asks, a Goddess before God? And why even ask, if we evolved from monkeys? "The reason is that history, real or imagined, provides a charter, a basis for identity, a sense of direction, particularly when it claims to represent the primary order, the natural order, of things. So questions about the primacy of the Goddess are being asked insistently and urgently throughout this searching and somewhat addled country."[68]

But we can think of a more important reason for the sudden interest in archaeology among those who would otherwise never have bothered to learn the difference between a runestone and a rhinestone. At a time when women are exploring every possible way of affirming their femaleness, it is hardly surprising that many of them want to repudiate the notion of a god who supposedly represents male consciousness in favour of a goddess who supposedly represents female consciousness.

Belief in female superiority is now securely encoded, at any rate, in a myth, or secular myth, that is at least potentially attractive to all women. Even academics in women's studies take goddess movements seriously as manifestations of feminism. Some have gone further, lending their academic authority to it by arguing, for instance, that goddess worship arose because of a universal human experience: being born of woman.[69] This is particularly true of feminists who teach and write about some schools of psychoanalysis.

Accepting the complexity and ambiguity that shapes reality would mean rejecting not only sentimental nostalgia for a lost golden age of women in the past but also – and much more saliently – political leverage in the struggle for a new golden age of women in the future and therapeutic advantages in the effort to forge a new identity for women in the present. Many feminists now argue that women must withdraw into "womanspace."[70]

PART II

From Reform to Revolution:
Restoring the Goddess

We turn now to the moral and practical implications of what goddess ideologues say in the name of feminism or even women. This problem is familiar to every minority community. When Jews, for instance, say or do anything unsavoury, other Jews find it necessary to challenge them publicly for fear that the larger society will fail to notice that not all Jews think or act in the same ways. In an ideal world, this measure would be unnecessary, but this is not an ideal world. So far, most feminists have tried to distance themselves from the extremists. When it comes to religion, for instance, many feminists want merely to bring about reforms. But some want reforms that would amount to revolution. Others truly want revolution.

In chapter 4, we examine a Christian movement that promoted religious revolution implicitly. Knowing that the language of reform is more acceptable than that of revolution to most religious people, leaders used the former as a front for the latter (which is not surprising, given that one antecedent of feminist ideology, and therefore also of goddess ideology, is Marxist "critical theory"). In this case, they promoted "Sophia," the feminine Greek noun that means wisdom, but also the female divine principle that some Christians now associate with the Holy Spirit. This promotion provoked a polarizing controversy in one Presbyterian denomination. Many of those who might have begun by trying to restore the feminine side of a god ended up by flirting with the worship of a goddess – what we call Sophianity. But the choice of monotheism over polytheism was a defining one in the development of biblical religion; abandoning monotheism means abandoning Christianity or Judaism.

Most Presbyterians, in this case, understood that they had encountered revolution masquerading as reform.

Our point here, though, is that Sophianity affected men. Sophians
explained the change as a remedy for misogyny, branding men who
disagreed, let alone their ancestors, as haters of women. Inherent in
the new order, therefore, was an attack on men. Sophians preferred
to ignore, trivialize, excuse, or condone this misandry. Even those
who took it seriously and explicitly opposed it, moreover, often
failed to acknowledge or even to see some underlying parallels with
their own theories. Like their explicitly secular counterparts, feminist ideologues, they saw no links between goddess ideology's conspiracy theory of history and their own misandry.

In chapter 5, we examine goddess ideologues who advocate revolution not implicitly but explicitly. They want to change Western
religions in truly radical ways. Mary Daly, a former Catholic, has
long been an icon for both goddess ideologues and feminist ideologues. One of her books, *Beyond God the Father*, has become part
of the feminist canon among academics in the field of religious
studies. Daly argues there that women cannot remain Christians or
Jews without denying the value of their own femaleness and therefore participating in their own oppression. In later books, Daly has
gone much further. She argues that all patriarchal religions, even
those that include both gods and goddesses, are inherently evil. She
sees no point in trying to reform them, not even if reform is a front
for revolution. Instead she urges women to worship a goddess and,
in doing so, not merely to empower themselves but to worship
themselves. What about men in the new world? Daly daydreams
cheerfully about women decimating the male population through
parthenogenesis – or, at the very least, waiting for "nature" to do
the job for women.

4

The Green Goddess:
Feminism for a Therapeutic Age

The New Age is a vast, amorphous, and unstable congeries of closely interconnected movements. Some are explicitly religious but implicitly secular, others explicitly secular but implicitly religious. Some focus primarily on the personal, others primarily on the political. Some attract both men and women, others mainly women. All of them, however, are in some way about health or healing. In this chapter, we examine two feminist versions of New Age movements that often flow together, one linking religion and feminism (either egalitarian or ideological) with psychotherapy to promote *personal* healing for women, and the other linking religion and feminism (either egalitarian or ideological) with environmentalism to promote *collective* healing not only for women but for all species on a female planet. Though now moving toward the political centre, environmentalism clearly originated on the left. So did its offshoot, ecofeminism,[1] which is what most people call this second feminist version of the New Age. Green, therefore, is the new red.

Some academic feminists turn to psychoanalysis as a way of understanding the current mainstreaming of goddess religion. Jean Shinoda Bolen, a clinical professor of psychiatry at the University of California in San Francisco, has presented parts of her book, *Goddesses in Everywoman*,[2] at conferences of the International Association for Analytical Psychology, the American Academy of Psychoanalysis, the American Psychiatric Association, the Women's Institute of the Orthopsychiatric Association, the Association for Transpersonal Psychology, the C.G. Jung Institute, and so on. For three years in the 1980s, she was also on the board of directors of the *Ms* Foundation for Women. Gloria Steinem, who founded the *Ms* Foundation, has written a glowing foreword to Bolen's book.

According to Steinem, the best-known advocate of mainstream feminism in America, Bolen is "a gentle revolutionary whose healing calm and accepting spirit [is] testimony to the better world that a feminist revolution might bring."[3] Actually, Bolen is a brilliant popularizer whose trendy "sharing" testifies to the intellectual vacuity that any ideological revolution can bring. Reducing religion to a form of psychotherapy, she describes goddesses as clever labels that women can adopt in order to describe ways of thinking or feeling. This provides women with a convenient taxonomy by which to classify their intellectual and emotional possibilities. It provides them also, albeit indirectly, with a convenient excuse for trivializing those of men.

Bolen makes it clear that women should never imagine themselves restricted to one goddess. Because the primordial great goddess has local manifestations, women can see in themselves a whole range of personalities. This is her version of "pluralism," evidently, or "cultural diversity." Bolen believes that the Greek goddesses are metaphors "for diversity and conflict within women ... they are complex and many sided. All the goddesses are potentially present in every woman."[4] She points out that "which goddess or goddesses (several may be present at the same time) become activated in any particular woman at a particular time depends on the combined effect of a variety of interacting elements – predisposition, family and culture, hormones, other people, unchosen circumstances, chosen activities, and stages of life."[5]

A woman who keeps changing her mind is not confused or inconsistent, therefore, but merely taking on various goddesses. A woman who sends out double messages is not duplicitous, but is merely engaging in a kind of dialogue between two goddesses. Still, a woman can have a greater affinity for some goddesses than others. She might be primarily an Artemis woman, for example, or a Hera woman. "The 'goddesses' are powerful, invisible forces that shape behavior and influence emotions ... When she knows which 'goddesses' are dominant forces within her, a woman acquires self-knowledge about the strength of certain instincts, about priorities and abilities, about the possibilities of finding personal meaning through choices others might not encourage."[6]

Who are these "others"? Obviously, they are men (along with "man-identified" women).

Bolen has clearly adopted a dualistic approach; no wonder that she writes only for women. Lecturing on her discovery of mythology as a therapeutic resource for women, Bolen observes that "audiences were turned on, intrigued, abuzz with the excitement of using myth as an insight tool. This was a way for people to understand women."[7] Elsewhere, she writes that the "Jungian perspective has made me aware that women are influenced by powerful inner forces, or archetypes, which can be personified by Greek goddesses. And the feminist perspective has given me an understanding of how outer forces, or stereotypes – the roles to which society expects women to conform – reinforce some goddess patterns and repress others."[8]

Bolen relies on the work of Marija Gimbutas, which we have discussed in previous chapters. Referring to universality, for instance, Bolen writes: "Known by many names – Astarte, Ishtar, Inanna, Nut, Isis, Asthoreth, Au Set, Hathor, Nina, Nammu, and Ningal, among others – the Great Goddess was worshipped as the feminine life force deeply connected to nature and fertility."[9] On supremacy, she writes that "before the coming of patriarchal religions the Great Goddess was regarded as immortal, changeless, and omnipotent. She took lovers not to provide her children with a father, but for pleasure. Fatherhood had not yet been introduced into religious thought, and there were no (male) gods."[10] No wonder that Bolen addresses only women. Her great goddess would have nothing to offer modern men except a divine mandate for their service as women's toys. After decades of empowering single mothers and celebrating mothers single by choice, even fatherhood is not significant enough to require a divine model. Unfortunately, some feminists believe that the goddess represents not only what Jung called the Great Mother archetype – one of several, including her direct counterpart for men, the Wise Old Man – but also the archetype of all archetypes: "Paralleling the power held by the Great Goddess when she was worshipped, the archetypal Great Goddess has the most powerful effect of any archetype."[11]

Bolen relies also on Jungian theory, which she uses in the service of feminism – the former modified, of course, to eliminate conflicts with the latter. For Bolen, like Jung, all deities are really local or historical manifestations of primordial archetypes embedded in the collective unconscious. But she ignores Jung's inclusion of gods as well as goddesses. The trouble is not that Bolen ignores the gods – after all, she is addressing women – but that she rejects them. This is because she relies almost as heavily on Gimbutas as she does on Jung, and Gimbutas says that all goddesses were and are local or historical manifestations of a primordial great goddess. Yet there is no real parallel between the "collective unconscious" defined by Jung and the great goddess that Gimbutas discusses; Jung's collective unconscious provides men no less than women with a distinctive and valuable perspective of their own, while the great goddess provides one only for women. For Bolen as for Gimbutas, therefore, the gods are like dead-end streets leading nowhere, certainly not to primordial wisdom. And how could it be otherwise for those who believe that "in the beginning" was a great goddess but not a great god? Even if the Greek gods exist somehow in everyman, they are mere usurpers and imitators of the Greek goddesses in "everywoman." They have no legitimate or even authentic voices of their own. For Bolen as for Gimbutas, only women have direct access to the well-springs of truth, wisdom, compassion, and so forth.

The sexual asymmetry in Bolen's work is no accident. It is a direct result of her uncritical reliance on goddess ideology, not merely on the psychology of women. She condemns the Greek gods and heroes as the legacy of patriarchal mythology, which "reflects the encounter and subjugation of peoples who had mother-based religions, by invaders who had warrior gods and father-based theologies."[12] In doing so, she refers explicitly to Gimbutas herself, who relied on half-truths rather than acknowledge the ambiguity of ancient evidence.

Naomi Goldenberg, who teaches psychology of religion at the University of Ottawa, has popularized the great goddess by appealing to another school of psychology: object-relations theory (to which we will return). In a collection of essays called *Returning Words to Flesh*,[13] Goldenberg's aim is to link religion and psychoanalysis with feminism: "Besides sharing the subject of sexuality ... psychoanalysis and feminism have a similar soteriology, a similar way of approaching human salvation. Both analysis and feminism are fundamentally messianic; both are concerned with developing methods and visions of transforming self and world."[14] In view of this messianic urge to restore the ancient goddess cult, we would classify Goldenberg as an "archeologian."

Her introduction, "Apocalypse in Everyday Life: The Cultural Context in Which We Do Theory," establishes the political goal by revising an old nursery tale. In the traditional version, she observes, Henny Penny gets hit on the head by what she takes to be a piece of the sky. With Turkey Lurkey, Ducky Lucky, and Chicken Licken – but also, according to versions of the story that she ignores, with Cocky Locky, an obviously male inhabitant of the barnyard[15] – Henny Penny runs off to warn the king. What they should have done, writes Goldenberg, was set up a consciousness-raising group! There they could have discussed the more immediate problem of Foxy Loxy, who was lurking nearby and preparing to gobble them up. Why did they not see the real danger? Why did they waste time appealing to the distant ruler? (Does this mean that Goldenberg would oppose the enormously successful efforts of feminists to influence male presidents, prime ministers, and other administrative authorities?) Because, answers Goldenberg, false consciousness has duped them.

Goldenberg's point is that the friends represent women, who are innocent victims; Foxy Loxy represents men, on the other hand, who are evil victimizers. For her, then, the story becomes a cautionary tale with an overt political and ideological message. Instead of running to some authority in the male hierarchy, women had better use their own unique and superior female "ways of knowing" to solve the many urgent problems that men have caused. Having warned readers of the coming apocalypse, she urges them to explore the possibility of averting it by combining feminist analysis, psychoanalytical theory, and religious imagination.

In fact, she writes, many women have already begun to do so. This is particularly true in the realm of religion. Reformist feminists have tried to adapt older religions. Revolutionary feminists have established new religions for women. Academic feminists have formulated new theories to account for the origins of religion. All of these approaches converge, however, on the great goddess. This phenomenon has made "the return of the Goddess a definite cultural event – an event which religious leaders, theologians, and scholars of religion are beginning to notice."[16]

Goldenberg believes that her own contribution is to show how psychoanalytical theory explains this phenomenon and how the latter, in turn, explains some current trends in psychoanalysis. To do this, she examines four tendencies common to both ways of thinking: recycling the past as a source of new meaning; emphasizing the communal dimension of human development instead of the personal; glorifying female symbols of power and desire while deconstructing male ones; and proclaiming that *fantasy* is a primary structure of rational thought – which is to say, of *scholarship*.

Discussing the first of these, the past, Goldenberg establishes a link between the archetypal mother of what she considers psychoanalysis and the primordial goddess of what she considers archeology. To do so, as we say, she resorts to object-relations theory. According to advocates such as founder Melanie Klein and D.W. Winnicott, the most important factor in early development is not the innate "drives" that dominate the internal world, as Freudians would have it, but relationships with others in the external world – that is, with the objects of their attention. Because everyone's mother is the earliest object, they say, she is also the most important one (even though there is no logical connection between chronology and importance). Goldenberg needs to find support for this theory, and she does so by ransacking religious lore (which hardly ignores mother goddesses).

Object-relations theory's intense interest in the deep past is, in broad terms, quite similar to that of the contemporary goddess ideologues. Both psychoanalysis and the new "theologies" involve participants in extensive discussions of what happened long, long ago. Psychoanalysis emphasizes the pre-verbal past. Goddess ideology emphasizes the collective prehistoric past.

Both philosophies cultivate a sense of connection to the past, which heightens involvement in the present. In the case of goddess ideology, this focus on the past confers a sense of reality and legitimacy on the experiences of modern women. Books about goddess mythology provide them with prototypes of female passions and sensibilities; myths call their attention to the complexity of female experience and dignify the experience by revealing its primordial roots. To a great degree, therefore, goddess ideology follows the pattern that Mircea Eliade describes in his work on myths of "eternal return."

Even more significant than their shared reverence for the deep past is the fact that both "thealogy" (goddess theology) and object-relations theory agree on what, or rather who, is the most important part of the past. Unlike classical analytic theory, which focuses on the father, object-relations theory focuses on the mother. Like

goddess ideology, in fact, object-relations theory places a woman at
the Beginning and thus champions a shift from male symbols to
female ones. Both ways of thinking undermine the value of fathers
and of maleness itself.[17]

Goldenberg relies not only on a gynocentric reading of psychoanalytical theory but also on a gynocentric reading of evidence
from history, archaeology, and religious studies. With all this in
mind, she stresses the importance of believing that the biblical rejection and denigration of female imagery was *politically* inspired:
"Women are there. Things female are there. But they have been
*inverted or cloaked in order to be appropriated by male phallic his-
tory and mythology.*"[18] The result of this belief is a combination of
psychological insight and religious ecstasy. The female principle
lives, she exclaims, and rediscovering it is a therapeutic and inspir-
ing experience for every woman.

As for the second tendency, the communal dimension of human
development and human existence, Goldenberg observes that object-
relations theory emphasizes the infant's dependence on others –
especially, she argues, the mother:

> Since every human life begins in the body of a woman, the image
> of a woman, whether thought of as mother or Goddess, always
> points to an early history of connectedness: Mother-*mater*-
> matter-matrix. "Woman" is the stuff out of which all people are
> made. In the beginning was her flesh, and, after the beginning,
> she continues to suggest human historicity, to suggest human
> connection to and dependence upon the outside world ... It is
> pre-birth experience and post-birth mothering which destined
> feminist theory to expand awareness of the context which sup-
> ports everything human. At a basic level, the image of woman is
> the image of human context, the image of human connection to
> the world.[19]

Relying heavily on Carol Gilligan[20] and Nancy Chodorow,[21]
Goldenberg explains that feminist theory extends this "connectedness" to the larger context of personal interactions with others.
Goddess ideology, moreover, extends it to the still larger context of
human interaction with nature. "Like objects-relations theory in
particular and feminist theory in general," she says, it "is concerned
with expanding awareness of the conditions which make lives what

they are. Thealogy, however, focuses on some other, nonhuman aspects of the context of life. The goddess movement takes seriously the ancient pagan perception that human life is part of a larger web of life that includes all of nature ... The entire earth is conceptualized as the body of the goddess and thus is sacred. No part of the ecosystem is separate from her."[22]

Believing the great goddess primordial and thus eternal, "thealogians" believe also that they can rescue her from the past. Therapy in the present is more important, however, than any constraints imposed by available information about the past. Even if historians could show that the great goddess was *not* primeval and primordial, in other words, Goldenberg would still be willing to convince people of the opposite in order to end the tyranny of patriarchy. She explicitly indicates that "by stressing those ignored or suppressed portions of collective religious history which refer to female figures of power, Goddess thealogy chips away at the monolith constructed by patriarchal history. *Even if particular facts or arguments about the history of goddess worship are disputed, the work of writers like Merlin Stone, Savina Teubal, Charlene Spretnak and others loosens the male monopoly on religious power.*"[23] The end, apparently, justifies the means.

The face of humanity and even of the planet is female, as Goldenberg describes it, not male or even androgynous. This is feminist egalitarianism? There is no room in this worldview for men in general or fathers in particular. She might paraphrase Shakespeare as follows: If all the world is a stage, all the women are actors and all the men are extras.

Of greatest importance here, though, are the third and fourth tendencies that unite feminism with both the object-relations school of psychoanalysis and goddess ideology. The former emphasizes female symbols by deconstructing male ones. The latter emphasizes fantasy as an acceptable or even desirable feature of scholarship by deconstructing the supposedly male emphasis on reason. Because these are two sides of the same coin, we discuss them together.

Goldenberg wants women to replace Christian theology's Father, Son, and Holy Spirit with pagan "thealogy's" Diana, Luna, and Hecate. This shift away from male symbols, as distinct from the egalitarian *addition* of female ones, creates a real problem for men. At the moment, few men are consciously aware of it; even so, the supposedly firm foundation on which their worldview rests is not as firm as either they or some of their adversaries imagine. Three examples should make this clear.

At one time, men could believe that the penis represented a vital force, or essence, to be celebrated. Now, feminists argue that glorifying the penis is really only the result of a frustrated desire to return to the mother and overcome the original separation from her breast. At one time, men could make a distinction between the public realm of men and the private realm of women, legitimating sexual segregation. Now, because "the personal is political," feminists acknowledge no legitimately separate space for men (although they still demand a separate space for women on the false assumption that men have traditionally maintained all space as their own). At one time, men could define knowledge in the objective and abstract terms that feminists now like to identify with maleness (terms that did, however, create serious problems for women). Now, academic feminists define knowledge in the subjective or embodied terms they like to identify with femaleness (terms that create serious problems not only for men but also for women in the academic world). Without affirming these features of manhood, we would still ask how men are supposed to live in a world stripped of any public affirmation of maleness. Goldenberg has no advice for them. Presumably they should just step out of the way and let women get on with things.

Like other postmodernists, Goldenberg refrains from an outright rejection of all claims to objective knowledge. Like them, moreover, she rejects these claims only when it suits her – that is, when she cannot rely on verifiable facts that support her own claims. (Just because she plays this game openly does not, of course, make it acceptable on scholarly grounds.) Realizing the danger that relativism poses for her own cause, she uses deconstruction only to prove that "patriarchal discourses" are inherently "privileged" and unstable. Convinced that gender is a political category, she makes use of a political strategy: inverting the hierarchy rather than abolishing it. Having deconstructed male privilege and androcentric hegemony, she refuses to allow deconstruction of either her own conclusions or her own methods. In short, she deconstructs men but tries to prevent anyone from deconstructing women in general or herself in particular.

Goldenberg explains that revealing connections between the prehistoric and the subconscious through therapy or recalling connections through ritual, as a kind of "eternal return," creates psychological distance from patriarchal symbols and customs.[24] Accuracy about the past is unnecessary, because it is *fantasy* about the past that empowers women in the present. No wonder, then, that she considers all of this therapeutic! Self-indulgence, self-righteousness, and self-delusion always feel therapeutic (at least for the moment).

It is easy to explain the preference among women, among feminists, and especially among feminist theologians, for goddesses over gods.[25] It is not so easy to explain the preference among contemporary academics for fantasy, or myth, over scholarship. Ultimately, of course, the buck stops here: with those who lead the way. Susanne Heine points to the dangers of feminist fantasy:

> I regard the popular variants of feminist theology, in which I include more than just the Christian positions, as being politically dangerous. The false syntheses arouse false hopes in that they falsify reality. Deceptions, illusions and schematizations are always more popular consumer goods than the stubborn fight on the field of confusing reality. Whatever ... roles ... the wholly evil and the wholly good are assigned, where dogmatic schematizations reach around themselves, regress disguises itself as progress ... The logic of the reactionary also contains the step from reason to magic. And experience confirms that argument, cross-checking, self-critical questioning are virtually impossible in this kind of feminist circle. In that circle it is said that criticism strengthens the forces of reaction. But the opposite is the case: Reactionaries have always been characterized by the way in which they brand criticism as "destructive"... Those who dream of the matriarchy and feminine spirituality produce opium for women."[26]

Goldenberg tries to conflate myth – sometimes she calls it "thealogy" or even "fantasy" – and history. Unfortunately, she understands neither. Apart from anything else, myths are communal stories about how things are in connection with how things were in the primeval past and often in connection with how things will be in the eschatological future. In other words, they confer meaning, purpose, and identity on communal life, especially in connection with festivals and rites of passage. Myths present (sacred) time as a cyclical or circular series of events in the remote past (or remote future), which people can re-experience (or pre-experience) in the context of communal purpose and meaning. History presents (secular) time, on the other hand, as a linear series of events, which archaeologists or other scholars can study scientifically in terms of cause and effect. Myth and history do overlap, in a way, but they are hardly synonymous to modern scholars. There is nothing to be achieved, except political gain, by evaluating myth as if it were history (or history as if it were myth). As many people have understood, however, there is something to be gained by evaluating myth (or history) on psychological and moral grounds. Not all myths are necessarily either healthy or good. The Nazi myth, for instance, relied on both fear of and hatred for the Other. We suggest that the Nazi myth is a lamentable analogue of the myth, or collective fantasy, that goddess ideologues have produced and that Goldenberg has promoted.

Goddess ideologues do not always conflate myth and history implicitly; sometimes, they have the audacity to do so explicitly. Refusing to acknowledge the distinction between myth (or "fantasy" or "thealogy") and history, goddess ideologues promote the idea of an ancient matriarchy as a wish about history, one that they intend to realize in the near future. They are fond of quoting these lines from Monique Wittig's Les Guérillères: "There was a time when you were not a slave, remember. Try hard to remember. Or, failing that, invent."[27] Wittig's cleverness lies in her recognition that belief in a golden age for women in the past can empower women in the present. That is, *an invented past not only can but should replace a remembered one.* After all, she implies, faith is simply a very strong wish.

From Goldenberg's therapeutic perspective, wishing that matriarchy existed in the past is a good enough reason for claiming that it did. As she points out, people "build their 'real' worlds ... to correspond to their deepest inner expectations."[28]

Instead of conceiving of a fairly separate line between "reality thinking" and "fantasy thinking," as did Freud and many of his followers, object-relations analysts conceive of fantasy as the basis or context of all thinking. What is felt to be real in the inner, psychic world, they say, tends to be what is created in the external world. Fantasy is seen as determining the blueprint of a life ... These analysts, therefore, like many witches,

see the entire external, human world as something constructed
upon a stratum of internal fantasy ... they both maintain that
the inner world of anticipation and wish is the basis of all
human thought and action.[29]

Crucial here is the idea that both goddess ideologues and psychoan-
alysts "understand fantasy or wish as constituting the primary
matrix for all mental processes."[30] Feminists who follow this line of
thinking are eager, not surprisingly, to recover historical truth from
the past when it legitimates their own views and proves therapeutic.
When it does not, of course, they resort to fantasy. If you believe
that fantasy is the basis for all thinking, and that the external world
is built on nothing more solid than a psychological stratum of wish-
fulfillment, then you can easily claim fiction as fact. But what this
means for scholarship is that anyone can create fantasies and try
to convince others that they are true. But does this *make* them
true? Is there any room for knowledge provided by anthropology,
archaeology, religious studies, and other disciplines? Or, in this age
of postmodernism, is the very notion of knowledge, even partial
knowledge, obsolete?

Goldenberg addresses *Returning Words to Flesh* directly and only
to women: "If we women are to be successful at creating more
humane social institutions ..."[31] It is just as well. How many men
would expose themselves to 125 pages of feminist self-glorifica-
tion? In one passage, it is true, Goldenberg does acknowledge that
women have yet to attain perfection.[32] Having covered herself with
the necessary disclaimer, though, she still indulges in the kind of
female self-adulation that might well embarrass many women. It is
hardly surprising, then, that she so eagerly welcomes worship of a
great goddess. Its corollary is the worship of women – which is to
say, self-worship.

In her comments on feminist methodology, Elizabeth Schüssler
Fiorenza writes that the "notion of objective and disinterested
research must be replaced by *conscious partiality* ... Rather than
reproducing the scholarly rhetoric of impartiality and value-neu-
trality, feminist biblical scholars need to spell out our commitments
and challenge our colleagues to do the same."[33] Most of the scholars that we discuss do indeed spell out their political motivations.
But does this make their work scholarly? Does acknowledging bias
legitimate it? If feminists think that they can achieve legitimacy for

gynocentrism merely by identifying it as such, why should men not do the same for androcentrism?

The answer to this last question is usually that feminists are merely doing what men have already done. But since when do two wrongs make a right? Besides, doing this sort of thing now is not the same as doing it was in the past. Scholars have only recently become aware of androcentrism. In earlier times, few people noticed that kind of bias; they simply absorbed most beliefs (though not necessarily all) from their cultural environments. Succumbing to bias in that context was lamentable, but the conscious choice of bias by the very people who have recently become so aware of that problem is another matter entirely. The former was naïve. The latter is hypocritical and opportunistic. It all adds up to expediency. And we make this claim on both logical and moral grounds. If it is wrong for men to do something, it is surely wrong for women to do the same thing. And no context can turn something that is wrong or false into something that is right or true. Even oppressed people, after all, can acknowledge intellectual and moral standards that transcend their own experience. Being oppressed does not give them carte blanche to say or do anything at all. Otherwise, terrorists really could legitimate their behaviour by pointing to their version of history, which revolves around the wrongs that others inflicted on them. In doing so, of course, they would destroy both scholarship and morality. The end does not justify the means.

"Can a committed participant in a cause," asks Gayle Graham Yates, "also serve as its scholar?" – a good question in this context. She answers in the affirmative (although part of her answer refers to theologians, who are not scholars per se), by arguing that even the most personally involved feminist can discuss historical material about women descriptively and objectively.[34] As we observe elsewhere, however, many feminist academics reject the idea of objectivity as a by-product of patriarchy.[35]

But Yates's point is well taken. Without mentioning it by name, she refers to the anthropological technique of *epoché*: consciously bracketing out personal attitudes in order to hear precisely what informants tell them. By definition, scholarship assumes that attaining some level of objective knowledge, a significant level, is possible. From this it follows that scholars must account, to the best of their ability, for demonstrable facts. As finite beings, to be sure, they cannot expect to produce results that are more than provisional; other scholars might come along with new information or new interpretations that explain the facts more fully. Even so, scholars assume that they should and can seek useful knowledge of the external world. Otherwise, they would be merely playing intellectual games.

It is true that perfect objectivity is impossible. Does this mean that we should stop striving for it? If so, then we should embrace totalitarianism. After all, perfect democracy is impossible. But are we children? Must we adopt an all-or-nothing mentality? To the extent that these feminists (and other postmodernists) deny the value of even searching for objective truth, they reject scholarship itself. At the very least, then, honesty should compel them to abandon the claim to being scholars. They might be doing something valuable or even necessary, but it is not scholarship. If we accept the idea that there is no point in seeking objective truth, moreover, moral responsibility should compel us to disband all universities. After all, why should we allow academics to defraud taxpayers by forcing them to pay for institutions that produce nothing but political propaganda? If we acknowledge, on the other hand, that there are objective criteria for knowledge, then we should not expect universities to hire those who openly reject the *sine qua non* of scholarship (and those who openly advocate the demise of academic freedom in the interest of "political correctness").

We suggest that intellectual life is now under siege not by the masses, as in the past, but by academics. Special-interest groups consider themselves immune to any standards of judgment. They ignore facts that contradict their own views. They attack canons of scholarly proof and circumvent reason by asking rhetorical questions: Whose truth? Whose standards? Whose logic? By doing so, they expediently shrug off any challenge as nothing more than a reflection of "the dominant culture."

The postmodernist method par excellence is deconstruction. Many feminists (but certainly not only feminists) have found Jacques Derrida's trademark deconstructive games very useful. Their aim is to show that society has identified the derivative, supplementary, or "subaltern" with women, with oral traditions, and with goddesses. To do this, they must show that the reverse has been true for men. Their aim, in other words, is to show that society has identified the normative and thus the privileged with men, with male traditions, and with gods. This androcentric "discourse," they argue, represents a conspiracy of silence intended to hide the brutal reality of male dominance and oppression that originated in a usurpation of female power at the dawn of history. Another aim, though, is to replace the androcentric discourse with a *gynocentric* one. Served up to women on a silver platter would be their own normative and "privileged" status: biologically, historically, morally, intellectually, and spiritually.

It is true, as postmodernists charge, that scholars have been heavily involved in the Enlightenment task of discovering objective truth. They really do gather facts and try to interpret them. Yes, they have had biases such as ignoring women's perspectives, and they have needed feminist and other critiques. But they have seldom been stupid enough to confuse observation with revelation. Today, for example, those in the field of religious studies have learned to reduce the likelihood of superimposing their own worldviews – that is, their own biases – onto the people whose religion they are studying. This method, *epoché*, involves them in self-conscious and disciplined attempts to establish empathy by "bracketing out" preconceived ideas. Obviously, they can never be completely successful. Even so, they can point to major improvements in scholarship since the adoption of this method.

Is there really no significant difference between the studies of Hinduism produced by missionaries in the nineteenth century, for example, and those produced by scholars in our own time? The dispute over psychoanalytic interpretations of Hinduism notwithstanding, many Hindus agree that Western scholars now produce better studies of Hinduism than those of the colonial period.[36] Moreover, scholars need not confine themselves to particularities governed totally by context. To some extent, they can discern underlying patterns that disparate cultures have in common and, with these in mind as well as whatever is unique to each, make responsible generalizations. They do so very effectively by considering the evidence of large and representative samples.

In short, scholars can indeed know something about the past. They maintain high standards for the collection and interpretation of information, standards that they periodically review. It bears repeating here that goddess ideologues themselves rely on scholarship, when it suits their needs. When it does not, many resort

openly to fantasy, making that "the basis or context of all thinking." This is intellectual laziness at best and intellectual opportunism at worst.

But who is to judge the "conscious partiality" of feminists if we
cannot evaluate truth claims according to either an ultimate criterion (objectivity being a pernicious illusion that the "male model"
generates) or a transcendent authority (goddess ideology representing what some people might call "the female model")? To argue
that the search for objective truth is irrelevant to theory is to argue
for all practical purposes that anything goes – anything, that is, if it
helps "us." Not everyone finds that position convincing. "What
feminists claim to be feminine science," writes Heine, "is a false
kind of thinking which takes short cuts, and if one were to judge
these women by the criterion of their own thinking only one conclusion would be possible: once again it emerges that women have no
logic. However, one can make a virtue of feminine illogicality by
declaring logic itself to be a vice and disqualifying all those who
concern themselves with it, both men and women."[37]

The implicit goal of some theologians has been to legitimate their
own assumptions, which amounts to letting the tail wag the dog.
Some conservative theologians look for scriptural or other evidence
that supports their conservative worldviews, for instance, and some
liberal theologians look for scriptural or other evidence that supports their liberal worldviews. The explicit goal of theologians,
however, has always been to discern divine will and articulate it
in ways that make sense both of scripture (or tradition in some
broader sense) and of everyday life. And if they discern something
that challenges their own assumptions, then so be it; the best of
them, at any rate, seek truth wherever the search might lead them.
The goal of Carol Christ, however, is explicitly to find scriptural or
other evidence that supports her own feminist worldview – which is
to say, a worldview that makes women feel better about themselves
as women.

Christ[38] looks for religious myths or texts that women can appropriate to satisfy their spiritual needs. Like Gimbutas, she believes
that women cannot flourish within traditional religions – that is,
"patriarchal" ones – such as Christianity or Judaism. Instead, she
argues in *Why Women Need the Goddess*,[39] women must either
create or recreate some form of goddess religion. Unlike Bolen and

Goldenberg, however, Christ tries to avoid secular reductionism by making a distinction between women's psychological needs and their spiritual needs. The latter include cognitive dimensions, deeply rooted beliefs, and moral principles that define worldviews (what some people call "values"). In theory, therefore, she is a "thealogian"[40] and not a therapist, but this distinction is more apparent than real.

She uses theological rhetoric, in short, for therapeutic purposes. Here her underlying syllogism is: Ancient people worshipped a great goddess before the rise of patriarchal gods; women cannot flourish without a great goddess; ergo, women today must either restore the ancient goddess cult or create a new one.

Unlike Christian and (religiously) Jewish feminists, Christ insists that anthropomorphic language – to be precise, gynomorphic language – is not merely a concession to patterns of human habits but a tribute to the patterns of female thought. The goddess is not merely like a woman, in short, but *is* a woman – not a goddess but a woman – *every* woman. In this way Christ moves not only beyond transcendence but also beyond immanence. Scholars in religious studies (and many theologians too, for that matter) understand immanence as an experience of the sacred or even of God within the natural order. God appears to Moses from within a burning bush, for instance, and holiness pervades a home on the Jewish Sabbath and festivals. God actually takes on human flesh as Jesus of Nazareth, moreover, and Catholics can experience his immediate presence during Holy Communion. But even Catholics insist that Jesus was unique in being, paradoxically, both fully human (Jesus) and fully divine (the Christ). They can be like him as followers of Jesus, but they cannot *be* him as the Christ.[41] Christianity, like Judaism, involves both transcendence and immanence – although some forms of Christianity, especially some forms of Protestantism, try to eliminate immanence. On the other hand, goddess ideologues such as Carol Christ (and Mary Daly, whom we discuss in chapter 6) try to eliminate transcendence.

As Gayle Yates points out, moreover, Carol Christ's theology is more radical even than liberation theology. The latter insists that God (or at least the idea of God) as known through scripture (or at least some Marxist interpretation of scripture) is an independent source of authority. In other words, God remains the source of accountability and therefore of legitimacy. For Christ and her followers, however, the only source of authority or accountability, let alone legitimacy, is each woman's "story" – and therefore the collective story of women. In *Diving Deep and Surfacing*,[42] she applies that theory to literature by women.

Now consider Elinor Gadon, who teaches at Brandeis University. In *The Once and Future Goddess*,[43] she uses both religion and the arts to create a therapeutic environment for women. She acknowledges her debt to Marija Gimbutas and her own existential attraction to goddess religion (though not necessarily to the point of any personal experience of or metaphysical assertion about the goddess). The primordiality of a great goddess is the linchpin of her work, as these opening words reveal:

> Mine is a tale about the Goddess as she was in ages past, as she continues to be in many parts of the world today, and as she is reemerging in late twentieth-century Western culture ... While the Goddess has indeed had many names, many manifestations throughout human history, she is ultimately one supreme reality. Only after the patriarchal Indo-Europeans overthrew the cultures where the Goddess had flourished from earliest times and imposed the worship of their sky gods was her identity fractured into myriad goddess, each with an all-too-human personality ... The death blow to Goddess culture was delivered by monotheism in which one male, all-powerful and absolute, ruled both the heavens and the earth. And yet, "the religion of the Goddess never completely died out despite the brutal persecutions of the Inquisition and the witch burnings, but was kept alive by a handful of the faithful who practiced their rituals in small bands and preserved their knowledge of nature's teachings. The Time of Burning, of paranoia and superstition led by a fanatical and threatened Christianity, was followed by the Age of Reason, a time of disbelief. The Old Religion went underground and became the most secret of religions."[44]

Of interest here is the great goddess's "return." This return, Gadon argues, would not only solve the closely related problems of nature versus culture (ecological disaster) and women versus men (patriarchy) but also "empower" women. Gadon encourages that end by linking the goddess with female bodies, female sexuality, and female creativity. If women absorb those links, they will be able to overthrow patriarchal religions and therefore patriarchal societies (although she concedes the possibility of deconstructing and reconstructing them from within, a strategy, as we will show, that other goddess ideologues have chosen). In short, says Gadon, "the melding of spirituality and politics holds promise of revolutionizing [sic] our attitude toward life on earth."[45]

Using documentation based on interviews, biographies, and autobiographies, Gadon tries to demonstrate a connection between the art of modern women and that of neopagans. She and her colleagues are very self-consciously creating a new iconography to suit this religion by encouraging women to visit goddess sites, interpret dreams, or imagine fantasies and then express themselves through painting, sculpture, and performance art. She refers often to a woman's own body as the sacred source, the sacred site. According to Gadon, various women refer to their own eggs as their sources of artistic creativity; they paint themselves as nudes to reveal the goddess within, carve their images onto the walls of an archaic goddess cave in Cuba, journey to an ancient goddess shrine on the island of Hvar in the Adriatic, use time-release photography to document their own bodies as the great goddess, and so on. One woman becomes the goddess and proceeds to enact a ritual on the streets of New York City, where a crowd instantly gathers for the performance. As she puts it, the "images were presented aggressively as sexuality, mind and spirit comfortable in one body. I was summoning Goddess to make house calls, talking to Goddess with the body, and ending the dialogue with being."[46] Some women perform at national and international gatherings of professional or academic women. Others perform at goddess shrines around the world, syncretistically blending the folk rituals of women with contemporary gestures. Still others, we would add, travel to China and visit the matrilocal Na people, whose "alternative" social structure attracts Western tourists.

The therapeutic focus on self is clearly at the heart of this movement, not worship of a deity. To put it another way, this is self-worship masquerading as worship of a deity. (Apparently, self-worship is evil in connection with men worshipping a god but not in connection with women worshipping a goddess.) "Re-imaging the Goddess in their own likeness," says Gadon, "was a path of self-discovery for many women artists, at times a painful confrontation with the discrepancy between the power inherent in the image and the powerlessness they felt. Each woman tapped into the power of the Goddess according to her own priorities."[47] This "self-imaging," viewers learn, belongs to women's effort to resacralize their sexuality and bodies, making the person public. Associated with ritualistic artistic performances are the edifying (but standardized) feminist code words: "relationship," "communication," "caring," "sharing," "loving," "thanksgiving," "justice," "body," and "immanence."

But where do men fit into all of this? To her credit, Gadon uses gender-inclusive language when reporting this phenomenon. On closer examination, though, doing so turns out to provide nothing more than a thin veneer of respectability. She includes only a few references to the participation of men. She notes, for instance, that some neopagans are men who worship an ancient horned god of the hunt. No further details. Are these men "independent" neopagans with their own "men's spirituality" groups? Are their rituals united with those of female neopagans in some way (even though not all feminists approve of hunting)? She either does not know or does not care.

Gadon does draw on the writings of one man: Matthew Fox. He advocates a goddess-sympathetic Christian theology, the notion of God as a mother no less than a father. Christians have ignored this theology for too many centuries and must recover it, he says, just as Christian men must recover their "feminine side" and thus their (metaphorical) creativity. The notion that God is *like* a mother has indeed always been part of the Christian tradition, albeit a minor part in specific traditions such as Protestantism. Fox avoids charges of heresy, although he comes dangerously close, by using non-Christian examples such as Wicca. For Gadon, at any rate, it is a simple matter for men to grow beyond patriarchy by linking up with a goddess. The main point is this: When men become like women, and women become like goddesses, the result is to "empower" women (although she says little about women becoming like men or men becoming like gods). What would the result be for men in daily life? She must assume that men would be better off with less power than they already have or perhaps even with less power than women. If so, however, then she must assume in addition that all men are alpha males. This would be a contradiction in terms, because alpha males are by definition those with more power than most other men.

Attacking mythologist Joseph Campbell for eulogizing the hero's journey, not the heroine's journey, Gadon says that the "quest of everyman for his maleness has not served men of our time well. The hero's journey glorified in Western tradition ... is a journey away from the Mother. The quest in search of the Father is one of exile from his female source and has led to alienation and estrangement between men and women ... Seen from this point of view, it is clear that any attempt to counteract the alienation we experience in this culture must be an attempt to restore the so-called feminine aspect of men's nature and to stop demeaning the femaleness in ourselves."[48] It is destructive for men to seek the source of their maleness, in other words, but not for women to seek the source of their femaleness. Gadon concludes nonetheless by suggesting that men and women could live in peace and as equals, again, but only if they return to the kind of goddess religion that Gimbutas described.

But precisely how could men and women be "equals" under a goddess in this context? If Jews and Christians can argue that all people, including men and women, are equal under their god, why not make the same claim for a goddess? And, for some Wiccans, the analogy is legitimate. But it is easy to take this analogy too far. Despite some linguistic conventions, after all, Jews and Christians do not claim that their god is male; on the contrary, they claim that "he" transcends both maleness and femaleness (and all other human features). The feminists under discussion here, though, claim that their goddess is indeed female. It is precisely *because of her femaleness* and thus her ability to empower *women* that they gather in her name. Back then, to our question. How could a religion that fosters only femaleness support the needs of men? And why would this religion be better than one that fosters only maleness? One answer would be to create a religion with (at least) one god and (at least) one goddess. That is the Wiccan solution. Whether or not Wicca is the ultimate answer to human needs, at least it makes sense from the perspectives of both women and men.

Other feminists prefer to use bisexual imagery for the deity of Christianity and Judaism, relying on the traditional belief that all human imagery is inadequate in the face of an ineffable divine reality. Unlike their (even) more radical sisters, they believe that Christianity and Judaism are not irredeemably patriarchal – that is, misogynistic. They see themselves as reformers, not revolutionaries.

But when does reform become revolution? In one way this solution does seem less radical than the neopagan one. These are familiar and traditional religions to most Americans and Canadians, after all, not alleged revivals of dead religions, modern creations, or foreign imports. And yet for Christians or Jews to turn their religions into something other than monotheism, or even seemingly other than monotheism, would be radical indeed.

Like other therapeutic feminists of her generation, Gadon intertwines worship of a goddess and the earth, a tree, or an animal. For her, the goddess inspires comments on problems such as science (which has presumably destroyed all sacrality) and industrialization (which has presumably done nothing more than ravage the earth). Not surprisingly, Gadon's work pays homage to feminist visionaries, high priestesses, and goddess ideologues such as Starhawk and Zsuzsanna Budapest. Gadon's interest in the goddess aligns her with the second movement that we discuss in this chapter: environmentalism to promote *collective healing* not only for women but for all species of a female planet.

Those who associate nature with the female body, as if the male body were either unnatural or a mere "social construction," often refer to both the Gaia movement and ecofeminism. "Gaia Consciousness is a growing movement that holds promise," writes Gadon, "of healing our planet. In the late twentieth century, with our very survival as a planet and species threatened by nuclear holocaust and environmental pollution, the Goddess is returning as a symbol for the resacralization of the earth. Once again we are honoring her as the source of all life."[49] As for ecofeminism, it combines feminism, either egalitarian or ideological, with environmentalism (instead of psychotherapy) and often religion as well. Women do not by any means have a monopoly on environmentalism; among the most prominent environmentalists, after all, are Al Gore and Matthew Fox. And yet women have identified themselves with environmentalism much more successfully than men have. Why? Because many feminists would have us believe that women are simply more "connected" than men with nature and "ecological balance" (even though they react angrily to the same idea about women in the context of early and medieval Christianity: associating women with nature and men with culture). With that (and often much more) in mind, they call themselves "ecofeminists."

This brings us to Rosemary Radford Ruether. She grew up in a liberal family, partly Catholic and partly Protestant, which encouraged her to think about ecumenism. She taught for many years at Garrett-Evangelical Theological Seminary, which is part of the Graduate Theological Union at the University of California, Berkeley, and now teaches at the University of San Diego. Eventually, her major focus became a combination of "ecological spirituality" and feminism. More to the point here, she has become an advocate of the Gaia Hypothesis.

Before proceeding, we should note that James Lovelock and Lynne Margulis coined the term "Gaia Hypothesis,"[50] using the name of an ancient Greek goddess. According to this theory, the earth, or "biosphere," is not a collection of separate organic beings and inorganic things but a unified and living organism, a self-regulating super-organism. Each component, closely related to all others, helps to keep the whole in a state of homeostasis. Humans are parts, therefore, of something much larger than themselves. Environmentalists now use this theory to promote awareness that human activities have already led to widespread pollution and could lead in the near future to ecological catastrophe. This much is not particularly controversial among laypeople.[51] Many societies have observed that humans interact with animals, plants, and even rocks or rivers – that we are all interconnected and interdependent – even though some people have found ways of ignoring the obvious.

Very controversial, on the other hand, is the idea that the earth is a *conscious* organism. We have no scientific evidence to demonstrate that. Most controversial of all, however, is the idea that this conscious organism is a *divine* one. Not only do we have no scientific evidence to suggest that, but we never could have it. That is because scientific hypotheses do not and cannot rely on religious ones. (For that matter, religious hypotheses about the supernatural do not and cannot rely on scientific ones.) In any case, feminists have found the Gaia Hypothesis very useful for their own purposes by linking treatment of the earth with treatment of women. And many societies have indeed made symbolic links between the two – usually the subjugation of women with the subjugation of nature. Some people up the ante. "Raping" the earth, for instance, is symbolically tantamount to raping a woman. In the early 1980s, Elizabeth Gray wrote about this link.[52] Why, she asked, do people think of ships as women? Because, she answered, we step on them, just as we step on the ground, on dirt. (Never mind that referring to a ship as "she" or "her" has been an act of endearment, not of contempt.)

A decade later, in a similar context, Ruether's *Gaia and God* appeared.[53] Unlike many ecofeminists, or goddess ideologues, Ruether remains Christian, sort of, mainly in order to provoke "healing" (change) from within. To do that, as she says in *Gaia*, she searches through not only Christian sources but also Hebrew[54] and Greek ones (and encourages non-Westerners to ransack their own traditions) for ideas that support ecofeminism.[55] In other words, she sees no reason to discard everything Christian or Western as irremediably evil. After all,

> these classical traditions did not only sacralize patriarchal hier-
> archy over women, workers, and the earth. They also struggled
> with what they perceived to be injustice and sin and sought to
> create just and loving relations between people in their relation
> to the earth and to the divine. Some of this effort to name evil
> and struggle against it reinforced relations of domination and
> created victim-blaming spiritualities and ethics. But there are
> also glimpses in this heritage of transformative, biophilic rela-
> tionships. These glimpses are a precious legacy that needs to be
> separated from the toxic waste of sacralized domination.[56]

Note here that what makes an idea "salvageable," "reclaimable," or "re-usable" for Ruether is not its legitimacy within Christianity but its legitimacy within ecofeminism.[57] Her source of authority is secular, in short, not religious (even though she is generally considered a theologian).

Unlike most ecofeminists, or goddess ideologues, Ruether explicitly rejects dualism. Since *Faith and Fratricide* (1975),[58] for instance, she has rejected the Christian dualism that generated anti-Judaism and eventually anti-Semitism. In *Gaia*, she rejects even the feminist dualism that has generated what we call misandry (in addition to the older dualism that generated misogyny).

Whether she rejects dualism consistently or effectively, of course, is another matter. Consider a major form of Christian dualism. On the one hand, Christian feminists correctly point out that Jesus attacked many assumptions of first-century Judaism and especially those that produced or sustained injustice. They point out that

Jesus, unlike other Jews, made no distinction between men and women. In fact, they argue, he accepted women as disciples. Like them, Ruether sees Jesus as a proto-feminist. On the other hand, Christian feminists separate Jesus from his Jewish context and thus support Christian triumphalism. From this point of view, Jesus was the one good Jew for opposing traditional Judaism and thus liberating women and other oppressed groups from its deadly grip. In other words, Christianity replaced Judaism. This fits, as Ruether herself explains brilliantly in *Faith and Fratricide*, into an ancient pattern in Christian theology.[59] Ruether is always careful to place Jesus in his cultural or historical context (partly because she wants to undermine his theological context) and therefore to acknowledge Jewish precedents – mainly those of the prophetic tradition – for his theology and thus also for the liberation theology of modern Christians. But this is an inherently tricky operation, so even Ruether, despite her caution and good intentions, sometimes forgets about it.

Among the main problems that feminists see in Christianity, after all, is its theological assertion that Christ took the form of Jesus – a man, that is, not a woman or a hermaphrodite. In *Gaia*, Ruether fails to provide an adequate explanation for the great importance that she attaches to Jesus's Jewishness, however, and the *lack* of importance that she attaches to his *maleness* – what she calls the "*kenosis* of patriarchy."[60] Given the importance that first-century Jews attached to embodiment (daily life in this world) and Christians to incarnation (divine participation in this world), this problem is by no means easy to solve. We applaud Ruether's insistence on trying to do so. But would Jesus, a first-century Jew, really have agreed with modern feminists that the *fatherhood* of God has no intrinsic value at all, being merely a cultural residue of the ignorant society into which he happened to born? Would a first-century Jew really have wanted modern feminists to rewrite his own prayer – which is to say, the Lord's Prayer – with that in mind? Would a first-century Jew really have agreed with modern feminists that sex and reproduction are purely mechanical processes, which just happen to require two kinds of genital equipment (but not even that for same-sex couples), and are therefore devoid of ontological or even symbolic importance? Despite her explicit insistence on referring to Jesus's cultural or historical context, Ruether does not really care one way or another. What matters for her is *our* context. His context matters only to the extent that it explains ideas that we can therefore "reclaim" for our own purposes.

By giving environmentalism a divine mandate in *Gaia*, that of what she calls "God/ess" (which everyone must pronounce, of course, simply as "goddess"), Ruether has a lot of clout among Christian or Jewish advocates of ecofeminism. And yet, as a principled scholar, she sees no reason to ignore the problems that she finds in that movement. She rejects its dualistic central doctrine, as we say, that men succumbed to "original sin," causing the "fall"[61] into patriarchy, and that they have been responsible for evil throughout history. She rejects the movement's two essentialistic doctrines, moreover, that some "great goddess" inspired a feminist utopia in the remote past and that "nature," left to its own devices, is inherently benevolent. Though psychologically useful to women, she argues, these doctrines do not rest on scholarly foundations. On the other hand, she acknowledges their importance and thus legitimates them as the means to an end: motivating the creation (though not the recreation) of an ecofeminist society.

Ultimately, therefore, Ruether finds it expedient not only to support the Gaia hypothesis but also to promote the worship of Gaia – that is, God/ess – either within the churches or without. Doing so within the churches is not merely a matter of changing the divine name or even changing the entire theological vocabulary. It is a matter of filling old wineskins with new wine or, in effect, creating a new religion. The bibliographical structure of *Gaia*, therefore, replaces some traditional keystones of Christian theology (such as creation, judgment, sin, and redemption) with ecofeminist ones (creation, destruction, domination, and healing). These notions do parallel their Christian prototypes, but they are more specifically modern and secular. They focus attention on relations not only between humans and the environment but also between men and women.

Of greatest importance here is the former pair: relations between men and women. Ruether clearly makes a distinction in *Gaia* between men and patriarchy – the latter a synonym, of course, for evil, and more specifically, the evil that men inflict on women, minorities, and the natural order.[62] Once again, moreover, she clearly rejects dualism. She refuses to denounce all men of today for the crimes of all or even some of their ancestors. Consequently, she allows men to enter the Promised Land with women (on condition, of course, that they become honorary women by converting to feminism). But her analysis relies heavily on feminism (and thus indirectly on Marxism), which explains the keyword "domination." According to virtually all feminist theories, men have intentionally or unintentionally dominated women, although Ruether adds (albeit inconsistently) that the real culprits have been elite men, not other men. (She might mean by "other" men all ordinary men of today, as distinct from the alpha males.[63] According to a less generous interpretation of her words, though, she might mean only men who suffer outright persecution due to race, religion, or sexual orientation.) As we have explained in two earlier volumes,[64] however, women have always found ways of dominating men in some ways – and clearly do so now. To bring about reconciliation between men and women, which Ruether does promote, she would have to do two things. First, she would have to provide more than perfunctory remarks on the participation of *women* in sin or "destruction" (and not merely as the victimized dupes of men). Second, she would have to provide more than perfunctory remarks on the distinctive contributions that *men* could make to redemption or "healing" and the creation of a new society.

Unlike many ecofeminists, Ruether does not want to repeat past errors. "Some see the Jewish and Christian male monotheistic God," she writes, "as a hostile concept that rationalizes alienation from and neglect of the earth. Gaia should replace God as our focus of worship. I agree with much of this critique, yet I believe that merely replacing a male transcendent deity with an immanent female one is an insufficient answer to the 'god problem.'"[65] Her answer in *Gaia* is "God/ess." But even in this egalitarian and therefore relatively benign version of feminism, gynocentrism replaces not only androcentrism but even anthropocentrism. This problem is worth an explanation here.

In theory, the new and egalitarian society that Ruether proposes would indeed be open to men and women alike, because the sexes would be interchangeable except for the specific purpose of reproduction. This is not merely equality, however, but sameness. The trouble is that men and women are not the same. Every society must be able, as we have suggested elsewhere,[66] to provide each sex with a healthy collective identity, no matter how minimal. And that means allowing each sex to make *at least one distinctive, necessary, and publicly valued contribution to society.* Unlike equality, same-ness, or interchangeability, is an illusion. That is because women can do at least two things that men cannot do: gestate and lactate.

Exacerbating this genetic asymmetry is a *cultural* asymmetry that originates in a contradiction at the heart of Ruether's own analysis. She says that men and women are the same, except for the purpose of reproduction, but she also *implies* that they are not the same by describing one way of thinking that she approvingly ascribes implicitly to women in general (and that most societies have either approvingly or disapprovingly ascribed explicitly to women in gen-eral) and another way of thinking that she disapprovingly ascribes implicitly to men in general (and that most societies have approv-ingly ascribed explicitly to men in general). Not all men are patri-archs, she admits in one way or another on several occasions, but all patriarchs are men. In other words, men can indeed have a dis-tinctive identity – but only a *negative* one. To the extent that men have contributed anything at all to society *as men*, at least since the Neolithic period, they have contributed patriarchal systems that damage the environment and oppress women (along with some men).[67] Ruether says that men are free to repudiate that unhealthy identity and to live in harmony with women and the environment, to be sure, but she suggests no healthy *alternative* identity. On the contrary, she hopes that men will become more like women.

In fact, therefore, most men would see no point in entering this new and ostensibly egalitarian society – not because they hate women but because they happen to be men. It would allow for no significant distinction between men and women and thus would deprive them of any identity *as men*. They could enter this new soci-ety only by parking their collective identities *as men* at the front door. Women would not need to do this as women, of course, because the new society would rely almost entirely on their distinc-tive ways of thinking, feeling, being, and so on.

Ruether does present one very interesting and useful idea about men, including those who established patriarchies in the remote past, although she does not do much to develop this idea in *Gaia*:

> The root problem lies in the extension of the female childbear-ing and suckling functions into making the mother the domi-nant parent, together with primary food-gathering and food-sharing roles. Males are then somewhat auxiliary to the life-sustaining processes, both in food production and in reproduc-

tion, and can experience this as uncertainty about the male role. While the female role is built into the process of life-reproduction and food-gathering, the male role has to be constructed socially. Societies that fail to develop an adequately affirmative role for men, one that gives men prestige parallel to that of women but prevents their assuming aggressive dominance over women, risk developing the resentful male, who defines his masculinity in hostile negation of women. The symbolic negation of women in conflictual societies provides the myths through which actual dominance over women is promoted and justified ... One has to ask whether elements of male resentment are not built into the matricentric pattern. The matricentric core of human society remains, even under male hierarchies, and continually reproduces the insecure, resentful male, who emancipates himself from his mother by negation of women.[68]

As she (along with many psychologists) points out, all boys must grow apart radically from their mothers in order to become men, something that girls need not do to nearly the same extent, obviously, in order to become women. Whether boys must do so by becoming misogynistic, however, is another matter.

Ruether argues in *Gaia* that misogyny is an inherent possibility as long as mothers (or women) are primarily responsible for the physical and emotional care of their sons.[69] To solve the problem, she proposes a family structure in which both mothers and fathers provide physical and emotional care for their children. This would align her[70] with egalitarian feminists, including those who draw the conclusion that, because mothers and fathers are interchangeable after birth, children can do just as well with two fathers, two mothers, single fathers, or single mothers.[71] So, there goes fatherhood as the only potential source of a healthy masculine identity, one that (unlike provider and protector) could offer modern men a distinctive contribution to family life and thus to society as a whole. From our perspective, the inability to establish a healthy identity *as men* is what causes misogyny. This is why we say that Ruether does not do enough to develop the idea. She understands the problem but then ignores it. Only a few pages later, she writes:

If, as I have suggested, this matricentric pattern is itself the breeding ground of male resentment and violence, rooted in male strategies of exploitative [*sic*] subversion of women's

power, then a new pattern of mutual parenting must balance
maternal primacy in reproduction ... Men and women must
share fully the parenting of children from birth and the domestic work associated with daily life. A genuine change in the
pattern of parenting must be understood, not as a slight adjustment toward males "helping" females with childcare, but a
fundamental reconstruction of the primary roots of culture,
transforming the gender imaging of child-parent relations and
the movement into adulthood for both males and females ...
New egalitarian family patterns will be essential to shaping
new psyches in which women can be affirmed as partners, and
men commit themselves to sustaining ongoing life on earth.[72]

That sounds very edifying. Who would oppose such an egalitarian
ideal? Unfortunately, Ruether fails to see the significance of her
own words. If the problem really is that men lack the basis for a
healthy identity, and if fathers really should be more than mere
assistant mothers, then how could equality – in the sense of same-
ness – possibly solve the problem? Instead of using culture to make
men more like women, or fathers more like mothers, why not use it
to make men *less* like women, fathers *less* like mothers, but also neither more nor less valuable to society than women? This, we suggest, is the kind of equality that society needs.

We suspect that any society's level of misogyny – negation of
women – depends also, perhaps mainly, on the definition of manhood. To the extent that manhood requires stoicism – physical and
emotional self-denial in order to withstand the rigour of hunting or
warfare – it probably does involve some degree of envy and therefore hostility toward women, who need not keep proving both to
themselves and to society, beginning with coming-of-age rituals,
that they can endure severe forms of self-denial. But our point here
is that Ruether has at least acknowledged a possible explanation for
patriarchy, one that might involve something other than, or at least
more than, some innately and uniquely male inclination toward
evil. In another volume, *Transcending Misandry: From Feminist
Ideology to Intersexual Dialogue*, we will add that "patriarchies"
solved some real problems for our remote ancestors, even though
they replaced those problems with new ones – including problems
for both women and men.

When Ruether mentions the needs of men at all, moreover, she usually does so in connection with a rebuke. "It is the male rather than the female life-style that needs, however, the deeper transformation. Males need to overcome the illusion of autonomous individualism, with its extension into egocentric power over others, starting with the women with whom they relate. Men need to integrate themselves into life-sustaining relations with women as lovers, parents, and co-workers. They need to do regularly what they have hardly ever done, even in preagricultural societies: feed, clothe, wash, and hug children from infancy, cook food, and clean up wastes."[73] It is unnecessary to assume that Ruether uses "male" here in a genetic sense; she probably uses that word merely as a synonym for "men." At any rate, she says that men need to act like women. We have no problem with men doing these things. We do have a problem with men being unable to do anything that identifies them, in *healthy* ways, *as men.*

In *Gaia* Ruether lauds goddess ideology but explicitly rejects its pervasive conspiracy theory of history. In *Integrating Ecofeminism, Globalization, and World Religions,*[74] she does not always bother to do so. Implicitly, therefore, she is just as misandric as the ecofeminists whose work she discusses. She notes here and there, in effect, that "patriarchy" is not a synonym for "men." Nonetheless, she keeps repeating historical and theological paradigms – if not her own, then those of feminists whom she clearly admires, such as Starhawk,[75] Carol Christ,[76] and Carolyn Merchant[77] – that do indeed link some male principle with the cause of all suffering and oppression. To be blunt, she recites these paradigms but does not challenge them on moral grounds as misandric. She admits that some feminists criticize Vandana Shiva's version of ecofeminism,[78] to be sure, but she adds that they do so because Shiva's theory is too Hindu (and thus misogynistic);[79] she says nothing about it being too misandric. She applauds Catherine Keller's theory, first promulgated in *From a Broken Web,*[80] that maleness is innately inferior to femaleness, and she remains untroubled by its obvious misandry. According to Ruether herself, Keller "identified a dualism of two kinds of self, the male self whose goal is separation and autonomy and the female self or rather no-self, which both supports and serves as the scapegoat for the separative male self." Men are full of themselves by nature, in other words, and women selfless. We

would be unlikely to notice from Ruether's description the contradiction between Keller's hostility to misogynistic dualism and her
own use of misandric dualism.[81] On the contrary, Ruether continues to praise Keller: "Her proposal is a transformative integration
of these dualistic selves, self-in-relation, which is neither false
autonomy nor self-sacrificial support for the selfhood of another
bought at women's expense."[82]

But even when Ruether does acknowledge the misandry of other
ecofeminists, she tries to tone it down in her own words. "[Carol]
Christ seeks to avoid any essentializing of the female," says Ruether
of that author's conspiracy theory of history, "as 'naturally' more in
harmony with nature. One should not simply reverse patriarchal
hierarchical dualisms, lifting up body, femaleness, and feelings as
the superior side. Rather one has to bring together male and female,
mind and body, heaven and earth, feeling and thinking, light and
dark, the one and the many, transcendence and immanence in an
interactive relationality."[83] The trouble is that, moralistic caveats
notwithstanding, misandry is inherent in the conspiracy theory of
history. Dualism, in other words, is inherent in that theory. Whether
Carol Christ intends to essentialize the female positively (and therefore the male negatively), or not, that is precisely what she and
many other ecofeminists have done.

It is hard to imagine any man – even a minority man, to whom
Ruether would allow respectability as an honourary woman – reading her book and coming away with any sense of being able, as a
man, to make any distinctive and necessary contribution to either
the human world in particular or the natural world in general. On
the contrary, he would come away with a profound sense of otherness (the very "alterity" that feminists have noted for decades about
their own predicament as women). After all, the most fundamental
feature of ecofeminism – its *sine qua non* – is its premise about the
history of men: that the subjugation of nature and the subjugation
of women are two forms of the same problem. That problem is
patriarchy. But women, according to ecofeminists such as Keller,
did not create patriarchy; only men could have done that, because
only men can think of themselves as autonomous individuals instead
of interconnected beings in the "web" of life, as outside observers
instead of participants in the natural world, and so on. The title of
Keller's first major opus, *From a Broken Web* (which is all about
men), makes it clear that being male means being inwardly

deformed, perverted, distorted, twisted, or, well, broken. Moreover, at least some of these ecofeminists would add, despite evidence to the contrary, that only men continue to benefit from patriarchy in our time and refuse to let go of their "dominology" (which sounds a lot like the word "demonology").

Ruether herself, ever the egalitarian on a conscious level, would probably admit that many elite women have found ways of benefiting from the patriarchal status quo and thus continuing its sway over other women and other races. But even Ruether would not – and does not – admit that anything much has changed for most women in our society. Because she and other ecofeminists equate the subjugation of nature with the subjugation of women, they believe that one form of subjugation cannot disappear without the other. And because the subjugation of nature is obviously still rampant in connection with high technology and globalization, the subjugation of women must be rampant as well – even if that is by no means self-evident to those who analyze current legislation and statistics on male suicide and school dropout rates (let alone negative stereotypes of men in popular culture, advertising, and journalism). Throughout her career, Ruether has carefully and insightfully exposed the ways in which women suffer from theological and other forms of misogyny. Egalitarianism notwithstanding, however, she gives no indication of ever having entertained the possibility that men might now suffer from misandry in our society. Nor does she consider that "patriarchy" might have created problems for women in the attempt to solve problems for men – even though she does admit that "matricentric" societies might well have been very problematic for men.

What leaves us dissatisfied with Ruether (as distinct from many of the ecofeminists whom she discusses) is not misandry per se on her part but rather her unquestioning, a priori acceptance of patriarchal theory, which leads directly to hatred of men. Ruether rejects that in the personal sense (hating individual men, as such, in daily life) but unwittingly accepts it in the abstract sense (hating men as a class). She rejects some primitive explanations for the initial rise of patriarchy and some crude expressions of dualism, it is true, but she assumes nonetheless that "patriarchy" has been and remains the defining feature of our society and of every society since the transition from horticulture to agriculture. Instead of relying at least partly on the messy but often surprising information that social scientists collect, Ruether relies on the elegant but often misleading symbolic patterns that theologians, philosophers, and psycho-analysts use (albeit reversing their meaning when it comes to sex and gender). To put it another way, Ruether sees the misandry in ecofeminism and is somewhat embarrassed by it but considers it a marginal or trivial byproduct. We suggest that misandry lies near the core of ecofeminism, most obviously in the form of god-dess ideology.

This is why we have devoted a few paragraphs to Ruether's ear-lier work on anti-Judaism within traditional forms of Christian the-ology. Unlike many well-meaning Christian theologians (at least until recently) for whom anti-Judaism has been a lamentable but also marginal or trivial by-product of Christendom – that is, Chris-tianity as an established and therefore powerful state religion – Ruether believes that it has been a central feature of Christianity, its symbolic cornerstone, from the beginning. Yet for some reason she fails to see the analogical centrality of misandry in both ideological feminism and goddess ideology – which is to say, in ecofeminism.

Without misandry, without a negative foil (maleness, masculinity, men, patriarchy, or whatever), she and her colleagues would have to rely mainly on moral arguments for compassion toward other living things and practical arguments for the conservation of natu-ral resources. What gives ecofeminism its emotional and political power is its link between environmentalism and ideological femi-nism. Why? Because the latter supplies women with a positive iden-tity as goddesses, or at least as the benevolent devotees of their immanent goddess, in contrast to the negative identity of men as the malevolent devotees of their transcendent god. Feminists have understood that identity always implies both likeness (the suppos-edly life-affirming community of other women) and unlikeness (the supposedly death-affirming isolation of men). And no feminists have used that inherent duality of identity more effectively in favour of women than have goddess ideologues.

History, Herstory, or Heresy?
Sophianity and the New Reformation

By the 1990s, some goddess ideologues had become religious separatists. They wanted nothing to do with institutionalized religion,
especially Western forms. Of interest here, though, are those goddess ideologues who *rejected* separatism. They wanted instead to
take charge within those religions. Using the rhetoric of religious
reform, albeit to promote religious revolution, they tried to "restore"
feminine imagery, including goddesses that had been rejected by
these religions.

Some Jewish feminists, eager to restore female imagery to their
tradition, borrowed terminology from alien sources. "Rabbi" Leah
Novick,[1] for instance, refers to her own "rabbi craft." Others call
themselves "Jewitches."[2] But most tried to reinterpret traditional
terminology, especially the *shekhinah*. That word refers in early
rabbinic literature to God's immediate presence and in later commentaries as an intercessor who argues with God on behalf of people. Jews of the kabbalistic (mystical) tradition have gone further
by identifying the *shekhinah* as one of God's ten *sefiroth*, which
are analogous to God's three "persons" in Christianity. This one is
female. Every Friday night, God unites with her on the cosmic level
just as husbands and wives do on the microcosmic one (which turns
the dinner into a nuptial banquet on both levels). Not surprisingly, modern Jewish feminists have tried to popularize and reinterpret the *shekhinah*. They have tried to remain Jewish, or at least
monotheistic, but also to celebrate a Jewish version of Canaanite
goddesses such as Asherah and Anath.[3] They have aligned both
themselves and the *shekhinah*, accordingly, with new-moon and
harvest festivals. But they have seldom mentioned the fact that

kabbalistic Judaism has by no means led to the "liberation" of
Jewish women from what feminists consider the misogyny of orthodox Judaism.[4]

Christian feminists, too, have tried to restore female imagery.
Sometimes, this has meant rehabilitating (or almost deifying)[5]
iconic Christian women. The classic example would be Mary
Magdalene. According to the New Testament, she was not only a
disciple of Jesus but also a witness to his death on the cross and
his resurrection at the empty tomb. Commissioned by a risen Jesus
to tell the others, she became an "apostle to the apostles." No wonder that the New Testament refers to her more than to any other
woman except the mother of Jesus. And yet later Catholic (but not
Eastern Orthodox) tradition turned her into a prostitute – conflat-
ing her with the sinful woman in Luke 7: 36–50, say, or the adulteress in John 7:53–8:11 – who found salvation and even sainthood as
a reformed follower of Jesus. Why have Catholics attributed a dis-
honourable past to her?

The answer is obvious, says Jonathan Darman in a 2006 cover
story for *Newsweek*[6] (which indicates the extent of current interest
in Magdalene). To some feminists, "she was a figure with equal (or
even favored) status to the men around Jesus – a woman so threatening that the apostles suppressed her role, and those of other
women, in a bid to build a patriarchal hierarchy in the early
church."[7] Feminists claim that Catholicism refuses to acknowledge
female leadership, past or present, because it is a profoundly and
possibly irredeemably misogynistic tradition.

According to Elaine Pagels, who teaches early Christian history
at Princeton and pioneered in research on the gospels of gnostic
Christians (gnosticism being a pervasive worldview that emerged
during the Hellenistic period and influenced both Judaism and
Christianity to some extent), the answer is more specific: jealous
hostility from a power-hungry and misogynistic Peter. In the Gospel
of Thomas, for instance, he keeps attacking Magdalene and even
tells Jesus to dismiss her from the community of disciples, "for
women are not worthy of life." With this in mind, no doubt, she
tells Jesus her side of the story in another gnostic gospel: *Pistis
Sophia*. "He threatens me and hates our race" (which implies that
Jesus and Magdalene were not Jews, thereby foreshadowing an
anti-Semitic claim that the Nazis found helpful).[8] The heterodox
tradition of gnosticism emphasized the importance of Magdalene

and denied that of Peter, according to Pagels, while the orthodox tradition of Catholicism has emphasized the importance of Peter and denied that of Magdalene.

Feminist ideologues, including goddess ideologues, find it easy to believe not only that the church suppressed gnostic gospels (which it clearly did by the very act of distinguishing between canonical and non-canonical ones) but also that it suppressed the truth about Jesus and his earliest followers (which it might or might not have done, because the mere existence of non-canonical texts says nothing at all about their accuracy). Kenneth Woodward puts it this way:

> Just as a feminist hermeneutics of suspicion – biblical scholar-ship based on suspicion of male authorship – dictates that the text of the New Testament, being the work of males, must be distrusted *for that very reason*, so a feminist hermeneutics of retrieval – in this case, retrieving the suppressed evidence of the party of Mary Magdalene – must go to other sources. These sources are the various texts that did not make it into the New Testament as it was fixed in the fourth century. And the very fact of this exclusion by male church hierarchs make the extra texts *all the more authoritative* for scholars whose aim is show-ing that patriarchy suppressed female leadership in the church.[9]

As Darman observes, though, this alleged personal conflict between Peter and Magdalene – or even, as Woodward says, an alleged gender war between the Peter party and the Magdalene party – would have reflected a much more important theological one, which surfaces even within the canonical gospels. In that of John, for instance, the risen Jesus appears to Magdalene as an almost unrecognizable ghost and warns her not to touch him. Later on, though, he appears to other disciples as an easily recognizable man and even urges "doubting" Thomas to touch him.[10] John pres-ents not one notion of resurrection, therefore, but two: that of the body and that of the spirit. He identifies the former with male disci-ples, the latter with a female disciple. And that dichotomy corre-sponded in turn to one between orthodox Christians (who, relying on Hebrew scripture, insisted on resurrection of the dead) and het-erodox Christians (who, relying on Hellenistic philosophy, insisted on immortality of the soul). Luke puts it this way: "Handle me, and see," Jesus tells the disciples, "for a [disembodied] spirit has not flesh and bones as you see that I have."[11] Darman refrains from adding two thoughts. First, it was this fundamental theological controversy over the material world that motivated orthodox Christianity to reject gnostic Christianity. Second, it was gnostic Christianity, at least as much as orthodox Christianity, that associated suspicion of the material world in turn with Magdalene and thus by extension with women in general.[12]

For those who see the Christian gnostics as innocent victims of patriarchal oppression, of course, it makes sense to believe that the church would go to any lengths – even murder, as it does in the Dan Brown's *Da Vinci Code* – to conceal its darkest secrets and that Magdalene was actually not only a respectable woman (whatever that means to feminists) but also the wife of Jesus and mother of his children. Jane Schaberg and Melanie Johnson-DuBaufre take that approach.[13] Interestingly, though, they note that the Catholic legend is no worse than Brown's novel. The former turned Magdalene into a repentant whore, to be sure, but the latter has turned her into a respectable mother; both have emphasized her body and ignored her mind. Both have failed, in other words, to acknowledge her as a leader.

But not all advocates for Magdalene have endorsed either cynicism about the church or wishful thinking about her. Elizabeth Johnson endorses neither, although she does say that "most [perhaps unwitting] distortions about Magdalene can be laid at the feet of men." Her main point is that Catholics should consider the importance of this woman (and every woman).[14] All of these authors, though, have one thing in common. As Woodward puts it, even modern reconstructions of the former repentant prostitute "can be prostituted for polemical purposes."[15]

Mary Magdalene is still making headlines. The publication of a best-selling novel and the release of a blockbuster movie about her provoked many, to be sure, but so have less controversial events – if not always in national dailies, then at least in religious monthlies and quarterlies.[16] Christine Scheck, for instance, has encouraged American Catholics to emphasize Magdalene's feast day every 22 July. Countless reading groups, moreover, discuss the many new books and websites about Magdalene.

Catholics and other Christians can defend themselves ably enough from anti-religious attacks. They had already done so in no fewer than nine books[17] and countless websites on the *Code* within only two years of the book's publication. So far, though, men have not defended themselves from that book's anti-*male* attacks.

In this chapter, we discuss (1) Jewish and Christian attempts to (add or) restore female imagery, (2) a case study of one church that became polarized over this topic in the 1990s, and (3) an update on this topic.

Some Christian feminists have ransacked the Hebrew Bible for female imagery. Elizabeth Johnson,[18] for instance, a nun who teaches at Fordham University, builds her case for female imagery on the apocryphal Book of Wisdom 10:15–17:

A holy people and blameless race
Wisdom delivered from a nation of oppressors ...
she guided them along a marvelous way,
and became a shelter to them by day,
and a starry flame through the night.
She brought them over the Red Sea,
and led them through deep waters;
but she drowned their enemies,
and cast them up from the depth of the sea.[19]

Bemoaning women's marginalization in the Bible, Johnson insists that Christians must replace its patriarchal images of king, father, master, and so on. As modern biblical scholars have done for well over a century, she dismisses the idea that Christians need to take biblical imagery at face value as eternal truth. But those biblical scholars interpreted scripture in the light of contemporary science or critical analysis. Postmodernist scholars do so in the light of contemporary needs or desires, usually psychological or political ones. "In this perspective, when the interpreting community today is women themselves, or women and men together in the struggle for emancipation from sexism, then what ensues is interpretation guided by a liberating impulse."[20] She argues that just as Christians can reject creationism and slavery despite biblical passages that support both, they can reject sexism despite passages that support it. She tries to make her case by using a Christian criterion of the nineteenth century: "For the sake of our salvation: on the wings of this principle feminist hermeneutics lifts off from imprisoning discourse and flies around the scriptures seeking what has been lost, to practical and critical effect."[21]

After promoting the idea of God as liberator of the oppressed, Johnson turns to the Holy Spirit. This is supposedly the Christian equivalent of the Jewish *shekhinah*, at least in the sense of dwelling with the people in the form of cloud, fire, or light. Johnson writes that "it signifies no mere feminine dimension of God but God as She-Who-Dwells-Within, the divine presence in compassionate engagement with the conflictual world, source of vitality and consolation in the struggle."[22]

Next, Johnson explores the biblical notion of wisdom, claiming that it is the most common female personification of God's presence. Known in Greek as *sophia* (wisdom), this feminine noun can refer to "sister, mother, female beloved ... preacher, judge, liberator, establisher of justice, and a myriad of other female roles wherein she symbolizes transcendent power ordering and delighting in the world. She pervades the world, both nature and human beings, interacting with them all to lure them along the right path to life."[23] And Johnson connects either *sophia* or the personification Sophia with the act of creation. According to her translation of Proverbs 8:22–31, "Sophia existed before the beginning of the world as the first of God's works. Then she is beside God at the vital moments of creation as either a master craftsperson or God's darling child (the text is disputed). In either case, God takes delight in her."[24] Johnson concludes that creation is "not simply the act of a solitary male deity."[25]

In connection with one text, the Wisdom of Ben Sira (Ecclesiasticus), Johnson summarizes the story of "how [Sophia] came forth from the mouth of the Most High and covered the earth like a mist; how her throne was in a pillar of cloud; how alone she made a grand proprietary tour of the heights and depths of the created world and its people; how she then searched the world for a resting place, and was told by the Creator to pitch her tent in Israel. Once there, she flourished, and issued her compelling invitation: 'Come to me, you who desire me, and eat your fill ... whoever obeys me will not be put to shame, and those who work with my help will not sin (24: 19, 22).' At the climax of Sophia's song, the author of Ben Sira breaks in to make a momentous identification. Sophia represents Torah, the book of the covenant of the Most High God (24: 23)."[26] Moreover, Johnson points to yet another ancient text, the

Wisdom of Solomon, where Sophia takes on the attribute of omnipotence (7:25–26). From these and other passages she concludes that *sophia* – or Sophia – is the Holy Spirit.

Suggesting that the image of Jesus draws from the tradition of a personified Sophia, Johnson refers to "Jesus-Sophia," the incarnation of God's wisdom or Jesus as Sophia's child, and cites several New Testament passages to support the idea. In the end, she claims, Philo displaced this tradition, substituting the idea of *logos* for *sophia*. This, she claims, was part of the transition from matriarchy to patriarchy; after that, Christology emphasized the "maleness"[27] of Christ and thus led to the subordination of women. The imagery of Sophia has historical precedents, at any rate, that refer to God (who is nonetheless ultimately incomprehensible). Therefore, says Johnson, Christians, or at least Christian women, should restore this imagery to its rightful place. She endorses, in other words, what we call Sophianity.

Johnson argues that the Judeo-Christian tradition interpreted Exodus 3:14, "I Am Who I Am," as "He Is Who He Is." Now, she says, the tradition should reinterpret the same words as "She Is Who She Is," or simply "She Who Is." In short, femaleness is no mere dimension of God or even a mere Holy Spirit of the Trinity. It is worthwhile quoting her at length.

> *She Who Is* can be spoken as a robust appropriate name of God. With this name we bring to bear in a female metaphor all the power carried in the ontological symbol of absolute relational liveliness that energizes the world ... linguistically this is possible; theologically it is legitimate; existentially and religiously it is necessary if speech about God is to shake off the shackles of idolatry and be a blessing for women. In the present sexist situation where structures and language, praxis and personal attitudes convey an ontology of inferiority to women, naming toward God in this way is a gleam of light on the road to genuine community. Spiritually, *She Who Is,* spoken as the symbol of ultimate reality, of the highest beauty and truth and goodness, of the mystery of life in the midst of death, affirms women in their struggle toward dignity, power, and value. It discloses women's human nature as *imago dei,* and reveals divine nature to be the relational mystery of life

who desires the liberated human existence of all women made in
her image. In promoting the flourishing of women *She Who Is*
attends to an essential element for the well-being of all creation,
human beings and the earth inclusively. Politically, this symbol
challenges every structure and attitude that assigns superiority
to ruling men on the basis of their supposed greater godlikeness.
If the mystery of God is no longer spoken about exclusively or
even primarily in terms of the dominating male,
a forceful linchpin holding up structures of patriarchal rule is
removed. In a word, *She Who Is* discloses in an elusive female
metaphor the mystery of Sophia-God as sheer, exuberant, rela-
tional aliveness in the midst of the history of suffering, inexhaust-
ible source of new being in situations of death and destruction,
ground of hope for the whole created universe, to practical and
critical effect.[28]

Although Johnson briefly admits that male imagery is neither
more nor less adequate than female imagery, because divine reality
is beyond all human perception and thus beyond all imagery, she
focuses on female imagery: spirit, wisdom, mother, and so on. This
is ostensibly a corrective, but it could just as well be a sleight of
hand to give Christianity both a feminist "thealogy" and a goddess.

Like Jewish feminists, moreover, some Christian feminists find
the *shekhinah* useful. Like their Jewish counterparts, however,
Christian feminists must reinvent it to suit their own needs. Gershom Scholem, the classic authority on kabbalistic literature, never
suggests that the *shekhinah* is a distinct goddess in Judaism:

In Talmudic literature and non-Kabbalistic Rabbinical Judaism,
the *Shekhinah* – literally in-dwelling, namely of God in the
world – is taken to mean simply God himself in His omnipres-
ence and activity in the world and especially in Israel. God's
presence, what in the Bible is called His "face," is in Rabbinical usage His *Shekhinah*. Nowhere in the older literature is a
distinction made between God himself and His *Shekhinah*; the
Shekhinah is not a special hypostasis distinguished from god
as a whole. It is very different in the usage of the Kabbalah,
beginning with the *Bahir*, which already contains most of the
essential Kabbalistic ideas on the subject. Here the *Shekhinah*

becomes an aspect of God, a quasi-independent feminine element within Him.[29]

Of course, the important adjective here is "*quasi*-independent." Scholem admits that the *shekhinah* created paradoxes and ambiguities, even a mythic realm at the heart of a religion that had closed itself off to myth. Moreover, because of its great popularity with the common people, it inspired controversy and necessitated apologetics.[30] Nevertheless, the *shekhinah* was always understood within a gnostic or theosophical interpretation of Jewish monotheism. This consisted of the dynamic unity of God as a theogonic process, the ten modes of action (*sefirot*, otherwise understood as potencies or hypostases) of the one living God:[31]

But while in all other instances the Kabbalists refrain from employing sexual imagery in describing the relation between man and God, they show no such hesitation when it comes to describing the relation of God to Himself, in the world of the Sefiroth. The mystery of sex, as it appears to the Kabbalist, has a terribly deep significance. This mystery of human existence is for him nothing but a symbol of the love between the divine "I" and the divine "You," the Holy one, blessed be He and His Shekhinah. The ... "sacred union" of the king and the Queen, the Celestial Bridegroom and the Celestial Bride, to name a few of the symbols, is the central fact in the whole chain of divine manifestations in the hidden world. In God there is a union of the active and the passive, procreation and conception, from which all mundane life and bliss are derived ... Dimly we perceive behind this [*sic*] mystical images the male and female gods of antiquity, anathema as they were to the pious Kabbalist.[32]

Much of what medieval kabbalists thought and said would be repugnant to modern feminists. It is true that both male and female elements interact in connection with these *sefirot*. But the ninth, a "male potency, described with clearly phallic symbolism, [is] ... the 'foundation' of all life, which guarantees and consummates the *hieros gamos*, the holy union of male and female powers."[33] In other words, the phallic symbolism prevails. Furthermore, when the *shekhinah* is female, as the soul, she has a terrible aspect, a dark face, representing death and the demonic.[34] The *shekhinah* even goes into exile, representing human guilt and sin, an exile that she overcomes through divine marriage.[35]

In his discussion of the *shekhinah* as an archetypal image of the divine and as the soul's imaginative faculty, Elliot Wolfson notes the *shekhinah*'s secondary status not only to the divine unity but also to the male aspect of that unity: "The feminine aspect of the Godhead is the optical apparatus through which the masculine aspect, and particularly the *membrum virile*, is seen."[36] Elsewhere he writes that "the forms become visible through the feminine, but their ontic source is actually in the masculine, the *Saddiq*. There are kabbalistic sources that explicitly connect the phallic aspect of the divine and the production of images."[37]

Similarly, not all Christians or academics have accepted Sophia as an *imago dei*. Mary Aquin O'Neill,[38] for instance, admits that Johnson has impressive academic credentials, a command of the sources, even poetic language. But by the end of the book, according to O'Neill, Johnson has risked "conjuring up another God ... one who sometimes complements, sometimes corrects, sometimes bests the traditional male God. Moreover, male images of God, when alluded to, are almost universally cast as negative. 'Patriarchal' becomes the code word for an image of God that is unfeeling, controlling, distant."[39] This is not Christianity, as we say, but Sophianity. O'Neill observes that Johnson has removed virtually all notions of justice along with Mary as the Mother of God. Mary McClintock Fulkerson,[40] too, begins her review by complementing Johnson for her elegance, theological astuteness, and power of language. But she as well worries that Johnson's ostensible replacement of gender polarity with "multipolarity" actually focuses only on the female side.

In many early states, at any rate, femaleness was a divine attribute along with maleness. And female symbols increased at times of reduced stress.[41] Even without feminist attempts to deconstruct patriarchy, divine couples became popular. Supreme gods developed female attributes and sometimes, as in the Hindu case of Shiva, androgynous ones.

Monotheistic traditions, however, are not necessarily monolithic. By definition, they have room for the worship of only one deity, usually a god represented in primarily masculine terms. Nevertheless, a surprising number of female symbols have found their way into both biblical and post-biblical texts.[42] This, according to Tikva Frymer-Kensky, was no accident: "The development of monotheism is not simply a form of subtraction. Eliminating other gods and jettisoning old religious practices changes fundamental ideas about the workings of the cosmos. The image of God must expand to include all the functions previously encompassed by an entire pantheon. The religious and philosophical systems must adapt to form a coherent picture of the universe that no longer includes multiple divine powers. The biblical system had to replace both goddesses and gods, and as it did so, it transformed its thinking about nature, culture, gender, and humanity."[43]

Functions that the god of Israel took over included, for example, both providing agricultural fertility (the rain that other societies associated with gods such as the Canaanite Ba'al or the Babylonian Marduk) and producing human fertility (the procreative abilities that other societies associated with goddesses such as the Canaanite Anat or the Sumerian Ninhursag). Unlike its Mesopotamian neighbours, ancient Israel was prone to underpopulation, not overpopulation. Families were small. Given the climate and terrain, they had good reasons for encouraging reproduction. How else could they expect to continue tilling their fields, building their cisterns, terracing their hills, and defending their cities?

Of reproduction, Frymer-Kensky writes that the "whole enterprise was too doubtful and precarious to take place without divine supervision. Because no other god could be invoked, the God of Israel had to oversee this vital function."[44] The Bible often mentions God's active involvement in procreation. From God, therefore, come "blessings of breast and womb."[45] Over and over again, in fact, God actually intervenes. He opens the wombs of Sarah, Rebecca, Rachel, and Hannah to produce the founders of Israel:

This story of the once-barren mother repeatedly conveys the message that God and God alone can cause conception. All children are gifts of God ... God's role in childbirth extends beyond conception to all functions previously under the supervision of the mother goddesses. God oversees the entire process of gestation and childbirth: God forms and shapes the child in the womb, God takes note of the child in the womb, cares for it there, and may call the child into service there; God is midwife, bringing on the labor and bringing forth the child.

There is no more need for a mother goddess, or for divine midwife-assistance and divine labor-attendants. God, the master of all the other elements of the natural world, is master of human reproduction as well.[46]

The Bible attributes to God, who transcends both maleness and femaleness, both male and female qualities. Speaking in the name of God, (deutero-)Isaiah[47] exclaims: "Hearken to me O house of Jacob, all the remnant of the house of Israel, who have been borne by me from your birth, carried from the womb ... I have made and I will bear; I will carry and will save."[48] Later, (trito-)Isaiah uses the same maternal imagery. In the words of God, he declares: "As one whom his mother comforts, so I will comfort you."[49] From out of the whirlwind, God asks Job: "Who shut in the sea with doors, when it burst forth from the womb, when I made clouds its garment and thick darkness its swaddling band?"[50] Elsewhere God asks him: "Who has begotten the drops of dew? From whose womb did the ice come forth, and who has given birth to the whore frost of heaven?"[51] And listen to the psalmist, grateful for divine compassion: "But I have calmed and quieted my soul, like a child quieted at its mother's breast."[52] Even Moses, greatest of all the patriarchs, uses maternal imagery when referring to God. "You were unmindful of the wrath that begot you," he tells the children of Israel, "and you forgot the God who gave you birth."[53]

In the post-biblical period, Jews began to personify God as the *shekhinah* (although this word, referring to the immediate presence of God, was not a new one). We have already mentioned the *shekhinah* as God's female aspect. This notion found its way from kabbalistic theology into the Sabbath liturgy.[54] There, God is the cosmic bride or queen. Not surprisingly, mystically oriented communities understand the Friday evening meal as a nuptial banquet celebrating a sacred marriage between the Holy Community of Israel and God. At the microcosmic level, husbands and wives have intercourse on that night to celebrate their own marriages. Almost every Jewish liturgy, moreover, refers to the God of mercy (*el ha-rahamim* or simply *ha-rahaman*), and the Hebrew word for mercy and its variants (*rahamim* and *rahaman*) derive etymologically from the word for womb (*rehem*).

But is all this talk about "absorbing the goddesses" just another way of talking about a patriarchal "takeover"? As usual, the matter is far more complex than it might first appear. For one thing, neighbouring societies had already marginalized their own goddesses by elevating gods such as the Babylonian Marduk and the Canaanite Ba'al to supremacy. The Israelites, on the other hand, refrained from excluding female aspects of God. More importantly, the process of eliminating goddesses did not involve further marginalization of women in ancient Israel (a process that had already begun earlier in Babylonia) as some academics have claimed. Nor did it leave women with an ontological status that was inferior to – or even different from – that of men. This is worth examining in more detail.

Frymer-Kensky points out that the transition from polytheism to monotheism involved a far deeper change than merely uniting many functions under one umbrella: it involved a revolution in relations between the divine and the human. It is true that the god of Israel absorbed the functions of many gods and goddesses. It is true also, however, that the *people* of Israel absorbed other functions. In Sumerian myths, for example, the gods and goddesses establish agriculture. In the biblical tradition, though, Cain establishes agriculture and Abel pastoralism. The same is true of other skills. Jubal is the founder of music, Tubal-Cain of metallurgy, and so forth. Yet of greatest importance here is that some "elements of culture that were once goddess-linked, such as storage, administration, lamentation, song, and wisdom-writing [were] entirely within the domain of humankind. They [were] neither divinely granted nor divinely supervised."[55]

Frymer-Kensky argues that the transition from polytheism to monotheism, which involved the transfer of some power from gods and goddesses to mortals, benefited everyone – including women. "Throughout the Bible, in every aspect of biblical thought, human beings gain in prominence in and because of the absence of goddesses. In Israel's philosophy of culture, humans have a greater role in the development and maintenance of the array of powers, functions, occupations and inventions that constitute civilized life than they ever did in ancient Near Eastern myth."[56] Moreover, monotheism promoted egalitarianism:

The narrative sections of the Bible reinforce the impression of male privilege conveyed by the laws even though at the same time they modify our impression of the extent to which women acted as subordinates. These stories reveal the women of Israel as both victim and actor, and provide some insight into Israel's conception of gender. They show that beyond the realities of Israel's [hierarchical] social structure, the Bible presents a remarkably unified vision of humankind, for the stories show women as having the same inherent characteristics [as] men ... There is nothing distinctively "female" about the way women are portrayed in the Bible.[57]

No goals of women, whether good or bad, are characteristically or distinctively "female" in the Bible.[58]

Every liberal denomination of both Judaism and Christianity has discussed the restoration of a great goddess. With the academic debate over all this in mind, consider the following case study.

A 1993 issue of *Christianity Today* showed signs of trouble within the Presbyterian Church (USA). The lead article, about feminist God-talk in the church, is by Elizabeth Achtemeier.[59] Even though she acknowledges centuries of discrimination against women in Christianity, and even though she acknowledges the importance of reform – the use, for instance, of gender-inclusive language – Achtemeier argues that changing the sex of God would be going too far. "By attempting to change the biblical language used of the deity, these feminists have in reality exchanged the true God for those deities which are 'no gods,' as Jeremiah put it (2:11)."[60] She attacks the claims by well-known feminists in the field of religion – these would include Rosemary Ruether, Sallie McFague, Lettie Russell, Isabel Carter Heyward, and Dorothee Sölle – that female or asexual images can replace the male ones in view of the fact that all biblical images are metaphorical in the first place. God is not a mother but *like* a mother, not a king but *like* a king. Behind these revealed images is a personal deity who is really beyond both maleness and femaleness.

This "otherness" of God is a primary and distinctive characteristic of the biblical tradition. "I am God and not man," reads one biblical passage, "the Holy One in your midst"[61] Another asks to "whom then will you liken God, or what likeness compare with him?"[62] The creator is not the creation but different from it. Virginia Mollenkott notwithstanding, this is not the "undivided One God who births and breast-feeds the universe."[63]

A picture of Mary Daly and her now-famous statement, "If God is male, then the male is God,"[64] appear at the top of one page in *Christian Century*. Achtemeier's discussion suggests that Daly has turned the tradition on its head. In the same context, she opposes Zsuzsanna Budapest's claim that "'this is what the Goddess symbolizes – the divine within women and all that is female in the universe ... The responsibility you accept is that you are divine, and that you have power.' If God is identified with his creation, we finally make ourselves gods and goddesses, the ultimate and primeval sin"[65]

Given their fierce opposition to Near Eastern or Greco-Roman gods and goddesses, Achtemeier surmises, the Israelites came to establish their religious identity quite early. Actually, it took between five hundred and a thousand years for them to establish monotheism on an enduring basis. Scripture records that lengthy and painful process and therefore enshrines a polemic against polytheism. The fact that some Israelites continued to support polytheism, or that they kept backsliding even after adopting monotheism, hardly means that the biblical tradition ever *approved of* polytheism.

Then Achtemeier throws down the gauntlet: "The result is that Ruether and all those feminists who want to erase the distinction between God and his creation finally share with the most radical feminists, who have abandoned the Christian church and faith altogether, a view of divinity that is at home in modern witches' covens."[66] The result is a reversal of biblical thinking: life is a paradise; there is neither fall nor sin; death is reintegration into the cosmos, not eternal life.[67] In short, this is no longer Christianity (or Judaism). Nowhere is this rejection of scripture more evident, she argues, than in the claims of some feminists to be goddesses, divine manifestations, embodiments of love, not mere creatures who serve God. She concludes by warning that when human beings think of themselves as all-powerful, with no awareness of human finitude and capacity for sin, a law onto themselves, who can "by their own power ... restructure society, restore creation, and overcome suffering,"[68] they are foolishly and arrogantly ignoring human history.[69]

Achtemeier's article includes two sidebars. One is by Thomas Oden, who writes about his personal experience in the United Methodist Church. There he found himself participating in a service led by a female pastor at the theological seminary where he teaches. After a hymn to Sophia, she preached a sermon about the victory of "a pious Methodist lay leader and other members [who] ... were driven out of her church and forced to join another after they challenged her authority to offer the Lord's Supper in the name of the goddess Sophia. She recounted triumphantly how she had preached on the virtues of doctrinal diversity and invited all members who did not agree with her to look for another church."[70] After this declaration of Sophianity, the pastor likened the Christian notion of discipleship to sadistic and masochistic sex and invited the congregation to communion in the name of the goddess speaking through Christ. At that point, Oden left. We will return to him, however, in due course.

The other sidebar is by Dale Youngs, the pastor of Forest Hills Presbyterian Church in Helotes, Texas. He too throws down the gauntlet, saying that "the call for goddess worship is no mere corrective to the worship of Yahweh; it is a call to a new religion. More precisely, it is an old religion in new clothes."[71] He then reminds readers that the ancient Near Eastern goddesses were not what feminists now imagine. They were not supreme. They were always connected with motherhood and fertility. They were nonetheless sometimes warriors. And they presided over profoundly patriarchal societies.

Clearly, then, the Presbyterian Church (USA) and the United Methodist churches were well aware in 1993 of a coming crisis. Conflict came to a head in November of that year with an event in Minneapolis that shook the crumbling foundations of liberal Christianity in America: a feminist conference called Re-Imagining 1993. The World Council of Churches had convened this conference as part of its Decade in Solidarity with Women. Over two thousand women (and a few men) attended. Coming from twenty-six countries, they formed a roster that looked like a who's who of women in both national and international ecclesiastical circles: members of committees serving the (American) National Council of Churches and the World Council of Churches, editors of church publications, professors at theological seminaries, bureaucrats at denominational head offices, and so on. Fully recorded on tape, the conference was very much a late twentieth-century event. These tapes include not merely words but also applause and cheering to supply the context in which they were spoken.

For some reason, many outside observers were shocked when they found out what this conference was all about. In its lead edito-

rial, the *Presbyterian Layman* summed up the situation by observing that "participants and speakers angrily denounced the Christian
church, charging that its teachings about Jesus Christ constitute the
chief source of women's oppression, human violence, racism, sexism, classism, and the abuse of the earth. They called for the 'reima-
gining' of the church and its theology and then, if it cannot be
transformed, for its destruction."[72]

What most needed "re-imagining," according to delegates at the
conference, was no one less than God. The result was an attack on
theologies of divine transcendence (in which God exists *beyond* the
cosmos but intervenes occasionally in the guise of providence) and
a call for theologies of divine immanence (in which God is *part*
of the cosmos). Citing a feminist author, Rita Nakashima Brock
celebrated "not transcendence, that orgy of self-alienation beloved
of the fathers, but immanence, god working out god's self in
everything."[73]

Actually, the dichotomy is not quite as clear as advocates of both
often imagine. If God were totally transcendent, after all, no contact with human beings would be possible. At the heart of both
Judaism and Christianity, therefore, is the seeming paradox of a
transcendent god who takes a passionate interest in the cosmos as
we experience it in daily life – so passionate, in fact, that this transcendent god becomes incarnate (as Torah for Jews and as Jesus for
Christians). An incarnate god is an immanent one, of course, albeit
one whose ultimate being remains a mystery. Jews and Christians
have chosen a middle way, therefore, insisting on transcendence in
some ways but acknowledging immanence in others.

Those who attended the conference and those who were already
interested in theological debates were well aware of what was at
stake. After all, it was nothing new. Mary Daly, whom we discuss
in the next chapter, had long been campaigning for the position
affirmed at this conference. And readers of the *Layman* did not
have to know much about Catholicism to know what she was all
about. "At Re-Imagining 1993 Mary Daly's creed, 'If God is male,
male is God' reached its ultimate apotheosis. The guiding spirit of
the event seemed to be, 'Since women are gods, god is a woman.'
By turns ignoring and excoriating God's self-revelation, and by
(rather unimaginatively) redefining God in their own images,
what conference participants declared most clearly to the Church
and the world was not what they believe, but what they reject."[74]

To illustrate this debate, the *Layman* printed Michelangelo's famous painting from the Sistine Chapel ceiling, God creating Adam in his own image, and labelled it *imago dei*. Printed next to that is the same painting in reverse: Adam creating God in his own image, labelled *imago hominum*.

At any rate, the conference linked immanence (God *within* the cosmos) with monism (God *is* the cosmos). But the founders of biblical religion had rejected this idea too, denouncing it as "idolatry" (worshipping objects, including but not restricted to those made by human hands). What could be more central to the biblical way of thinking than the idea that human beings, by definition, are finite (not infinite and therefore not divine) beings?

Virginia Mollenkott, from the National Council of Churches (which had commissioned a study on gender-inclusive language), was among the speakers at this conference. She made her Sophian position very clear: "The monism I'm talking about assumes that god is so all-inclusive that she is involved in every cell of those who are thoughts in her mind and embodiments of her image ... Like Jesus, we and the source are one."[75]

Pui-lan, who teaches theology and spirituality at Episcopal Divinity School in Cambridge, Mass., and is renowned for her feminist and post-colonial theology,[76] said much the same thing (but much less clearly): "If you bring out what is within you, what is within you will save you. But if you cannot bring out what is within you, what is within you will destroy you."[77]

Not surprisingly, the conference linked immanence also with polytheism but forgot to link biblical religion with what had once been a shockingly new way of thinking: monotheism. The latter refers not only to one deity but to one principle of order in the cosmos – physical, spiritual, moral, and so on – that unifies what would otherwise be a fragmented realm of competing and conflicting principles. Speakers not only referred respectfully to polytheistic Asian and African religious traditions (which all Christians, except for the narrowest of fundamentalists, would consider appropriate) but also declared them superior to the monotheistic Christian one (which no Christians, except for the most secular and radical of liberals, would consider appropriate). At any rate, speakers made no secret of promoting a female pantheon. According to Pui-lan, Christ was like the Big Mac "prepackaged and shipped all over the world. It won't do. It's imperialistic."[78] Much more acceptable to her was another religion, that of her own country. What could be more "diverse" or "pluralistic," after all, than 722 gods and goddesses? Never mind that the World Council of Churches had appointed Pui-Lan to represent a specifically Christian point of view. When it comes to the "diversity of women's voices," apparently, anything goes.

Moreover, many conference participants linked immanence with concreteness and transcendence with abstraction. But that link is itself an abstraction. It all boils down, in practical terms, to the assumption that concreteness is somehow female and abstraction somehow male. No wonder that participants made extensive use of ritual, which gave their theories concrete expression. One ritual involved "telling stories" or "sharing." Explicitly or implicitly, these stories of women functioned as replacements for the scriptural ones of men. Another ritual was more "traditional" – that is, traditional for Hindus: women placing red dots on the foreheads of other women "to signify their divinity" (or at least their devotion to goddesses).[79]

All of this had little or nothing to do with Jesus, of course. No longer the incarnation of (a patriarchal) God, he had become nothing more than an elder brother and trailblazer. Dolores Williams, a professor at Union Theological Seminary in New York, put it this way: "I don't think we need a theory of atonement [the reconciliation of God and humans through Christ, especially his death on the cross] ... at all. I think Jesus came for life and to show us something about life ... I don't think we need folks hanging on crosses and blood dripping and weird stuff."[80]

Not even that was enough for some participants at the conference. Mollenkott, for example, solemnly announced that "as an incest survivor, I can no longer worship in a theological context that depicts God as an abusive parent and Jesus as the obedient, trusting child."[81] Aruna Gnanadason, director of the sub-unit on Women in the Church and Society of the World Council of Churches, opined that Christianity "centered its faith around the cruel and violent death of Christ on the cross, sanctioning violence against the powerless in society."[82] Just how did this act of Roman tyranny, condemned by scripture in the strongest possible way, sanction violence? It obviously did nothing of the kind. But that was not Gnanadason's point. We would summarize her point, like that of Mollenkott, as follows: Christian imagery (Jesus on the cross) glorifies self-sacrifice; self-sacrifice fosters passivity in women who would otherwise actively oppose domestic violence; ergo, Christian imagery fosters domestic violence. Never mind that the same Christian imagery glorifies self-sacrifice among men and has been used by the state most effectively to glorify the death of men in battle. Never mind that choosing to sacrifice yourself in any Christian sense must be motivated by freedom, not subservience; must involve active choice, not passive resignation; and must be expected to have a redemptive effect on someone, not a placating one. Some participants might have thought about these things, but no one mentioned them.

One delegate noted with a bizarre mixture of metaphors that "women take the nothing which results from destructive injustice, from violence, from accidents, and we wash away the blood and at the table of creative necessity, we make the strands of life emerge."[83] She meant that women had little or nothing to learn from or to value in Christianity. She spoke, nevertheless, as a Christian. What we could call "non-Christian Christians," secular people who leave their churches even if they retain some residual interest in or respect for Christianity, have long been a feature of modern societies. What we could call "anti-Christian Christians," secular people who remain as members or even leaders of their churches but offer only contempt for Christianity, have emerged more recently. Among them are the Sophians.

To outsiders observing these events with some detachment, the whole discussion might have seemed like the height of hutzpah. After all, people either want to be Christians or they do not. If not, they can always leave their churches and establish new ones, join other churches, convert to other religions, or abandon religion altogether. But where is the logic or honesty in denouncing Christianity from a specifically Christian platform? To insiders, those who have been either doing that very thing or opposing it for the past twenty years, it might have seemed like business as usual. But to people in the middle, those who went to church on Sundays, the whole controversy must have seemed shocking.

This conference was held during the week of Reformation Day, which provided an ideal (and no doubt carefully planned) opportunity to call for a "second Reformation." But were the new protesters really demanding reforms, asked one observer, of the kind that Luther and Calvin had demanded? Was this call for a "second Reformation" really about destroying a decadent bureaucracy and returning to the purity of what Jesus had originally taught? On the contrary, he argued, it was about destroying a tradition and displacing Christ. This would require supporters not only to reopen the canon (which might have been an interesting possibility, at least in theory, because both Christians and Jews had done that very thing in the remote past) but to proclaim their own divinity (which, given the fact that even Jesus made only ambiguous remarks about his identity, would have had no obvious precedent).[84]

For anyone who still misunderstood what was going on, however, Hyun Kung Chung,[85] a Presbyterian theologian from Korea who teaches feminist and ecofeminist theology at Union Theological Seminary in New York, defined both her position and that of the conference in very explicit terms. Describing herself as an "Asian feminist liberation theologian," she opined that "the Christian church has been very patriarchal. That's why we are here together, in order to destroy this patriarchal idolatry of Christianity."[86] Johanna Bos, who teaches at Louisville Presbyterian Theological Seminary, referred to a biblical passage in which "the prophetess predicted the destruction of Jerusalem"[87] – a recitation that received roars of approval from the audience.[88]

There was an aftermath to the conference. Everyone knew perfectly well from the start that *any* critique of it would generate a storm of controversy (which was, of course, precisely what participants had wanted and still wanted). In the same issue of the *Layman* that broke the story was an article called "Get Set for the Spin." In fact, the general assembly council's executive director called in a public relations firm to help prepare for rebuttals from feminists. These were "imaged" in several ways: "All we did was attend a conference." "How could we have known that controversial statements would be made at the conference?" "It's unfair to take a few quotes out of context and smear the entire conference with them." "What's the big deal over one conference that would have faded into oblivion had the *Layman* not made such a fuss about it?" "We didn't worship the goddess Sophia; we just pointed to an attribute of God that's biblical (found in the wisdom literature of the Old Testament)." "We live in a broad church, not a fundamentalist one." "The Lay Committee is trying to take our agenda away from us by imposing another one." "You can't believe anything you read in the *Layman*; everyone knows it distorts the truth."[89]

One reply, suggested the *Layman*, might be that the speakers at this well-planned conference had hardly been passive bystanders. Not only had they not objected to anything said or done, after all, but they had actively participated, hooting and cheering.

This controversy did not make the cover of *Time*, true, but it did generate several articles in its theological equivalent among Protestants, *Christian Century*. In the opening comments of one, David Helm[90] discussed the importance of dialogue between people in conflict. According to him, both the *Layman* and its Methodist counterpart, *Good News*, had prevented dialogue. And the reason was very simple: Both publications were run by conservatives. Clearly, Helm supported the goals of this conference. Sophia, he pointed out, refers to nothing alien or blasphemous. A personification found in the Book of Proverbs, it refers to a "master architect" working with God to create the world. For Helm, moreover, women had good reasons for rejecting traditional Christian theories of atonement. Women have had difficulty, he noted, with the idea of God's self-sacrifice "in which we should participate by way of imitation," because it can lead to self-abnegation and can "shackle women in abusive relationships."[91] He did criticize female participants for playing "the gender card" and critics of the conference for playing "the heresy card," but only because both strategies would lead men to reassert their own control by silencing the conference. As a self-appointed mediator, nevertheless, he claimed that each side considered itself under attack. Besides, most people did not align themselves with an extreme position on either side. The church should be ready, therefore, to learn from feminists even as it tested their ideas according to scripture.

The next article was by Catherine Keller,[92] a "self-avowed and practicing" member of the United Methodist Church who teaches at Drew University's Theological School. After studying "process theology" under the guidance of John Cobb, she took up "constructive theology." This latest form of systematic theology includes a "deconstructive" phase as well as a "creative" one in the interest of "reconstructing" the history of Christian doctrines. Although Keller uses many hermeneutical tools, the most important is probably feminist ideology in the form of goddess ideology. It is one thread, at any rate, that links her first book with all later ones.[93] Keller attacked a retired bishop's statement that had recently appeared in the *United Methodist Reporter* under the headline "Sophia Theology Worst Heresy in 1,500 Years of Christianity." For Keller, all criticisms of the conference were the destructive acts of a "radical conservative" minority. Observing that the board of global ministries had received thousands of protest cards, she dismissed their importance on the grounds that those on the political right had long attacked this board for its stand on social justice. As far as she could tell, the controversy was a battle between evangelical right wingers and liberal pluralists. And she did not shrink from calling on the reforming zeal of John Wesley (the male founder of Methodism) to legitimate the "activism" that had inspired the conference.

But much of Keller's article was a response to more specific attacks on the conference. She defended it for turning to "women's experiences" as a way to celebrate "the sacredness of women's lives as reflecting the image of God in which we are all created."[94] Responding to attacks on liturgies held at the conference, she observed that critics had taken words out of context. Yes, they had used specifically female images for God, she continued, but anyone could find those words in the Song of Songs. Besides, she added, these liturgies never actually mentioned a goddess.

But one image in particular, Keller knew, had provoked hostility. Even though participants had carefully referred to God's *sophia* (wisdom), many had almost certainly been thinking about a goddess named Sophia. Why else introduce a Greek word to replace the common English one? Given "their allegiance to the goddess 'Sophia,' participants catapulted their rhetoric well beyond commonplace themes of women's equality. Instead, they heralded a more radical agenda: to promote a new religion with a new god."[95] The more precise reference was to a goddess, not a god. According to Keller, of course, that was nonsense. "What goddess," she asked rhetorically, "Whose goddess?" No one, she explained, had ever intended to introduce a goddess into Christianity: "Sophia advocates have chosen to remain within the hermeneutical force field of the Hebrew and Christian texts."[96] Somehow this defence does not amount to much; anyone who reads a transcript of the conference can see that the delegates had either explicitly or implicitly gone far beyond the "force field" of Christianity and embraced that of Sophianity.

Observing that real goddess ideologues have dismissed Sophia as a "mere cosmic handmaid of Yahweh" or "the inner feminine of a dominant masculinity,"[97] Keller discussed the history of *sophia* in

more detail. She emphasized that the word refers to nothing more
than an attribute of God, a mere female metaphor for the Holy. In
fact, she argued, it was the heresy hunters themselves who had created the goddess Sophia. This goddess was "their projection, their
construction, their obsession. This fantasy of the Mediterranean
fertility goddess Sophia allows them to relegitimate the rather
un-Methodist and immoderate concept of heresy. By itself, the 'fem-
inist/womanist/lesbian' omnibus may provide them a scapegoat,
but not yet a heresy."[98] That, for Keller, was what it all came down
to. There was no heresy, only a right-wing plot that involved neuroticism and scapegoating.

It is easy now to misunderstand the word "heresy." It has become
a dirty word. People associate it with "blind faith," rigid conformity, authoritarian intolerance, implacable cruelty, and – maybe
worst of all – failure to value "diversity" or "pluralism." In the pluralistic atmosphere of postmodernism, of course, the whole idea of
heresy (and therefore, not incidentally, of truth) seems ludicrous. If
nothing can actually be either true or heretical, it follows that anyone who warns against either must be doing so for some sinister
ulterior motive.

Keller used several arguments against those who had called the
conference heretical. For one thing, she claimed, the rhetoric of heresy has nothing to do with the compassionate language of Jesus. Yet
in actuality, the language of Jesus was very nasty when addressed to
his adversaries; he used the rhetoric of hypocrisy and evil, not
merely of error. For some reason, people prefer to think of Jesus as
"meek and mild," conveniently forgetting his habit of throwing
savage rebukes at those who disagreed with him. This sugary image
of Jesus owes much to what nineteenth-century critics called the
"feminization" of Christianity (as distinct from the "muscular"
Christianity that they hoped would attract men). Not surprisingly,
therefore, Keller was happy to perpetuate this feminized image
of Jesus.

Not satisfied with theology, Keller appealed to psychiatry. According to her, in effect, "heretic" is just another word for "scapegoat"
or "victim." Why talk about heresy now? According to Keller,
(male) people are afraid of change, (male) pastors are afraid of losing their parishioners, (male) leaders are afraid, "perhaps above
all," of losing the "traditional modes and symbols of masculine
power." Two explanations never occurred to Keller. One is that

men do have legitimate reasons for their fear. The other is that some (male and female) Christians actually care about the faithful transmission of their tradition from one generation to the next. Ironically, moreover, Keller created her own scapegoats: everyone who disagreed with her. And even though she made a brief allusion to the fact that some women create their own orthodoxies, she defiantly dismissed as a patriarchal plot, or "backlash," all criticism of women.

Finally, Keller resorted to a clever (but distorted and opportunistic) version of communication theory. Those who warned of heresy, she claimed, were really trying to "silence" their opponents and thus prevent debate. Actually, the reverse was true. The fact is that heresy trials *are* debates. The judges hear *both* sides. Therefore, these trials can hardly stifle debate. On the contrary, they provide a forum for debate. Why a forum? To ensure that debate is carried out fairly and responsibly (because a church, like every other institution, can function effectively only when participants pay attention to "due process") and to ensure that debate, once argued thoroughly, does not go on indefinitely (which could fracture a community just as surely, and with far more devastating results, than a clean break). Those who fail to convince an ecclesiastical court are no longer burned at the stake; they either accept the court's decision and remain within the church or reject it and move on. Heresy trials allow communities to clear the air and then get back to the business of living. What Keller advocated, on the other hand, would do nothing to improve communication. On the contrary, it would result in a lengthy war of attrition. In this kind of struggle – what amounts to siege warfare – victory usually goes to those who are prepared to hold out the longest. Keller consequently concluded with a call to arms:

> The power of women can appear overwhelming to men and
> some women who are on the defensive. As women gain power,
> men who feel that their own power is diminished are tempted
> to stress the 'her' of 'heresy.' As for feminists, we sometimes
> collude with our own victimization, both by succumbing to the
> ways of fear and defensiveness, and by resorting to orthodoxies
> of our own making with their complementary conservative here
> sies. But we have gained some wisdom during the decades: we
> know that we are not helpless victims of a patriarchal plot;

that the strength of the backlash is testimony to the power of
our accomplishments; and that our diversity gives us an unprecedented healing force especially as we mature in solidarity with
like-minded men. If we remain together and vigilant, this movement of the Spirit will remain strong.[99]

A third article in *Christian Century*[100] by Joseph Small and John
Burgess was the only one to take the heresy accusation seriously.
And even they were very careful to preface their criticism of the
conference by noting the importance of "challenging and expanding horizons." Their main point, however, was that not even those
who do all this challenging and expanding are immune to critique.
Those who claimed that conference liturgies had indulged in nothing more than the use of imagery from the Old Testament, according to Small and Burgess, were (at best) naive. Far from attacking
this imagery out of context, critics did so precisely by placing it *in
context*. The liturgies had failed to make clear, they argued, the distinction between wisdom motifs in the Old Testament and God's
ultimate self-disclosure in the New Testament – which is to say, in
Christ. And who could accuse them of hair-splitting?[101] "The New
Testament proclaims 'Christ the power of God and the wisdom of
God' (I Corinthians 1: 24), *not* wisdom as a divine manifestation
apart from Jesus Christ."[102] Small and Burgess pointed out, moreover, that the frequency of references to Sophia and their specific
formulations clearly indicated something way beyond metaphor.
One liturgy at the conference, for example, had concluded as follows: "Through the power and guidance of the spirit of wisdom
whom we name Sophia." As for the "Ritual of Sunday," it had been
a parody of the Eucharist. Instead of consuming bread and wine, for
instance, participants had consumed milk and honey, and Sophia
"was the only one to whom thanks and praise were offered."[103]
This conference had a divisive effect, to say the least, on politics
within the Presbyterian Church (USA). Officials were incensed on
learning that $66,000 from the church had helped to pay for the
conference. They moved quickly, alerting churches across the country to what many were now acknowledging as heresy. They
reminded leaders of a duty to defend their doctrines, their constitu-
tion, and their *Book of Order*. One after another, congregations
called for a full investigation, passed resolutions calling for the discipline or dismissal of representatives at the conference, curtailed or

withheld funds from the denomination, and adjusted their budgets to contribute funds only for church programs that conformed to established theological principles. They threatened the general assembly council with judicial proceedings, moreover, unless it acted quickly and effectively against this "second Reformation." They included protest cards in the *Layman* for readers to tear out and send to ecclesiastical authorities.

Eventually, the church established one national committee to examine its participation in ecumenical gatherings and another to explore distrust between the national staff and local congregations.[104] At last, after at least fifteen years of dithering complacency, many people were taking the problem seriously. Not only had this conference indicated the return of an ancient goddess, after all: it had in addition indicated the return of ancient controversies over heresy. Not surprisingly, the *Layman* carried an additional article on gnostic heresies.

In its *Journal of the General Assembly*, the Presbyterian Church (USA) established the following recommendations: to publish all complaints that people had sent to national headquarters; to recommend ways of dealing with them; to clarify how officials had made them; to describe what actually happened during their presentation at the general assembly; and to describe the national council's response, a council that people had accused of complicity in the conference.[105] Although the general assembly voted nearly unanimously to accept the recommendations, it did so in a highly charged atmosphere. In the *Journal*'s preamble, readers discovered that several events had followed the vote: prolonged and repeated rounds of applause, two renditions of the doxology, various prayers, the joining of hands, hugging and kissing, and a spontaneous rendition of "Amazing Grace." According to the report, these events had moved many to tears. In the words of one spokesman, the Holy Spirit had enabled people to bring about "reconciliation."[106]

Just what were the terms of this reconciliation? The recommendations consisted primarily of politically expedient doubletalk. Although the authors admitted that the conference had provoked a crisis by introducing theology that was not in the Reformed (Calvinist) tradition or even the Christian tradition, they said, people should have seen this event within the historical context of Protestantism. There had been precedents within the Presbyterian tradition itself, after all, for rethinking theology and adapting it to the times. The use of imagination (including art, music, and literature) belonged to the theological task of expressing the truth of Jesus Christ in every age by engaging society in "conversation," critique, and reform. Human theological statements cannot be absolute, in any case, because only God can be absolute.

Those who convened the conference had originally intended to provide an opportunity for engaging in "dialogue," the report continued, not rewriting creeds. "Women theologians from 10 denominations, 12 countries, and 8 racial ethnic backgrounds were invited to address aspects of this theme as it pertains to God, Jesus, church, creation, community, and world. Other areas, such as family, sexuality, arts, language, ethics, work, and ministry were also included."[107] The recommendations affirmed, in other words, the importance of participation in (and the right of access to) ecumenical, cross-cultural, and interfaith "conversations" that, by definition, might challenge traditional beliefs and practices.

Moreover, the recommendations called for more theological convocations within the Presbyterian Church (USA) to be held annually just before the general assembly. Presbyterian theologians should address topics such as the church's position on atonement, incarnation, and language about God. Moreover, the church should publish and disseminate all forthcoming discussions widely. We would explain these recommendations in connection with the need for better public relations no less than for public accountability.

In its response to accusations of complicity, the national council discussed its role and responsibility. The council admitted a need for greater scrutiny of what the church's money was used for. In fact, the council admitted that it had been slow in its response to the protests of local churches (although it blamed this slowness partly on the turnover of members that year). Finally, the council admitted its irresponsibility in using undesignated bicentennial-fund money for a controversial project, allowing staff participation without adequate guidelines, and participating in theological and liturgical innovations that were problematic for many church members. In addition, the council took measures to ensure that this problem would not happen again.

Despite these conciliatory gestures, the council offered another spin on the affair by implying that no one could hold it completely responsible. There were many interpretations, after all, of what had gone on at the conference. Besides, there were many theological positions within the general Presbyterian one. Finally, the council appealed to freedom of conscience, albeit within "boundaries," and the continuing need for "dialogue" and ecumenical participation.

In another section, this *Journal of the General Assembly* more directly addressed the underlying problem.

> Presbyterian women who are our ministers and elders, who are ordained by our church, have been hurt by the assumption that they are not capable of critical theological judgement. A consequence of this controversy has been the impression that the church is indifferent to the pain and estrangement of women and has ignored the fact that women's concerns are not always welcome at the center of the church's life. We affirm that Scripture and Reformed speech about God include feminine and masculine images. We affirm in the strongest possible terms that the body of Christ is made up of women and men. God calls both women and men to ministries in the life of the church. An attempt to silence or marginalize any voices is not worthy of Christ's body. We reaffirm our church's commitment to solidarity with women, especially in the important task of thinking theologically.[108]

After asking again for reconciliation, the report concluded by calling on "the women of the Presbyterian Church to hear the depth of our hope and strength of our commitment that this will not be the last opportunity for ecumenical, cross-cultural, and interfaith conversation. We affirm the importance of women's voices and work in the church and the important task of developing and articulating our theology."[109]

Was this merely a masterpiece of double-talk? Was it something for everyone? Was it a definition of boundaries that all Presbyterian feminists and their supporters would have to take note of, at least for a while, because money and jobs were at stake? As if to mollify the critics, the report argued that the church's intention had been merely to explore new language, not a new god. "Just as clearly, however, conference presentations and rituals used language, including the term 'sophia,' in ways that imply worship of a divine manifestation distinctly different from 'the one triune God ... whom alone we worship and serve."[110]

In 1995, the Sophian contingent published a book entitled *Re-Membering and Re-Imagining*.[111] It tells the stories of women who attended the conference. Editor Nancy Berneking provides an apologetic explanation for this collection in the name of "imagination."

> Imagination, one of the gifts of a wildly imaginative Creator, helps us reach beyond the boundaries of what we know to embrace the possibilities of exploration. We are invited by the gospel to do that exploring within a community of differences, trusting that the community's process will lead to wisdom. The stories of the community of people who attended the Re-Imagining Conference call us to imagine what church can be. Evoking stories, listening and speaking, calling and recalling, remembering and re-imagining will all be necessary to build a community of faith where justice finds a home. Listen to the stories.[112]

Some of the stories are descriptive, recalling women's religious experiences at the conference. Others are defensive, telling their side of a controversy.

One contributor, Heather Murray Elkins, an associate professor of worship and liturgical studies at Drew University and an ordained United Methodist, did not attend the conference. At the last moment she had given her registration to another woman, but her name tag had remained at the conference. This worried her because of her own involvement in a similar controversy, one described at the beginning of this section in connection with Thomas Oden, who had found it necessary to leave a church service because of its polytheistic content. Elkins had arranged the printed liturgy of that service and presided with Reverend Cady at the communion table. According to Elkins, Cady had expressly pointed out in her lecture at Drew University the evening before that she would not use the word *sophia* as the name of a goddess. Oden had not attended this lecture. In any case, the church had vindicated Cady and Elkins. A jurisdictional joint review committee that consisted of liturgical scholars and bishops had analyzed the text of the service and pronounced it "orthodox."

But the church did not vindicate Mary Ann Lundy for her role in the Re-Imagining Conference. She begins her story by announcing that the church's general assembly council fired her. She states that the council questioned her extensively in February 1994 as part of its fact-finding procedure but did not follow due process. The charges against her were vague. And the church did not allow her to respond in a public forum. She blames the right wing of the church, which was still locked in conflict with the church's more liberal wing. In short, she became a scapegoat. Personal attacks and even physical threats had ensued as pressure mounted for her to resign. Even though many rallied to her cause, and even though the general assembly tried to arrange a reconciliation later that year, the church had not forgiven her. When some commissioners asked the assembly to express its appreciation for her eight years of service to the church, in fact, the assembly declared them out of order.

The saga of Sophia did not end in 1993. Between 16 and 19 April 1998, what was billed as a "Re-Imagining Revival" took place in St Paul, Minnesota, as a response to a conference that the World Council of Churches had convened in Harare, Zimbabwe, to mark the Ecumenical Decade of Solidarity with Women. According to Parker Williamson of the *Presbyterian Layman*, delegates included many of those who had been delegates to the original Re-Imagining conference and therefore did not represent most members of the Presbyterian Church (USA). Over the preceding five years, after all, the church had actually rejected the delegates' worldview, declaring it "beyond the boundaries" of Christianity. In fact, the church had begun to investigate the National Network of Presbyterian College Women for promoting lesbianism and theologies that rejected the doctrine of Christ's atonement.

Since then, other conservative Christians have set up websites that monitor syncretistic movements – mainly attempts to meld Christianity with neopaganism – within the churches. Although these churches had always opposed liberalism, they could now focus on a dramatic case study. Under "apostasy," for instance, one website[113] presents a five-page discussion of Presbyterian churches. It carefully distinguishes the Presbyterian Church (USA) from traditional Presbyterian churches in connection with its emphasis on the following topics: ecumenism (supporting the National Council of Churches and the World Council of Churches, both of which promote theological compromises in the name of Christian unity); modernism (promoting a "false social gospel" and denying the divinity of Jesus); abortion (supporting the Religious Coalition for Abortion Rights); homosexuality (ordaining gay men and women); feminism (actively promoting feminist causes such as "women's

spirituality," contributing $66,000 to the Re-Imagining Confer-
ence); paganism (inviting Starhawk, under the auspices of its Feminist Perspectives Committee, to address the San Francisco
Presbyterian Theological Seminary; actively promoting not only
Wicca but also goddess religion in general); and immorality (con-
doning rampant divorce, for instance, and even adultery). More
than most other Presbyterian churches, this liberal church supports
"charismatic renewal," which originated as an American movement in conservative Pentecostal churches.

Another five-page article from a closely related site[114] focuses
specifically on the Re-Imagining conference. First, it discusses the
churches that supported it. These included not only Presbyterians,
Methodists, Anglicans, and Lutherans but also Baptists, Catholics,
and even Moravians. Clearly something very powerful must have
united women – and continues to unite women – from such different traditions.

Then, the article discusses clearly heretical claims of delegates
such as Delores Williams ("I don't think we need a theory of atonement at all. I think Jesus came for life and to show us something
about life. I don't think we need folks hanging on crosses and blood
dripping and weird stuff ... we just need to listen to the God
within"), Virginia Mollenkott ("As an incest survivor, I can no longer worship in a theological context that depicts God as an abusive
parent and Jesus as the obedient, trusting child."), and Chung
Hyung Kyung ("My bowel is Buddhist bowel, my heart is Buddhist
heart, my right brain is Confucian brain, and my left brain is Christian brain"; "The Bible is basically an open book, and I want to add
the next chapter."). The site warns specifically against the lesbian
heresies of delegates such as Nadean Bishop, a Baptist minister who
believes that Mary and Martha were lesbian lovers, and Janie
Spahr, a Presbyterian minister whose theology is informed primarily by making love with her female partner.

The article concludes by discussing the claim that Sophia is not
merely a metaphorical reference to divine wisdom but a divinity
in "her" own right. This is why David Cloud notes that Sue Seid-
Martin identified Sophia with Jesus – whom Christians identify
with God. Cloud refers also to the following prayer, which was
addressed directly to Sophia: "Our maker Sophia, we are women in
your image ... Sophia, creator God ... shower us with your love ...
we invite a lover, we birth a child; with our warm body fluids we

remind the world of its pleasures and sensations ... Our guide, Sophia, we are women in your image ... With the honey of wisdom in our mouths, we prophesy a full humanity to all the peoples." As Cloud observes, this prayer owes at least as much to feminism and New Ageism as it does to Christianity.

From all this, we conclude that the Re-Imagining conference actually fostered polarization within the Christian world, in addition to polarization of the sexes. If it leaves a lasting legacy, it will probably be for Christian fundamentalism as a potent symbol of the continuing divide between religion and secularity, tradition and modernity, conservatism and liberalism, "us" and "them." In their own words, after all, the delegates actually confirmed the worst nightmares and the most heated rhetoric of the most fiery nineteenth-century revivalists.

6

A Hag for All Seasons:
The Ultimate Revolution

Mary Daly is an academic who taught radical feminism at Boston College. Her refusal to allow male students into her classes led to a lawsuit, which she and the college settled out of court.[1] This controversy led to her retirement. She made her reputation by attacking men, however, not ignoring them. In one of her best-known books, she states, "The divine patriarch castrates women as long as he is allowed to live on in the human imagination." The remedy: "The process of cutting away the Supreme Phallus."[2] Elsewhere, she writes that "Phallocracy is the most basic, radical and universal societal manifestation of evil, underlying not only gynocide but also genocide, not only rapism but also racism, not only nuclear and chemical contamination, but also spiritual pollution."[3]

Daly's implacable and relentless hostility to "patriarchal religions" such as Christianity, especially Catholicism, became the cornerstone of her worldview and therefore of her teaching (although she believes that every world religion is inherently patriarchal and therefore inherently evil).[4] She could have left Boston College, which is run by Jesuits, but she chose to stay and undermine the institution from within. At least she had the intellectual and moral integrity to leave the Catholic Church, however, which is more than we can say of many other feminist ideologues – including some of her followers, who remain affiliated with or even paid by churches that they despise, precisely in order to help destroy them. Ironically, Daly's worldview relies heavily on ways of thinking that are very similar in some ways to those of Catholicism and many other "patriarchal religions." If these ways of thinking seem unfamiliar, that is because Daly has inverted and distorted them.

To be sure, Daly is not a mainstream feminist. She calls herself, with good reason, a radical and a revolutionary. (She uses many additional labels for herself and like-minded feminists: "hag," "crone," "spinster," and so on. One of her most characteristic strategies, along with reversal and ridicule, is reclamation. She reclaims these labels from the linguistic oppression that men have supposedly foisted on women.) Despite her status as a radical, possibly because of it, Daly has become a feminist icon. Even those who disapprove of this or that aspect of her worldview, after all, see her as a touchstone. To paraphrase an old song from *Oklahoma!*, Daly and her entourage have gone about as far as they can go. Feminists can "situate" themselves somewhere along a continuum, in short, between Betty Friedan at one end and Mary Daly at the other.

In this chapter, we discuss Daly's worldview in connection with the biblical paradigm of return to paradise on (1) a personal level, (2) a collective level, and (3) a cosmic level. We continue with a discussion of (4) her admiring fans and (5) her ambivalent critics, concluding with (6) a moral critique of our own.

In the first three chapters, we discussed the biblical paradigm of return to paradise on a purely chronological basis: first paradise lost, then the Fall, and finally paradise regained. Our goal now is to discuss this paradigm at several levels of interpretation.

Apart from anything else, the Bible is a literary anthology that has shaped the West's collective imagination for thousands of years. In *The Great Code*, Northrop Frye[5] discusses biblical literature in connection with patterns, observing that some motifs – characters, symbols, stories – appear over and over again in various guises. Like their ancestors, post-biblical readers have traditionally applied these paradigms to everyday life in their own times. Among the most important and deeply embedded paradigms is that of return to origin.[6] It appears several times within the Bible itself and several more times in the stories that Jews and Christians have told about themselves as individuals, communities, nations, and so on.

In the Bible, our primeval ancestors originate in a garden paradise called Eden. Due to disobedience, they enter the chaos and conflict of history but then learn through tradition (Torah or Gospel) how to live in harmony with others and with God. Finally, our eschatological descendants will end up once again in paradise (to be called the Messianic Age or the Kingdom of God). Or: The Children of Jacob (Israel) originate in Canaan. After an ugly episode in which they sell one brother to passing traders, they migrate to Egypt, endure slavery, and then escape into the desert. There, they learn how to live in harmony with others and with God. Finally, they end up once again in Canaan (now called the Promised Land). Meanwhile, every one of us originates as a soul in paradise. We enter at birth into the chaos and conflict of daily life, albeit through no fault of our own, but learn through experience and tradition how to live in harmony with others and with God. Finally, we will end up once again in paradise (known as Eden, the World to Come, Heaven, or whatever).

This paradigm, despite many variations, is so deeply embedded in Western culture that it has found expression in countless religious and secular ways. One example, ostensibly at the individual level but also, just below the surface, at several additional levels, is the story of a young girl in *The Wizard of Oz*. Dorothy lives in Kansas. Then, because of her inability to understand the meaning of home (she has also had a nasty bump on the head), she enters the chaos and conflict of Oz but learns through her new friends about the importance of wisdom, compassion, and courage. Finally, she ends up back home in Kansas. This same story is one that Americans have traditionally told about themselves as a nation. Their ancestors, as either refugees or entrepreneurs, find themselves in the primeval paradise of a New World. Then, due to some flaw in the new society (such as the practice of slavery), they enter the chaos and conflict of history but learn how to live in harmony with themselves (and, in most versions, with God). Finally, their descendants will end up once again in a either a millenarian paradise or a technological utopia.

Back now to Daly. In the story of her own life, even as someone who rejects the biblical tradition root and branch, Daly recapitulates this paradigm. And she argues that every woman can experience, and should experience, the same journey to self (and Self) realization. In Daly's case, the outline of this journey is clearly indicated by her books. Each is a landmark on the way back to a female "homeland." She often comments on her earlier books, in fact, from precisely this point of view.

Daly was born to a Catholic family in Schenectady, New York, in 1928. In 1950, she graduated from the College of St Rose with a BA in English. Two years later, she received an MA in English from the

Catholic University of America in Washington, D.C. But Daly was interested primarily in theology and philosophy, which led her to a PhD in religion from the School of Sacred Theology at St Mary's College in Notre Dame, Indiana. What she really wanted, however, was a PhD in Catholic theology, something that no university in the United States offered to women. The University of Fribourg, in Switzerland, did. A new university by European standards, it was state run and therefore could not legally prevent women from any course or degree program. Daly stayed there for the next eleven years and earned several degrees, including doctorates in both theology and philosophy. In 1966, she became an assistant professor of theology at Boston College, a Catholic school, and published her first book, a study of French philosopher Jacques Maritain. But it was her next book that made her name.

In *The Church and the Second Sex*,[7] written as a radical response to *The Second Sex* by Simone de Beauvoir,[8] Daly reveals what has become her lifelong fascination with language. She calls for a *"castrating* of language and images that reflect and perpetuate the structures of a sexist world."[9] At this stage, though, she still hopes that women will be able to reform the Catholic Church – or any other "patriarchal religion" – by building on beneficial aspects of tradition. As outsiders, she believes, women must be well equipped with defiant "courage to be" (an expression that she borrowed from Protestant theologian Paul Tillich)[10] in the face of patriarchal evil.

Beyond God the Father[11] marks a watershed in Daly's life, because she realizes that women cannot be both Christians and feminists. Reform, she now believes, is impossible. God's maleness is inherent in Christianity and provides the ultimate legitimation for sexism in all forms. Like her, women must choose between rival worldviews. She urges them to follow her in rejecting Christianity and replacing it with her existentialist interpretation of religion – one that amounts to her version of feminism. She describes her journey:

I moved on to other things including a dramatic/traumatic change of consciousness from "radical Catholic" to post-Christian feminist. My graduation from the Catholic Church was formalized by a self-conferred diploma, my second feminist book, *Beyond God the Father: Toward a Philosophy of Women's Liberation*, which appeared in 1973. The journey in time/space that took place between the publication dates of the two books could not be described adequately by terrestrial calendars and maps. Experientially it was hardly even a mere trip to the moon but more like leap-frogging galaxies in a mind voyage to further and further stars. Several women-light years had separated me from *The Church and the Second Sex* whose author I sometimes have trouble recalling.[12]

Even though Daly still acknowledges a few sources of hope for Christian women, she makes it clear that these are too few and too late. Worse, they might lead women to "premature reconciliation" with men. "What is at stake," she claims, "is a real leap in human evolution, initiated by women."[13] Even at this early stage in her career, Daly believed that trying to reform Christianity would be a waste of time. "The appearance of change is basically only separation and return-cyclic movement."[14]

In *Gyn/Ecology*,[15] she once again attacks traditional religions as patriarchal and therefore not only deceptive but also oppressive. They impose a false ideal of femininity on women and thus undermine the self-esteem and autonomy of women. Much of the book illustrates this thesis: foot-binding in China, widow-burning in India, witch-burning in Europe, and so on. But in this book she moves beyond attacking to advocating. What was somewhat vague in *Beyond God the Father*, her notion of what women could actually do once they moved beyond Christianity, is now both more sophisticated than it was and less focused on the West. Clearly, she has reached a new stage in her own life. For Daly now, the true spiritual journey of women is a radical revolution that will lead them to establish a new language (or at least a specialized vocabulary) of their own, a new religion of their own, and a new society of their own. If these goals are not revolutionary, what would be? "My purpose," she writes, "is to show that the women's revolution insofar as it is true to its own essential dynamics, is an ontological spiritual revolution, pointing beyond the idolatries of sexist society and sparking creative action in and toward transcendence."[16]

Of great importance to Daly from this point on, moreover, is language. Why language? Because every language is a symbol system. Creating their own language and "naming" things from their own female perspective (instead of continuing to let men do so from their male, alien, and hostile perspective) will empower women more fully than any tinkering with the existing social order. Naming things is tantamount, Daly says, to creating them. What she wants to rename, or recreate, are not ordinary things such as vegetables or furniture, of course, but those things that a patriarchal society has associated lin- guistically with women, femaleness, and femininity. Her preoccupa- tion with language takes several forms: inventing new words (such as "snools" for men and also for women who have not yet seen the light), re-appropriating or reversing of others ("hag," "crone," and "spinster" now being good words instead of bad ones), and empha- sizing still other words by capitalizing them or modifying their spell- ing ("Realization," "Weaving," "Spinning," "Be-ing," "Sin-tactics," "Crone-ology," "Gyn-ecology," and so on).

Ironically, Daly's approach is like that of traditional religion – most obviously that of Eastern religion but also that of Western reli- gion[17] – in some important ways. For her, as for the ancient gnostics (but also for Hindus and Buddhists), life is a journey from igno- rance to enlightenment and therefore to liberation. The big differ- ence, of course, is that enlightenment and liberation are possible only for women.

At this time, moreover, Daly discovered that she could communi- cate with animals – that is, with "familiars" (which medieval clerics associated with witches) such as cats – or that they could commu- nicate with her. Animals, she believed, were like women outsiders (relegated to the background) in a patriarchal world (the fore- ground).[18] At this time, moreover, Daly travelled to Crete and dis- covered what she construed as remnants of a pre-patriarchal society, one that worshipped a great goddess and represented her symbolically as the labrys (a double-headed ax). Both discoveries led to her later preoccupation with returning to some primordial form of paganism – that is, a goddess cult – as the ideal way of replacing all existing traditional religions.

In *Pure Lust*,[19] Daly continues her attack on men (making no consistent distinction between men and patriarchy, the ultimate and universal source of evil) and the ways in which they deliberately and systematically torture women. At the same time, she elaborates on the history of various religions by identifying three ages (ones that correspond precisely, ironically, to the temporal paradigm of Western religions): that of a primordial women's religion under the aegis of a great goddess, that of current "phallocentric" religions under the aegis of sinister gods, and that of a re-emerging women's religion under the aegis once more of a great goddess. Only a goddess can represent female power and female essence, she insists, so even the Virgin Mary is merely a pale and distorted (but still evocative) remnant of the great goddess in primeval society. Women must therefore rediscover their own past.

Admirers have called *Websters' First New Intergalactic Wickedary of the English Language*,[20] which Daly wrote with Jane Caputi, a "final triumph of naming."[21] Words are of primary importance in a book that arranges them alphabetically. By "wickedary," Daly refers to a "wicked and Wiccan dictionary," which interprets Wicca as goddess ideology. It provides women with a religious vocabulary that opposes and reverses not only Christian theology but also Christian morality. "The entire conceptual systems of theology and ethics, developed under the conditions of patriarchy, have been the products of males and tend to serve the interests of sexist society."[22]

As usual, Daly relies heavily on clever word games and alliterations, fanciful etymologies, and mythological associations. These new words (or old words with either new or reasserted pagan meanings) allow women to experience their own female essence without imposing on them the Christian and therefore patriarchal baggage of Original Sin. On the contrary, Daly reminds women that "Be-ing is Sinning."[23] To be women in any meaningful sense, according to her, requires them to repudiate traditional religions such as Christianity by rejecting not only their theological abstractions but also their moral principles. Daly is no innovator in this sense, because the founders of religious movements often make similar claims about the virtue of overturning virtues.[24] Part of Daly's appeal for women, probably, is the childlike fun of transgressing. When adults indulge in transgression for its own sake, though, the results can be devastating. During the 1920s and early 1930s, for instance, new converts to National Socialism surely found it very satisfying to transgress against bourgeois propriety by openly attacking Jews in the newspapers or in the streets.

Of particular importance for those who want to know how Daly understands her own life is *Outercourse*,[25] a kind of non-fictional bildungsroman. Daly looks back at her journeys, both spiritual and professional – the latter includes the protracted conflict at Boston College over her policy of refusing to admit male students to her classes.[26] She sees each stage (marked by the publication of a book) as one of increasing participation in what she has come to call "Be-ing" (another word that she borrowed from Tillich, who usually referred not to God but to the more abstract "ground of being").[27] In view of the fact that Daly sometimes calls this phenomenon "Self," it is not surprising that she reveals a preoccupation with the evolution of her own self and the selves of other women.

Quintessence[28] is Daly's theological magnum opus. In it, she uses metaphysical terms to describe her own attainment of enlightenment, one that all women can attain. Her focus is now on the ontological essence, or quintessence, of womanhood more than the illusory and sinister essence of manhood. But her approach to this topic too is like that of traditional religion – most obviously that of Western religion – in some important ways. For Daly, as for Jews and Christians, life – that of the cosmos no less than that of the individual or the collectivity – is ultimately and eschatologically a return to primeval origin; the life-cycle on all three levels – personal, collective, and cosmic – is a circle (even though Daly prefers to call it a "spiral"). The big difference is that everyone has access to the restored paradise of Judaism and Christianity, but only women have access to that of radical feminism. In *Amazon Grace*,[29] Daly repeats much of what she says in *Quintessence*.

On the social or historical level, Daly relies primarily on other feminists to demonstrate that women once enjoyed a golden age in paradise under the aegis of a great goddess before succumbing to the myriad forms of patriarchal oppression. Listen to the preface of *Pure Lust:* "This book is being published in the 1980s – a period of extreme danger for women and for our sister the Earth and her other creatures, all of whom are targeted by the maniacal fathers, sons and holy ghosts for extinction by nuclear holocaust, or failing that, by chemical contamination, by escalated ordinary violence, by man-made hunger and disease that proliferate in a climate of deception and mind-rot. Within the general context of this decade's horrors, women face in our daily lives forces whose intent is to mangle, strangle, tame and turn us against our own purposes."[30]

Daly is supposed to be a philosopher, not an archeologist or social scientist, but her work consists mainly of ranting dualistically about the innate and eternal evil of men or raving essentialistically about the innate and eternal goodness of women. Not surprisingly, she refers over and over again to men as "they" or "them" and to everything negative as "their" creation. For her, men are the archetypal "others." She traces every basic problem, at any rate, to "the living out of patriarchal myth. They live it out through their technology as well as through their religion, their art, their societal structures, their economies and their wars. It's always the same. Their wars are the same. Its infinitely the same. 'Getting their big gun off,' as Valerie Solanas said."[31] (Solanas, who clearly influenced Daly,[32] was the woman who tried to murder Andy Warhol after establishing the Society for Cutting Up Men [SCUM] and writing its manifesto.)[33]

And if that does not sound dualistic enough, listen to this: "But I'll argue," Daly replies in defence of her own essentialism,

> that whether or not they're inherent, the fact is that the differences between men and women are there, even if it's just through millennia of conditioning. I, of course, think it's inherent. But even if it were cultural, the fact is that this [my feminist point of view] is the way to go if you're biophilic. What I'm concerned with is the war between biophilia and necrophilia. It's love of life versus hatred of life. Necrophilia translates directly into love of death, or loving the dead – actually f—-ing corpses. And in general, patriarchal culture is necrophilic, fixated on hatred of life and love of death.[34]

Or try this: "'Human being' I got rid of a long time ago ... I wanted to liberate 'human beings' and I found out that the whole thing was fallacious because there's a false inclusion, as if there were greater similarity between women and men than there is difference."[35]

In one of her interviews, she opines that "insofar as our experience gives us images, certainly the female is more appropriate [than the male] for talking about nurturing life, loving and creativity on every level. If you have to choose between the two, female obviously is better [than male]. And I don't even have to choose between the two; I mean, the other isn't worth consideration any more. It's just hanging all over putridly."[36] So men, as such, are "false inclusions" in the human race. In other words, they are subhumans – or would be if Daly did not believe that women had transcended the human race altogether and were therefore superhumans. Just as dualism goes along with essentialism, it goes along also with hierarchy.

But the future is already dawning. Daly has envisioned a way to restore the golden age of women: radical separation from men. She makes this clear in several ways. First, women should be physically and psychologically separate from men. "I don't think about men," she told one interviewer (forgetting for the moment that she attacks men virulently at other times and therefore obviously thinks about them a great deal). "I really don't care about them."[37] Moreover, she says, women should be reproductively separate from men. And they can do so, she adds, by resorting to parthenogenesis.

This story differs significantly from its biblical prototype and its spinoffs in that women, according to Daly, are not responsible for their own fall into the chaos and conflict of history and therefore have no need to repent. They do need to learn something, sure, but that is not how to live in harmony with others. The archetypal "others," after all, are men. What women need to learn, says Daly, is more about themselves (and about a goddess who, however, is really a hypostatized female Self).

For the time being, Daly believes, women must do whatever they can to resist the (male) forces of darkness and death. What can they do? For one thing, they can rewrite history. When asked about the archaeological evidence on goddess cultures indicating that ancient goddesses presided over some very brutal societies, Daly's first response is evasion. Those societies – the ones that practised slavery, forced labour, human sacrifice, or whatever – were actually patriarchal. "Prepatriarchal would be really ancient – gynocentric ... I'm talking about a *really* woman-centered society of which we have no direct memory."[38] Her next response is even more revealing. "But as Monique Wittig said, 'If you can't remember, invent.'"[39] And when all else fails, she says elsewhere, women can throw tantrums: "Our Rage enables us to recognize the reality which is hidden by the foreground. It triggers our breakthrough to seemingly esoteric, yet utterly available knowledge."[40] Elsewhere in the same book, she shows how radical feminists can transform grief – the grief of all women at all times and in all places – into both rage and hope.[41] Hope through rage.

This brings us to Daly's main interest: the ontological and metaphysical implications of this story – that is, the same story but on a cosmic instead of a personal or collective level.

Ironically, Daly's view of cosmic evolution is very similar to that of the Christian theologians whom she despises: paradise lost, history (patriarchy), and paradise regained. Within history, therefore, women are voyagers, pilgrims. "Ignoring phony promises of a 'better future,' Wayward Women *will* to find and create a Real Future. We Time-Space travel beyond archetypal deadtime and reach deep into our own Memories, our Deep Past, to Dis-cover the roots of an Archaic Future, beyond the limits of patriarchal time."[42]

As the protagonist of the novelistic *Quintessence*, Daly "leaps" ahead in time to a "Lost and Found Continent." There, or then, she sees the future and female world order. Not surprisingly, the inhabitants – spiritually evolved women – are republishing one of her books with a new commentary on what now amounts to scripture! Discussing history, they tell Daly about the courageous and wise women of her own time who had foreseen momentous changes and acted accordingly. At this point, Anowa (Daly's new friend) presents readers with a mythic – which is to say, a thinly veiled – version of the feminist movement's eventual triumph. Guided by their innately female prescience, radical feminists from all over the world make plans for a new order. They learn new skills, leave home not only with their daughters but also with their "familiars," and embark on a collective odyssey to some new land. The functional equivalent in some ways of mythical Atlantis, this new land has emerged from the sea because of the geological upheavals. These occurred as a result of global warming – that is, as a result of patriarchal evils such as industrial pollution, genetic engineering, and technology run amok.

In *Amazon Grace*, Daly once again leaps forward in time to the lost continent. She leaps back too, and meets a philosopher of the nineteenth century: Matilda Joslyn Gage. Daly's point, as usual, is that "Wild Women" must continue their heroic struggle against the "patriarchal" world order. Her enemies include the usual list of suspects: religious fundamentalists, Bushites, and men in general. Her chapter titles too include the usual vocabulary: "The Courage to Hear, Name and Create Nemesis," "The Self-Destruction of Patriarchy and the Re-Emergence of Female Power," "Seeing through Phallocracy's Biggest Lies and Reversing Its Rotten Reversals," "Keeping Hell at Bay," "We Can Stop It Now," and so on.

We discuss some of these topics more fully elsewhere in connection with two other levels of interpretation. Our point here is merely that Daly has gradually come to see her own journey through life as the paradigm for those of women as a class or community (the collective level) and that of either self or Self (the cosmic level).

This daydream about an all-female world makes sense to Daly, who is a lesbian in real life. "Female Presence is powerful," says her fictional counterpart, "and it is expanding everywhere. The world today is Gynocratic and Gynocentric. Many people Survived the Earth changes, and the Quintessential requirement for survival was and continues to be knowing and profoundly rejecting the evil of patriarchy and acknowledging one's own part in it. Such knowledge is inherently transformative. The Earth's transformation has required that her inhabitants grow through profound psychic changes."[43] In other words, no men (or even women who reject conversion to the true faith) need apply for admission.

Women's goal, she says, is "to Realize our own biophilic reality."[44] By the word "biophilia," of course, she refers to the love of nature and the ability to commune directly with it. This ability is innate in women, she says, but hidden or thwarted by the patriarchal culture of men. "The Wanderers of this Work meander through three Realms of Spheres, coursing first through Archespheres, the Realm of Origins; then through Pyrospheres, the Purifying Realm of Fire; and last through Metamorphospheres, the Realm of grace-less/Graceful transformations."[45] Of course, this biophilia is now in short supply. Patriarchy has carefully hidden it from women, who must therefore rediscover it. In a future paradise, in other words, they will restore quintessence to its rightful place. Daly describes this once and future paradise as a "Lost and Found Continent" or an "Archaic Future" world in which only (or almost only) women will live. Men will disappear just as patriarchy will wither into nothingness, she adds, because the male principle has no ontological status. The presence of men in history, therefore, has been an ultimately inconsequential aberration.

Men in Daly's work are essentially demons, beings whose function is to do evil. Demons are ontologically and metaphysically evil. This is how Daly explains her claim that men not only afflict women in order to attain other ends – to assert personal or collective power over women, to exploit their labour, or what have you – but also and ultimately to revel in doing so as an end in itself. They truly want to afflict women. To put all this another way, Daly externalizes evil. Ironically, the fact is that Christians have tended to do the very same thing by making the chief demon – Satan, Lucifer, Mephistopheles, or (simply) the Devil – a supernaturally sinister being who actively tempts people to thwart the will of God. Daly's point is that doing evil is not a possibility inherent in all humans but only in male humans.

In this way, Daly's worldview is unlike that of Christianity. For Christians, after all, sin is a defining feature of humanity and therefore of every human being. Not even the most misogynistic Christian has ever argued that only women are subject to sin and therefore that only women are in need of salvation through Christ. For Daly, however, the seven deadly sins – another motif that she borrows from Christianity – belong to men alone:

> *Gyn*-Ecologists will recall that the processions of demons who try to block our way are the personifications of the Deadly Sins of the Fathers ... These are: Processions (deception); Professions (pride); Possession (avarice); Aggression (anger); Obsession (lust); Assimilation (gluttony); Elimination (envy); Fragmentation (sloth). All of these sins, manifesting themselves as demons, appear and reappear in the course of the metapatriarchal Journey. The primary demons to appear in *Gyn/Ecology* were/are Processions, followed closely by Professions and Possession. These were/are warded off/defeated by the Spinning Spinsters and Amazing Amazons, Hags, Harpies, Crones, and Furies of the Gyn-ecological phase of the spiraling Journey ..."
>
> In *Pure Lust*, the main demonic attackers are Aggression and Obsession. As the voyage continues, the Furious Fighters of these infernal molesters increase in numbers and in spirit force. Moving onward, upward, downward, we enter, now, New Realms ... Recognizing that deep damage has been inflicted upon consciousness under Phallocracies' myths and institutions, we continue to Name patriarchy as the perverted paradigm and source of all social evils. Our Naming/analysis becomes even more direct and urgent as we confront the advanced stages of nuclearism ... Refusing to be distracted by the fathers' perpetual State of Emergency their frenzied foreground fixations the proud Prudes who prance through the Realms of Pure Lust fiercely focus on Fury, Firing/inspiring our Selves and each Other with renewed commitment to the cause of women and all elemental be-ing ...[46]

But Daly's main interest is not in the horrors of history under patriarchy or even in the joys of paradise lost but in the joys of paradise regained. What links paradise lost and paradise regained is the female principle, or essence. In *Pure Lust*, she describes this cosmic female principle: "She is the shimmering Substance – Real Presence – that shines through appearances. She is the root of connectedness in the female Elemental Race. In mythic terms 'Archimage' Names the Triple Goddess."[47] Elsewhere, she calls it "biophilia" or "quintessence." For the Pythagorean philosophers of ancient Greece, she says, this was "spirit that fills the universe and gives it life and vitality. In ancient and medieval philosophy, Quintessence Names the fifth and last or highest essence, above fire, air, water, and earth."[48] For her, it "is Universal and Cosmic harmony that transcends and includes this integrity of the five elements."[49] She sees quintessence as realization. "Quintessence ... Names the unifying Living Presence that is at the core of the Integrity and Elemental connectedness of the Universe and that is the Source of our power to Realize a true Future – and Archaic Future."[50]

In an interview, Daly says that "the word I commonly use for the ultimate reality – I won't say 'God,' that's dead – is 'the universe.' I'll say 'spirit' but meaning a principle of life within all being, including rocks. And I have used capital 'B,' *Be*-ing, to represent the *verb* God."[51] When asked about her philosophy of "sensitivity to and a connectedness with the life force or presence in everything, animate and inanimate," she responds, "Yes, and it's a recognition of our connection with the entire universe – microcosm and macrocosm. We don't necessarily have to know everything that's out there – that isn't the point – but it's a sense of striving for connectedness and a *joy* in that. I look at the sunset here, or the experiences of nature, aesthetic experiences, and experiences of creativity and of the power of fighting, overcoming fear."[52] Trendy words and capital letters aside, this is warmed-over "perennial philosophy"[53] for feminist New Agers.

The term "Mother Nature" takes on new meaning in the works of Daly. She means it literally, not merely metaphorically. Nature – this refers not only to plants and animals but also to the universe as a whole – is female. Moreover, everything in nature is interconnected. This is why only women, she says, can ever attain true communion with nature or even with each other. In addition, it establishes the context for her version of feminism. Just as women suffer under patriarchy, so do all other natural beings. "We grieve for our Foresisters and our contemporary Sisters who seem to be lost in the diaspora over time and space. We grieve for those burned alive ... We grieve for our sisters who have been raped, sexually abused and harassed, beaten, driven insane, mutilated, murdered. We grieve [likewise] for our Sisters the Animals who have been tortured in laboratories, hunted down, destroyed by agribusiness. We grieve for our Sisters the Trees who have been slaughtered and for our Sisters the Seas, the Lakes, the Rivers that have been polluted."[54]

Women "in touch with Quintessence ... become more than ever like trees and like angels. Extending our roots deeper, we are free to expand and participate in the creation of the universe."[55] "Memory-Bearing Women are Here and Now charged with the responsibility of blasting open the walls that have been installed in our minds/souls and opening the way to participate in the Biophilic Elemental Integrity of the Universe which is Quintessence."[56]

Known for her linguistic playfulness, Daly is just as metaphysically playful – so much so that many readers must find it hard to differentiate her philosophy from science fiction. It involves both space travel and time travel, at any rate, whether literally or metaphorically (or both). At the cosmic level, every woman's journey requires her to "spiral" from one "galaxy" and one "element" to another. By the time that women discover their true selves (centres, in some passages, or essences), they have left the realms of earth, water, air, and fire. They are "voyaging in the Fifth Spiral Galaxy" (wherever and whenever that is). This is the realm of "ether,"[57] which Daly associates with "the ground or field from which the other Elements arise."[58] Some readers might be reminded of the mystical voyages in such patriarchal religions as Judaism.[59]

Reviewers of Daly's books routinely introduce her with superlatives such as "the eminent theologian, philosopher, and author,"[60] "the leading philosopher-theologian of the radical feminist movement,"[61] or even "the most important Radical Feminist thinker around."[62] According to Susan Bridle, "if you want to speak with someone unrelentingly passionate about liberating women from the confines of patriarchal institutions and unabashedly zealous about establishing a feminist vision, all roads lead to Mary Daly."[63] At the American Academy of Religion's conference in 1987, Daly spoke to a vast, admiring crowd. This event took on the atmosphere of a religious revival meeting. The crowd broke into a chant: "Mary, Mary, Mary, Mary."[64] According to Manfred Hauke, a German dictionary of theology cites Daly more often than anyone except Jesus.[65] As Catherine Madsen points out, Daly's work is "heady stuff, especially for young women testing their intellectual powers for the first time or for women long frustrated in their search for feminist allies. The very intimacy of the language makes it unanswerable; one must meet it either with resistance or with conspiratorial glee."[66]

At the academy's conference in 1998, one panel was about Daly. Although some panelists pointed out that Daly tended to forget about race, class, sexual orientation, "ableism," and age,[67] most did not. They celebrated Daly and her newest book, *Quintessence*, but also paid tribute to her life and work. According to Carol Anderson and Jennifer Rycenga, co-chairs of the Lesbian Feminist Issues and Religion Group, feminists owe a "debt of gratitude to her activism." Daly spurred women on to "greater levels of engagement," they exclaimed, by her "empowering hag presence." They described the event as "lively and playful."[68] But they went further. "It was amazing for us to see how Mary Daly herself (not to mention her work) remains a 'litmus test' for radical feminists, distinguishing clearly those who recognize and remember her unparalleled contributions to feminist theology from those who have forgotten.[69]

Mary Hunt offers the following encomium: "I thank Mary Daly ... for the brilliant humor, deep commitment to women's well-being and explicit concern for animals and the planet."[70] Animals and the planet, yes, but not men. "I am proud," writes Rycenga, "to be immediate and immoderate in my anger and rage at patriarchy and immediate and immoderate in loving and valuing women."[71] When Daly "speaks to the Grief that awakened women share," opines Diane Rae Schulz, "I could not help but cry out 'YES! She truly knows how I feel!' ... We can't be reminded too many times of the challenge we all face in transforming the current nightmare into a positive future that worships the Life Force."[72] "I have been an avid participant in her [Daly's] spiraling voyage," writes Schulz, "beginning with my 'discovery' of *Gyn/Ecology* a few years ago. As I often do when I become enthralled with a book, I located all the author's published work and read them in sequence, becoming increasingly excited as Daly's unique and brilliant expression of ontology grew, unfolding more delightfully with each book. She is not only a crafted weaver of words, but a creatrix of language, as well as undeniably logical, all qualities that satisfy my intellectual longing."[73]

At the same conference, Carter Heyward, the first female Angli-
can priest and someone who supposedly promotes the teachings of
Jesus, said not a word about Daly's attitude toward men:

Well, Mary, your work was Fire among us in the twentieth century. It caught on. It burned. It bothered us and made us hot,
and fierce and dangerous. Most of all, it encouraged us. There
were Christian priests, pastors and ministers like myself who,
because of you, Mary, knew very early in our professional
sojournings that God the Father was a necrophilic overseer of
nothing but Lies. And a number of us Harrowing Harpies spent
much of our lives speaking this Truth in a thousand indifferent
ways to our Sisters who for a thousand different reasons – some
good, some not so good, but all real, reasons – were in the
church. Being a Radical Feminist Christian seemed as much like
an oxymoron to many of us as it did to you, I suspect. Year
after year, I stayed, we stayed, those of us who did stay in the
churches, to help those who needed to leave find their way out
– often through your books – and to help those who needed to
stay find the courage to stay on their own Elemental Feminist
terms, making no peace with their own or others' oppression.
Thank you for your Creative Courage, Mary, which not only
made many of our lives easier – in or out of the church – but
also, I am sure, in some cases possible. Your work was literally
a life-line.[74]

Daly's admirers are not exactly put off by the dream of an all-
female world, even one that women attain by deliberately preventing male births. "While not all women would agree with the idea of
living out their lives in a place inhabited only by women, her supporting evidence of the condition of life on Earth at the end of the
millennium, particularly the condition of life for women, makes
one take pause."[75]
    Daly herself has admitted that enemies would inevitably call her
books "anti-male,"[76] but she does not care. On the contrary, she
tries to legitimate that as self-defence. If people think that she is
anti-male, in short, then so be it. But here is the point: her "theology" is propagated by what purports to be a mainstream trade pub-
lisher, HarperSanFrancisco, not a radical press supported only by
true believers. (This is the same press, incidentally, that published

the works of Marija Gimbutas and of Riane Eisler, who popularized Gimbutas in *The Chalice and the Blade*.) No one can dismiss Daly effectively, therefore, as nothing more than a marginal or "kooky" figure. Even among feminists who disagree with her, almost all are prepared to cite her work, and many are prepared to defend her. Despite her own sense of radical apartness, despite her implicit assumption that the only true feminist is a lesbian feminist,[77] despite the slightly veiled condescension of some other feminists, Daly has become a significant force in mainstream feminism. She gives poetic potency to the avant-garde.

However, some feminists, such as Helen McNeil, have suggested that Daly is more trouble to feminists themselves than she is worth. Among the problems that these critics cite are the following: Daly's dualism, or sexism (her implacable hostility toward men); essentialism (her relentless glorification of women); metaphysical speculation; comparative suffering (her habit of ranking forms of oppression); anglocentrism (her exclusive focus on the English language); logocentrism (her exclusive focus on words rather than other linguistic units); theoretical orientation (her withdrawal from political activism); and, in other parts of the world, her misunderstanding of non-Western religious traditions.[78]

A few feminists have acknowledged that Daly's dualism and essentialism have created or exacerbated problems for both sexes. "The fallout from [her] revengeful explosions," writes Anne Doherty, "does not encourage social or emotional reconciliations between women and men. Still needed for victims of a mutually demeaning sexist past is a healing dialogue. Hopefully, we can begin to learn together that affirmation of one sex does not require degradation or rejection of the other."[79] But Doherty was writing in 1980. Since then, ideological feminists and some egalitarian feminists have found it politically expedient to condone or at least ignore Daly's sexism.

Even those who acknowledge these problems – among them very serious ones, to say the least – often find ways of excusing her. Some argue that Daly's dualism – they seldom refer explicitly to sexism – represents a mere phase in the evolution of a new and better society. This might or might not be so, but we can hardly use history to support the notion that reconciliation is likely to follow polarization. Others argue that Daly's challenge to traditional forms of religion will result in better ones. Even Virginia Mollenkott, who calls Daly sexist, tries to get her off the hook. She ends up justifying Daly's sexism with a "nevertheless": "Unfortunately, Daly herself is rather brutal in her contempt for male-to-female transsexuals, male homosexuals, lesbians who are not sufficiently 'woman-identified,' and more or less everybody who [is] not a radical/Lesbian feminist ... Nevertheless, Dr. Daly is voicing the most passionate challenge Christianity is likely to receive in many years. Theologians, take note!" Mollenkott's position is based on the notion that ends can justify means.

Consider an interesting historical analogy. There are those (both Jews and Christians) who point to the obvious historical fact that the State of Israel would not have come into existence had it not been for international guilt over the Nazi Holocaust. The assumption is that good came out of evil. But the conscious or unconscious implication is that, somehow, Auschwitz was "worth it." Theologians such as Elie Wiesel have correctly pointed out that this makes a mockery of both ethics and theology; only a thoroughly contemptible God would allow six million people to be brutally murdered in the interest of some greater good. If good comes out of evil, in short, it does so accidentally. Rejoicing in that is not the same thing as deliberately planning evil in order to bring about that good. Nor is it the same as deliberately ignoring, tolerating, or even excusing evil in the name of that good. Instead of supporting feminism, apologists for Daly's radical feminism bring even mainstream feminism into disrepute.

Despite her call for wholeness, Daly's thought is firmly based on a pervasive dualism: man the evil victimizer versus woman the virtuous victim. Like every dualist, she sees all of human history as a titanic struggle between "us" and "them." "Mary Daly's thesis," writes Mollenkott, "is that the 'normal mode of existence of the patriarchal male' (by her definition, *every* male) is a sado-masochistic, split consciousness, which is totally unable to relate to the inner mystery or integrity of the Other, and which has for centuries sapped women of their native strength ... She implies throughout [*Gyn/Ecology*] that men are irrevocably inferior to women and therefore irrevocably intent on destroying women. Because she assumes that for men, anatomy is destiny, Daly is deeply sexist."[80]

Helen McNeil writes that "for Daly, society (inevitably patriarchal) often appears to exist solely to give structure to male hatred of women. *Gyn/Ecology* abjures androgyny as a goal, and mocks those women who hope for partnership with what Daly, quoting Robin Morgan, sardonically calls the 'exceptional' man. Whatever Daly's personal politics, Gyn/Ecology is an anti-social book. Also, despite its concluding call for women to Spook/Speak, Spin and Search, Gyn/Ecology is obsessed with the enemy, less a book about women than a book about what men do to women."[81] In short, Gyn/Ecology indicates that women will transform their worlds only by triumphing over men.

Some feminists are put off by Daly's metaphysical claims. "Despite her insistence upon the constructed-creative character of these symbols and visions," writes S.G. Daveney, "Daly, no less than [Elisabeth] Shüssler Fiorenza and [Rosemary Radford] Ruether, refuses to understand such feminist perspectives as merely alternatives to male-construed interpretations of reality ... Daly argues for the validity of feminist visioning on the grounds that it participates in and corresponds to ultimate reality."[82] Marsha Hewitt makes the same point: "Daly's feminist philosophy at best is capable of providing only an abstract unity *among* women at the expense of the concrete differences that exist *between* women."[83]

Paradoxically, Daly continues to see herself as a peaceful partner of "Mother Earth" even as she speaks of herself as a dragon slayer. In short, this high priestess of feminist ideology uses the language of war and appropriates the imagery of warrior women but refuses to name herself a warrior. Consequently, she accepts no responsibility for her own warlike behaviour. This anomaly is possible, of course, only because she conveniently projects all negativity onto the external world (that is, onto men). As in all dualistic (ideological) worldviews, the source of evil is out there, not in here.

Is it a mere coincidence that the very first page of Daly's *Pure Lust* has a drawing of a butterfly's shadow at the centre of a spiral leading to the butterfly itself? Obviously, Daly sees the shadow as woman's old self, which she has left behind. But the shadow is not gone. According to a more appropriate interpretation, the butterfly has not yet recognized that the shadow is really part of itself. Women must still name the shadow and reclaim it. Yet the butterfly is gentle and fragile, so Daly's metaphor is not very illuminating. After all, her talk of "Furious Fighters" really suggests a woman with a gun pointed at the head of a man. The fact is that Daly shares with many other feminists the view that women are inherently morally superior. That is because, she argues, women are

connected through their "spinnings" to others and can thus experience "the intense joy of woman-identified bonding."[84] They are
linked not only with their sisters, in fact, but also with the basic elements of earth, air, fire, and water, with the rhythms of stars, sun,
and moon.

The penultimate implication of Daly's work is the complete separation of women from men. Every discussion of relations between
men and women is by definition a political one. Consequently, one
way to deal with the pervasive tyranny of men is simply to withdraw from their patriarchal institutions and establish institutions or
communities for women alone. In such communities, separatists
maintain, the "nurturant, life-giving qualities that allow men to
oppress women under patriarchy are thus turned toward each other
and used to create a new kind of society."[85] If men are the class of
enemies and women that of victims, then women would logically
have to withdraw from male society, establishing their independence. By this of course they mean independence *from men*. Not all
feminists actually say this, but intentionally or otherwise, the logic
of their arguments often implies it. Even if this advice were practical, however, there is still the moral problem of defining all men as
oppressors. Does the end justify the means? On what basis can we
be so naively optimistic? Does hatred leave a lasting legacy to future
generations? Can we learn nothing from the legacy of nationalist
hatred in Europe?

The ultimate implication of Daly's work is the decimation or elimination of men. Even women who choose to live in a separate society,
after all, might still bear sons. In that case, they would have to live
with an anomaly. But if sons are demons, how could these women
bear them in the first place? Daly credits Sally Miller Gerhart with
the answer.[86] For the sake of logical consistency, ridding their world
of demon men would mean ridding it of men altogether. And this, of
course, would involve women in some very un-biophilic activities. At
the moment, for example, they would have to abort their sons after
amniocentesis, or they would have to use cloning or avoid sperm in
other ways. In the future, they might find it more palatable to rely on
parthenogenesis, a high technology that produces females but no
males. (It is surely not coincidental that Daly calls *Pure Lust* the
"parthenogenic daughter" of her previous books.[87])

In any case, Daly resorts to a new double standard. When an
interviewer criticized women, Daly agreed with the criticism but

excused women "because their lives are so empty and they've had no opportunities. Because their self-image has been so damaged. I can go on and on about the damage that has been done to women under patriarchy."[88] Indeed she could, and does. This particular passage indicates that Daly is not nearly as radical as she would like to believe. The ploy, blaming men for whatever is wrong with women, is common. Margaret Atwood, the best-selling – and therefore mainstream – Canadian author, has made the same point. When a reviewer observed that her book, Cat's Eye,[89] is critical of women, Atwood responded that unattractive features in her female characters represent not so much a critique of women but a critique of the patriarchal culture that makes them that way. But Atwood, unlike Daly, must have realized that she had inadvertently undermined her own moral vision, and added, "I wanted to deal with the idea that women somehow are more morally wonderful than men. There is no gene for moral wonderfulness. To buy into that is to be back in the nineteenth century."[90]

Blaming men for women's faults raises a larger question: Can we assume that patriarchy – which is to say, men[91] – are morally responsible for everything that is wrong with the human condition? At what point must women take responsibility for their own behaviour? Now that the rhetoric of equality has begun to subside in some circles, the rhetoric of sexual differences has re-emerged, only now the differences are all in women's favour. What these women dislike about themselves, if anything, is whatever they can explain away as the result of cultural conditioning in a society created by men. In connection with men, they turn this reasoning upside down. What these women dislike about men (just about everything) is innate. But what they like about men (if anything) is merely the result of cultural conditioning – that is, the impact of feminism. These men are what we call "honorary women."[92]

Aside from the methodological problems of essentialism and determinism, we challenge this mentality on both logical and moral grounds. To say that human nature – our innate characteristics – can be either good or evil makes nonsense of any moral system, because good and evil make sense only in terms of the free choices that we make as informed and competent people (as distinct from sin, which is an ontological category and might have little or nothing to do with good and evil). If women were "innately good," they would surely deserve no credit for it. Similarly, if men were "innately evil," they would surely deserve no blame for it. But instead of drawing the logical conclusion that society should protect men from their own dangerous impulses, radical feminists succumb to both self-righteousness and misandry. This is not only immoral but also illogical.

Daly uses the same double standard. Many women are amused by her overtly sexist remarks such as those about cutting off penises. These "jokes" might seem acceptable in some circles because men have made sexist jokes about women. It would be considered profoundly offensive, of course, to make jokes about cutting off women's genitalia.[93] To justify this double standard, women must assume that men deserve abuse – including legal abuse.[94] In moral terms, however, this is not justice but revenge.

Apologists for radical feminism claim that in recent years it has become self-critical. Feminists now generally recognize, for example, that their predecessors did not pay enough attention to the needs of lesbians and women with sexual identities "in transition," women with physical or mental "challenges," women of ethnic or racial minorities, and women in poor countries. Few critics have summed up Daly's baneful effect on women as brilliantly as Catherine Madsen, who writes, like Daly, as a lesbian:

> [Daly's] idiosyncratic language has done what idiosyncratic language will do and created a sect; it is extraordinarily easy for women to use her terms to dismiss other women as insufficiently radical. She has added heavily to the lexicon of female contempt for the male anatomy, an amusing pastime as long as one doesn't object to forming the habit of contempt ... One can't explain to a totally committed person what it is to stand suddenly just outside the commitment: to see it comparatively, to recognize that the euphoric hopes and unheard-of liberties are becoming a new set of repressive boundaries, that the giddy bravado coming out of one's mouth has begun to sound like other forms of bravado one does not want to indulge. When I was thirty or so – an insignificant library clerk desperate with pent-up intellectual strivings that seemed to have no good outlet in "Womyn's Culture" – I encountered a book on the Nazi effort to delimit a German aesthetic; I recognized in one breath the parallels to my own earnest effort to develop a lesbian aesthetic, and woke to the prolonged intellectual hangover that

anyone suffers who has given too much of herself to a political movement. One does not want, after a shift like that, to be invited into a conspiracy; one does not want to bolster one's serious love of a woman with sneering caricatures of men. One begins to mistrust altogether the impulse toward purity.[95]

But recognizing the dangers of this "impulse towards purity" represents self-criticism only in a limited sense. For one thing, feminist ideologues such as Daly believe that moral problems have resulted from not taking their theory to its logical conclusion, not from any contradictions or forms of blindness that might be inherent in that theory itself. They acknowledge moral problems only if they affect women, moreover, not men. Very few feminists question the basic premise of feminist ideology, including goddess ideology, that human history is nothing less than a conspiracy of men against women. There are good reasons for subjecting Daly to a critique on the grounds of sexism, but few feminists do so. (Even when they acknowledge sexism on the part of women, they usually explain it as "reverse sexism" to suggest either that it is not real sexism or that it is excusable for some reason.)

Many feminists explain that Daly has merely been expressing anger. But there is a profound difference between anger and hatred.[96] Anger is an emotion, a spontaneous response to people or (immediate) situations. Hatred, on the contrary, is not primarily an emotion but a *result* of anger or fear. A sustained response to (groups or classes of) people or (long-term) situations, it must be deliberately fostered (reinforced culturally). One function of any dualistic worldview is to identify and legitimate hatred of the "enemy." The hatred that Daly consistently expresses can easily be explained in historical terms, but it cannot be *excused* in moral terms without distorting the whole notion of morality.

Daly's attitude represents a glorification of women as victims. This presents several ethical problems. In the first place, being a victim per se confers no moral status. That is, we can deduce from it neither intrinsic moral superiority nor exemption from moral standards. When *The Man in the Glass Booth*[97] made its screen debut in 1975, survivors of the Nazi death camps picketed the movie theatres that showed it. They were outraged by the fact that the protagonist experiences so much guilt over his own survival that he poses as a Nazi in order to have himself punished. Although his guilt is clearly neurotic, the survivors, as victims, believed that the film was calling their innocence into question. They felt disturbed by the implication that guilt cannot be contained in neat categories. It would be the height of insensitivity to argue this matter with a survivor. Nevertheless, the fact remains that we can deduce nothing whatsoever about the moral status of victims from the behaviour of their victimizers.

It is true that victims should not be blamed for the actions of their victimizers; yet they surely should be held accountable for their own actions. One must assume that Jews are neither more nor less inclined toward malice than any other group of people (although for historical and cultural reasons they have, at least until recently, been less likely to express it through violence).[98] If being a victim has any value at all, that value must originate in two lessons that any victim can learn: not to be victimized again, and not to victimize others. Unfortunately, most victims never learn the second lesson. The victims of child abuse, for example, often become child abusers themselves.

To conclude, it should be clear by now that Mary Daly has had a profound impact on feminism. Even those who dislike this or that aspect of her work still acknowledge her as an icon and bask in the glow of her fame – or, better still, of her infamy. Moreover, Daly has had a profound impact on religious communities in this part of the world – even on the particular one that she has rejected, we should add, in view of the civil war that is now raging between radical and conservative Catholics. Says Mary Hunt about Daly's influence, "We are decades into that work, with lesbian feminist values of community, inclusivity and equality finding their way into religious discourse in virtually every major tradition."[99] Almost every mainstream religious community – certainly Jewish[100] and Christian ones – must now accept, modify, or reject a worldview that originated with Daly but is now ubiquitous.

Those communities – liberal ones – that accept the new worldview must by definition replace their traditional sources of authority. The ultimate revelation now comes from Daly and her direct or indirect followers, not from God. This means discarding anything in divine revelation that does not correspond to feminist revelation, not the reverse. At what point does an explicitly religious but implicitly political worldview become, in effect, a quasi-religion?

The same question applies to people who reject religion, even the new religion. At what point does their explicitly political and explicitly secular worldview become, in effect, a quasi-religion?

We have already suggested in the prologue that feminist ideology, whether it uses or rejects explicitly theological terminology, *is* a quasi-religion – that is, a secular (or implicit) religion. In a review of *Beyond God the Father*, Lois Livezey says much the same thing (albeit approvingly). She writes that Daly's book "is not ... just a critique of the sexism of the Christian faith. It is also an attempt to articulate an alternative faith, the faith of feminism. 'Feminism,' writes Mary Daly, 'is not merely an issue but rather a new mode of being.' Throughout the book and especially in the final three chapters ... she describes the women's movement as the locus of newly emerging religious meanings. These are expressed, in this interpretation, in the revelatory 'courage to see' ... in the ontological and existential struggle of being with nonbeing ... in the soteriological role of the women's movement as the context of self-actualization and as the catalyst for the revolution of the social order ... and in the theistic symbolization of God as 'Verb' or 'Be-ing.'"[101]

If Livezey is correct, and we think that she is, then Daly's version of feminism corresponds almost perfectly to quasi-religion (although a perfect correspondence to any theoretical "ideal type" would, of course, be impossible). If agnostics can belong to traditional religious communities for a wide variety of social, political, and other secular purposes, after all, then they can just as easily belong to Daly's religious community. Some might have authentic religious experiences, at least in theory, but some might not. What links those who do and those who do not (feminist ideology) is more important than what separates them ("thealogical" terminology).[102]

Daly has withdrawn from the Catholic Church, in short, but many of her disciples – Heyward being one obvious example, and Rosemary Ruether[103] – have chosen to stay on. They meet the classic definition of infiltrators: those whose explicit or implicit intention is to undermine a community or institution and thus promote revolution. To argue that Daly is nothing more than an embarrassing anomaly or a marginal anachronism would be to indulge in wishful thinking at best and intellectual dishonesty at worst.

7

Gynotopia:
Goddess Ideology and Misandry

Goddess ideology is more than a bunch of ideas, theories, or symbols. It is a coherent worldview. But apart from anything else, of course, it is a gynocentric one in reaction against an androcentric one; history revolves around women instead of men. But neither gynocentrism nor androcentrism, per se, is a major problem; individuals and communities can be preoccupied by their own needs and problems, after all, without hating others. Misandry and misogyny, however, really are major problems; they undermine human solidarity morally, socially, and politically. What sort of worldview fosters the link, then, between either gynocentrism and misandry or androcentrism and misogyny?

In this chapter, therefore, we (1) apply the nine characteristic features of ideology, as outlined in the prologue, to goddess ideology, and (2) show how these characteristic features have generated misandry.

Even the word "ideology" is contentious because of its political connotations. These are always pejorative, but the precise meaning depends on who uses the word. Karl Marx understood ideology as a collection of assumptions that most people leave unexamined. Taken together, these assumptions make the way things are seem to be the way things have always been, should be, and even must be. In other words, real change is impossible. Marx attributed these hidden assumptions to "false consciousness," which the ruling classes invent and propagate through a symbolic and institutional "superstructure" in order to perpetuate their own power and privilege. They hoodwink the masses, in effect, by preventing them from understanding their own reality and thus from rebelling against it – that is, from seizing the "modes of production." For Marxists, ideology is always "their" sinister plot to perpetuate hegemony over "us."

This definition has given rise to another, albeit closely related one. For non-Marxists, the word "ideology" can refer to any systematic re-presentation of reality (by "exposing," "unmasking," "subverting," "transgressing," or "deconstructing" traditional assumptions) in order to achieve specific social, economic, or political goals. The names of participants in this political drama change from one ideology to another, of course, but the polarization remains, amounting to a titanic struggle between "us" and "them." According to this definition, the word "ideology" can refer not only to worldviews on the political right, such as nationalism or racism, but also to those on the political left. In that case, Marxism itself is an ideology. (It is an ideology according to the first definition as well, ironically, because Marx himself made several unverifiable and dubious assumptions about both human nature and history.)

The ideological branch of feminism derives partly from Marxism (but also from Romanticism). For ideologically oriented feminists, "gender analysis" is the precise counterpart of "class analysis" and the "patriarchy" of the "bourgeoisie." They want to abolish culturally propagated notions of masculinity and femininity, believing that these are insidious notions subconsciously carried, as it were, by both men and women as "false consciousness" – but in the interests only of men.

With this second definition of ideology in mind, consider its nine distinguishing characteristics in feminist ideology, especially goddess ideology: (a) essentialism, (b) dualism, (c) hierarchy, (d) collectivism, (e) consequentialism, (f) utopianism, (g) revolutionism, (h) selective cynicism, and (j) quasi-religiosity.

Essentialism refers to the idea that people have inherent qualities. These qualities link them together as groups, similarities being more important than differences. Here, essentialism relates to the belief that "we" are inherently good. For ideologues in general, the gold standard, both biologically and morally, has become femaleness. For Sophians in particular, that means adding symbols of femaleness to Christian or Jewish theology. For Mary Daly and her disciples, it has meant *replacing* symbols of maleness with those of femaleness – and ultimately withdrawing from contact with men or even cooperating with nature in the destruction of men. But women have not deified themselves and rewritten history in a cultural vacuum. This mentality has been supported increasingly by both popular and elite culture since the 1970s. Some women have been demanding complete reproductive and parental autonomy for themselves. Scientists have been trying to make it possible through technologies such as parthenogenesis.[1] One scientist has even declared men unnecessary for "human" survival.[2]

Dualism is simply the other side of that essentialistic coin. Although it refers properly to both "them" and "us" (just as essentialism does), it focuses attention on the latter (just as essentialism focuses attention on the former).

Dualism should not be confused with duality, which refers merely to the presence of two forces – usually in harmony with each other as in the relation between yin and yang. Dualism refers, on the other hand, to two forces in *conflict* with each other. In religious forms, it sees the cosmos as a battleground between two rival deities and therefore between the two human communities ("us" versus "everyone else") that worship them. Although dualism probably originated in central Asia as Zoroastrianism, it exerted a profound influence on both ancient Judaism and ancient Greek philosophy. It exerted a profound influence on Christianity, therefore, which drew heavily on both sources. We define dualism as a worldview in which "they" (sinister aliens or "others") are inherently evil and must be either destroyed or marginalized.

In *Beyond Power*,[3] for instance, Marilyn French describes not one but three forms of dualism: culture versus nature, transcendence versus immanence, and maleness versus femaleness. Though not goddess ideologues, she and other feminist ideologues have adopted a similar worldview. It is not only gynocentric (glorifying femaleness) but also misandric (opposing maleness). These feminists blame men not only for our "necrophilic patriarchy" or "rape culture," after all, but for the idea of transcendence too, and indeed for everything else that they believe is wrong with the world. They define "otherness," or "alterity," explicitly in terms of maleness. For all intents and purposes, therefore, men are innately evil[4] (even though that would be a contradiction in terms, because moral agents must be free to choose evil).

A characteristic feature of dualism is the conspiracy theory of history. We use the latter term here in connection with feminist or goddess ideology, not in connection with history itself. We suggest that patriarchy originated with the profound changes brought on by economic or technological innovations, not with conspiracy. These innovations included domestication of the horse and development of agricultural technologies such as the iron plough and irrigation. Climate change was sometimes an additional factor, provoking mass migrations and the resulting conflicts. In coping with so much stress, tribal traditions broke down. Chaos at the collective level provoked ambition at the individual level. Alpha males – chiefs and early kings – recognized no authority but their own. They consolidated their power over male rivals, who imitated them by consolidating their power over low-ranking men and women. Even though androcentrism actually solved some problems, therefore, it generated major new ones (including those arising from urbanization, social stratification, and war). Eventually, the world's great religions responded to rampant injustice. What feminist and goddess ideologues call "patriarchy," in short, arose from the pressing need to solve new problems, not simply from misogyny, greed, or sheer malice.

Hierarchy is an inherent feature of any worldview that relies on essentialism and dualism. Assuming that good is better than evil, after all, it makes sense to rank "us" (as defined by essentialism) higher than "them" (as defined by dualism). Given the notion that women are good and men evil, moreover, it follows that the former are superior and the latter inferior. For many goddess ideologues (and other feminist ideologues) it would be just as unthinkable to acknowledge their own worldview's hierarchy as to acknowledge its dualism and essentialism. After all, they project those things onto men as aspects of "the male model" that produced patriarchy. Nonetheless, almost everything that they have said or written about their great goddess, in connection with either the lost golden age or the restored one, says directly or indirectly that men (with the exceptions, possibly, of male converts to feminism) are inferior to women. This is hierarchy.

Attempts at sexual equality in the goddess movement are evident in neopagan communities (such as Wicca) that worship both gods and goddesses but not in those that worship only goddesses. The latter group attribute every problem of the modern world, without exception, to the alleged shift from peaceful, natural, and egalitarian societies under the aegis of their goddess to warlike, unnatural, and hierarchical societies under the aegis of one or more gods. Leaders routinely attack specifically masculine attributes of patriarchal gods, for instance, although they sometimes honour these very attributes in their own goddess. Supremacy is desirable in the goddess, apparently, but undesirable in a god. Motherhood is desirable in the goddess, similarly, but fatherhood is undesirable in a god.[5]

Collectivism is inherent in any worldview that involves a collectivity – a formal or informal community – but not every collectivity places the same emphasis on this perspective. No society can say that the needs of society should always take priority over those of individuals, of course, without succumbing to totalitarianism. Those that do succumb reduce individuals to nothing more than the means to collective ends. Many societies, including our own so far, have tried to balance the needs of individuals with those of groups and society; one or the other might take precedence, depending on circumstances, but the goal is to maintain a balance. Feminist and goddess ideologues have tried another solution. They have argued that the needs of their own community should take precedence over those of other individuals, other communities, and even the larger society. They are collectivists, like other ideologues, because they focus exclusively on the needs and problems of their own collectivity. But that collectivity is not the nation.

Consequentialism characterizes several schools of ethics and law. We refer here specifically to the belief that ends can justify means. Some means do not require any justification, because they are morally acceptable, but means that would ordinarily be unacceptable do require justification. Almost all people consider killing justifiable, for instance, in the specific context of personal or collective self-defence; it is never good, of course, but it is sometimes a necessary evil or the lesser of two evils. Even though killing is sometimes justifiable, we suggest, spreading hatred toward any group of people is never justifiable. It is hard to see how doing that is an acceptable form of self-defence.

At the very least, we must all avoid double standards. If women justify themselves on therapeutic grounds for indulging in fantasies of male inferiority or evil, as Daly does, then they have no reason to be shocked if men – who obviously need collective therapy at least as much as women do – justify themselves on the same grounds for indulging in fantasies of female inferiority or evil. In this context, remember *The Protocols of the Elders of Zion*. Not long after its publication in Russia in 1905, this book was revealed in court as a forgery. Nonetheless, it has been translated into many languages and been reprinted many times. It purports to divulge the secret minutes of a Jewish organization plotting to take over the world. Anti-Semites, no doubt, find this fantasy profoundly therapeutic, but that does not make it scholarship, nor even an acceptable alternative to scholarship.

Utopianism is not merely about the improvement of society. It is about perfecting society, creating a perfect society. One problem with utopia, a secular version of paradise, is that it can account for neither human finitude nor the complexity and ambiguity of human existence. Another problem is the continuing existence of dissenters – those who, if left alone, would question or even attack the project.[6] Noble rhetoric and visionary ideals notwithstanding, those who offer us utopia have never yet delivered the goods; perfection eludes us now, as it always did in the past. This historical datum should not prevent people from continuing to seek better ways of organizing the world, but it should prevent them from succumbing to the naive and arrogant belief that *their* utopia will do what no other utopia has ever done: create a paradise *within* history. No feminists make stronger claims about a coming feminist utopia than Daly and the goddess ideologues. Their entire project, after all, is premised on the possibility of "restoring" an earlier state of perfection.

Revolutionism is an inherent feature of utopianism and therefore of ideology as well. Some feminists, including goddess ideologues, make no secret of their revolutionary intentions. Because their branch of feminism relies so heavily on Marxism, especially the "Frankfurt school" of critical theory, we should take seriously its revolutionary rhetoric.[7] For Marx and several generations of his followers, revolution was something that took place in the streets. For Marx's more recent and more sophisticated heirs, though, revolution is something that takes place in churches, universities, courthouses, legislative assemblies, and even venues of popular culture. This is certainly true of goddess ideologues, because the sort of change that they propose is a matter not merely of degree but of kind. They do not foresee a violent revolution, to be sure, but they do foresee a religious one that would generate social and political revolutions. Like Marxists of all stripes, they intend to bring about a new world order (social, economic, and political), a new age, a new paradise under the aegis of their goddess: "Their language is not always explicitly eschatological, but it is always implicitly eschatological."[8]

For some feminists, especially religious ones, the call for revolution is too alienating. So they do what Marxists have always done:
use the less scary rhetoric of reform. Marxists themselves used the
notion of a "front" to disguise and shield their political activities.
One example was the infiltration by Marxists of cooperatives that
Father Divine had set up for his religious community.[9] In connection with the movement that demands a "restoration" of Sophia to
Christianity, for instance, goddess ideologues use religious reform
as a front for religious revolution. They are at least honest by
openly rejecting Christianity in order to start fresh.[10]

Selective cynicism is yet another aspect of dualism and essentialism. Cynicism, in its modern sense and taken to its logical conclusion, means that *everyone* is up to no good. This position can
have a moral value, actually, even though it can be socially desta-
bilizing (let alone psychologically depressing). After all, it is inherently egalitarian. But some ideologues do not take cynicism to its
logical conclusion. They apply it to "others" but not to themselves.
This gives rise to the double standards that we have discussed in
two other books.[11] But consider the double standards that we discuss in this book. If supremacy is a positive attribute of the goddess,
for instance, why is it a negative attribute of gods? And if men are
really worshipping themselves when they worship one or more god,
as goddess ideologues have claimed, then are women who worship
their goddess not worshipping themselves? Actually, as we have
shown, some feminists are very open about doing precisely that.[12]
Jews and Christians have long understood idolatry as self-worship
in disguise, of course, and secular writers in our time often dismiss
religion itself as nothing more than self-worship in disguise. Either
way, self-worship is less than admirable, and if it is wrong for men,
it is surely wrong for women. But goddess theory in the West relies
on a double standard; its advocates lose no more sleep over moral
inconsistencies than they do over historical anomalies.

Quasi-religiosity is of particular importance here for two reasons. Some secular forms of feminism, we suggest, are implicit religions. To put it another way, they are secular religions. We prefer
the latter term, because it highlights the apparent paradox of being
both non-religious (in popular parlance, secular) and religious. Many
are overtly secular[13] but nonetheless function in almost all of the
ways that traditional religions do. The only religious function that
they lack happens to be the defining feature of religion: mediating

what religious people experience as the sacred. They are secular religions, therefore, not religions.

Other secular religions are overtly religious, on the other hand, but nonetheless function in almost all of the ways that secular – especially political – ideologies do. We suggest that the goddess movement (though not neopaganism in general) is overtly religious with its myths, rituals, pilgrimages, and so forth. It nonetheless functions in almost all of the ways that other political ideologies do. Both provide adherents with the sense of belonging to a community, a coherent picture of the way things are (along with the way things were and the way things will be once more), a moral code, personal and collective identity, personal and collective purpose, times and places that are set off from ordinary ones, authoritative writings, initiation, and so on.

Consider those who join ideological communities. Like religious initiates, ideological ones attend "consciousness raising" groups, read magazines, watch talk shows, and so on – activities that lead to conversion. Like religious initiates, ideological ones experience liberation from oppressive illusions and see the possibility for the first time of salvation – which is what evangelical Protestants call "being born again." Like religious initiates, ideological ones cannot fully experience the new without first breaking with the past – what Christians call "dying to sin."[14]

Some women have come to identify themselves heavily with goddesses and even to think of themselves in effect as goddesses. But it is unlikely – although no one could ever prove this – that members of this movement have suddenly discovered the sacred in any sense that would be recognized by phenomenologists in the field of religious studies (although "thealogians" might well do so in churches that are prepared to elide the sacred with almost anything considered worthy in moral, political, or psychological terms).[15] Any criticism of goddess religion calls forth a polemic on the historic marginalization of goddesses, the persecution of their high priestesses, the hunting of witches, and so on. By claiming religious status, moreover, goddess ideologues can claim protection by the state as a minority religion.

The feminists whom we discuss in this book have explicitly adopted a gynocentric worldview. All of human history, they believe, revolves around women – which is to say, around themselves. The implication is that society needs to worry only, or at least mainly, about their needs and problems (although they do link those with the needs and problems of their political allies: minorities).[16] It is thus the counterpart of androcentrism, which refers to a worldview in which all of human history revolves around men, the implication being that society needs to worry only, or at least mainly, about their needs and problems. And our society really has traditionally been androcentric. Over the past thirty years, however, it has become increasingly gynocentric (a process that we have documented elsewhere).[17]

The transition has been gradual, though very quick in terms of human history as a whole, and uneven. At the moment, many people – including both women and men, though for different reasons – are unaware, or not fully aware, of what has been happening. They do not always realize that goddess ideology, like feminist ideology in general, relies on a thoroughly gynocentric approach to history and therefore to men. Its seed, as it were, is the feminist notion of patriarchy, which has become a slogan and discourages historical analysis of the complex factors that led to androcentrism. It does so in two ways. First, it indulges in essentialism by reducing all factors to the power inherent either in maleness or in masculinity. Second, it indulges in dualism by claiming that the primary motivation of men is and always has been precisely to subordinate and therefore oppress women. The "root cause" of women's problems is not the complex of cultural forces that often generate androcentrism, in other words, but the *evil* of men that *always* generates misogyny.

A gynocentric worldview does not necessarily lead to misandry, just as an androcentric worldview does not necessarily lead to misogyny. But it does so often enough, whether implicitly or explicitly, to warrant detailed analysis. This became clear to us after realizing that some feminists were not only rewriting history and reversing biblical mythology (which we discussed in part 1 of this book) but also politicizing religion with that in mind.

The ideological paradigm is overt, or explicit, in revolutionary religious movements but sometimes covert, or implicit, even in reformist ones. Some movements are ambiguous, moreover, in this respect. Like other neopagan movements, for example, Wicca can be either gynocentric and misandric (if it welcomes only women to worship only a great goddess) or not (if it welcomes both men and women to worship both gods and goddesses). The same is true of reform movements within established religions such as Judaism and Christianity.

But not all feminists turn to religion of any kind, let alone goddess ideology; most, probably, do not. Many (though by no means all) of those who do not, however, have a very similar worldview. Goddess ideology has a secular counterpart in feminist ideology. Both are ideological. Both are the children, as it were, of a marriage between Marxism (emphasizing reason in the Enlightenment tradition, identifying false consciousness, engaging in class struggle, using fronts to infiltrate institutions, working toward the classless society, and so on) and Romanticism (glorifying the emotions, the remote past and either the nation or the race).

Misandry refers to hatred directed toward men. (As a frequent but not quite inevitable byproduct of gynocentrism, it is the sexist or even racist[18] counterpart of "misogyny.") Precisely what, however, is "hatred"? We do not use that word as a synonym for either "intense dislike" or "anger," which are emotions and thus both transient and personal. "Hatred" refers here to a *culturally propagated worldview*, a profoundly dualistic one, that identifies an entire group of people as the source of all evil and suffering and therefore as the legitimate target of implacable hostility (whether direct or indirect). No feminist, not even the most ideologically oriented one, would ever admit to promoting hatred. And yet it is hard to imagine anything other than hatred as the result of accepting what goddess ideologues such as Daly, for example, have written about men. But, as we have shown in chapter 5, faced with this charge, some feminists try to justify or at least excuse it by arguing that misandry among women is an inevitable result of misogyny among men. This response leads to another moral problem for those who refuse to believe that two wrongs can make a right (even if they reject that Golden Rule as a "patriarchal construct"). Other feminists claim to disapprove of misandry but remain silent about it all the same. By doing so, of course, they implicitly condone the rhetoric of the goddess ideologues.[19]

Unlike most Wiccans and some other neopagans, who glorify both gods and goddesses, goddess ideologues deny any legitimacy whatsoever to gods. They thus deny any legitimacy whatsoever to maleness and therefore, as Daly makes clear, to the continued existence of men. But consider Hinduism: Hindu goddess worship has not spawned the kind of dualism, goddess versus god or women versus men, that has crept into monotheism in the West. This, we suggest, is because Hindu polytheism has offered many more possibilities than Western monotheism: one or more gods, one or more goddesses, androgynous deities, or a supreme principle that transcends any sexual categories.[20] Moreover, just as women feel free to worship gods, men feel free to worship goddesses. In the past, their collective identity as men was secure enough, thanks to the strong patrilocal and patrilineal family system and male dominance in the public sphere, that they felt no threat from the divine feminine. From a sociological point of view, this trade-off is unattractive to Western women and even to a growing number of Hindu women. It will be interesting to see whether goddesses remain attractive to Hindu men as a result of Indian reforms for women in both public space and domestic space. If men feel a threat to their collective identity as men, they might feel less inclined to worship goddesses.

To the extent that other women expect to live in societies with men, at any rate, they will have to find ways of affirming their own collective identity without destroying that of men. Many women – including egalitarian feminists – would like very much to do so. The problem is that nature does not present us with equality. That is a moral or philosophical or theological category that people impose, at least to some extent, on nature. We use culture,[21] in other words, to create various forms of equality in response to natural inequalities. The most obvious one involves reproduction, which would otherwise marginalize men in family life and give them no obvious stake in either the stability or the future of society.[22] To succeed, therefore, we must do more than make laws that *assume* equality (although we certainly need those). We must *explain the need* for equality. Women have learned this much after decades of using law to eliminate androcentrism and "level the playing field." Men now have to eliminate gynocentrism and thus level that same playing field. Feminist ideology, including goddess ideology, is the ultimate barrier to reciprocity or even coexistence between women and men.

Unlike misogyny, misandry tends to be invisible, although that situation has begun to change. Men in general lack not only the analytical tools to discern the underlying cultural patterns but also the will to do so, because that would reveal their vulnerability and therefore undermine their sense of masculinity. Women in general do have the analytical tools but lack the will to discern the underlying cultural patterns, because that would undermine the assumption that only women are victims of stereotyping or discrimination and therefore would undermine their feminist ideological world-view (including its political goals). So even those who do discern the underlying cultural patterns of misandry, unlike those of misogyny, seldom challenge them publicly.

Misandry, in short, still amounts to an ugly secret, the true equiv-alent in our time to what Betty Friedan diagnosed as a women's "disease with no name."[23] By identifying it as a problem and giving it a name, the "feminine mystique," Friedan enabled women to explore – and revise – cultural assumptions about women that had made their identity as girls and women so problematic. So far, boys and men have few resources to help them overcome the "masculine mystique." On the contrary, the advent of feminist ideology has made it harder than ever for them to create either healthy identities at the personal level or a healthy identity at the collective level (let alone at the ontological or metaphysical levels).

As we say, though, undermining the identity of another group is not only a practical problem but also a moral one. The problem is not that some women worship a goddess but that they have launched an attack on men – and on women, for that matter – who worship a god. Their attack is total: moral, to be sure, but also spir-itual, intellectual, psychological, existential, and even biological. As a result, the ideal world that goddess ideologues want to build – the primeval paradise that they want to "restore" – is one in which men can make no contribution and therefore can have no identity, no value, and even no existence. Meanwhile, men do still exist. To the extent that goddess ideologues allow them a collective identity at all, it is a negative one: as the incarnation of cosmic evil or, at the very least, of innate inadequacy. This is the same problem that they attack, correctly, when it affects women. Generally speaking, this problem is *hatred* (known as misandry when the targets are men and misogyny when the targets are women).

In *Spreading Misandry: The Teaching of Contempt for Men in Popular Culture*, we argued that misandry – culturally propagated contempt, or hatred, toward men – was at least as common as misogyny in popular culture during the 1990s. In *Legalizing Misandry: From Public Shame to Systemic Discrimination against Men*, we argued that misandry is even more common than misog-yny (at least implicitly) in legal matters. In *Transcending Misandry: From Feminist Ideology to Intersexual Dialogue*, we will argue that our society can move beyond both misandry and misogyny through intersexual dialogue. We argue here, in *Sanctifying Misandry*, that goddess ideologues have tried to legitimate misandry both ontologically and metaphysically. In doing so, they have generated hostility not only toward men but also toward maleness itself. Daly and her supporters have taken misandry to its logical conclusion, the elimination of men, but other feminists have colluded with them by not even acknowledging that gynocentrism is as likely to generate misandry as androcentrism is to generate misogyny.

This ideological mentality, as we have said, provides no firm basis for self-criticism.[24] So goddess ideologues are unlikely to acknowledge, even to themselves, the inherent moral problems of a gynocentric and misandric worldview. Of course, acknowledging the inherent problems of an androcentric and misogynistic worldview has proven very hard for Jews and Christians. Whatever its flaws, though, the biblical tradition that lies at the root of each at least established a transcendent source of moral authority. Whether in the present or the future, whether in this world or another, *everyone* must conform to justice according to a divine standard: Israelite and Canaanite, rich and poor, powerful and powerless, male and female. Because everyone knows the principles of divine justice, moreover, everyone can appeal to them when earthly justice fails. In fact, the Israelites *institutionalized* self-criticism by preserving in scripture the accounts of prophets who ferociously condemned their own kings and, by implication, their own people for tyranny just as they condemned the kings of foreign nations, including their bitterest enemies.

Androcentrism or even misogyny notwithstanding, traditional religious communities have always *needed* women. Feminists dislike the roles that Judaism and Christianity have assigned to women, to be sure. However, the fact remains that both traditions have indeed assigned to women roles that, no matter how limited from a feminist perspective, allow them to make contributions to the community that are *necessary, distinctive*, and *publicly valued*. These women can establish identities as Jews or Christians (even though feminists try to convince them that religion has deluded them). Otherwise, no Jewish or Christian woman could maintain a healthy sense of identity. And many, in fact, do.[25]

But the same level of reciprocity, no matter how far from the ideal, is not characteristic of goddess ideology. After all, what *necessary, distinctive,* and *publicly valued* role has this movement assigned to men? Disaffected from Judaism and Christianity, some men join Wicca and other forms of neopaganism that worship both gods and goddesses. But what would men have to gain by becoming goddess ideologues (assuming that they would be allowed to do so in the first place)? In other words, what can they offer that movement *as men*? This would not make much difference if the movement were content to remain a gynocentric ghetto, even one with strands of misandry. But goddess ideologues are much more ambitious than that. Advocates want to generate a spiritual revolution that would affect all of society and ultimately generate a political revolution. This means that its understanding of men has far-reaching implications for everyone.

Misandry, the result of both feminist ideology and goddess ideology, is a major problem in connection with the formation of collective identity among boys and men. But that is by no means the only major problem. Another one originated long before any modern ideology, although both feminist ideology and goddess ideology have greatly exacerbated it. Having a healthy identity, as we keep saying in order to reinforce our most basic premise,[26] requires the ability of a person or group to make *at least one distinctive, necessary, and publicly valued contribution* to the larger society. We regard this statement as self-evident, or axiomatic. It has both practical and moral implications.

In the past, men could make three contributions: they could be providers, protectors, and progenitors. But the prevalent assumption today is that women can do all of these things as well as men or better than men, either by themselves or with help from the state and from sperm banks. (Men are involved in both the state and the sperm bank, but generally neither institution involves direct personal relationships between men with women. It is easy for women to ignore the fact that most legislators are men, therefore, and that all sperm contributions come from men.) Worse, feminist ideologues – including goddess ideologues – have argued cynically and opportunistically that all three contributions are nothing more than excuses to oppress women or children: as husbands who provide their wives with material support but at the cost of denying them independence ("autonomy," or "agency"); as husbands or fathers who offer protection only to satisfy their own egos or to assert their own superiority; and as rapists, who impregnate women – even within marriage – against their will. The picture is complicated by a combination of common sense and identity politics. As everyone knows, men cannot do everything that women can do (at least not yet).[27] Men cannot gestate, after all, and they cannot lactate. This asymmetry that nature imposes, without any of the compensations that culture once provided, means that identity has now become a bigger problem for boys and men than at any time since the agricultural/urban revolution.[28]

Consider the notion of fatherhood,[29] both divine and human. By now, our society has trivialized the whole idea of human fatherhood to the point of absurdity (and not only or even primarily because of goddess "thealogy"). And yet our attachment to the concept is still powerful on some level. Millions of people – both men and women, both Catholics and non-Catholics – experienced the death of Pope John Paul II as an intensely moving event. Although this was partly the case because they valued the personal characteristics of this particular pope, we suggest that it was partly because many intuited the archetypal characteristics of a "holy father" and maybe even the underlying notion of a "divine father."

Why would anyone value that? Precisely, we suggest, because many people have come to believe that compassionate fatherhood is not as obvious an attribute of men as compassionate motherhood is of women. Whatever its roots in the natural order, the cultural order must strongly reinforce fatherhood. Very few commentators, if any, observed that John Paul II was not only a great pope and a great person but also a great *man* – that is, a male person who excelled at disciplined but loving and even self-sacrificial care for his children. At a time when many people, both men and women, have come to believe that fatherhood means nothing more than a moral and legal obligation or the proverbial teaspoonful of sperm or a walking wallet, the pope asked people to believe that fatherhood is a way of experiencing holiness by imitating a transcendent and compassionate father, a belief that ultimately affects not only men but also children and women. In view of what amounts to a non-violent civil war within the Catholic Church, one that reflects equal polarization in other communities throughout the West, this was no small achievement.

Beyond the Fall of Man

In our time, the word "man" no longer refers to people in general but only to men in particular. We chose "the Fall of Man" as our main metaphor with that in mind, because it describes the central doctrine of goddess ideology. Despite the metaphor, our ultimate goal in writing this book is to convince readers of the need to move *beyond* the Fall of Man and thus restore this description of the human condition to its original and inclusive sense.[1] This would mean, above all, moving beyond dualism (and therefore also essentialism, the other side of that coin).[2] Only by means of stereoscopic vision, as it were – seeing from two points of view and therefore in "three dimensions" – can we sustain egalitarianism.

Moving beyond dualism, in turn, would mean rejecting religious revolution and continuing the historical process of religious reform. By "reform," we do not mean embracing change for its own sake or as an end in itself[3] but changes that would suit the needs of both men and women. Meanwhile, extremists on both sides have spoken. Some reject divine femaleness (more or less) in order to retain monotheism. Others reject monotheism (more or less) in order to satisfy feminism. This puts other Jews and Christians in the unenviable position of having to steer a course between the Scylla of androcentric fundamentalism and the Charybdis of gynocentric revolution. But as long as no one promotes hatred of any kind, including misandry and misogyny, we should be able to find room for all religious movements. After all, people are free to choose any religion or no religion at all.

Goddess ideology has not merely reversed Judeo-Christian symbols, we suggest, but gone one step further in the opposite direction.

It has replaced the *dominance* of male symbols, for instance, with the *exclusivity* of female ones. It has replaced the post-biblical notion that women (as daughters of Eve) are *more* guilty than men (as sons of Adam), moreover, with the misandric notion that men *alone* are guilty (which means, of course, that women alone are innocent). Goddess ideologues have upped the ante, in short, by replacing androcentrism not merely with gynocentrism but with extreme gynocentrism – which is to say, with misandry.

We refer briefly in this epilogue to some problems that goddess ideology creates for (1) scholarship, (2) equality, and (3) religious communities.

Our critics are quick to point out that not everyone in the goddess movement is what we consider a goddess ideologue. Riane Eisler seems egalitarian, for instance, not only because of her promotion of the "partnership model" and the therapeutic industry that it has spawned but also because of her attempt to rescue men from the accusation of innate evil:

> For millennia men have fought wars and the Blade has been a
> male symbol. But this does not mean men are inevitably vio-
> lent and warlike. Throughout recorded history there have been
> peaceful and nonviolent men. Moreover, obviously there were
> both men and women in the prehistoric societies where the
> power to give and nurture, which the Chalice symbolizes, was
> supreme. The underlying problem is not men as a sex. The root
> of the problem lies in a social system in which the power of the
> Blade is idealized – in which both men and women are taught
> to equate true masculinity with violence and dominance and to
> see men who do not conform to this ideal as "too soft" or
> "effeminate."[4]

In addition, she acknowledges sexually egalitarian societies such as the BaMbuti, the !Kung, and the Swedes.[5]

Then, however, Eisler makes Neolithic cultures, which glorified goddesses and women, the origin of both civilization and religion. In fact, she resorts to the conspiracy theory of history by adding that "one of the best-kept historical secrets is that practically all the material and social technologies fundamental to civilization were developed before the imposition of a dominator society."[6] She loads the dice not only by making men mainly responsible for the "dominator model" (and thus everything evil) but also by making women mainly responsible for the "partnership model" (everything good). The Neolithic brought every major breakthrough, she claims, in connection with social organization, the domestication of plants and animals, architecture, town planning, healing, law, administration, religion, and the arts, trade, administration, education, clothing, pottery, metallurgy, writing, the arts, and so on. Also making these claims are feminists such as Gerda Lerner, Marilyn French, Carol Gilligan, Carol Christ, Rosemary Ruether, Catharine MacKinnon, and others.[7] So much, then, for the "partnership" with men and "egalitarianism." In our opinion, Eisler is – they all are – trying to have their cake (claiming the equality of men and women) and eat it too (claiming that women are superior to men). Eisler's solution is to change the way that men and women are socialized by teaching men to be more like women. The new model for men, in effect, would turn them into male feminists – in other words, "honorary women."[8]

In her conclusion to *The Myth of Matriarchal Prehistory*, Cynthia Eller challenges common feminist claims about matriarchal and patriarchal societies in prehistory:

Prehistoric human societies may have been different from all those that came after them, but any such assertion runs into three perhaps insurmountable obstacles: first, there is no evidence that they were [different]; second, there is no reason to expect that they would be (at least not when we are talking about the past thirty to forty thousand years of *Homo sapiens sapiens*, as feminist matriarchalists typically are); and third, if they were utterly different, and universally so, we need a compelling explanation of why things changed so drastically. Feminist 'matriarchalists' make their strongest case for Patriarchal Revolution in Southeast Europe and the Near East, where it is at best one possible explanation among others. Elsewhere in the world, patriarchal revolution is an even less likely scenario. Feminist matriarchalists' arguments explaining how, why, or even when patriarchy became a worldwide phenomenon simply do not square with the available evidence.[9]

So far, we agree with Eller. And she could have stopped there, setting the historical record straight. But she goes on to dismiss history. The record is so obscure, she says, that we might never know what really happened at the dawn of human history. And she has a point. But she goes even further, dismissing even historical evidence of more recent times as useless in the effort to understand gender. She dismisses cross-cultural evidence of gender, moreover, claiming that in any case feminists need not worry about gender. Gender varies greatly from one culture to another, after all, in both content and importance. Not all cultures, she says, understand even motherhood in the same way. Not surprisingly, she argues that heterosexuality is "sometimes the norm" and sometimes "only a grudging necessity."[10] "If there are no inherent barriers to women's equality," she says, "then the future of women does not rest on biological destiny or historical precedent, but rather on moral choice."[11] And even if male dominance were really genetically determined, she adds, every culture would still have to find its own solution. Women need neither prehistoric nor anthropological evidence (although both might be helpful) to get on with feminism.

We argue that both historical and cross-cultural evidence can be useful indeed, because some solutions to social problems have succeeded and others failed. We are referring at least partly to the historical record of societies that have found it expedient to promote hatred.

This takes us to Eller's discussion of myth. To soften her critique of goddess myth-making, she pays a back-handed compliment: she praises goddess ideologues for their "imagination," which is an "impressive achievement."[12] But then she opines that their "house of cards" will embarrass feminists. Moreover, she says, goddess ideology's origin stories use timeless archetypes, totalizing images of "patriarchy," nostalgia for the remote past, and Romantic notions about nature – all carrying the danger of escapism, which could deter the feminist cause to improve the lives of women. She concludes that we do not need "matriarchal myth to tell us that sexism is bad or that change is possible. With the help of all feminists, matriarchalist and otherwise, we need to decide what we want and set about getting it."[13] Eller does not seem to care that the new ideological goddess myth is morally problematic because it promotes hatred of men either directly or indirectly. This takes us back to our central concern: equality.

Eller does refer in her conclusion to the feminist struggle for "equality." But her notion of equality is meaningless, we suggest, because she has no interest in the people to whom women are equal. No less gynocentric than her informants, she focuses only on women's problems, the solidarity of sisterhood, and solutions proposed by women. She comes close to social constructionism, moreover, by insisting that gender systems are highly malleable. She sees nothing in maleness, for instance, that might prove problematic in the formation of masculine identity – certainly nothing that women would have to account for in any attempt to create a truly egalitarian society. Not surprisingly, the problem – the moral problem – that we have identified as misandry does not show up on her radar screen. Goddess ideologues are wrong, she says, but only because of the damage that their theories might inflict on women. They are not wrong, in other words, because of the damage that their theories have already inflicted on men.

Rosemary Ruether takes a slightly different approach at the end of *Goddesses and the Divine Feminism*. She repudiates not only Christianity *in toto* but every historic religion; all are hopelessly contaminated, she argues, by patriarchy. Moreover, she ignores the identity of men as such; they can prosper in a new world order, but only to the extent that they become like women. Her book ends with a sermon on the evils of patriarchal religion. Women should invent new myths, she says, but avoid feminist fundamentalism – taking those myths literally as history. By combining immanence and transcendence, these myths could undermine the likelihood of "a twenty-first century world threatened by military violence, economic exploitation, and ecological collapse."[14]

Using ideas and even words that come directly from both feminism (of the kind that Marilyn French, in particular, made popular) and neopaganism (of the kind that New Age made popular), she calls for recognition that "the divine is to be a matrix of life-giving energy that is in, through, and under all things, sustaining and renewing life, re-creating relationships of mutuality ... [which] can be imaged as female or male in ways that celebrate our diverse bodies and energies, rather than in ways that reinforce traditional gender stereotypes. But it is neither male, female, nor anthropomorphic in any essential or exclusive sense. It calls us to repent of power over others and to reclaim power within and power with one another."[15] Once again, it is hard to see how men could buy into any of this as men; their only way into the future would be as honorary women.

There is an alternative, one that religious people (except for fundamentalists) have already begun to explore. We refer to science. By that, we mean not devotion to scientism, which is an implicit religion and has led to dangerous technocracies, but devotion to the scientific method of inquiry. At this point, surely, we have no need for new myths, no matter how creative, that clash with verifiable empirical evidence. We will always need to *interpret* empirical evidence, of course, to provide us with helpful ways of living in the world that science describes or explains. But if we allow these interpretations to *compete* with science as "alternative truths," we will not only undo centuries of learning (which benefits women no less than men) but also end up in relativistic chaos.

Throughout this book, we have emphasized flaws in the scholarship of academics who promote goddess ideology. This ideology is not merely a matter of carelessness or jumping to the wrong conclusions. It is a matter of deliberately either ignoring or trivializing evidence that ideologues find hard to explain or inconvenient. In other words, it is a matter of intellectual dishonesty.

Some of these authors (such as Gerda Lerner, Marija Gimbutas, and Riane Eisler) pretend that they can prove their theories the old-fashioned way: with hard evidence from objective research. Others (such as Naomi Goldenberg and Mary Daly) openly acknowledge that they are more interested in creating therapeutic myths for women than in being accountable to objective methods and standards, which they reject in any case as "patriarchal" or "phallocentric" and replace with subjective methods that are equally biased but in favour of women. Admitting bias, however, hardly legitimates it as scholarship.

Goddess ideologues are not troubled by or even interested in the moral implications of hatred. Rejecting Judeo-Christian religion, after all, means rejecting much more than Judeo-Christian theology. It means rejecting Judeo-Christian morality – including and even especially the most basic moral principle of all: the Golden Rule in either its negative form (the Jewish version being "Do *not* do unto others as you would *not* have them do ...") or its positive form (the Christian version being "*Do* unto others as you *would* have them do"). Because the Golden Rule relies as much on common sense as on divine authority, it is very widespread cross-culturally in connection with both religious and secular philosophies. Rejecting its fundamental premise of ethical reciprocity amounts to far more, therefore, than rejecting any particular version of it. No wonder, then, that Daly wants "nature" to exterminate all men, so that she and other women can look delicately the other way and not have to get their hands dirty. The obvious parallel with Nazism is interesting in view of the fact that the Nazis too explicitly rejected both Judeo-Christian religion – they considered Christianity not only a rival religion but also a stifling version of Judaism and Judeo-Christian morality. They too had no use for "do unto others," "love your enemies," or "turn the other cheek."

Over the past forty years, however, many Jews and Christians have become used to the idea of reforming their monotheistic traditions in various ways – including their attitudes toward sex and gender. With this in mind, they have replaced generically masculine pronouns with gender-inclusive ones, added androgynous or even female metaphors for God to their liturgies, renewed emphasis on female saints or female contributions, ordained women as religious leaders, created new liturgies for female life-cycle events, and so on. These reforms will never satisfy goddess ideologues such as Daly who have rejected all world religions. Moreover, they might not satisfy many of the feminists who have chosen as Jewish or Christian women to live with ambivalence. Nonetheless, these reforms have satisfied or at least not alienated many Jews and Christians. But will they succeed in the long run? More specifically, will they retain both men and women or become the preserves of women? And will they remain religious or become secular fronts for political ideologies?

To answer these questions, we must allude to what many people prefer to ignore: some religious changes amount to revolution, not merely to reform. Acknowledging this is not easy, because the combination of postmodernism and political correctness makes it very risky to criticize *anything* to do with women, let alone to argue that goddess ideology is gynocentric, ideological – that is, misandric – or even secular. Many of those who concede that goddess ideology is indeed all those things would still balk at the idea that introducing goddess symbolism into Judaism or Christianity is actually a front for goddess ideology. Although doing so might look like reform – not only in the sense of change but also in the sense of purification by returning to the remote past – it would actually amount to revolution. It would require Jews or Christians to reject not only the founding principle of biblical religion, after all, but their identities as Jews or Christians as well.

Being troubled by gynocentrism and misandry does not mean that we advocate a return to androcentrism and misogyny. On the contrary, we argue that members of every religious community sometimes have a moral responsibility to campaign for reform.[16] But if their proposed reforms amount to revolution – that is, to the destruction of existing traditions, then they have a moral responsibility to leave and start new religions.[17] In this sense, the Wiccans and even Daly have done the right thing.[18]

It is true that male imagery has dominated Western religious traditions (although female imagery is by no means absent in some of them). If this problem did not originate as part of a titanic conspiracy of men against women, then how did it originate? As we have said, ancient Near Eastern religions were agricultural and fertility cults, which is why they featured both gods and goddesses. We suggest that androcentrism originated with the shift from belief in both gods and goddesses, sometimes headed by supreme goddesses, to supreme gods. The next step was from supreme gods to *one god*. This was the monotheistic revolution that we now associate primarily with the Israelites.[19] When they replaced polytheism with monotheism,[20] they had to choose either a single god or a single goddess. (They could have chosen some philosophical or metaphysical principle instead of either, to be sure, but that would not have been theism at all.) They chose a god, although they associated that god with some attributes of goddesses and eventually produced theologies that transcended gender attributions.

Adopting monotheism was not merely one choice among many in the evolution of Western religion. It was the *founding* choice, the *defining* one. The constant struggle to affirm that choice, instead of going back to the old religion by assimilating into neighbouring societies, went on for hundreds of years. In fact, scripture recorded it as a *paradigmatic* story. Extensive upgrading of female imagery would ultimately have involved a return to some period *before* the Israelites made that fateful choice and became Jews, thus making it possible for others eventually to become Christians (or Muslims for that matter). Adding a goddess, as we have explained, would amount not to reform but to revolution. The result would no longer be Judaism or Christianity but something else: the road not taken.

Jews and Christians who resist attempts to turn God into God-dess, therefore, are not necessarily being misogynistic. They might simply be saying that they can stretch historical continuity, cultural identity, communal loyalty, and spiritual integrity only so far. It is unfortunate that some Jewish and Christian feminists have drawn a line in the sand where they have, because they have made it as clear in modern times as it was in ancient times that the extreme femin-ization of Western monotheism leads ultimately to its dissolution. Jewish and Christian feminists, therefore, are left between a rock and a hard place. If they add a goddess, then they must abandon monotheism. If they retain monotheism but switch allegiance from one god to one goddess, on the other hand, they must still abandon Judaism and Christianity.[21] Most, not surprisingly, prefer to leave traditional monotheism alone but reform it in ways that enhance the lives of women.

One specific advantage of biblical monotheism over goddess ide-ology (although the same could be said of polytheistic traditions that feature both gods and goddesses) is the support that it can pro-vide for fatherhood. It has always been very easy to glorify mother-hood but much harder to glorify or even to understand fatherhood. The meaning of fatherhood varies, both historically and cross-cul-turally, considerably more than that of motherhood. Despite the lin-gering popular assumption that fathers are either assistant mothers or walking wallets, and despite even the opportunism of feminists who want the law to presume maternal custody after divorce, researchers have begun to take fatherhood seriously.[22] It is no lon-ger self-evident to many people – not only to goddess ideologues and feminist ideologues but also to feminist egalitarians, to some social engineers and state bureaucrats, to many men, and to most boys growing up in "dysfunctional" families – that fathers have any important function in family life or even that they are necessary at all. This is the pervasive message today, at any rate, about single mothers who either do not need or do not want the fathers of their children. But if we are to maintain a human society – that is, accord-ing to all historical and cross-cultural precedents, a community of both men and women – we must find a way of either affirming or reaffirming the importance of fatherhood. This is not the place to discuss what fatherhood has meant, could mean, or should mean. It is the place, however, to point out that every society has relied on religion in one way or another to define and support fatherhood.

Because the raison d'être of goddess ideology is ultimately to empower women and secondarily, at best, to experience the sacred – which is the defining feature of religion – we suggest that goddess ideology as not only explicitly religious but also implicitly secular. In fact, it is a quasi-religious version of Judeo-Christian religion despite its surface deposits of pagan motifs. But implicit secularity is not its main characteristic. Its main characteristic is ideology, especially two of its most important characteristic features: essentialism and dualism.

Women often leave Jewish or Christian communities because their identities as women (or feminists) are more important to them than their identities as Jews and Christians, which is why many of them either abandon religion or become goddess ideologues. Men often leave for a similar reason, identity conflict, although they seldom articulate it at the conscious level. To put the matter bluntly, men need to affirm their collective identity as men just as women need to affirm theirs as women. The maleness of Jesus or the "maleness" of God notwithstanding, many men have felt like intruders in liberal Christian churches – those that replaced intellectuality with sentiment in the nineteenth century, for instance, and those that replaced androcentric theology with gynocentric theology in the twentieth. In short, religious communities that expect to endure will have to find ways of acknowledging and then satisfying the distinctive needs of both women and men.[23]

What can we do about all this? Male monotheism[24] could attract both sexes by fostering the affirmation of feminine identity (albeit under the constraints of monotheism). To the extent that religion matters at all – some people deny that it matters – we need to become more conscious not only of what is going on in both theological and academic (or ideological) circles but also what is at stake for the larger society. As religious feminists have pointed out, religion can have a dramatic effect on the ways in which people see both themselves as men or women and other people as men or women. Goddess ideology, preached exclusively to women, is profoundly hostile to men (unlike neopagan movements such as Wicca, which feature both gods and goddesses). In itself, that might not matter. Goddess ideology does not seek men as converts, after all, and is unlikely to become a mass movement even among women in an increasingly secular age. But its leaders have been very influential in other religious communities – and even, as we have shown, in popular culture – as promoters of gynocentrism and misandry.

Every modern democracy assumes, at least in theory, the legal equality of all its citizens. No individual is above the law; no class deserves special privileges. Everyone knows what equality is – in this case, legal equality between men and women – but even that is not as simple as it sounds. Some people refer glibly to "women's equality." This makes no sense, because both equality and inequality can exist only in the context of two or more groups (men and women, for example, or rich and poor). The implication, of course, is that women should be equal to men.

Other people refer to "gender equality" (which refers implicitly to culturally produced characteristics of masculinity and femininity) or "sexual equality" (which refers implicitly, and more helpfully in connection with legal rights, to the genetically produced characteristics of maleness and femaleness). By not referring explicitly to both women *and men*, however, all of these expressions foster political opportunism. They allow people to assume that only women need to worry about equality with men and therefore that men do not need to worry about equality with women. But that second assumption is false. In some important ways, men do indeed need to worry about equality. By referring explicitly to "equality between men and women," we at least encourage people to think about that.

Almost everyone acknowledges the legitimacy of equality of all before the law in a democratic society, although not everyone sees (or chooses to see) inequality in some of its forms or actually cares enough about inequality to do anything about it. Goddess ideologues, on the other hand, acknowledge no such thing. Unlike egalitarian feminists or even the more prudent of feminist ideologues, they openly repudiate the equality of men and women. Daly refuses even to allow the co-existence of men and women. And whether they say so or not, many of her ardent fans agree.

The logical conclusion to goddess ideology is not necessarily for women to exterminate men, but for women to separate from men. That might work for gay women, some of whom feel no compelling reason at all to mingle with men. But it would not work so well for straight women, most of whom want healthy relationships with men. Besides, separatism – whether sexual, religious, racial, linguistic, or any other kind – presents a profound *moral* problem to those who, like egalitarian feminists, include the fear of "otherness" and the resulting desire to exclude "others" among the most fundamental human problems. Even if we could engineer two truly separate but equal realms, we could do so only at the cost of a truly historic moral defeat.

Defining Religion

Is goddess ideology religious or secular? For that matter, is goddess *religion* religious or secular? Both could be religions, but we suggest that neither religion nor secularity is an adequate classification for these phenomena. We propose a definition of religion that would place goddess ideology on a continuum between religious and secular worldviews. At the centre of this continuum are hybrid worldviews. In this section, accordingly, we (1) define worldviews and discuss goddess ideology in connection with (2) religious worldviews, (3) secular worldviews, (4) hybrid worldviews, and (5) ideological feminism and goddess ideology as hybrid worldviews.

All social groups (families, communities, and so forth) inherit or produce worldviews, general orientations that bind people together by giving them enough meaning and purpose for life to make sense. These worldviews include the following characteristic features: (1) both cognitive *and* experiential dimensions; (2) both conscious and unconscious dimensions; and (3) both personal and collective dimensions. There are now two main kinds of worldview: religious, hybrid, and secular.

RELIGIOUS WORLDVIEWS

Religious worldviews[1] have all the characteristic features of every worldview, of course, *plus* the following ten. These additional characteristics emerge from cross-cultural and historical evidence, which allows for an empirical definition.

1 They presuppose either supernatural dimensions[2] or ultimate
    experiences (or both) that transcend but also transform
    everyday life.[3]

2 They help people live with fundamental paradoxes of the
    human condition (such as the apparent conflict between order
    and chaos, life and death, self and others, male and female;
    nature and culture, mind and body, finitude and infinity) and
    respond to existential questions that emerge from the human
    condition (such as why injustice exists, why the innocent
    suffer, why compassion requires sacrifice, and so on).

3 They rely on symbol systems that give coherence to both
    personal and communal life. Apart from doing anything else,
    religion provides the symbolic glue that holds communities
    together.

4 They presuppose both sacred time (as distinct from profane,[4]
    not secular, time) and sacred space (as distinct from profane,
    not secular, space).

5 They find primary expression in forms such as myths,[5] scrip-
    tures, hagiographies (sacred biographies), and rituals.

6 They find secondary expression in their interpretations and
    applications of primary ones;[6] these secondary expressions
    include kinship, taboo, theology, and philosophy, morality,
    law, the arts,[7] and so on.

7 Considering the characteristic primary and secondary fea-
    tures of religious worldviews together, it becomes clear that
    they are comprehensive or nearly comprehensive ways of life.

8 They sustain groups (defined by birth or choice), not merely
    isolated individuals. Every community has a public dimen-
    sion, for instance, which involves face-to-face encounters.

9 They claim sources of authority[8] for these ways of life and
    thus for belonging to the group.[9]

10 They are successful enough to endure for a long time.[10]

SECULAR WORLDVIEWS

Like religious worldviews, secular worldviews[11] have all the characteristic features of every worldview. They differ from religious
ones, however, by (1) presupposing only the natural or cultural
order,[12] and therefore (2) acknowledging only reason in general
and science in particular as the ultimate authority. Consider

one example, which most people call "secular humanism." Says Ninian Smart,

> At its most articulate level, this worldview typically is scientific humanism ... As humanism, it believes that the highest values are found in human beings and their creation. But it does not hold that humans survive death or have any kind of immortal nature; nor that they exist because they have been brought into being by a God ... It means that there is nothing higher than the human race ... But such humanism is also in an important way thought to be scientific. The person who holds to this worldview believes that all true knowledge about the world is ultimately to be found through science, or at least within the framework of a scientific outlook.[13]

According to Charles Taylor,[14] the theory of secularization holds that modernization[15] allows non-religious or even anti-religious ways of holding society together and protecting people. But recent history has diminished the legitimacy of that theory. True, secularization has destabilized traditional forms of religious life, as Taylor notes, but it has also led to "recomposition and new forms." Some are explicitly secular. Others are more complicated.

HYBRID WORLDVIEWS

Modernity generates hybrid worldviews. These combine (1) explicit religiosity with implicit secularity, (2) implicit religiosity with explicit secularity, or (3) explicit religiosity *and* secularity.[16]

Hybrid worldviews usually emerge in connection with the civil religions[17] of states,[18] ethnic communities,[19] secularizing religious communities,[20] political movements,[21] popular culture,[22] transient or virtual communities,[23] and "personal spirituality."

Taylor makes no distinction between religious and hybrid worldviews. Rather, he continues to think of the latter as new (but "thin") religious forms in "the post-secular age." These coexist, he says, with non-religious and anti-religious worldviews as a "new plurality." In any case, all of these worldviews have become extremely fragile. Since the cultural upheavals of the 1960s, many people have tried to find their own ways of being human – that is, to create their own "identities," find their own answers to the big "existential" questions, establish their own "authenticity," and so on. They refer to all of this as "spirituality," not religion (which they consider merely external, institutional, and rule bound).

As we say, Taylor has collapsed the distinction between religious and hybrid worldviews. Much of what he describes as "spiritual" belongs in the hybrid category. By using the word "spiritual" so loosely, he has ignored the eclectic mix of religious and secular characteristics. Moreover, he has ignored the fact that many hybrid worldviews are largely secular.

Personal spirituality, especially as New Agers understand it, is much more radically individualistic than any other hybrid worldview. Notwithstanding its historical relation to religion (the origin of spirituality), it focuses almost exclusively on the personal search for meaning, purpose, and identity. It relies on a continually shifting congeries of attitudes, feelings, ideas, and archetypes or other symbols (from new religious movements, therapy groups, and even traditional religions). Characteristic of this worldview is experimentation – that is, selecting attractive features from everywhere (the "cafeteria" model of religion). The result of experimentation is not merely eclectic but also both amorphous and ephemeral. Appearance notwithstanding in some cases, this phenomenon is often remote from religion. It is a kind of frontierland that reduces religion to psychology or even sentiment. It is radically individualistic too, which takes it (strictly speaking) beyond the category of worldview altogether.

Although hybridity has influenced some religions, it has not influenced all of them to the same degree. Many immigrants are intent on preserving the "authenticity" of their religious traditions precisely to prevent disintegration.

Notes

PROLOGUE

1 Paul Nathanson and Katherine K. Young, *Spreading Misandry: The Teaching of Contempt for Men in Popular Culture* (Montreal: McGill-Queen's University Press, 2001).
2 Feminism does include divergent and even conflicting schools of thought about the one thing that they all have in common: creating a society that makes life better for *women* than it is. But two of these schools are of particular importance here – that is, from the perspective of *men* (along with those who care about men and boys as the equals of women and girls). Both are gynocentric (focused on women). One is also misandric (hostile to men).

   The original form of second-wave feminism was and remains egalitarian, at least in theory. Advocates believe not only in the equality of men and women but also in the interchangeability of men and women. They acknowledge one problem, however, aside from prejudice against women due to conservative mentalities, religious beliefs, or sheer ignorance. Only women can bear children, after all, and many women want very much to do so. Because that takes them out of the workforce, a truly egalitarian society must find ways to help them find the security and personal fulfillment that men find in professional careers. In the practical vision of egalitarian feminists, the state intervenes in ways that allow women to participate in public life just as fully as men do.

   A slightly later form of second-wave feminism (although it has roots in some versions of first-wave feminism) was and is anything but egalitarian. On the contrary, it is hierarchical (although few advocates would admit that, because they see hierarchy as an innate feature of maleness). Instead of believing that men are superior to women, of course, they believe that women are superior to men: physiologically, psychologically, and – most important of all – morally. From this, they conclude that the blame for all of human (and even non-human) suffering has rested throughout history on the patriarchal societies that men have created to serve their own selfish interests and malicious urges. This is ideological feminism.

3 See Nathanson and Young, *Spreading Misandry*, 200–18.

4 Paul Nathanson and Katherine K. Young, *Legalizing Misandry: From Public Shame to Systemic Discrimination against Men* (Montreal: McGill-Queen's University Press, 2006).

5 Goddess *religion* includes Wicca; some forms of it are egalitarian and generally welcome men.

6 Though probably less numerous than other feminist ideologues, just as feminist ideologues are less numerous than egalitarian ones, goddess ideologues have been very influential (partly because many of them are either academically trained professionals or academics) – so influential that their ideas have filtered down from academic treaties, through popularized versions of those, into the popular culture of talk shows, sitcoms, commercials, movies, and so on.

INTRODUCTION

1 Riane Eisler, *The Chalice and the Blade: Our History, Our Future* (Cambridge, Mass.: Harper and Row, 1987).

2 Ibid., xvi.

3 Dan Brown, *The Da Vinci Code* (New York: Doubleday, 2003).

4 Sectarian Christians produced these gnostic gospels two or three centuries after the canonical ones.

5 Ashley Montagu, *The Natural Superiority of Women* (New York: Macmillan, 1968).

6 *The Da Vinci Code*, directed by Ron Howard, 2006.

7 The most notorious example is probably *The Protocols of the Elders of Zion*, which in most Western countries is available only with the analyses and commentaries that expose the original text as a forgery.

8 Kenneth L. Woodward, "A Quite Contrary Mary," *The Da Vinci Code* (2006), www.beliefnet.com/story/131/story_13188.html (accessed 21 June 2007).

9 In one interview, Deborah Caldwell explains the political "agenda" that underlies this book. It is "an attempt to – and I'm going to use this term

on purpose – relegate Christianity to a level that is like other religions. There are a lot of things Christianity claims are unique about what Christians believe and what Christianity is about – particularly the focus on Jesus Christ and his uniqueness. And it's those elements that tend to be relativized by this kind of material. We have a novel that's claiming that the divine Jesus was originally a human Jesus. That's the major re-visioning that's going on" ("Da Vinci's Secret Agenda," *Beliefnet* [undated]: 2, www.beliefnet.com/story/145/story_14506_1.html [accessed 10 March 2005]). Not a word about feminism, ideological or otherwise. According to Sandra Miesel, moreover, Brown is "writing in a particular way best calculated to attract a female audience. (Women, after all, buy most of the nation's books.) He has married a thriller plot to a romance-novel technique. Notice how each character is an extreme type ... effortlessly brilliant, smarmy, sinister, or psychotic as needed, moving against luxurious but curiously flat backdrops. Avoiding gore and bedroom gymnastics, he shows only one brief kiss and a sexual ritual performed by a married couple. The risqué allusions are fleeting although the text lingers over some bloody Opus Dei mortifications. In short, Brown has fabricated a novel perfect for a ladies' book club" ("Dismantling the Da Vinci Code," *Crisis* [2003]: 2, www.crisismagazine.com/september2003/feature1.htm [accessed 10 March 2005]). Once again, not a word about feminism.

10 *Conspiracy* is a major part of any ideology, including both ideological feminism and goddess religion. Many people have come to think of conspiracies in psychological terms. Everyone is now familiar with the notion of paranoia, a psychotic and delusional state in which people are tormented by the irrational fear of sinister enemies or implacable conspiracies. For political purposes, some people have expanded this clinical definition of paranoia. They accuse those who point out either real conspiracies or real conspiracy theories of paranoia – of mental derangement. The fact remains, however, that not all conspiracies are imagined by paranoids. Historians show that every real conspiracy has had at least four characteristic features: groups, not isolated individuals; illegal or sinister aims, not ones that would benefit society as a whole; orchestrated acts, not a series of spontaneous and haphazard ones; and secret planning, not public discussions. This pattern lies at the root of a feminist conspiracy theory of history. It refers to the belief that men conspired in the remote past to control and oppress women under patriarchal regimes. Charging whole groups of people with conspiracy, however, has unfortunate historical associations with forms of racism such as anti-Semitism

(which often involves the idea that a cabal of Jewish bankers is plotting to take over the world). In short, conspiracies always have negative connotations. Consequently, most feminists avoid the word "conspiracy" in connection with their own behaviour.

Why, then, do we use this word in connection with both ideological feminism and goddess religion? Mainly because it is the best word to describe a central feature of their worldview: the belief that all human suffering, especially female suffering, is due to the usurpation of power from women by men and the establishment of patriarchies. We do not deny that one by-product of the newly risen states was androcentrism. Nor do we deny that androcentrism presented more problems for elite women than for elite men. These are not paranoid delusions. But we do argue that the ideological explanation for those problems – that this amounts, no matter what words they use, to a titanic conspiracy of men against women at the dawn of history – really is false and, in some cases, possibly paranoid. Not being psychologists, we cannot get into the minds of those who advocate this theory. What concerns us is not the remote possibility that some are clinically paranoid but the fact that they deliberately and carefully foster illusions that distort history and, by doing so, poison relations not only between religious and non-religious people but also between men and women.

Some of those who espouse either ideological feminism or goddess religion do acknowledge that they accuse early men of a conspiracy against women, but they usually try to soften the effect by pointing out that the word "conspiracy" generally indicates a relatively small number of participants. This would mean, presumably, that their accusation is directed only at a few men of the remote past, not all of them, or all men of today. In fact, however, they themselves often make a very different point when it comes to the small fry. All men, they either say or imply, were and are guilty for continuing to *benefit* from what leaders or ancestors have done. In other words, the guilt applies not only to those who actually engineered and carried out the plot but also to those who were politically unaware, those who were subconsciously motivated, and even those who were knowing but passive onlookers. These feminists maintain the notion of conspiracy, therefore, and they expand its scope. And they apply precisely the same reasoning to the conspiracy of silence that has allegedly passed down the guilt of men from one generation to the next for thousands of years. Whether they actually use the word "conspiracy" or not, then, the historical analysis presented by feminist ideologues and goddess ideologues does indeed fit the definition.

Advocates of both ideological feminism and goddess ideology insist on classifying the rise of patriarchy as a conspiracy of ancient men against women. Explicitly or implicitly, they make three fundamental claims. First, they claim that patriarchy originated and continues not merely as the personal enterprise of a few men but as a collective enterprise of all men, because all men have allegedly benefited from it. Second, they claim that it is a well-orchestrated intellectual and political movement, not merely a series of purely spontaneous events. Third, they claim that its goal of stealing the power of women and using it to oppress them has been covert, not overt. Although both ideological feminists and goddess ideologues realize that not all women agree with or even approve of their theory, they nonetheless speak in the name of all women on the assumption that all women will one day see the truth about their own condition and who caused it.

But we think that their theory of patriarchy itself amounts to a conspiracy of modern women against men. First, we claim that it is a collective enterprise of some women in the name of all women. Second, we claim that it is a well-orchestrated intellectual and political movement, not merely a series of spontaneous events. Third, we claim that some of its aims have been covert, not overt. This last point requires an explanation.

In some ways, they operate overtly. Feminist ideologues and goddess ideologues do not hide in cellars to lay their plans in secret; they publish books and articles, speak at public gatherings, and use every resource of the democratic state and open society. On the other hand, they rely heavily on covert activities. As we explain elsewhere (Paul Nathanson and Katherine K. Young, *Legalizing Misandry: From Public Shame to Systemic Discrimination against Men* [Montreal: McGill-Queen's University Press, 2006]), they accomplish many of their goals not by campaigning for legislative changes that overtly discriminate against men but by convincing administrators – bureaucrats, judges, lawyers, courts, police chiefs, and so on – to interpret legislation in ways that covertly discriminate against men (despite the gender-neutral language of laws and policies). Only when they are involved in legal conflicts with women do many men become aware of the extent to which the procedural deck is stacked against them. This is particularly true not only in connection with divorce and custody but also in connection with domestic violence and sexual harassment.

11 Dan Brown, "An Interview with Dan Brown," *Beliefnet* (undated), www.beliefnet.com/story/127story_12775_1.html (accessed 10 March 2005).

12 Brown, "An Interview," 1.

13 "Cracking the Da Vinci Code, *Catholic Answers* (8 March 2005): 16, www.catholic.com/library/cracking_da_vinci_code.asp (accessed 10 March 2005).

14 Robert Richardson, "The Priory of Sion Hoax," *Alpheus* (2002), www.alpheus.org/html;/articles/esoteric_history/richardson1_print.html (accessed 10 March 2005).

15 Brown, "An Interview," 244; his emphasis.

16 Ibid., 444.

17 Jewish feminists, of course, have noticed this phenomenon. See Judith Plaskow, "Blaming Jews for Inventing Pagtriarchy" and "Feminism and Faith: A Discussion with Judith Plaskow and Annette Daum," in *Lilith* 7 (fall 1980): 11–12, 14–17. More important, several Christian authors, including Christian feminists, have acknowledged this problem. See, for instance, Katherina von Kellenbach, *Anti-Judaism in Christian-Rooted Feminist Writings: An Analysis of Major American and West German Feminist Theologians* (Ann Arbor, Mich.: University Microfilms International, 1987). Lisa Isherwood makes a similar point, extending the argument in ways that refer directly to Mary Daly: "Of course, the mistake that we have all made, I am sure, is to imply that Judaism is in some way a prologue for Christianity and therefore ceases to be truly valid in the present day. Worse still that as Christian feminists we can somehow take the bits from the Hebrew Scriptures that suit our arguments and interpret them completely in our own context, not paying attention to their historic and cultural roots. Appropriation works towards the elimination of difference and is essentially a non-feminist activity, but it is something that feminists do. Equally worrying is the way in which some feminists develop a hierarchy of oppression and place anti-Semitism on the list below sexism. It is regrettable, yet understandable, that such ways of thinking would develop. Understandable only because the ways of oppression are so many that one can feel overwhelmed if all are faced at one time, and this ends in list mentality whereby we try and decide what needs tackling first. However, the compilation of the lists says more about the person than about the need. Thankfully, there is increasing feminist awareness that all oppression is linked and while it is not possible to make lists, it is necessary to prioritize one's own action ... There could be no excuse today for Daly or any other feminist theologian to suggest that sexism is more important than the Holocaust" (*Introducing Feminist Christologies* [Cleveland: Pilgrim Press, 2002], 121).

18 Brown, "An Interview," 246.

19 Elaine Pagels, *The Gnostic Gospels* (New York: Random House, 1979).

20 Brown did not, of course, invent this idea. Catholic and other Christian feminists have long made the same argument. In a review of books on feminist Catholics, Margaret Steinfels refers to one in particular: "*The Resurrection of Mary Magdalene: Legends, Apocrypha, and the Christian Testament*, by Jane Schaberg, written some 30 years after Daly, may, in time, inform and broaden the Catholic tradition. It is a dense, scholarly examination of texts (and possibly missing texts), putting forth conjectures and reconstructions that the author thinks 'privilege that tradition of the women at the tomb ... and of the appearance to Mary Magdalene, [who] had a visionary experience of Jesus which empowered her with God's spirit.' Schaberg's bottom line: Mary Magdalene may have been the first apostle, and a tradition of her centrality was erased from history, suppressed in the formation of the early Church and of the canonical accounts of Jesus' ministry" (Margaret O'Brien Steinfels, "What Catholic Women Want: A Survey of Recent Books," *Boston College Magazine*, [fall 2003]: 6, www.bcm.bc.edu/issues/fall_2003/c21_women.html [accessed 7 January 2007]).

21 Brown, "An Interview," 125; his emphasis.

22 See Robin Briggs, *Witches and Neighbors: The Social and Cultural Context of European Witchcraft* (New York: Viking Press, 1996); Deborah Willis, *Malevolent Nurture: Witch Hunting and Maternal Power in Early Modern England* (Ithaca, NY: Cornell University Press, 1995).

23 Bruce Boucher, "Does 'The Da Vinci Code' Crack Leonardo?" *The New Age Center* (undated): 3, www.newagepointofinfinity.com/new+page_10.htm (accessed 10 March 2005).

24 Brown, "An Interview," 256.

25 Nathanson and Young, *Spreading*, 194-233.

26 *Chalice* has been in print since 1988. As a novel, *Code* had sold approximately 36 million copies as of 2005, making it a best-seller by any standard (and appearing for approximately two years on the *New York Times* list). Moreover, it has been translated into approximately forty languages ("Q: Da Vinci Code Sales Figures," *Google Answers* [27 December 2005], www.answers.google.com/answers/threadview/id/610195.html [accessed 19 November 2008]). The filmed version of *Code* cost approximately $125 million to make. It earned approximately $218 million at home and $541 million abroad. From its opening weekend in May 2006, when it earned $77 million at home, experts classified it as a "blockbuster" (Brandon Gray, "'Da Vinci' Almighty," *Box Office Mojo* [26 May 2006], www.boxofficemojo.com/news/?id=2072&p=.htm [accessed 19 November 2008]).

27 For practical reasons, we have limited our scope to the "goddess movement" in connection with Christianity and Judaism, which have long his-
tories in the United States, but not included religions that have arrived
here more recently. The earliest Jews and Christians had to think about
goddesses in connection with their rejection of polytheism. Today they
must do so all over again in connection with current goddess movements.
The earliest Muslims too had to think about goddesses in connection
with their rejection of polytheism. So far, however, they have not had to
do so in connection with current goddess movements. (They have had to
discuss goddesses in early Islam, to be sure, but that topic would take us
into the recent controversy over Salman Rushdie's *Satanic Verses*. We
prefer not to go there.)

28 The Library of Congress lists sixty-seven books on the Gaia hypothesis.

29 Cynthia Eller, *Living in the Lap of the Goddess: The Feminist Spirituality
Movement in America* (New York: Crossroad, 1993).

INTRODUCTION TO PART ONE

1 Charles Dickens wrote *A Christmas Carol* in 1843. Since then, it has
become a modern classic, a secular myth. On Christmas Eve, the ghost of
Christmas Past shows Ebenezer Scrooge, a notorious miser, the world of
his childhood and youth. Scrooge's father was uncaring, but Fan, his sister, was very loving. His boss, Fezziwig, was poor but also joyful; preserving the traditional ways of merry old England, moreover, he treated
his employees kindly. Scrooge rejected all that in order to succeed in the
cynical new industrial order. The next ghost, that of Christmas Present,
guides Scrooge through the current world of misery that he has created
for himself and others. The ghost of Christmas Yet to Come shows
Scrooge a bleak future: dying alone and unmourned even by his business
associates. But this inspires Scrooge to repent and thus avert that bleak
future. The book ends instead with a reformed Scrooge finding love and
joy once again.

Dickens did not invent this notion of time. On the contrary, he relied
on a very ancient notion of time, one that reached him through Christianity. In this story, he presents time and therefore history as a circle.
Christmas Yet to Come (destiny) would be bleak indeed and therefore
unlike Christmas Past (origin), were it not for Scrooge's conversion. But
Scrooge does convert, and so Christmas Yet to Come really is a return to
a past Christmas (and way of life) he once found so warm and fulfilling.
The middle (Christmas Present) is familiar to all of us from the experi-

ence of chaos and confusion in daily life. This is what Scrooge fails to understand at first. He feels locked into the present, unwilling or unable to remember his past and therefore unable to choose his future. Only the present moment "exists" for him. The three ghosts (four, if you include that of Jacob Marley) must open him up to a deeper and richer sense of time (apart from anything else). Without this temporal framework, Dickens could never have written his story.

The same pattern shows up in *The Wizard of Oz*, another modern and secular myth. It begins with Dorothy in Kansas, continues with her odyssey through Oz, and concludes with her return to Kansas. In the Kansas prologue, Dorothy lives with people who love her, but she has yet to understand what that means. Worse, evil in the form of Miss Gulch threatens her way of life. In the Kansas epilogue, Dorothy once again lives with people who love her. Now, though, she does understand what that means. And Miss Gulch no longer threatens her. Nothing has changed in Kansas, but Dorothy has changed due to what she has learned in Oz. (See Paul Nathanson, *Over the Rainbow*: The Wizard of Oz *as a Secular Myth of America* [Albany: State University of New York Press, 1991]).

This temporal framework has generated many politically motivated variants as well. Marxists omitted the first stage, for instance, retaining the notion of progress toward a utopian future. But the result is therefore linear rather than circular yet incorporates the notion of sacred time. In the mythic and ritualistic contexts of holy days such as Shabbat or Christmas, people re-experience the remote past and pre-experience the remote future. (See Mircea Eliade, *The Sacred and the Profane: The Nature of Religion* [New York: Harcourt, Brace, 1959].) Many secular feminists have adopted that model. Other feminists, though, have retained the traditional circular paradigm, and their version is what concerns us in this book. Consider it in relation to the one that Dickens used. Dickens told the story of someone who needed to repent in order to restore what he had lost. Goddess ideologues, on the other hand, tell the story of those people – that is, women – who need *not* repent in order to restore what they lost at the dawn of history; only men, they believe, need to repent.

2 Few scholars use "BC" and "AD" nowadays, because these terms refer specifically to Christianity: Before Christ and Anno Domini (in the year of our lord). They use "BCE" and CE" instead, because these terms refer to a supposedly universal system: Before the Common Era and Common Era. But this "common era" is no such thing; it is merely a disguise, because the numbering of years remains that of Christianity.

CHAPTER ONE

1 Revelation 22: 14.

2 *The Goddess Remembered*, directed by Donna Read; script and narration by D.C Blade, Donna Read, and Gloria Demers, 16 mm, 54 min. (Montreal: National Film Board, 1989).

3 Ibid., 1.

4 Ibid., 3.

5 Ibid., 3–4.

6 Ibid., 5.

7 Ibid.

8 Ibid.

9 Ibid., 6.

10 Ibid.

11 *Behind the Veil: Nuns*, directed by Margaret Westcott, script and narration by Gloria Demers, 16 mm., 130 min., part 1: 106C 0184 049; part 2: 106C 0184 050 (Ottawa: National Film Board of Canada, 1984), 2: 2.

12 Ibid.

13 *The Burning Times*, directed by Donna Read, script by Erna Buffie, 16 mm., 58 min. (Montreal: National Film Board of Canada, Studio D, 1993).

14 See Johann Jakob Bachofen, *An English Translation of Bachofen's Mutterrecht (1861): A Study of the Religious and Juridical Aspects of Gynecocracy in the Ancient World*, abridged and translated by David Partenheimer (Lewiston, NY: Edwin Mellen Press, 2006).

15 Ibid.

16 Gerda Lerner, *The Creation of Patriarchy* (New York: Oxford University Press, 1986).

17 Ibid., 148–9.

18 Ibid., 39; our emphasis.

19 According to Lerner, archaeologists have indeed found many female figurines from the seventh millennium BC. These usually show women in squatting positions to emphasize the breast, navel, and vulva. Lerner implies that this pervasiveness establishes their great age. For some reason, though, she begins with the Neolithic period rather than the earlier Palaeolithic one. It was during the Palaeolithic, between 35,000 and 8,000 years ago, that representational art first appeared. Even though she acknowledges that "we need to look more closely at such societies in the Palaeolithic ... and early Neolithic periods" (39), she refrains from actually doing so.

Archaeologists have been doing precisely that. And the most recent findings have included an even earlier female figurine, 5,000 years earlier (which means it is approximately 35,000 years old). It depicts humongous breasts and hips, along with genitalia, but a tiny head. Goddess ideologues notwithstanding, many feminists would be appalled by a modern image of this kind: a woman who has been grotesquely or even pornographically "objectified." But in any case, goddess ideologues such as Lerner would be disappointed by these recent discoveries, because archaeologists have found phalluses at the very same Paleolithic sites. All of these objects were carved from bone or ivory. Clearly, our remote ancestors were preoccupied with both female *and male* fertility (Paul Mellars, "Archaeology: Origins of the Female Image," *Nature* 459 [14 May 2009]: 176–7).

20 Ibid., 40.

21 Feminists have reacted to psychoanalytical theories with suspicion and even hostility. Many repudiate Freud's theory of "penis envy," for example, as nothing more than a characteristic form of misogyny.

22 Marija Gimbutas, *The Language of the Goddess* (New York: Harper and Row, 1989).

23 Susan G.E. Frayser, *Varieties of Sexual Experience: An Anthropological Perspective on Human Sexuality* (New Haven: HRAS Press, 1985), 286–8. Judging from her study of many ethnographies, Frayser says that "Although the details differ, many societies give a physiological explanation for conception (62 per cent of 26 societies) ... In some societies, intercourse is not explicitly mentioned as necessary for conception, but its role is strongly implied. Sperm is repeatedly mentioned as one of the main elements out of which the child is formed ... In other societies, the relationship between frequency of intercourse and conception is more clearly specified ... A second category of beliefs about conception consists of those that assert that intercourse is a necessary not a sufficient condition for the conception of the child (27 per cent of 26 societies). Other factors, especially supernatural ones, are thought to play an important role ... The last category of beliefs about conception is associated with societies in which ethnographers have claimed that the people have *no* idea of the relationship between intercourse and conception (12 per cent of 26 societies) ... Nevertheless, I am particularly uneasy about the validity of this category because of the lack of supplementary information to corroborate the writers' statements" (286–7).

24 Gimbutas, *Language*, 175; our emphasis.

25 Gimbutas, ibid., 181. She continues: "The phallus is often used with the female body, whose inherent power is enhanced by the life force manifested in the column. On this Upper Palaeolithic figurine of steatite (or serpentine marble), the head is replaced by a featureless phallus ... The Old European phallus is far from being the obscene symbol of our days. Rather, it is close to what is still found in India, the *lingam* a sacred cosmic pillar inherited from the Neolithic Indus valley civilization ... One of the earliest such representations in Europe is a fusion of the phallus with the divine body of the Goddess, which begins in the Upper Palaeolithic. Some of the "Venuses" of this period have phallic heads with no facial features ... The same phenomenon is encountered in southeastern Europe during the Neolithic until about 5000 BC ... Among the Starcevo figurines of the mid-6th millennium BC are some whose form is that of male genitals; the upper part is phallic and the lower buttocks are shaped like testicles" (230–1).

26 Ibid., 231–2. Elsewhere, Gimbutas argues that "divine bisexuality ... [stressed] *her* absolute power." In other words, the great goddess is bisexual but nevertheless female, a meaningless contradiction in terms. When confronted with the undeniable presence of a penis, Gimbutas routinely explains it away as something attached to a female form and thus, despite the absence of any logical connection, inessential; the male force enhances the female, she believes, but does not fuse with it. One example is particularly strange. She describes something with a high cylindrical neck, a "mushroom" head and no facial features. "When viewing the object from the back," she notes, "we see an anatomically correct rendition of the male genitalia, an erect penis and scrotum with the genital ridge represented by a deep groove ... When viewed from top and bottom ... however, the sculpture resembles female genitalia" (232). Strangely enough, she marvels at its perfect combination of female and female imagery, rejecting the very idea that it might be "the obscene symbol." No, she insists, it is not a penis at all but a cosmic pillar! Why should anyone consider male genitalia obscene, though, but not female genitalia? Although Hindus believe that *lingam* is a cosmic pillar, moreover, they also believe it is a form of the supreme god Shiva. Examples of this kind establish beyond a doubt that phallic imagery was commonplace.

27 Gimbutas, *Language*, 265.

28 From evidence presented by Jean Clottes in a lecture for the Department of Anthropology at McGill University on 22 March 1996.

29 Gimbutas, *Language*, 265.

30 Dorothy O. Cameron, quoted in Gimbutas, *Language*, 265.

31 "Autumn Comes and Leaves Fall," *Westmount Examiner*, 26 September 1991: 6; this artwork stands in Westmount, a suburb of Montreal.

32 Frayser, *Varities*, 284. Carl Ernst von Baer first observed the ovum in 1827.

33 Gimbutas, *Language*, 266.

34 Peggy Reeves Sanday, *Female Power and Male Dominance: On the Origins of Sexual Inequality* (Cambridge: Cambridge University Press, 1981).

35 Ibid., 68.

36 Ibid., 66. She examined ninety-nine societies for which information is available on both their origin myths and the type of game animals that they hunt. Of those societies that have male imagery, 72 per cent hunt small game or several types of game and 28 per cent hunt mainly big game; of those that have both female and female imagery, 61 per cent hunt small game and 39 per cent hunt mainly big game; and of those that have female imagery, 48 per cent hunt small game and 52 per cent hunt mainly big game. Forty-three societies hunt mainly big game. In all but five of these, moreover, she found either male or both male and female symbols of origin. Fifty-six societies hunt big game and gather plants or hunt small game, fish, and gather plants. Because Sanday's anthropological study was both comparative and thorough, we have used it extensively for this and other books.

37 Although Gimbutas refers to some Palaeolithic sites, she concentrates on Neolithic ones in southwestern Europe dating from 6500 to 3500 BC and in western Europe from 4500 to 2500 BC.

38 Gimbutas, *Language*, 258–63. Neolithic artists usually depicted a fish either within the goddess's womb or alone to represent a goddess.

39 Barbara Ehrenreich too is critical of Lerner, noting that she assigns to the Neolithic period cave paintings and sculpture – the famous "Venus figurines" – that actually belong to the Palaeolithic (*Blood Rites, Origins and History of the Passions of War* [New York, Metropolitan Books, 1997], 103). But Ehrenreich herself has trouble establishing the Palaeolithic origins of goddess worship. She assumes, for example, that the Venus figurines and the paintings in upper Palaeolithic cave art are goddesses. (Like many of the feminists that we discuss, she seizes on every indication of female imagery and goddess worship but either ignores or trivializes every indication of male imagery and god worship. She hardly mentions gods, which leaves readers with the impression that goddesses were universal or at least dominant.) In addition, she assumes that the figurines symbolize predation. As we say, however, the figures are notoriously

hard to interpret. Ehrenreich argues lamely that they need not refer to
fertility. By doing so, she hopes to create enough scope for her own theory that they refer instead to predation. As for the painted figures, she
downplays the possibility that these are mistresses of animals. For her
they are supreme goddesses.

Like Gimbutas and Lerner, moreover, Ehrenreich offers an ahistorical
analysis. Most of her material comes from civilizations – that is, from the
large-scale cultures that states generate. "Anthropologists," writes Bruce
Trigger, "distinguish early civilizations from less complex chiefdoms or
tribal states and from still simpler tribal agricultural and hunter-gatherer
societies. The smaller-scale societies tended to be integrated primarily by
kinship networks, and social relations rather than religious concepts
played a leading role in mediating all other forms of activities ... [These
proto-states] can be subdivided into two general types according to the
nature of their political organization. I have labeled these city-state systems
and territorial states" (*Early Civilizations: Ancient Egypt in Context*
[Cairo: American University in Cairo Press, 1993], 8). Very little of
Ehrenreich's material comes from Neolithic societies or even from their
modern-day horticultural counterparts, much less from Paleolithic ones.
By pushing goddess worship back to the Palaeolithic, she can argue that it
was primeval; if the great goddess was not there at the very dawn of human
history, as image and artifact, she was surely there before most others.
Ehrenreich admits that archaeologists have found both male and female
figurines, but she scarcely mentions the male ones. In fact, she devotes a
whole chapter to the female ones: predators with the faces of women. The
implication is that these female figurines might have predated the cave art,
although her evidence must be later than both the cave art and the figurines.
But her main point is that they represented female hunters, because women
participated in mob hunting (in which whole bands participated in driving
animals over cliffs or into pits or bogs).

It was the blood of women during menstruation and childbirth,
according to Ehrenreich, that people associated with predators that left
bloody wounds on their prey. They associated the blood of women also
with their monthly cycles and in turn with the moon's monthly cycle,
which produced a sense of time. But it was the fact that women could
bleed without loss of life that, for Ehrenreich, contributed most to their
power and, by extension, the power of goddesses.

There is a far more likely explanation. As Ehrenreich notes, animal
populations might have declined during the Mesolithic period (*Blood
Rites*, 110, 117, 123). In that case, people might have associated god-

desses with the renewal of herds. Why? Because they had already associated women with pregnancy – new life – and with sustaining life in spite of periodic bleeding. If so, they would have worshipped goddesses as mistresses of animals and thus symbolically renewed the dwindling herds of stags, bears, and so forth.

Because the people of Neolithic states believed that goddesses enjoyed eating sacrificial meat, Ehrenreich assumes that the same was true of goddesses in the Palaeolithic. This would mean that the ritual sacrifice of animals also had been common in the Palaeolithic. Never mind that Palaeolithic evidence of sacrifice – or evidence of any kind – is scarce. (Ehrenreich offers no convincing evidence in *Blood Rites* for predatory deities in the Palaeolithic period and none at all for sacrifice. For example, she tries to make a case for predatory deities, but her evidence is nothing more than a bear skull found near what could have been an altar [73]. It could just as easily have represented a deity who replenished the animals. Similarly, deposits of bones need not be the remains of sacrificial animals; people might have used them in rituals to replenish animals. Today's hunting and gathering societies, uninfluenced by horticultural ones, do not practise animal or human sacrifice, which suggests that Palaeolithic ones did not do so either.)

40 See Katherine K. Young, "Creation Myths/Cosmogonic Myths" in the *Oxford Encyclopedia of Women in World History*, ed. Bonnie G. Smith (Oxford: Oxford University Press, 2008).

41 Tikva Frymer-Kensky, *In the Wake of the Goddesses: Women, Culture and the Biblical Tradition of Pagan Myth* (New York: Free Press, 1992), 32.

42 Ibid., 12.

43 Gimbutas, *Language*, 316.

44 Ibid., xix. "A remnant in the historical era of the goddesses' ruling power is indicated by the usage of the term *queen* for those who were not married to Indo-European deities but who continued to be powerful in their own right. Herodotus wrote of 'Queen Artemis' and Hesychius called Aphrodite 'the queen.' Diana, the Roman counterpart of the virgin Artemis, was invoked as *regina* ... The most inspired account in all ancient literature is contained in Lucius Apuleius' 2nd century A.D. *Golden Ass*, the earliest Latin novel, where Lucius invokes Isis from the depths of his misery. Then she appears and utters: 'I am she that is the natural mother of all things, mistress and governess of all the elements, the initial progeny of worlds, chief of the powers divine, *queen of all* that are in Hell, the principal of them all that dwell in Heaven, manifested alone and under

one form of all the gods and goddesses. At my will the planets of the sky, the wholesome winds of the seas, and the lamentable silences of hell be disposed; my name, my divinity is adored throughout the world, in diverse manners, in variable customs, and by many names'" (318–19).

45 Like Lerner and Gimbutas, Ehrenreich refers occasionally to a goddess's "reign" (*Blood Rites*, 110). This word indicates royal rule, that of a queen. In the art of archaic states in both the ancient Near East and India, lions and tigers – or figures riding these powerful predators – often represent royalty. Most of Ehrenreich's textual references to goddesses and predators are from the period of archaic states. But because the predatory goddesses of these states were supreme, she implies, so were the earlier predatory goddesses of the Neolithic period (or even the Palaeolithic): pure speculation.

46 Gimbutas, *Language*, 318.

47 There is an exception: *Urmonotheismus*, an archaic monotheism that Wilhelm Schmidt described. It occurs among some hunters and gatherers (Charles H. Long, "Silence and Signification" in *"Myths and Symbols: Studies in Honor of Mircea Eliade*, ed. Joseph M. Kitagawa and Charles H. Long [Chicago: University of Chicago Press], 143–4).

48 Hindus, for example, have often represented the supreme god, Vishnu, as a king. The idea that he had many names and incarnations made it easy for him to absorb formerly separate gods such as Rama or even local tribal ones such as Jagannath in Orissa. Vishnu's rise to the status of supreme god, at any rate, clearly paralleled the rise of states in India. The transcendent and omnipotent divine ruler corresponded closely to the majestic and omnipotent earthly ones of Hindu kingdoms. But Vishnu was not the only god to claim supremacy – so did Shiva, and the two were rivals for centuries.

49 Goddesses that have similar forms are not necessarily identical. We can explain their similarities in many ways. When people migrate, for instance, they take their ideas and customs with them. The same symbol can mean one thing here, moreover, and another thing there. Similar forms can have different functions. Similar shapes or associations can generate different forms. And what about dissimilarities? Gimbutas herself divides "Old Europe" into cultural zones. If everything had been uniform and "monistic," why study separate zones? Because we are dealing with prehistory – which is to say, the period before written records that might have explained precisely how people actually understood female symbols – interpreting what evidence we do have is inherently risky. For lack of an alternative, scholars look for parallels from other times and places.

50 Mary Lefkowitz, "The Twilight of the Goddess," *New Republic* (3 August 1992): 29. Lefkowitz refers to the mid-nineteenth century work of Johann Bachofen. In his introduction to *Mother Right*, Bachofen proposed a study of mythology that would unite what he called "the multiform and shifting manifestation" of myth under a single general description. But surely that multitude of forms and the shifting manifestations are not secondary things that students of myth should erase in the name of a theory. The analytical coarseness of this method is extraordinary, and it is nicely illustrated by all this recent literature on goddesses.

51 Lefkowitz, "Twilight," 33.

52 Lerner, for instance, writes that this goddess "is shown amidst pillars or trees, accompanied by goats, snakes, birds. Eggs and symbols of vegetation are associated with her. These symbols indicate that she was worshipped as a source of fertility for vegetation, animals, and humans. She is represented by the Minoan snake-goddess, with her breasts exposed. She was venerated in Sumer as Ninhursag and Inanna; in Babylon as Kubab and Ishtar; in Phoenicia as Astarte; in Canaan as Anath; in Greece, as Hekate-Artemis. Her frequent association with the moon symbolized her mystical powers over nature and the seasons. The belief system manifested in Great goddess worship was monistic and animistic. There was *unity* among earth and the stars, humans and nature, birth and death, *all of which were embodied in the Great Goddess*" (Lerner, *Creation*, 148–9; our emphasis).

53 Sam D. Gill, *Mother Earth* (Chicago: University of Chicago Press, 1991).

54 Ibid., 6.

55 Edward B. Tylor, *Primitive Culture: Researches into the Development of Mythology, Philosophy, Religion, Language, Art and Custom*, 2 vols. (London: John Murray, 1873).

56 Gill, *Mother Earth*, 126, 66.

57 Ibid., 146.

58 James Mooney, "The Ghost Dance Religion and the Sioux Outbreak of 1890," *14th Annual Report of the Bureau of Ethnology, 1892–1893* (Washington: Government Printing Office, 1896).

59 Something similar might have happened in connection with the Zuni story of creation, says Gill, even though it includes both an earth mother and a sky father. This story was really the creation of another scholar, Frank Hamilton Cushing, who claimed that it was common not only among the horticultural tribes of the American southwest but also throughout North America.

60 Hubert Bancroft, Andrew Lang, Albrecht Dieterich, Hartley Burr Alexander, James Frazer, Frederick Heiler, Joachim Wach, Gerardus van der Leeuw, E.O. James, Raffaele Pettazzoni, and Mircea Eliade all drew from these few reports of an earth goddess in Amerindian religion in order to substantiate their theories about a universal and primordial goddess.

61 Eliade; quoted in Gill, *Mother Earth*, 116.

62 Ironically, feminist revisionism relies on a foundation laid by *men* (Bachofen, Marx, Engels, Frazer, Briffault, and so on) who contributed to the case for a matriarchal stage of history. But they had quite different goals in mind. Bachofen believed that matriarchy preceded patriarchy, for instance, but only as a more *primitive* stage in human evolution.

63 Lerner, *Creation*, 17.

64 G. Robina Quale, *A History of Marriage Systems* (New York: Greenwood Press, 1988) In fact, scholars now think that pair-bonding developed even *before* the origin of our species among hominids such as *Homo erectus* or *Homo habilis*. Nonetheless, culture has always cemented those pair bonds.

65 David C. Geary and Mark V. Flinn, "Evolution of Human Parental Behavior and the Human Family," in *Parenting: Science and Practice* 1, nos. 1–2 (January–June 2001): 5–61.

66 Geary and Flinn point out that one other explanation for the development of human families is the need to prevent infanticide: "When infanticide risk is high, females copulate with males who are likely to displace the dominant male and thus confuse paternity. Males generally do not attempt to kill the infants of females with whom they have copulated ... Although infanticide risk may have been present during hominid evolution, it is not, in and of itself, a sufficient explanation of concealed ovulation in humans" ("Evolution," 23). But Geary and Flinn argue that "this is because an evolved female strategy that confused paternity would be associated with little or no male parenting, which is inconsistent with the finding of male parenting in every human culture that has been studied ... and with the possibility that Austraolopithecine males parented."

67 Lerner, *Creation*, 39.

68 Ibid., 42.

69 Eisler, xvi.

70 Frymer-Kensky, 17–18.

71 Lerner, 45.

72 David D. Gilmore, *Manhood in the Making: Cultural Concepts of Masculinity* (New Haven: Yale University Press, 1990), 40–8.

73 Ehrenreich's reconstruction of history has a political implication. Modern women should realize that early women were indeed powerful hunters. Fierce and predatory goddesses, she believes, must have symbolically represented powerful women. Her aim is not to restore goddess worship, to be sure, but to restore women's power by arguing that the women of remote antiquity were hunters, not merely gatherers.

74 Morgan D. Maclachlan, *Why They Did Not Starve: Biocultural Adaptation in a South Indian Village* (Philadelphia: Institute for the Study of Human Issues, 1983).

75 But note also that masculine and feminine roles overlap considerably in small-scale societies, such as predominantly horticultural ones, which do not rely heavily for their food supply on male mobility, size, and strength.

76 Ehrenreich, *Blood Rites*, 108.

77 Some evidence does not support Ehrenreich. The *Daily Telegraph* reported on studies of Boxgrove, a lower Paleolithic site in West Sussex, England. Boxgrove contained a waterhole that attracted big animals such as rhinos, horses, bison, and giant deer. Archaeologists have found thousands of bones there, many of which have cut marks. This suggests that hunters speared and butchered them. See David Derbyshire, "Stone Age Man: Spear-Thrower or Scavenger?" *National Post*, 26 May 2003: A12; reprinted from the *Daily Telegraph*.

78 Ehrenreich, 108.

79 The !Kung lived in the Kalahari desert of southern Africa. Though now farmers, they were traditionally hunter-gatherers. The women collected plants and small mammals. The men hunted big game; this meant major expeditions of several days, because no big animals lived in the desert.

80 See McLachlan, *Why They Did Not Starve*, 242.

81 The detailed evidence of Linda Owen's study of this topic was convincing enough to Marta Camps. "Personally," writes Camps, "I approach 'feminist' perspectives to life in general with a bit of caution, because I could not disagree more with those whose aim is not to correct the extant biases that put women in a lower or less important position in many activities or situations than men, but instead, try to institute the reverse position, that women are superior in just about everything. In this respect I found Owen's study to be exemplary because it does not attempt this type of 'make-over.' If present biases about the roles of men and women in prehistory are to be corrected, it will not happen by trying to demonstrate that the correct version is to be found at the other end of the stick. Clearly, avoiding this pitfall is one of the strengths of Owen's study"

(review of *Distorting the Past: Gender and the Division of Labor in the European Upper Paleolithic*, by Linda Owen, in *PaleoAnthropology* [2008]: 91–2).

We are less enthusiastic about Owen's study. It corrects early academic attitudes toward "man the hunter," to be sure, but its title still indicates that male academics purposely distorted the past. Besides, Owen's book is about hunting in general, not about big-game hunting in particular. Hunters do need massive upper-body strength to throw their arrows or spears, and most men really do have more upper-body strength than most women. According to Bobbi Low, "Many human male-female physical differences are immediately obvious: compared with women, men on average have more upper-body strength and muscular development, larger jaws, and heavier brow ridges ... ("Biological Bases of Sex Differences," in *Encyclopedia of Sex and Gender: Men and Women in the World's Cultures*, vol. 1, ed. by Carol R. Ember and Melvin Ember [New York: Springer, 2003], 28).

And Owen still overstates the case for women's participation in some subsistence activities. "The similarity in gender stereotypes found cross-culturally," writes Deborah Best, "suggests that the psychological characteristics differentially associated with women and men follow a pancultural model with cultural factors producing minor variations around general themes. Biological differences (e.g., females bear children, males have greater physical strength) serve as the basis for a division of labor, with women primarily responsible for child care and other domestic activities, and men for hunting (providing) and protection. Gender stereotypes evolve to support this division of labor and assume that each sex has or can develop characteristics consistent with their assigned roles. Once established, stereotypes serve as socialization models that encourage boys to become independent and adventurous, and girls to become nurturant and affiliative. Consequently, these characteristics are incorporated into men's and women's self-concepts, aspects of their masculinity and femininity. This model illustrates how, with only minor variations, people across different cultures come to associate one set of characteristics with men and another with men. Pancultural similarities in sex and gender greatly outweigh cultural differences. Indeed, the way in which male-female relationships are organized is remarkably similar across social groups. The relatively minor biological differences between the sexes can be amplified or diminished by cultural practices and socialization, making gender differences in roles and behaviors generally modest but in some cases culturally important ("Gender Stereotypes," in

Encyclopedia of Sex and Gender: Men and Women in the World's Cultures, vol. 1, ed. Carol R. Ember and Melvin Ember, vol. 1 [New York: Springer, 2003], 11–23).

Moreover, the brains of men and women do differ in some ways, including spatial ones. Scholars suggest that men's tendency to use directional cues and women's to use landmarks originated because of evolutionary pressures. Men hunted for big game, which required them to travel far from home; women gathered plants and killed small animals close to home. The importance of male strength is found in other contexts.

Finally, men and women have different functions in agriculture. "Plow agriculture," says Morgan Maclachlan, "is usually male farming because its technology favors the exploitation of the male strength advantage. This occurs not because women are necessarily incapable of such work, but more likely for the following reason: if an activity enhances the material security of a population and if increased proficiency in it occurs with increases in muscular strength or aerobic work capacity, marital selection tends to favor those who cultivate their proficiency at the task ... If men can perform an important task more proficiently than women, women (or their families) will favor men who will do this work for women, and they will especially favor those men who can do it well, because such men offer benefits to wives and children" (*Why They Did Not Starve*, 242).

82 Lerner, *Creation*, 49.

83 David Aberle, "Matrilineal Descent in Crosscultural Perspective," in *Matrilineal Kinship*, ed. Kathleen Gough and David Schneider (Berkeley: University of California Press, 1961), 657–727.

84 Alice Schlegel, *Male Dominance and Female Autonomy: Domestic Authority in Matrilineal Societies* (New Haven: HRAF Press, 1972).

85 William T. Divale, *Matrilocal Residence in Pre-Literate Society* (Ann Arbor: UMI Research Press, 1984), 148–51.

86 Sanday notes the following figures gathered by Murdock and Wilson: "In the total Standard Cross-cultural Sample of 186 societies, 26 (14 percent) are classified in the matrilineal descent category and 38 (21 percent) follow the matrilocal rule of residence" (269).

87 In his foreword to *The Language of the Goddess*, Joseph Campbell supports the view that Neolithic societies were matrilineal or even matriarchal: "In the library of European scholarship the first recognition of such a matristic order of thought and life antecedent to and underlying the historical forms of both Europe and the Near East appeared in 1861 in Johann Jakob Bachofen's *Das Mutterrecht*, where it was shown that in the codes of Roman Law vestigial features can be recognized of a matri-

lineal order of inheritance. Ten years earlier, in America, Lewis H. Morgan had published in *The League of the Ho-de-no-sau-nee, or Iroquois*, a two-volume report of a society in which such a principle of 'Mother Right' was still recognized; and in a systematic review, subsequently, of kinship systems throughout America and Asia, he had demonstrated an all but worldwide distribution of such a prepatriarchal order of communal life. Bachofen's recognition, around 1871, of the relevance of Morgan's work to his own marked a breakthrough from an exclusively European to a planetary understanding of this sociological phenomenon. There is to be recognized in Marija Gimbutas's reconstruction of the 'Language of the Goddess' a far broader range of historical significance, therefore, than that merely of Old Europe, from the Atlantic to the Dnieper, c. 7000–3500 B.C." (in Gimbutas, *Language of the Goddess*, xiii.)

88 Gimbutas, *Language*, xx.

89 Ibid. Lineage societies in which the clan head assumes greater importance are common in the transition from Neolithic societies to chiefdoms and kingdoms.

90 Nevertheless, some of these societies were beginning the process of state formation. This involved the rise of chiefs resulting from the development of social stratification and lineages.

91 Lerner, *Creation*, 35.

92 Ibid., 29. Matrilocal societies, too, give women an advantage by allowing them to live with their kin; men arrive as strangers.

93 David M. Schneider and Kathleen Gough, *Matrilineal Kinship* (Berkeley: University of California Press, 1961), 22.

94 A.R. Radcliffe-Brown and Daryll Forde, *African Systems of Kinship and Marriage* (London: Oxford University Press, 1950), 283–4.

95 Schneider and Gough, *Matrilineal Kinship*, 22.

96 Karla O. Poewe, *Matrilineal Ideology: Male-Female Dynamics in Luapula, Zambia* (London: Academic Press, 1981), 50.

97 Ibid., 61. Note the following: "Some men are obsessed with the sexual activities of their wife. They might spend days scheming how to catch their wife and her lover during sexual intercourse ... Usually, [the] duration [of conflict] ... is shortened by outbursts of physical violence ... Of 250 civil court cases heard in Lukwesa during the year 1973, 103 refer to tensions between the sexes" (69).

98 Ehrenreich proposes a new goddess theory. She rejects the exclusive focus on the *gentle* goddess, like us, noting that Gimbutas "consistently slighted the goddess's *violent* side, even conjecturing wistfully that the Minoan and Sumerian goddess's double axe symbolized a butterfly!" Ehrenreich

observes that it "is tempting to discern, in myths connecting the goddess to the hunt and the menstruating woman to the hunting animal, a time when real women played a central role in the realms of both economies and religion: in the economy, as participants in the hunt; in religion, as beings whose bodies had the seemingly divine gift of bleeding without dying, and doing so regularly, in tune with the most salient of the night skies" (*Blood Rites*, 108). Women were powerful, she suggests, partly because their periods synchronized in groups. As predatory hunters, they personified goddesses. In her opinion, the link was direct and positive.

She observes that refusing to deal with the violent side of many goddesses – Artemis, Cybele, Sekmet, Innana, Astarte, Kali, and Durga – is just plain old gender bias. She refers to feminists who associate violence exclusively with men: "In the 'logic' of our own time, violence is an exclusively male attribute, so that the notion of a predator goddess can only be a cultural oxymoron" (*Blood Rites*, 103). Ehrenreich has a point. It really is important to acknowledge the ferocious imagery of goddesses, their association with fearsome animals, and their voracious appetite for meat or blood. Doing so respects the historical truth and casts doubt on any position that has no respect for historical truth or at least the quest for it as the *sine qua non* of scholarship.

In any case, advocates of the great goddess attribute the peace and harmony of paradise primarily to the influence of women. But taking other factors into account, we could argue that men were partially or primarily responsible not only for the violence and conflict of the current state of affairs but *also* for the peace and harmony of the one that *preceded* it along with some of those that followed it (because advanced states fostered peace within their kingdoms).

99 Marija Gimbutas, *The Civilization of the Goddess*, viii.
100 Ibid.
101 See Bruce G. Trigger, *Understanding Early Civilizations: A Comparative Study* (Cambridge: Cambridge University Press, 2003), 40–53.
102 Eli Sagan, *At the Dawn of Tyranny: The Origins of Individualism, Political Oppression, and the State* (New York: Knopf, 1985).
103 Paul Nathanson discusses this subject much more fully in *Over the Rainbow: The Wizard of Oz as a Secular Myth of America* (Albany: State University of New York Press, 1991).
104 This discovery was presented by Jean Clottes in a lecture at McGill University on 22 March 1996.
105 Jane Goodall was the first to describe what she called "chimp wars." The elimination of neighbouring unrelated males allows males to take terri-

tory with prime feeding areas as well as reproductive females. We lack archaeological evidence of widespread human warfare from the Paleolithic period (although even contemporary hunting and gathering societies are generally peaceful). Maybe our remote ancestors solved many of their conflicts with neighbouring bands by simply moving on (the flight rather than the fight response). *Homo erectus* learned to dominate all other species, which could have made possible the gradual migration out of Africa. Gleary and Flinn write that people are "unique in that social competition occurs in the context of ecological dominance. In most ecologies, human groups have achieved a level of control over essential resources (e.g., food, use of land) that is not evident in other species" (30). But the authors do mention at least one possible context for early wars: intra-species competition, in which *Homo sapiens* might have eliminated both *Homo erectus* and *Homo neanderthalensis* (27).

106 Gimbutas, *Language*, 223.

107 See Patricia McGee, "Challenging Women: Peaceful Women May Have Once Ruled the World," *Maclean's*, 12 February 1990, 66–7.

108 Actually, archaeologists do not know the precise life span. According to a paleontologist at McGill University, M.S. Bisson, early hominids had a life span of under twenty years. It is true that the average life span of those that archaeologists have found at burial sites was approximately thirty, but not everyone received elaborate burials. We might never find the burial sites of many people, including children. It seems likely, therefore, that thirty represents a *high* life span for this period. Even in classical Greece, the average life span was still approximately thirty years.

109 The ancient Israelites were highly unusual in recording their military defeats as well as their triumphs. They were even more unusual in recording their moral and spiritual defeats. Doing so, in fact, became a hallmark of the prophetic tradition.

110 Elizabeth Gleick, "When Having It All Is Not Enough," review of *What Our Mothers Didn't Tell Us* by Danielle Crittenden, *New York Times Book Review*, 31 January 1999: 9.

111 Hebrew scriptures – especially the prophetic books – record a long and bitter conflict between those who valued the austere way of life known to their nomadic ancestors and those who were happy to adopt the sensual customs of their agricultural neighbours.

112 Lerner, *Creation*, 222.

113 Ibid., 228.

114 McGee, "Challenging," 66–7.

115 Eva Keuls, book jacket of *Civilization*.

116 Lerner, book jacket of *Civilization*. See also her "How the Historical Profession Became a Male Preserve," review of *The Gender of History: Men, Women and Historical Practice* by Bonnie Smith, *Journal of Women's History* 11, no. 2 (summer 1999): 221–3.

117 Barbara Ehrenreich has a doctorate in biology. She has written or jointly written many books but has become best known as an essayist for *Harper's* and *Time*.

118 Barbara G. Walker, *The Woman's Encyclopedia of Myths and Secrets* (San Francisco: Harper and Row, 1983), 346.

119 "Perennial" philosophers and theosophists have come up with similar positions.

120 Katherine K. Young, "Goddesses, Feminists, and Scholars, in *The Annual Review of Women in World Religions*, vol. 1, ed. Arvind Sharma and Katherine K. Young (Albany: State University of New York Press, 1991), 105–79.

121 Ibid., 116–17.

122 Ibid., 158.

123 Lefkowitz, "Twilight," 31.

124 Rosemary Radford Ruether, *Goddesses and the Divine Feminine: A Western Religious History* (Berkeley: University of California Press, 2005), 300.

CHAPTER TWO

1 According to Julien Ries, the "theogonic aspect of the fall deals with the degradation of the divine and is found in the numerous myths concerning the origin of the gods, of their victory over chaos, or of the victory of the more recent forces of divinity over older ones. Coextensive with the creation, the fall as presented in theogony implies the identification of evil and chaos on the one hand and of salvation and creation on the other ... Anthropogony, however, offers the most important perspective on the fall. From this perspective, the contemporary human condition, a condition of degradation in contrast to that of the golden age of humanity, is explained as the consequence of a fall, a tragic event that bursts into human history ... Myths of the fall clearly show three essential elements ... the concept of a golden age in the beginning ... a break or degradation of original harmony ... [and] the explanation of the present human condition ... [A]ny conception of the fall has implications concerning the origins of evil, as well as intimations of a possible overcoming of evil through a recovery of the state that existed previous to the fall. Thus ...

[an] ethical dimension is grafted onto, and is coextensive with, the idea of the fall and forms an important part of a hermeneutical approach that tries to come to terms with its relationship to guilt or fault" (Julien Ries, "The Fall," *Encyclopedia of Religion*, ed. Mircea Eliade [New York: Macmillan, 1987], vol. 5: 256).

2 There was an intermediate version. This was articulated by Elizabeth Cady Stanton (1815–1902). This "mother of feminism," an early leader of the movement demanding suffrage for women and an end to discrimination against women, was the daughter of a congressman and the wife a lawyer and abolitionist. Realizing that the Fall had come to be associated with women, she argued that the whole idea of a Fall was both unnecessary and undesirable: "Take the snake, the fruit-tree and the woman from the tableau, and we have no fall, no frowning Judge, no Inferno, no everlasting punishment and hence no need of a Saviour. Thus the bottom falls out of the whole Christian theology. Here is a reason why in all the Biblical researches and higher criticisms, the scholars never touch the position of women" (Elizabeth Cady Stanton, quoted in Mary Daly, *Beyond God the Father: Toward a Philosophy of Women's Liberation* [Boston: Beacon Press, 1973], 69). In our time, goddess ideologues (and feminist ideologues) argue not for abolition of the Fall but for a *reversal* of it: blaming entirely on men what some post-biblical traditions once blamed primarily on women and what the biblical tradition originally blamed on both men and women.

3 For some reason, few people make this rather obvious argument. Nevertheless, it appears elsewhere at least once: "If the woman was the 'first' from both a biological and a historical point of view," writes Susanne Heine, "and therefore, so the argument goes, has to be the first again, as first cause she herself is responsible for all that follows, and is thus also responsible for the rise of the patriarchate" (*Christianity and the Goddess: Systematic Criticism of a Feminist Theology* [London: SCM Press, 1988], 87).

4 Elizabeth G. Davis, *The First Sex* (New York: Dent, 1973), 66; quoted in Susanne Heine, *Christianity*, 77.

5 Heine, *Christianity*, 77.

6 *The Goddess Remembered*, directed by Donna Read, script by D.C. Blade, Donna Read, Gloria Demers, 16mm, 54 min. (Montreal: National Film Board of Canada: Studio D, 1989).

7 *Behind the Veil: Nuns*, directed by Margaret Wescott, script and narration by Gloria Demers, 16 mm, 130 min. (Montreal: National Film Board of Canada: Studio D, 1984).

8 *The Burning Times*, directed by Donna Read, script by Erna Buffie, 16mm. 58 min. (Montreal: National Film Board of Canada: Studio D, 1993).

9 *Goddess*, 12.

10 Ibid.

11 Ibid., 12–13.

12 Ibid., 13.

13 Ibid., 13.

14 *Goddess*, 1.

15 Ibid., 10.

16 Gerda Lerner, *The Creation of Patriarchy* (New York: Oxford University Press, 1986), 53.

17 Ibid., 144–6.

18 Ibid., 151.

19 Queen Hatshepsut, the "female pharaoh," was an exception.

20 See Katherine K. Young, "Goddesses, Feminists, and Scholars," in vol. 1, of the *Annual Review of Women in World Religions*, ed. Arvind Sharma and Katherine K. Young (Albany: State University of New York Press, 1991), 137–42.

21 The rise of states always involved economic change, and economic change usually involved both symbolic and social change – including those affecting the status of men and women. But these changes occurred in various ways. "If the transition to agriculture [is] a consequence of migration or conquest," writes Peggy Reeves Sanday, "people face the decision of whether to adopt or reject foreign supernatural symbols along with the new technology. The choice is clearly a function of circumstances" (*Female Power and Male Dominance: On the Origins of Sexual Inequality* [Cambridge: Cambridge University Press, 1981], 70). Moreover, a group of hunters or warriors who migrate into an area of agricultural abundance might have changed the mythological charter to incorporate both masculine and feminine symbolism. If resources were scarce, on the other hand, they might have "accentuated masculine-oriented origin myths" (72). Advanced agricultural economies and increasing technological complexity usually accompanied a masculine orientation (69).

22 G. Robina Quale, *A History of Marriage Systems* (New York: Greenwood Press, 1988), 27–33.

23 Lerner, *Creation*, 49.

24 Quale, *History*, 33.

25 Because chiefs or kings had many women, this was a status marker. The democratization of this status marker, though, led to loss of status. In political terms, it undermined the hierarchy. Every chief or king had a

vested interest in ensuring that he alone retained the status of having many women or cattle or whatever. (Doing so did not prevent ordinary men, however, from occasionally seeking status in this way. Sometimes they became village headmen, local chiefs, or even kings.)

26 Quale argues that even chimpanzees "tend to move out toward other groups from their natal bands when they are receptive to intercourse ... It seems reasonable that expecting hominid females to move out, and hominid males to stay within the bands in which they had been born, would serve both incest avoidance (shown ... to be biologically advantageous) and the maintenance of bonds among groups of males who were accustomed to hunting together. It also seems reasonable that early hominid females would agree to such a move because they had recognized that collaborative hunting was more efficiently done by males who were familiar with one another as well as with the terrain, while females' gathering, though often done in company with one another, did not require as much practised cooperation as hunting ... It has been hypothesized that brother-sister avoidance comes naturally in human beings because of early familiarity, which tends to preclude the feeling of mild but discernible novelty that seems to be required for strong and lasting attraction ... It therefore seems fairly likely that at least by the time of Homo habilis a pattern had already been established by which females left at maturity to find mates in other bands, while males stayed together as a hunting team" (*History*, 30–3).

27 Ibid., 35.

28 As gathering yielded first to harvesting and storing and then to planting, which is the probable sequence, more children survived into adulthood. The human population nearly doubled in the six thousand years that followed the introduction of agriculture (in the sense of harvesting and storing), claims Quale, and it nearly doubled again during each of the next three millennia (47).

29 Ibid., 50. Tikva Frymer-Kensky too argues that women participated from the beginning in developing the notion of property, because the Sumerians believed that goddesses did on the divine plane what women did on the human plane (*In the Wake of the Goddesses: Women, Culture and the Biblical Tradition of Pagan Myth* [New York: Free Press, 1992], 34).

30 Even after the rise of states, women continued to have some economic power. In Sumer, elite women played an important economic role between 3000 and 2400 BC. Before marriage, according to Marc Van De Mieroop, women probably owned big estates. After marriage, they owned and ran their own households apart from those of their husbands.

Women participated in farming, irrigating, gardening, tending livestock, and producing textiles. Male slaves, captured in foreign campaigns, provided much of the physical labour. Women participated in trade and commerce, moreover, and also in court proceedings ("Women in the Economy of Sumer," in *Women's Earliest Records: From Ancient Egypt and Western Asia*, ed. Barbara S. Lesko [Atlanta: Scholars Press, 1989]). The Sumerians, not surprisingly, believed that goddesses controlled the storage and management of surplus food and goods (Frymer-Kensky, *Wake*, 56). Still later, during the neo-Babylonian period from 1894 to 1595 BC, women conducted their own legal, financial, and commercial transactions. In addition, they owned property and made their own donations to the temples (Rivkah Harri, "Independent Women in Ancient Mesopotamia?" in Lesko, 145–6).

31 Frymer-Kensky, *Wake*, 62.

32 Ibid., 63.

33 Ibid., 64.

34 Ibid., 65.

35 Lerner, *Creation*, 143.

36 Ibid.

37 Carol P. Christ, *The Laughter of Aphrodite: Reflections on a Journey to the Goddess* (San Francisco: Harper and Row, 1987), 80.

38 Frymer-Kensky, *Wake*, 66.

39 Ibid., 78.

40 J. Aistleitner, *Die Mytholgischen und kultischen Texte aus Ras Schamra* (Budapest: Akademiai Kaido, 1959: 41); quoted in Susanne Heine, 46.

41 Goddesses have ruled over prisons as well as battlefields. Frymer-Kensky points out that Nungal, another Sumerian goddess, controlled the dungeons. "Her prison is a place of sighs and groans, in which the distressed pass the day in tears and lamentations" (*Wake*, 34).

42 David Kinsley, *Hindu Goddesses: Visions of the Divine Feminine in the Hindu Religious Tradition* (Berkeley: University of California Press, 1986), 117.

43 Ibid., 118.

44 Campbell, foreword to Marija Gimbutas, *The Language of the Goddess* (New York: Harper and Row, 1989), xiii–xiv.

45 Gimbutas, ibid., xx–xxi.

46 The correct neologism would be "gylandric." But that would have made the word *andros*, referring to men, more visible.

47 Riane Eisler, *The Chalice and the Blade: Our History Our Future* (San Francisco: Harper and Row, 1987).

48 Patricia McGee, "Challenging Women: Peaceful Women May Have Once
   Ruled the World," *Maclean*'s, 12 February 1990, 66.
49 Gimbutas's theory of the fall has been embraced by many academics.
   Here, for instance, is Jean Bolen's summary of Gimbutas's theory of the
   Fall of Man: "Dating back at least 5000 years (perhaps even 25,000
   years) before the rise of male religions, Old Europe was a matrifocal, sedentary, peaceful, art-loving, earth- and sea-bound culture that worshipped the Great Goddess. Evidence gleaned from burial sites shows that
   Old Europe was an unstratified, egalitarian society that was destroyed by
   an infiltration of seminomadic, horse-riding, Indo-European peoples from
   the distant north and east. These invaders were patrifocal, mobile, warlike, ideologically sky-oriented, and indifferent to art. The invaders
   viewed themselves as a superior people because of their ability to conquer
   the more culturally developed earlier settlers, who worshipped the Great
   Goddess ... Successive waves of invasions by the Indo-Europeans began
   the dethronement of the Great Goddess ... The goddesses were not completely suppressed, but were incorporated into the religion of the invaders. The invaders imposed their patriarchal culture and their warrior
   religion on the conquered people. The Great Goddess became the subservient consort of the invaders' gods ... Rape appeared in myths for the
   first time ... The female goddesses faded into the background, and
   women in society followed suit" (Jean Shinoda Bolen, *Goddesses in
   Everywoman: A New Psychology of Women* [New York: Harper, 1984],
   20–1). Notice her use of loaded words such as "infiltration," "invaders,"
   "ideologically," "imposed," "dethronement," "suppressed," "conquered," "rape," and "patriarchal" to characterize the Indo-Europeans
   as barbarian bogeymen. The reference to rape is particularly interesting.
   It is based on an argument from silence. Who knows, after all, what
   myths from earlier times were *not* preserved? The implication is not only
   that the Indo-Europeans introduced *myths* of rape, of course, but that
   they introduced *rape itself*, the former being a mere reflection of the latter. At this level of speculation, anything goes. After the Indo-Europeans
   arrived, at any rate, "the attributes, symbols, and power that once were
   invested in one Great Goddess were divided among many goddesses"
   (21). Gradually, their attributes were "expropriated and given to a male
   deity" (20–1). Never mind that Bolen does precisely the same thing herself
   by "expropriating" the attributes of gods and conferring them exclusively
   on a great goddess and her divine daughters. Unlike the patriarchal Greeks
   and Romans, she makes no room at all for deities of the opposite sex.

50 Barbara G. Walker, *The Women's Encyclopedia of Myths and Secrets* (San Francisco: Harper and Row, 1983), 347.

51 Gimbutas, *Language*, 318–19.

52 Eisler, *Chalice*, xvii.

53 Ibid., 58.

54 Ibid., 61.

55 According to John Baines ("Origins of Egyptian Kingship," in *Ancient Egyptian Kingship*, ed. David O'Connor and David P. Silverman [Leiden: Brill, 1995]), "the state and especially the unified state of Egypt, was never envisaged without kingship" (105). "Three principles, interrelated aspects of early kingship can be identified at the risk of some circularity of argument. These are: associations with aggression, conquest, and defense; large-scale architecture; and general royal ideology ... Aggression and conquest are exemplified by the unification itself which can hardly have been completely peaceful by motifs of smiting enemies and heroes warding off wild beasts ... and by large numbers of symbolic and real weapons found in some royal contexts" (105–6).

56 See Eli Sagan, *At the Dawn of Tyranny: The Origins of Individualism, Political Oppression, and the State* (New York, Knopf, 1985), 277.

57 Sagan (ibid., 354–66) discusses the process of individuation at the level of society, adapting the psychoanalytic theory of M. Mahler, *On Human Symbiosis and the Vicissitudes of Individuation* (New York: International Universities Press, 1968).

58 We will discuss the male body, and its history of gradual obsolescence, more fully in *Transcending Misandry*.

59 Consider the views of Colin Renfrew. He thinks that the Indo-Europeans themselves were originally agriculturalists, not pastoralists. Renfrew challenges Gimbutas's reconstruction of an Indo-European (Kurgan) invasion. For him, archaeological evidence of a warrior culture in prehistoric Europe indicates that it developed *internally* among local agricultural peoples as a result of competition for scarce land and resources rather than externally, as Gimbutas would have it, due to invasion by a violent group of foreigners. In short, according to him, the Indo-Europeans were not a distinctively violent people who disturbed the idyllic existence of a peaceful society.

"Drawing on the evidence described by Childe and buttressing it with recent findings," writes Renfrew, "Gimbutas reconstructed a series of 'Kurgan invasions' flowing west from the lands north of the Black Sea ... Yet to my mind it is not a satisfactory story. My reasoning is several fold.

In the first place, the archaeology is not convincing ... Perhaps the strongest objection is simply the lack of conviction behind the whole story. Why on earth should hordes of mounted warriors have moved west at the end of the Neolithic, subjugating the inhabitants of Europe and imposing the proto-Indo-European language on them? What enormous upsurge of population on the steppes could have been responsible? Although its construction is elegant, the story does not ring true for this listener" ("The Origins of Indo-European Languages," *Scientific American* 261, no. 4 [1989]: 109). After discussing the evidence for other theories (including the process of cultural and linguistic change), Renfrew argues that people from Anatolia rather than the Russian steppes gradually migrated west after about 6500 BC, to Greece, the Balkans, central Europe, and southern Italy. They brought agriculture with them. Renfrew thinks that "there is considerably greater continuity in European prehistory than has previously been believed ... In this light the whole early history of Europe appears as a series of transformations and evolutionary adaptations on a common proto-Indo-European base augmented by a few non-Indo-European survivals. The story is not predicated on a series of migrations from without but on a series of complex interactions within a Europe that was already fundamentally agricultural in economy and Indo-European in language" (113). Of course, one could argue also that they might have had good reasons for migrating. What if their homeland had been unable to sustain its population? Domestication of the horse made travel easy or provided military advantages.

In any case, the mysteries of the Indo-Europeans – their origin and their migration patterns – are far from solved.

60 Gimbutas, *Language*, 318.
61 Ibid., 319–20.
62 Paul Nathanson and Katherine K. Young, *Spreading Misandry: The Teaching of Contempt for Men in Popular Culture* (Montreal: McGill-Queen's Unversity Press, 2001), 206–7.
63 See D. Howard Smith, *Chinese Religions* (London: Weidenfeld & Nicolson, 1968), 94–7, 140–8.
64 This is *wu-wei*, which means "without doing" or the "absence of action." It does not refer to passivity. It refers instead to acting in harmony with nature, without the expectation of results (Max Kaltenmark, *Lao Tzu and Taoism* [Stanford: Stanford University Press, 1969], 53–8).
65 Joyce Tyldesley, *Daughters of Isis: Women of Ancient Egypt* (London: Penguin, 1994).

66 For the position of women in classical Greece, see Elaine Fantham et al., *Women in the Classical World: Image and Text* (New York: Oxford University Press, 1994); and Raphael Sealey, *Women and Law in Classical Greece* (Chapel Hill: University of North Carolina Press, 1990).

67 For more on the maintenance of Hindu women, see Werner Menski, *Hindu Law: Beyond Tradition and Modernity* (New Delhi: Oxford University Press, 2003), 484–542. One problem that Jewish law has not solved is that scripture allows only husbands to initiate divorce. In modern times, the problem has become more complicated. Women may initiate divorces according to secular law but remain married according to Jewish law if their husbands refuse to grant them religious divorces. Very reluctant to contradict scripture, which would undermine the entire system, the rabbis have tried to work around it. When a woman's case is strong, a rabbi may threaten her husband, who must then choose between giving his wife a writ of divorce (*get*) and losing various privileges (along with social status) in his community. Occasionally, though, even this measure fails. Jewish feminists call the result "*get* abuse." The "anchored woman" (*agunah*), whose husband has disappeared or refuses to grant her a divorce, presents a similar problem. She may not remarry according to Jewish law without either a divorce or proof that her husband is dead (Janice Arnold, "Agunah Rights Group Deals with the Issue of Get Abuse," *Canadian Jewish News*, 25 March 1993, 4). For more on the maintenance of Muslim women, see Jane I. Smith, "Islam," in *Women in World Religions*, ed. Arvind Sharma (Albany: State University of New York Press, 1987), 247.

68 Smith, "Islam," 239–40.

69 According to early Hindu texts, the man should be intelligent and come from a good family. In addition, he should have a good character, auspicious characteristics, learning, good health, generosity, and wealth. He should practise celibacy until the time of marriage. The couple should have children, enjoy sexual pleasures, be dear to each other, and grow old together. Even an adulterous wife is no excuse to annul the marriage (Pandurang Vaman Kane, *History of Dharmasastra (Ancient and Mediaeval Religious and Civil Law)*, 2nd ed. [Poona: Bhandarkar Oriental Research Institute 1974], vol. 2, pt. 2, 434–5, 528, 620). Another Hindu text, the *Kamasutra*, endorses a double standard, advising men on how to conduct their extramarital affairs.

70 According to Islamic law, a man may marry up to four wives. Polygamy has often been criticized by other religions, but it takes on a special

meaning if understood in its original context. Many of the earliest Muslim men died fighting in battles. Muhammad declared that their wives should not remain widows. Men should marry one or more of them and thus protect them and their children as long as he can provide for each wife equally. In Islam, marriage is a contract. Women may negotiate it, dictating the terms, including the dowry, which they may keep. "It is considered one of the great innovations of the Qur'an over earlier practices that women are permitted to inherit and own property" (Smith, "Islam," 239). Today, it seems unfair that a woman's share amounts to only half that of her brothers.

71 After the rise of kingdoms in Tamil Nadu, South India (between the first century BC and the third century AD), poets began to chastise unjust kings by saying that their ancestors were always friendly toward seers. They criticized greedy kings who were generous to their protégés but ruthlessly stole land from others. According to chapter 39 of the *Tirukkural* (ca. fifth century AD), the king must be virtuous, gracious, generous, protecting, wise, and energetic.

72 In fact, the key moral principle for Hindus by the classical period (from the fourth century BC to the fourth century AD) was *ahimsa*, which means non-violence and connotes benevolence to all living creatures. People should show compassion to everyone, according to the *Mahabharata* (Striparva 7:25–8), because all creatures dislike death (Katherine K. Young, "Hindu Bioethics," in *Religious Methods and Resources in Bioethics*, ed. Paul F. Camenisch [Dordrecht: Kluwer Academic Publishers, 1994], 14). Traditionally, Hinduism has also opposed both abortion, except to save a mother's life, and infanticide (see J.J. Lipner, "The Classical Hindu View on Abortion and the Moral Status of the Unborn," in *Hindu Ethics: Purity, Abortion, and Euthanasia*, by H.G. Coward, J.J. Lipner, and Katherine K. Young [Albany: State University of New York, 1989], 41–69). See also Kane, "History," vol. 2, pt 1, 509–10, for laws on infanticide.

73 Frymer-Kensky, *Wake*, 102–4.

74 Mark 12: 31.

75 Luke 6: 27.

76 Matthew 5: 39; Luke 6: 29.

77 I John 4: 8.

78 Avot 1: 12.

79 Avot 1: 18.

80 This idea, used often for homiletical purposes, occurs not once but several times in classical texts such as the Talmud (Sanhedrin 4: 5), Avot de Rabbi Natan ([vers. 1] 31: 45b–46a), and so on.

81 *Veil*, 2: 34.

82 *Veil* 1: 1.

83 In theory, Hindu women have one role, that of wife-mother. In fact, though, they have had other ones: seer, saint, cultured courtesan, temple dancer, and tantric adept. The same is true of Hindu men. Caste dictates occupation: priest (*brahmin*), warrior (*kshatriya*), or merchant (*vaishya*). In addition, the ideal man of each caste should be a householder (*grihastha*) – that is, a husband and father. This way, he can fulfill his obligations to family and society before seeking enlightenment (*nirvana*) by pursuing the ascetic path. Most men never actually get to that stage. Other men skip the first stage, despite tradition, and become wandering ascetics (*yogins*).

84 Also thrown into the pot are some statements that make no sense at all. Discussing the rise of "patriarchy," the narrator argues that "strange taboos evolved as the bond with nature became more obscure. During liberal eras of the classical world, it was believed that menstrual blood could dim mirrors, rust iron, and make dogs rabid" (*Veil* 1: 24). These beliefs seem strange to us, indeed, but that is precisely because the bond with nature is "more obscure" – mediated and objectified – through the lens of science. Were it not for science, it would make just as much sense to believe these ideas as to believe that women are born with magical powers.

85 *Veil* 1: 17.

86 Ibid.; almost the same statement occurs in 2: 13. According to another source, "Statistics on the numbers of religious show that there are approximately 1,190,272 members of religious orders throughout the world, of whom 229,181 are men (including 156,191 clerics and 73,090 lay) and 960,991 women" (Sandra Marie Schneiders, "Reflections on the History of Religious Life and Contemporary Developments," in *Turning Points in Religious Life*, ed. C. Tingley [Wilmington, Del.: Glazier, 1987]). There are therefore nearly four female Catholic religious for every male religious in the world (Helen Rose Ebaugh, "Orders," [dated:] 1998, *Encyclopedia of Religion and Society*, [1998], hirr.hartsem.edu/ency/Orders.htm [accessed 18 October 2006]). Why do so many more women than men join up? At one time, people interpreted the notion of "vocation" very broadly. Families might place daughters in convents, for instance, if they could afford to pay for the dowries of only one or two other daughters – or if their daughters were unmarriageable for one reason or another. But the most plausible reason, at least in modern times, is that most of the men who enter monasteries end up instead as parish priests.

87 *Veil* 1: 20.

88 Galatians 3: 28.

89 Here is another example. Opposing hierarchy and the concentration of authority in one man, the narrator opines that the pope "is said to be infallible." In a very specific context, yes, but only in that context. Papal infallibility refers strictly to *ex cathedra* pronouncements on matters of doctrinal theology or moral principles, not to pastoral guidance on current social problems. The first Vatican Council defined this doctrine as recently as 1870. Only one pope has ever invoked it, in 1950, and that was about the Assumption of Mary.

90 *Veil* 1: 2A.

91 Ibid., 1: 26.

92 Matthew 26: 20.

93 *Veil* 2: 10.

94 Ibid., 2: 15.

95 Ibid., L: 27.

96 Because the poor received a dole from the state, they had an immediate stake in the system. Because they had little to lose in terms of wealth and prestige, however, they had no *ultimate* stake in it.

97 Some biblical scholars have suggested that Jesus was a "zealot." See *Jesus and the Politics of His Day*, ed. Ernst Bammel and C.F.D. Moule (Cambridge: Cambridge University Press, 1984). See the following essays in that book, especially: J.P.M. Sweet "The Zealots and Jesus," 1–10; William Horbury, "Christ as Brigand in Ancient Anti-Christian Polemic," 183–96; Matthew Black, "Not Peace but a Sword," 287–94; and Gerhard Schneider, "The Political Charge against Jesus," 403–14. Not surprisingly, liberation theologians have adopted the model of Jesus the zealot. See Gustavo Gutierrez, *A Theology of Liberation: History, Politics, and Salvation* (Maryknoll, NY: Orbis Books, 1973); and Juan Luis Segundo, *The Community Called the Church* (Maryknoll, NY: Orbis Books, 1973).

98 The Jesus who urged his followers to "turn the other cheek" has always inspired Christians. But with the possible exception of those ready to become martyrs in the very early period, few Christians have ever taken this teaching seriously, except in theory. Communal exceptions include the Mennonites, the Amish, and the Quakers.

99 For liberation theologians, Jesus is the prototypical socialist. Far from supporting the status quo, he openly challenged those "principalities and powers" that oppressed the poor.

100 In *The Man Nobody Knows* (New York: Grosset and Dunlap, 1925), Bruce Barton argued that Jesus succeeded so well in selling his message because he was a brilliant organizer, someone who knew how to manipulate people. Barton's book became a best-seller. Obviously, this version of "the real Jesus" seemed plausible enough to millions of ambitious people.

101 According to the Deutschekristen in Nazi Germany, Jesus and the Galileans were not Jews at all but Indo-Europeans – that is, Aryans.

102 Katharina von Kellenbach, *Anti-Judaism in Christian-Rooted Feminist Writings: An Analysis of Major American and West German Feminist Theologians*, dissertation, Temple University, 1990 (Ann Arbor, Mich.: University Microfilms International, 1997).

103 *Veil* L: 25.

104 Sifra, 90b.

105 Leviticus 20: 10.

106 Ibid. At issue here is a moral problem, however, not merely an archaeological one. Christian feminists who adopt an explicitly anti-rabbinic – and implicitly anti-Jewish – mentality echo more traditional Christians in adopting the idea that Christianity superseded Judaism or that Jesus superseded Torah. It is one thing for Christians to believe that Christianity is better than Judaism. Otherwise, why be Christian at all? And some do so without concluding that Judaism is contemptible and Jews either idiots or agents of Satan. But most goddess ideologues are not Christian!

107 *Veil* 1: 26.

108 John 11–18.

109 Matthew 28: 1–10.

110 Luke 5: 1–27.

111 I Corinthians 15: 5.

112 *Veil* 2: 8.

113 Ibid., 1: 11.

114 Ibid., 1: 12.

115 Ibid., 1: 29.

116 Ibid., 1: 31.

117 Ibid., 1: 32.

118 Ibid., 1: 24.

119 Ibid., 2: 2.

120 This kind of reductionism is not unique to the filmmakers. It is common among historians of this school, that of "women's history." Anne Llewellyn Barstow, for instance, uses the same explanation. At one point,

in fact, she says something very surprising for a historian. Analyzing the causes of these witch hunts is irrelevant, she argues, because it distracts readers (or viewers) from the only thing that really is relevant: the victimization of women ("Studying Witchcraft as Women's History: A Historiography of the European Witch Persecutions," *Journal of Feminist Studies in Religion* 4, no. 2 [fall 1988]: 15). Nor are female feminists unique in adopting this approach. William E. Monter ("The Historiography of European Witchcraft: Progress and Prospects," *Journal of Interdisciplinary History* 2 [1972]: 80) argues "that witchcraft accusations could best be understood as projections of patriarchal social fears onto atypical women, that is those who lived apart from the direct male control of husbands or fathers and were therefore defenceless, isolated, and unable to revenge themselves by the more normal means of physical violence or recourse to law courts" (Monter, quoted in Elspeth Whitney, "The Witch 'She'/The Historian 'He': Gender and the European Witch-Hunts," *Journal of Women's History* 7, no. 3 [fall 1995]: 80).

121 *The Burning Times*, 11.

122 Carlo Ginzburg, *Ecstasies: Deciphering the Witches Sabbath*, trans. Raymond Rosenthal (London: Hutchinson Radius, 1990).

123 Ibid., 100.

124 Whitney notes that "recent work has shown that in many of the outlying areas of Europe in which the accusation rate was more equal for men and women, a more medieval pattern of belief persisted in which male sorcerers rather than female witches were thought to have access to the supernatural, a distinction with important implications for gender analysis of the hunts ... This pattern of male sorcery and female witchcraft may have persisted in outlying areas of Europe including Iceland, Estonia, Finland, Romania, and Portugal" (Whitney, "The Witch," 90; also footnote 73 for sources).

125 Ginzburg, *Ecstasies*, 9–10.

126 In theory, the church could have classified these people as infidels. In fact, though, they were syncretistic Christians. As baptized members of the community, they received the sacraments and believed in salvation through Christ. Nonetheless, they practised archaic folk rituals on the side (and, for obvious reasons, often in secret).

127 *Burning*, 1.

128 Ibid.

129 Ibid., 3.

130 Melford Spiro, *Buddhism and Society: A Great Tradition and Its Burmese Vicissitudes* (Berkeley: University of California Press, 1982).

131 *Burning*, 3.

132 Ibid.

133 Ibid., 16.

134 Ginzburg, *Ecstasies*, 160.

135 Ibid., 166.

136 Joshua Trachtenberg, *The Devil and the Jews: The Medieval Conception of the Jew and Its Relation to Modern Antisemitism* (New York: Harper Torchbooks, 1943), 139.

137 Ibid., 144.

138 John Putnam Demos, *Entertaining Satan: Witchcraft and the Culture of Early New England* (Oxford: Oxford University Press, 1982).

139 Ibid., 14.

140 Ibid., 368–9.

141 Notable outbreaks of influenza occurred in 1670, from 1682 to 1683, and again in the 1690s.

142 Trachtenberg, *Devil and the Jews*, 184.

143 Ibid., 173, 206.

144 The crusades had failed to unite Europe. In their wake, during the twelfth and thirteenth centuries, came social unrest and ecclesiastical schism. Inquisitions rooted out heresy. To avoid shedding blood on its own, the Church called in secular authorities to execute heretics (ibid., 170–1.)

145 Rosemary Radford Ruether, *New Woman, New Earth; Sexist Ideologies and Human Liberation* (New York: Seabury Press, 1975), 90.

146 The obvious analogy is commonplace. See Debbie Nathan and Michael Snedeker, *Satan's Silence: Ritual Abuse and the Making of a Modern American Witch Hunt* (New York: Basic Books, 1996).

147 Moira Johnston, *Spectral Evidence: The Ramona Case: Incest, Memory and Truth on Trial in Napa Valley* (Boston: Houghton Mifflin, 1997).

148 See Paul Nathanson and Katherine K. Young, *Legalizing Misandry: From Public Shame to Systemic Discrimination against Men* (Montreal: McGill-Queen's University Press, 2006).

149 Sometimes the church granted life imprisonment instead of capital punishment to repentant heretics. Others suffered capital punishment. The pope gave direct authority to inquisitors, mainly Dominicans and Franciscans. Trials lacked what we now consider due process, of course, and often arose on the basis of public rumour. The accused had no opportunities to confront their accusers (Y. Dossat, "Inquisition," in the *New Catholic Encyclopedia*, vol. 7 [New York: McGraw Hill, 1967], 535–41).

150 As infidels, Jews belonged in the same category as Muslims. Not surprisingly, Christians accused both Jews and Muslims of very similar crimes.

But almost all Muslims lived in Islamic countries and therefore beyond
the reach of Christian authorities. See Jeffrey Richards, *Sex, Dissidence
and Damnation: Minority Groups in the Middle Ages* (London and New
York: Routledge, 1990), and R.I. Moore, *The Formation of a Persecuting
Society: Power and Deviance in Western Europe, 950–1250* (Oxford:
Blackwell, 1987). See also Whitney, "The Witch," 86, 98n57.

151 The Fourth Lateran Council, which met in 1215, imposed characteristic
restrictions. It forbade Jews to proselytize, marry Christians, hire Christian servants, build synagogues that were taller than the local churches,
and so on. In addition, it forced them to wear identifying badges or
clothing. Enforcement of these restrictions varied from one time and
place to another. Every now and then, therefore, rulers reintroduced
these regulations or similar ones.

152 All the same, Jews suffered no less than Christian heretics from organized
persecution by inquisitions. In other words, not everyone cared about the
theoretical distinction between infidels and heretics; after all, both denied
the truth of Christianity. Not surprisingly, rulers or mobs sometimes
attacked both groups. In southern France, for example, they attacked
Jews along with the Albigensian heretics. Moreover, they burned both
Jewish and heretical books in public squares. And they accused both Jews
and heretics of spreading dissent. In the fifteenth century, especially during the Hussite wars of 1419–36, preachers accused Christians throughout Europe of "judaizing." Judaism itself was not a Christian heresy,
according to the church, but it *fostered* Christian heresy.

153 Stanley M. Hordes, *To the End of the Earth: A History of the Crypto-
Jews of New Mexico* (New York: Columbia University Press, 2005).

154 This is the estimate of Johannes Nohl in *The Black Death: A Chronicle of
the Plague* (London: Unwin Books, [1926] 1961), 7. In *The Impact of
Plague in Tudor and Stuart England* (Oxford: Clarendon Press, 1985),
Paul Slack estimates that about a third of the population died (15) but
adds that we have no way of knowing whether more women died than
men: "In parts of Europe women were said to be more susceptible to
plague than men, and there is some evidence to support this observation.
In England, on the other hand, men were thought to be hit particularly
hard" (179), for "the larger towns had an abnormal excess of male over
female burials; in smaller communities the reverse was the case" (181).
Slack suggests also that "it would be premature to suggest that plague hit
either of the sexes disproportionately. If more women or men died in a
particular outbreak, it may well have been simply because there were
more women or men around" such as apprentices or maid servants (ibid.).

155 Nohl, *Black Death*, 21.

156 Ibid., 46.

157 Ibid., 79.

158 Ibid.. The church became richer at this time, ironically, because many dying people gave all their possessions to it either in the hope of a cure or, failing that, of salvation. Because ecclesiastical officials thought that these gifts were contaminated by the plague, they often refused to accept them. In desperation, people threw them over the gates into monastic grounds (92).

159 Ibid., 91.

160 Ibid., 97.

161 Satan had not been invented at this time. He appears in the Book of Job, but as a kind of divine advisor, not a divine rival. Belief in demons was ubiquitous in the biblical period and throughout the mediaeval period, but the rise of Satan as a cosmic prince of demons, the anti-Christ, became truly pervasive only in the late medieval period.

162 This too was an old idea. It appeared first in the later biblical books known as "apocalypses."

163 Nohl, *Black Death*, 114.

164 Ibid., 116. Moreover, "it was believed to be a good work if churches were repaired with bricks and stones taken from the burnt houses and destroyed graves of the Jews and new belfries erected. At Muhlhausen all the Jews were slaughtered, at Nordhausen at least a part of them ... At Basle, the town council was impelled, by the threatening attitude of the guilds, who with unfurled banners marches to the Town Hall, to burn the Jews and prohibit their settling in the town for two hundred years. The diabolical scheme was then conceived of imprisoning all Jews in a wooden shed on an island in the Rhine, outside the town, and then setting the shed on fire ... The inhabitants of Mayence made such fires for the burning of their Jews to the number of twelve thousand that the lead in the window-panes and the bells of St. Quirius church were melted. A part of the Jews of Speyer were massacred by a raving crowd and their bodies, placed in empty winebarrels, allowed to drift down the Rhine" (117).

165 According to Carlo Ginzburg, "The presence in the dialects of the Dauphine and the Savoy of terms such as *gafa*, 'witch,' etymologically linked to the Spanish *gafo*, 'leper' (in the area of Briancon) or *Snagoga*, 'nocturnal dance of unspecified mythical beings,' from *synagogue*, in the sense of 'gatherings of heretics' (in the Vaux-en-Bugey) recapitulate, together with the already cited assimilation of the *Vaudois* to male

witches, the complex chain of events that we have reconstructed" (*Ecstasies*, 80).

166 Trachtenberg, *Devil and the Jews*, 126–7.

167 Ibid., 164.

168 Ibid., 168.

169 It was due mainly, though, to the fact that Ferdinand and Isabella wanted to unite their kingdom by purging it of all foreigners, both Jews and Muslims.

170 Trachtenberg, *Devil and the Jews*, 138.

171 Ginzburg, *Ecstasies*, 77.

172 Ibid., 154.

173 Sagan, *Dawn of Tyranny*, 118–19.

174 This is true even in the Catholic Church, where laypeople usually receive only the bread, due to the belief that each "species" contains both the blood and the flesh of Christ.

175 Over and over again, the *Malleus* discusses reproduction. For example, "such hatred is aroused by witchcraft between those joined in the sacrament of matrimony, and such freezing up of the generative forces, that men are unable to perform the necessary action for begetting offsprings" [*sic*] (J. Sprenger and H. Kraemer, *Malleus Maleficarum*, trans. Montague Summers; quoted in Elizabeth Clark and Herbert Richardson, *Women and Religion: A Feminist Sourcebook of Christian Thought* [New York: Harper and Row, 1977], 126–7). Witches, it claimed, "impede and prevent the power of procreation" (Clark and Richardson, 127). Witches are said to cause impotence and sterility. Moreover, witches "collect male members [penises] in great numbers" (130). Whatever else these passages might indicate, they clearly indicate something very close to the surface: deep concern over a low birth rate. After the Black Death, how could it have been otherwise? The church might have been trying to legitimate the removal of midwives, therefore, who knew the secrets of abortion and contraception.

176 And sodomy. See Anne Llewellyn Barstow, "Studying Witchcraft," 16.

177 Ginzburg, *Ecstasies*, 1.

178 After the Nazi regime ordered most of the gas chambers dismantled, because they wanted to eliminate visible evidence of their project, psychiatrists and doctors continued to kill people on their own by lethal injections or starvation diets and without the consent of review boards. This led to an anarchic situation called "wild euthanasia." Moreover, some people reassembled gas chambers in the east. See Robert Jay Lifton, *The*

Nazi Doctors: Medical Killing and the Psychology of Genocide (New York: Basic Books, 1986).

179 Demos, *Entertaining Satan*, 392–4.

180 For instance: "In Rome," writes Nohl, "in the plague year 1522, a Greek, Demetrius, walked through the town with a bull which had been tamed by witchcraft, and sacrificed it according to ancient custom before the eyes of all the people at the Colosseum to propitiate the hostile demons. In Lower Lusatia, in the year 1612, the following custom prevailed among the Wend peasantry: Naive persons were selected: two young chaste farm labourers, a widow who had lived seven years in widow-hood, and six pure maidens. These foregathered at midnight at the end of the village. One labourer brought a plough on four oxen; another a rod of dead wood [and] with this he described a circle, into which the seven women stepped and in which they divested themselves of all their cloth-ing. Then the widow proceeded carrying the rod, the maidens harnessed themselves to the plough and drew a furrow round the whole village, fol-lowed by one of the labourers, the other remaining to guard the clothes. When the work was completed they returned home without uttering a word. This custom of ploughing round the village, by which it was believed that a barrier was set up against evil powers, persisted in the central and southern Volga Government and in Siberia in 1890. The belief in devils and spirits was also greatly stimulated by the plague. Even Martin Luther shared the opinion that all pestilence was brought upon the people of evil spirits, 'that they poisoned the air or otherwise infected the poor people by their breath and injected the mortal poison into their bodies" (*Black Death*, 32–3).

181 Ibid., 69.

182 Ibid., 5.

183 *Burning*, 8.

184 The Venetians cared more about business than about religion. Depending on what served their commercial interests, they allied themselves with either Christians or Muslims.

185 Whitney, "The Witch," 80; following Christina Larner. Whitney suggests that this kind of thesis receives support from Robert Muchembled. He observes that French authorities tried to extend official law and order into the villages. This displaced local models of social control. We agree that this could have contributed to the witch craze but not as its original cause.

186 Jewish communities had always lived in their own districts. Both Jews and Christians had found this arrangement of informal separation

acceptable. In the sixteenth century, however, authorities formalized and enforced this arrangement. They allowed Jews to live only in walled enclosures and locked them up at night.

187 The problem was "solved," temporarily, only with the advent of secular states following the French Revolution. Napoleon led the way by emancipating Jews. He and others were motivated by the inherent logic of the Enlightenment and the Revolution, not by compassion for Jews or even interest in them. The hope was that toleration for Jews as free citizens would lead to their assimilation; without Jews, they believed, "the Jewish problem" would solve itself. And many Jews did disappear through assimilation. But ancient stereotypes remained pervasive. After only a few generations, the Nazis were hunting down Jews in the streets.

188 *Burning,* 4.

189 Ibid., 4. Barstow on her own estimate: "The statistically based figure, while lower, still makes the same point, namely that this was an organized mass murder of women, and does so in a way that cannot be dismissed by historians" ("Studying Witchcraft," 7). But listen to Cynthia Eller: "Spiritual feminists report that a huge number of women were killed as witches during the European witch craze. The standard figure in spiritual feminist literature is nine million. The first reference to this figure appears in Mathilda Joslyn Gage's 1893 book *Women, Church, and State.* This number is not supported elsewhere, and is never to my knowledge found outside spiritual feminist literature. Scholars for the European witch burnings place the numbers far lower, the lowest estimate being 30,000 and the highest 'several million,' though all agree that firmer numbers cannot be determined." See Cynthia Eller, *Living in the Lap of the Goddess: The Feminist Spirituality Movement in America* (Boston: Beacon Press, 1993), 174.

190 Orthodox Jews prefer the Hebrew word *shoah,* which refers to calamity. The English word "holocaust" refers technically to burnt offerings at the temple in Jerusalem, after all, and Hitler's victims were neither sacrificial offerings of pious Jews nor self-sacrificial victims and thus martyrs; they were simply victims.

191 Actually, many Jews consider this word inappropriate even for their own collective experience of Nazi rule. The Hebrew word for it is *horban,* which refers specifically to a sacrificial offering. But the people who died under Nazi rule were victims, not sacrificial or self-sacrificial victims. The best word in English is *shoah,* which means simply "catastrophe."

192 *Burning,* 8. This argument has profound implications. We can, we should, challenge it on moral grounds. The context, however, trivializes

it. For the most part, men suffered no less than women. "Those who spoke out wore the mask of shame. If they gathered in groups, they were plotting against men. Husbands were advised from the pulpit to beat their wives, not in rage, but out of charity for her soul. Those who made a dress too ornate wore the dressmaker's collar. Those who fell asleep in church, the rosary necklace. Others faced the ducking stool" (8). No one expected wives to beat their husbands, to be sure, but they did expect husbands to face every other form of punishment. The community discouraged all people from speaking out over grievances, suspected all people who gathered furtively of heresy or treason, subjected all people to sumptuary laws (against clothing deemed inappropriate for one reason or another), and publicly humiliated all people who fell asleep in church, blasphemed, or made lewd remarks. At another point, *Burning* shows viewers graphic descriptions of torture by inquisitions. The implication is that inquisitions tortured only women. In fact, it tortured all people suspected of heresy. And most heretics other than witches were men, partly because men were more often literate and thus more likely to read or write heretical works.

193 Anne Llewellyn Barstow, "Studying Witchcraft," 7. See also Barstow's *Witchcraze: A New History of the European Witch Hunts* (San Francisco: Pandora, 1994).

194 We could list many additional wars, not all wars but many of them. We could certainly include the American Civil War in this category. Although World War II included a "men's holocaust," referring to the millions of male combatants on both sides, it included several additional ones.

195 Elizabeth G. Davis, *The First Sex* (New York: Dent, 1973), 351–2; quoted in Susanne Heine, *Christianity and the Goddess*, 79.

196 "Then I saw an angel standing in the sun, and with a loud voice he called to all the birds that fly in mid heaven, 'Come, gather for the great supper of God, to eat the flesh of kings, the flesh of captains, the flesh of mighty men, the flesh of all men, both free and slave, both small and great.' And I saw the beast and the kings of the earth with their armies gathered to make war against him who sits upon the horse and against his army. And the beast was captured, and with it the false prophet who in its presence had worked the signs by which he deceived those who had received the mark of the beast and those who worshipped its image. These two were thrown alive into the lake of fire that burns with brimstone. And who sits upon the horse, the sword that issues from his mouth; and all the birds were gorged with their flesh ... Then I saw thrones, and seated on them were those to whom judgment was committed. Also I saw the souls of

those who had been beheaded for their testimony to Jesus and for the word of God, and who had not worshipped the beast or its image and had not received its mark on their foreheads or their hands. They came to life, and reigned with Christ a thousand years" (Revelation 19: 17–21; 20: 1–5).This nightmarish vision has long inspired millenarian movements based on belief in a coming apocalypse and a new dawn of peace and harmony. Millenarianism comes in two main varieties. Pre-millenarians believe that a thousand years of peace and harmony will *precede* the second coming of Christ; post-millenarians believe that this period will *follow* the second coming. No matter what the precise sequence of events, the scenario always includes a catastrophe or battle of cosmic proportions.

197 Mary Daly, *Pure Lust: Elemental Feminist Philosophy* (Boston: Beacon Press, 1984), ix.

198 Toni Morrison, *Paradise* (New York: Knopf, 1987).

199 Lisa Schwarzbaum, "Tony, Tony Toni," review of *Paradise*, by Toni Morrison, in *Entertainment Weekly*, 23 January 1998, 57.

200 Ibid., 56.

201 Paul Gray, "Paradise Found," review of *Paradise*, by Toni Morrison, in *Time*, 19 January 1998, 58.

202 Ibid.

203 Nathanson and Young, *Legalizing Misandry.*

CHAPTER THREE

1 Many Christians believe that Jesus has already inaugurated the Kingdom in the hearts of believers but will return at the end of days to finish the job by creating a new world order.

2 The Christian Old Testament ends with Malachi, who offers what Christians believe is a prophetic reference to the birth of Jesus. The Jewish Tanakh (Old Testament) ends with II Chronicles, on the other hand, which offers what Jews consider a reference to an ultimate return from exile and restoration to the Promised Land. This reference is explicitly to the restoration under King Cyrus (described as an "anointed" one, or messiah) but implicitly to an ultimate restoration under an ultimate messiah.

3 Christians differ, however, on the precise order of eschatological events. Pre-millenarian Protestants, for instance, believe that Christ's victory will begin with a thousand years of happiness. Post-millenarians believe that Christ's rule will follow a thousand years of happiness.

4 Both traditions maintain a closely related belief in everyone's ultimate
return to paradise. This belief, known as immortality of the soul, is somewhat at odds with belief in resurrection of the dead (and has a different
historical origin). Both assume a state of being that could be described as
eternity – one that is beyond time, or history. But the former occurs
immediately after death (or judgment) and the latter at the end of time,
or history.

5 *The Goddess Remembered*, directed by Donna Read, script and narration
by D.C. Blade, Donna Read, and Gloria Demers (Montreal: National
Film Board, 1989).

6 Ibid.

7 Ibid.

8 Ibid.

9 Ibid., 7–8.

10 Ibid., 1.

11 Ibid., 13.

12 Robert Graves, *White Goddess: A Historical Grammar of Poetic Myth*
(London: Faber and Faber, 1948).

13 *Goddess*, 6–7.

14 Ibid., 8.

15 Ibid., 9.

16 Ibid.

17 Ibid., 3.

18 Ibid.

19 Ibid., 1.

20 Ibid., 10.

21 Ibid., 11.

22 Ibid., 4.

23 But remember that the word "reform" and its cognates are often deceptive. The paradigm of all modern "reform" movements in the West, the
Protestant Reformation, was actually both a religious revolution and a
political one.

24 *Goddess*, 2.

25 Paul Nathanson and Katherine K. Young, *Legalizing Misandry: From
Public Shame to Systemic Discrimination against Men* (Montreal:
McGill-Queen's University Press, 2006).

26 *Goddess*, 1.

27 Ibid.

28 Ibid., 8.

29 Ibid., 14.

30 Cynthia Eller, *Living in the Lap of the Goddess: The Feminist Spiritual Movement* (Boston: Beacon Press, 1995), 5.
31 Eller, *Living*, 3.
32 Ibid., 4.
33 Ibid., 6.
34 Ibid., 18.
35 Ibid., 55.
36 Zsuzsanna E. Budapest, *Holy Book of Women's Mysteries* (Oakland, Calif.: Z.E. Budapest, 1979).
37 If we could call anyone the founder of Wicca, it would be Gerald Gardner, a civil servant in England. In the 1930s, he established this new religion by drawing on many sources: esoterica in *The Golden Bough*, by James Frazer (1854–1941); the magic of Aleister Crowley; the Hermetic Order of the Golden Dawn (a nineteenth-century order of magicians who maintained ties with theosophy, alchemy, and free masonry); his own experience in what he claims was a secret coven of witches, which claimed to transmit teachings from late medieval Europe; and a few other occult groups. In the late 1950s, Gardner wrote several books about witchcraft. But his unpublished Book of Shadows (which supposedly contains information from an ancient community of witches) became the central text for his followers. This was Gardnerian Wicca. Gardner claimed, however, that Wicca was not a new religion at all but one that originated in the Celtic religion of ancient Britain.

The time was right. Britain had repealed its medieval anti-witchcraft laws during the late 1940s. Public interest in magic, especially spells, emerged there and in other highly industrialized countries such as Germany. Vivianne Crowley, a Jungian analyst, fused Gardner's esoterica with Jung's interest in archetypes and religious experiences.

During the 1960s, Raymond Buckland, a Gardnerian initiate, brought Wicca to the United States. He wrote *Witchcraft from the Inside: Origins of the Fastest Growing Religious Movement in America* (St Paul, Minn.: Llewellyn, 1971) and many other books. In some circles, Wicca – especially Dianic Wicca (for women only) – blended with goddess ideology. In other circles, it blended with Jungian analysis. In still others, it blended with New Age culture. Dianic Wiccans notwithstanding, most Wiccans accept not only both a god and a goddess but also both priests and priestesses (in whom the former manifest themselves). They celebrate the full moon every month along with eight other days on their sacred calendar.

For Wicca's relation to New Age culture, see Wouter J. Hanegraaff, *New Age Religion and Western Culture: Esotericism in the Mirror of*

Secular Thought (Leiden: Brill, 1996). For Wicca's relation to Jungian analysis, see Nicholas Dion, "Worshipping the Dark: The Manifestations of Carl Gustav Jung's Archetype of the Shadow in Contemporary Wicca," MA thesis, Faculty of Religious Studies, McGill University, 2006.

38 Eller, *Living*, 58.

39 Ibid.

40 Ibid., 59.

41 Ibid.

42 Ibid., 60.

43 *Signs out of Time* (Donna Read and Starhawk: Belili Productions, 2003).

44 "That the goddess is female," observes Eller, "is clear enough; what should also be clear by now is that there are male deities wafting in and out of the picture. Not all spiritual feminists worship male deities or even acknowledge their existence. But many spiritual feminists say gods exist, though they choose not to deal with them; some will worship or invoke gods when they are doing rituals with men; a few even worship gods on their own ... For some women, it is anathema to even consider the possibility that maleness could be polluting the divine; it is bad enough that men exist on the earthly plane. Others see male deities operating on an intermediate level, but believe they are secondary or subservient to the goddess, who is the ultimate divine force in the universe. Still others believe that the ultimate is without gender, but that gender either comes in at the intermediate polytheistic level or can be arbitrarily assigned to suit the needs of the practitioner or society as a whole. In any case, whether for reasons of ontology or choice, the goddess is always the central figure in feminist spirituality's theology" (*Living*, 135).

45 We have summarized the core beliefs of a very eclectic and even inchoate movement. More specific beliefs, commonly but not universally held, would include the following: everything is spiritually interrelated by a cosmic, or divine, energy; spiritual beings – these could include angels, gurus, or even aliens from outer space – can guide us to ultimate fulfillment; material reality is superficial; "all you need is love"; emotion or intuition has been underrated and reason overrated; we can survive death in one form or another; all religions, at least in their esoteric forms, teach the same thing; all religions ultimately agree with science, especially when translated into the methods of parapsychological and psychotherapeutic movements; dreams reveal hidden truths about the self; the female principle, long ignored, is as important as or more important than the male; historians have foolishly ignored evidence of ancient civilizations such as Atlantis, which have much to teach us; there is no such thing as a

coincidence, because every event "speaks" to us; if enough people follow the signposts and reach a higher state of consciousness, everyone will be transformed; all of history is moving slowly but surely toward a destiny of ultimate fulfillment; and so on.

46 See Abraham H. Maslow, *Religions, Values, and Peak Experiences* (Columbus: Ohio State University Press, 1964).

47 Invented by Ida Pauline Rolf during the 1950s (although she founded the Rolf Institute for Structural Integration in 1971), it involves the manipulation of soft tissues – fascia, or connective tissue – in order to realign the body in relation to gravity. Rolfing is a form of physiotherapy, not psychotherapy. Because by the 1970s many people had come to reject the "traditional" opposition between mind and body, however, it soon became just as popular and fashionable as any other form of therapy.

48 The acronym stands for Erhard Seminars Training. Werner Erhard, living in San Francisco, gave the first training session in 1971. Soon afterward, it went national and then international. The goal is personal transformation as a way of taking personal responsibility for behaviour.

49 Arthur Janov invented primal therapy in the 1960s, although it first became newsworthy in 1970 because of its influence on John Lennon. Janov believed that all people need recognition from others. When that need (or any other universal need) goes unmet, as it always does, the result is psychic pain. The nervous system stores – represses – this pain, often from infancy, against the day when it can be released appropriately. People can attain maturity and find fulfillment, in short, only after re-experiencing early traumatic experiences and giving full expression to them. Although most people identify Janov's method with "primal screaming," it does not actually require any one way of expressing pain.

50 Both yoga and transcendental meditation originated in Hinduism. Transcendental meditation, introduced by Maharishi Mahesh Yogi in 1958, became a form of mental exercise that could lead to higher states of consciousness – or, at the very least, could slow down physiological processes enough to promote good health. This form of meditation owed at least some of its popularity among Americans and Canadians to the fact that it required so little effort: silent repetition of a mantra twice a day for twenty minutes. For many Westerners, yoga soon became a regimen of physical exercises, a way to relieve stress.

51 *Practical Magic* (New York: Putnam, 1995).

52 Phyllis Curott; quoted in Suna Chang, "Rhymes with Rich," *Entertainment Weekly*, 30 October 1998, 12–13.

53 See Eric Caplan, *From Ideology to Liturgy; Reconstructionist Worship and American Liberal Judaism* (Cincinnati: Hebrew Union College Press; Wayne State University Press, 2002). *Kol Haneshamah* is the title of a liturgical series for various occasions; see, for instance, the prayer book for sabbaths and festivals: *Kol Haneshamah: Shabbat vehagim* (Wyncote, Pa.: Reconstructionist Press, 1994).

54 Katherine K. Young, "Having Your Cake and Eating It Too: Feminism and Religion," review of *Feminism and Religion: An Introduction*, by Rita M. Gross, *Journal of the American Academy of Religion* 67, no. 1 (March 1999): 181.

55 Andrew Schneider and Diane Frolove, "Cicely," *Northern Exposure*, CBS, WCAX-TV, Burlington, Vt., 18 May 1992.

56 See Nancy Chodorow, *The Reproduction of Mothering: Psychoanalysis and the Sociology of Gender* (Berkeley: University of California Press, 1978).

57 See, for instance, Mary Daly, *Pure Lust: Elemental Feminist Philosophy* (Boston: Beacon Press, 1984). We discuss Daly in chapter 6.

58 Nina Auerbach, review of *The Memoirs of Elizabeth Frankenstein* by Theodore Roszak, *New York Times Book Review*, 11 June 1995, 33.

59 From 26 October 1980 (eleventh place) to 15 February 1981 (fifteenth place).

60 Jean Auel, *The Clan of the Cave Bear* (New York: Bantam Books, 1980), 390.

61 Christa Wolf, *Medea: A Modern Retelling* (New York: Nan A. Talese, 1998).

62 Rita Much, "Maligned Medea: A Feminist Vindication," review of *Medea: A Modern Retelling* by Christa Wolf, *Montreal Gazette*, 4 July 1998, 1–5.

63 Ibid.

64 Ibid.

65 Sara Jasper Cook, "Letters," *New York Times*, 8 May 1994, H-4.

66 Mary Lefkowitz, "The Twilight of the Goddess," *New Republic*, 3 August 1992, 29.

67 Ibid.

68 Ibid.

69 Although Lerner and Gimbutas base their theories on Near Eastern and "Old European" evidence, they imply a universal scenario. They ignore the comparative studies of archaeologists and anthropologists, moreover, to substantiate the implication of universality. They resort, on the

contrary, to psychology (also Western based). So we need to find out if their theories apply to other cultural areas (let alone the larger course of human history) before accepting any claims about the creation of "patriarchy" or the historicity of a "great goddess."

70 See Mary Daly, *Beyond God the Father: Toward a Philosophy of Women's Liberation* (Boston: Beacon Press, 1973), 40–3.

CHAPTER FOUR

1 Francois d'Eaubonne coined the French word *ecofeminisme* in 1972. Two years later, she published *La Féminisme ou la mort* (Paris: Horay, 1974). Her point was that only women would take care of the natural environment; men were too busy making money by exploiting it. She must have been unaware of both the women who were quickly moving up the corporate ladder and those who were eagerly buying the products or using the technologies of "men."

2 Jean Shinoda Bolen, *Goddesses in Everywoman: A New Psychology of Women* (New York: Harper, 1984).

3 Gloria Steinem; quoted in Bolen, *Goddesses*, ix–x.

4 Bolen, *Goddesses*, 23.

5 Ibid., 26.

6 Ibid., 5.

7 Ibid., 9.

8 Ibid., 4.

9 Ibid., 20.

10 Ibid., 20.

11 Ibid., 22.

12 Ibid., 19–20.

13 Naomi Goldenberg, *Returning Words to Flesh: Feminism, Psychoanalysis and the Resurrection of the Body* (Boston: Beacon Press, 1990).

14 Ibid., 149.

15 Indeed, according to an early version from the mid-nineteenth century, the friends include males such as Drake Lake and Gander Lander. In that version, it is Chicken Licken (or Chicken Little) who gets hit on the head. (Humphrey Carpenter, *The Oxford Companion to Children's Literature* [Oxford: Oxford University Press, 1984], 110).

16 Goldenberg, *Returning Words*, 190–1.

17 Ibid., 193–5.

18 Ibid., 196; our emphasis.

19 Ibid., 202.

20 See Carol Gilligan, *In a Different Voice: Psychological Theory and Women's Development* (Cambridge: Harvard University Press, 1982).

21 See Nancy Chodorow, *The Reproduction of Mothering: Psychoanalysis and the Sociology of Gender* (Berkeley: University of California Press, 1978).

22 Goldenberg, *Returning Words*, 201–2.

23 Ibid., 41; our emphasis.

24 Ibid., 42–3.

25 Gayle Yates points out that the problem is particularly acute for feminists within Christian and (religiously) Jewish communities, because they must "work out of a double commitment to their feminism and their particular form of religious belief or practice. The distinction between these two motives may be somewhat easier to make when, as in reformist Christian and Jewish works, feminist ideas are used to critique or expand a previously defined subject. One premise, the boundaries of the field, at least remains constant when a new viewpoint is espoused. Such differentiation becomes more problematic when both the subject matter and the ground rules for studying it have changed – as they have in the kind of work being done by Kolbenschlag, Plaskow, Christ, Goldenberg, Daly, and Ruether" (Gayle Graham Yates, "Spirituality and the American Feminist Experience," *Signs* [special issue on women and religion] 9, no. 1 [fall 1983]: 65). But are the "boundaries" really so clear? It is true that feminist theologians are following Jewish tradition by writing imaginative commentaries on scripture (*midrashim*), but these focus on women by inventing details that neither scripture nor rabbinic commentaries have included. The tradition defines midrashic "boundaries" not merely by content (biblical stories), however, but also by method (hermeneutical rules). According to one rule, the most important one, no *midrash* is legitimate if it undermines individual or communal efforts to maintain the sacred law (*halakhah*). It may say unconventional or fanciful things about biblical characters or even about God, to be sure, but not about the sacred legal fabric that holds society together. (In this way, Judaism is unlike Christianity; the latter has traditionally insisted most urgently on theological conformity, the former on behavioural conformity.) But there are limits to what midrashists may say even about God. If any midrash ever stated or implied something about God that was likely to undermine the tradition – something about God being evil, say, or arbitrary, or one among many gods – the rabbis surely rejected it (which is why *midrashim* of that kind do not appear in any rabbinic collections). Most (religiously) Jewish feminists accept these ground rules. In fact, their goal is precisely

to place women alongside men at the centre of religious life and therefore to support the *halakhic* system. But goddess ideologues, who want not merely to add female metaphors for God but to say that God is actually female, would find it just as hard as those who want to say that God is actually male. In short, the commitment to Judaism must come first, not the commitment to feminism or any other political perspective.

26 Susanne Heine, *Christianity and the Goddess: Systematic Criticism of a Feminist Theology* (London: SCM Press, 1988), 159.

27 Monique Witting, *Les Guerilleres*, trans. David Le Vay (New York: Avon, 1971), 89; quoted in Goldenberg, *Returning Words*, 47. In chapter 5, we discuss Mary Daly's use of that passage by Witting.

28 Goldenberg, *Returning Words*, 48.

29 Ibid., 48–9.

30 Ibid., 47.

31 Ibid., 171.

32 Ibid.

33 Elizabeth Schüssler Fiorenza, "On Feminist Methodology," *Journal of Feminist Studies in Religion* 1, no. 2 (1985): 75.

34 Yates, "Spirituality," 65–6.

35 See Paul Nathanson and Katherine K. Young, "Ideological Feminism versus Scholarship," in *Legalizing Misandry: From Public Shame to Systemic Discrimination against Men* (Montreal: McGill-Queen's University Press, 2006), 269–308.

36 Hindus remain hostile, however, to psychoanalytical interpretations of Hinduism. To put that in a larger context, however, many Westerners are equally hostile to psychoanalytical interpretations of Christianity or Judaism. Apart from anything else, psychoanalytical interpretations are reductive; they reduce religion to something imaginary or neurotic.

37 Heine, *Christianity*, 152.

38 One of Carol Christ's early books was *Diving Deep and Surfacing: Women Writers on Spiritual Quest* (Boston: Beacon Press, 1980). Her most recent book is *She Who Is: Re-Imagining the Divine in the World* (New York: Palgrave Macmillan, 2003).

39 Carol P. Christ, "Why Women Need the Goddess: Phenomenological, Psychological, and Political Reflections," in *Womanspirit Rising: A Feminist Reader in Religion*, ed. Carol P. Christ and Judith Plaskow (San Francisco: Harper and Row, 1979), 273–86.

40 Carol Christ refers to "thealogy" in *Laughter of Aphrodite: Reflections on a Journey to the Goddess* (San Francisco: Harper, 1987), although

Naomi Goldenberg had already used it, en passant, in *Changing of the Gods: Feminism and the End of Traditional Religions* (Boston: Beacon Press, 1979).

41 Both Catholicism and Eastern Orthodoxy make a subtle point about the "divinization" of Christians due to divine grace and through the sacraments. This is not quite the same thing, however, as *being* Christ within the current world order. As in the case of eschatology, Christians within the current world order have *begun a process* that will reach its conclusion only in another world order.

42 Carol P. Christ, *Diving Deep and Surfacing*; see also her "Women's Liberation and the Liberation of God: An Essay in Story Theology," in *The Jewish Woman: New Perspectives*, ed. Elizabeth Koltun (New York: Schocken Books, 1976), 11–17.

43 Elinor W. Gadon, *The Once and Future Goddess: A Symbol for Our Time* (New York: Harper and Row, 1989).

44 Ibid., 233.

45 Ibid.

46 Ibid., 273, discussing New York artist Mary Beth Edelson.

47 Ibid., 264.

48 Ibid., 372–3.

49 Ibid., 341.

50 See James Ephraim Lovelock, *Gaia: A New Look at Life on Earth* (Oxford: Oxford University Press, 1979).

51 It is not universally accepted, however, by scientists. Among those who question it are Richard Dawkins and Stephen J. Gould.

52 Elizabeth Dodson Gray, *Why the Green Nigger?* (Wellesley, Mass.: Roundtable Press, 1981); later title: *Green Paradise Lost*.

53 Rosemary Radford Ruether, *Gaia and God: An Ecofeminist Theology of Earth Healing* (San Francisco: Harper, 1992). Egalitarianism notwithstanding, the title gives precedence to Gaia, even though it would have been easier to pronounce the other way around.

54 In her main book on this topic, *Gaia and God*, Ruether often refers critically to early Jewish (biblical) sources, but she seldom refers at all to later Jewish (rabbinic) sources. Readers could interpret this omission as an example of Christian triumphalism, assuming that Judaism produced nothing of value after the advent of Christianity. But it would probably be a false accusation, because Ruether consciously tries to avoid that bad habit. She might simply believe biblical material to be more accessible to Christians. In addition, she refers to Babylonian sources.

55 "I also sift through the legacy of the Christian and Western cultural heritage to find usable ideas that might nourish a healed relation to each other and to the earth" (ibid., 2).

56 Ibid., 3.

57 In some passages, Ruether reveals a frank opportunism: "Those too alienated from this tradition [Christianity] to allow it to speak to them have every right to seek other spiritual traditions that can nurture them. But the vast majority of the more than 1 billion Christians of the world can be *lured* into an ecological consciousness only if they see that it grows in some ways from the soil in which they are planted" (ibid., 207; our emphasis).

58 Ruether, *Faith and Fratricide: The Theological Roots of Anti-Semitism* (New York: Seabury Press, 1974).

59 The *Journal of Feminist Studies in Religion* 7, no. 2 (1991) was devoted to the issue of feminist anti-Judaism: Judith Plaskow, "Feminist Anti-Judaism and the Christian God," 99–108; Leonore Siegele-Wenschkewitz, "The Discussion of Anti-Judaism in Feminist Theology: A New Area of Jewish Christian Dialogue," 94–8; Marie Theres Wacker, "Feminist Theology and Anti-Judaism: The Status of the Discussion and the Context of the Problem in the Federal Republic of Germany," 109–16; Fokkelien van Dijk-Hemmes, "Feminist Theology and Anti-Judaism in the Netherlands," 117–23; Asphodel P. Long, "Anti-Judaism in Britain," 125–33. See also Margaret Robinson, "Anti-Judaism in Lesbian Christian Theology," course paper, University of Toronto (2002), www.margaretrobinson.com (accessed 2 December 2008); Judith Plaskow, "Christian Feminism and Anti-Judaism," *Cross Currents* 33 (fall 1978): 306–9; Susannah Heschel, "Anti-Judaism in Christian Feminist Theology," *Tikkun* 5, no. 3 (May–June 1990): 25–8, 95–7; and Elisabeth Schüssler Fiorenza, *But She Said: Feminist Practices of Biblical Interpretation* (Boston: Beacon Press, 1992). A great deal has been written about this topic in German or by Germans, an early example being Katharina von Kellenbach's *Anti-Judaism in Feminist Religious Writings* (Atlanta: Scholars Press, 1994).

60 Rosemary Radford Ruether, *Sexism and God-Talk: Toward a Feminist Theology* (Boston: Beacon Press, 1983), 137.

61 Ruether refers to this feminist version of the "fall" in *Gaia*, which came out in 1992. Nathanson and Young had already discussed it, however, several years earlier. Out of that discussion came an article by Young, "Goddesses, Feminists and Scholars," in the *Annual Review of Women in*

World Religions, vol. 1, edited by Arvind Sharma (Albany: State University of New York Press, 1991).

62 In one passage Ruether says that patriarchal "valuing of the male over the female means that families cannot rest content with having produced two children, if both of these children are female" (*Gaia*, 264). But do these societies value male over female unambiguously? We do not think so. In some ways, obviously, they do. In other ways, though, they do not. Otherwise, why would so many of these societies assign the most dangerous tasks, such as hunting and warfare, to men?

63 Here is one example: "The roots of this evil lie, as we have suggested, in patterns of domination, whereby male *elites* in power deny their interdependency with women" (*Gaia*, 200; our emphasis).

64 In both *Spreading Misandry: The Teaching of Contempt for Men in Popular Culture* (Montreal: McGill-Queen's University Press, 2001), and *Legalizing Misandry: From Public Shame to Systemic Discrimination against Men* (Montreal: McGill-Queen's University Press, 2006), we observed that women have either created or exploited pervasive misandry for their own purposes. In legal terms, at any rate, the law now indirectly supports women not only in ways that it does not support men but also in ways that undermine due process.

65 Ruether, *Gaia*, 4.

66 See, for example, Nathanson and Young, *Legalizing Misandry*, 66–7. Because identity is one of the major underlying problems for men today, we discuss it in many places.

67 Ruether rejects the overt misandry of goddess ideology, to be sure, but she promotes the covert misandry of gynocentrism. She is reluctant to admit that men might have made significant contributions to society, for instance, even in the remote past – that is, after the development, by women, of horticulture. Men might have occasionally supplemented the diet with a few big game animals during the Neolithic period, to be sure, but were of marginal importance by that time (and, by implication, have become increasingly marginal ever since). For at least ten thousand years, in short, history has revolved around women despite the nefarious attempts of men to hide that fact and persecute women. "As both mother and food-sharer, it was women who pioneered bipedalism in order to pick and carry food as they gathered, while also carrying children. They also were the inventors of containers, to carry both babies and food, or free their hands for gathering. Weaving grasses into carrying containers and then storage baskets is an essential invention by women related to

women's combined roles. Most early human tools were probably created
first by women, such as digging sticks to uncover insects and stone tools
for cracking, pounding, and grinding food. Such tool use began with
[female] chimpanzees, and thus preceded by millions of years the development of weapons by men to hunt larger animals. Women probably
also developed fire to cook food, as well as the arts of treating skins of
animals and weaving animal hair for clothing. As plant-gatherers they
were the ones who first began to scatter some grain they gathered to
assure new growth, and thus became the first agriculturalists. Women's
roles thus are key to human biological, social, and technological evolution" (*Gaia*, 157–8).

Because we actually know very little about our remote ancestors, the
appropriate words here would be "might have." Women might well have
invented some of these things in some historical contexts, to be sure, but
men might well have done so in other contexts. Why assume, in any case,
that only one sex used this or that utensil? And why assume that those
who used it must have been the ones who also invented it? How do we
know, moreover, that our remote ancestors used fire first, or only, for
cooking purposes? Maybe they used it also, perhaps first, to scare away
predatory animals or simply to stay warm. And how do we know in any
case that only women did the cooking? Maybe men did the cooking for
big game animals and women for small animals or plants. That is the pattern today, after all, when men do the outdoor cooking (barbecuing) and
women the indoor cooking. In short, it is hard to see how anyone could
build a truly egalitarian modern society on such a gynocentric hypothesis
about ancient societies.

Elsewhere Ruether does the same thing in connection with Western
religion. "In these two traditions, covenantal and sacramental, we hear
two voices of divinity from nature. One speaks from the mountaintops in
the thunderous masculine tones of 'thou shalt' and 'thou shalt not.' It is
the voice of power and law, but speaking (at its most authentic) on
behalf of the weak, as a mandate to protect the powerless and to restrain
the power of the mighty. *There is another voice, one that speaks from the
intimate heart of matter. It has long been silenced by the masculine voice,
but today is finding again her own voice. This is the voice of Gaia. Her
voice does not translate into laws or intellectual knowledge, but beckons
us into communion*" (*Gaia*, 254; our emphasis). This passage is problematic for not one but two reasons. In the first place, Ruether unwittingly
(and ironically, in view of her brilliant exposé in *Faith and Fratricide*)
supports classic religious stereotypes. Here is the old paradigm of "law"

(which Christians identify with Jewish "rules") versus "gospel" (which they identify with Christian "love"). Jews see no such conflict. Or, to put in another way, they hear only one "voice." More important here, though, is the fact that Ruether unwittingly supports classic gender stereotypes: men are all about ideas and women about feelings. Worse, she assigns negativity to the male voice (despite the fact that it can "protect the powerless and restrain the power of the mighty") but not to the female one (despite the fact that emotion can be manipulative, neurotic, and abusive). To be sure, she goes on to say that "We need organized systems and norms ... But, without the second voice, our laws have no heart, nor roots in compassion and fellow feeling" (*Gaia*, 255). But the fact remains that most people, certainly readers of Ruether's book, will understand the supposedly male "voice" of "thou shalt" and "thou shalt not" as a *necessary evil*, not as something inherently good.

68 Ibid., 167–9.

69 Although fathers in our time are becoming much more involved in family life than ever before, very few of them even now are as deeply involved with their infants as mothers – especially breastfeeding mothers – are. The primacy of mothers for infants and young children remains pervasive, and this is clearly a very ancient feature of human family life. Ruether adds that "Woman-blaming or the lost paradise [of infancy] may have psycho-familial roots, roots that go back to primal human social patterns" (ibid., 145).

70 Ruether does not refer to same-sex marriage in *Gaia*, but she does in *Christianity and the Making of the Modern Family* (Boston: Beacon Press, 2000). She argues there that family structures have come and gone throughout history and that the one that religious conservatives want to maintain by opposing same-sex marriage is by no means the only one that Christianity could support.

71 "We need to support a variety of family and household patterns. These include the single householder; the gay or lesbian couple, including partners raising children by adoption, former marriages, or artificial insemination; the single parent, male or feamle; the two-earner heterosexual couple; the three- or four-generation family; families blended through divorce and remarrriage; and cohabiting parternships of two, three, or more people that may or may not include a sexual pair. This diversity is already the reality of American life ... We need to unmask the rhetoric that claims that the affirmation of 'holy unions' for gay couples somehow demeans marriage for heterosexuals. All of our unions are made holier by expanding the options for faithful relationship[s] and taking seriously

their careful preparation and joyful blessing" (Ruether, *Christianity*, 212–13).

72 Ruether, *Gaia*, 172.

73 Ibid., 266).

74 Ruether, *Integrating Ecofeminism, Globalization, and World Religions* (New York: Rowman and Littlefield, 2005).

75 Starhawk, a Wiccan, appears in Donna Read's goddess trilogy, which we have examined in chapters 1, 2, and 3. Her first book was *The Spiral Dance: A Rebirth of the Ancient Religion of the Great Goddess* (San Francisco: Harper and Row, 1979). Two of her most recent books are *Webs of Power: Notes from the Global Uprising* (Gabriola Island, B.C.: New Society, 2002) and *The Earth Path: Grounding Your Spirit in the Rhythms of Nature* (San Francisco: Harper and Row, 2004). In *Truth or Dare: Encounters with Power, Authority and Mystery* (San Francisco: Harper and Row, 1987), she distinguishes between "power over" (the dominating power of men), "power within" (the inner power of women and oppressed groups), and "power with" (the soon-to-be-triumphant opposite of domination). Marilyn French made very similar distinctions two years earlier in *Beyond Power: On Women, Men, and Morals* (New York: Summmit, 1985).

76 Carol Christ differs from Starhawk only in explaining the "fall" into patriarchy in connection with a gradual transition from horticultural (and egalitarian) societies to agricultural (and hierarchical) ones rather than in connection with the invasion of horticultural (and not only peaceful but also gynocentric) societies by pastoral (and bellicose) ones. Either way, suddenly or gradually, what amounts to the "original sin" that led to this "fall" from grace under a great goddess was the sin of men.

77 Carolyn Merchant, a historian of science and of the environment who teaches at the University of California at Berkeley, has been a very influential figure in the world of ecofeminism. Merchant is less interested in the remote origins of patriarchy than in the relatively recent origins of science and technology. In *The Death of Nature: Women, Ecology, and the Scientific Revolution* (San Francisco: Harper and Row, 1980), she traces our current ecological nightmare to the Enlightenment and its immediate precursor in the seventeenth century (but also to industrialism, colonialism, and capitalism). Earlier, people had seen nature as an organism, a benevolent mother; now they began to see it as a mechanism or, worse, a passive and inert set of objects to be studied, molded, controlled, dominated, and "raped." Among Merchant's more recent books are *Earthcare: Women and the Environment* (New York: Routledge,

1996) and *Reinventing Eden: The Fate of Nature in Western Civilization* (New York: Routledge, 2003).

Ruether has no problem with Merchant's hostility toward science. In fact, she writes approvingly of Merchant's belief that the old paradigm of nature as an organism has survived the lamentable reign of reason in "alternative philosophies, such as Neoplatonism and romanticism [*sic*], as well as by artists and poets" (*Integrating*, 121). You would never know from this statement that Romanticism, for instance, has been the primary source of such scourges as nationalism and racism. Nor would you know that science has produced any valuable insights – valuable to women, that is, no less than to men. Would Merchant and Ruether really prefer to live in a world that could do nothing to prevent scurvy, say, or smallpox? Would they really prefer to live in a world that could explain suffering only in connection with either sin or demon possession? Would they really prefer to live in a world that, for most people, did not extend beyond the next village? And even if subsistence farming really were a better way of life than any urban one, where would we find enough arable land for everyone (after centuries of expanding populations due not only to improved medicine but also to industrialization and urbanization)? On the other hand, as beneficiaries of postmodernism, Merchant and Ruether do approve of scientific developments such as chaos theory, quantum mechanics, and complexity theory – even though these (including postmodernism) have emerged primarily among men (not women) who can trace their intellectual lineage right back to the Enlightenment.

At any rate, Merchant encourages those who want to reverse history by restoring Eden not by subduing nature but by entering into a "partnership" with it and acting on the basis of negotiation with all human and non-human parties. This sounds very edifying, except that Merchant, like so many other ideological feminists, includes every form of evil under the heading of "patriarchy." Ruether summarizes Merchant's theory of patriarchy, which matches her own, as follows: "All those ills are often spoken of collectively [by Merchant] as 'patriarchy,' the rise of societies dominated by a male elite who subjugated women, turned the majority of humans into slaves, serfs, or low-paid workers and redefined all these humans, as well as nature, as property." In theory, as usual, the bad guys belong to a male *elite* – not all men either then or now. However, no one could miss the link that she makes between patriarchy and men in general. This is at least partly, we suggest, because Merchant's theory (like so many similar ones) makes it clear that men can redeem themselves only by becoming women, or honorary women. Merchant presents

women's way as the only alternative, after all, to that of patriarchy –
which is men's way, by definition, even if most men (slaves, wage slaves,
racial minorities, and so on) do not benefit from it.

78 Vandana Shiva began her career as a physicist, a specialist in nuclear
energy. Convinced that Western development schemes were degrading
not only the natural environment of India but of the whole world, she
rejected all that in favour of political activism as an environmentalist. She
is now the director of India's Research Foundation for Science, Technology and Natural Resource Policy. Like her Western counterparts, she lays
all of the blame on men. This is a major feature of her landmark book,
Staying Alive: Women, Ecology, and Survival in India (New Delhi: Kali
for Women, 1988). Science is nothing other than a form of patriarchal
oppression: a continuation, when used to help developing countries
through "green revolutions," of colonialism. Like other ecofeminists, she
attacks Western science for its assumption that nature is inert and passive
(like women) and therefore something to be controlled, dominated,
exploited, and so forth. In other words, Shiva relies on the standard arguments of postcolonialism. One thing about her point of view is unusual,
however, for Westerners: her reliance on one Hindu cosmology – a specifically Tantric one that emphasizes the female. To recover the "feminine
principle," she refers to the union of *shakti* (female energy) and *purusha*
(male energy) to produce *prakriti* (nature), also female. Hindus personify
both Shakti and Prakriti as goddesses. Here is Ruether's comment:
Shiva's theory is "a rejection of the Western gender ideology that defined
males by a masculinity of disconnection from the body, women, and
nature, violent domination over it, and a distortion of women and nature
into passive objects of this violence. Men need to overcome their alienation and violence, and women their passivity and acceptance of denigration. Both men and women must see themselves as active participants in
nurturing life in partnership with nature's own vitality" (*Integrating*,
108). But does it make sense for postcolonialists to attack Western science and yet to rely on Western feminism? And precisely what can male
"partners" contribute, as such, to this profoundly gynocentric project?
This was not a major problem for Indian men, traditionally, because they
had considerable power in both public and private life in exclusively male
circles, which satisfied the need for a distinctive masculine identity. If
masculine identity were to become fragile in contemporary India, as it
has in the West, then goddess worship would seem much less attractive to
men than it does now.

79 Ruether notes other criticisms that Western feminists have made against
Shiva. But for details, she points to her own criticisms of (elite) Hinduism
in chapter 2. Most important is that Hinduism subordinates women,
viewing them as ignorant and impure (as it views low castes and out-
castes). Male asceticism, too, denigrates women, viewing them as seduc-
ers. And Hinduism's view that the world, including the natural world, is
illusory (*maya*) means that protecting it would be meaningless. Despite
Hinduism's bucolic view of nature, moreover, India today is massively
polluted – so much for goddess religion Hindu style, according to
Ruether. This is not the place to challenge her stereotypical view of Hinduism (which, like any stereotype, relies on a grain of truth). In view of
the fact that she has so much insight into Christian stereotypes of Judaism, she might have recognized Western stereotypes of Hinduism. The
causes of India's pollution include not only Hinduism but also overpopulation, for instance, thanks partly to Western medicine and industrialization. Despite her devastating critique of Hinduism, she sees in Vandana
Shiva new hope and attributes that to her (Western) feminist reinterpreta-
tion of Hinduism. What she fails to see is that Shiva draws on a traditional Hindu cosmology – the Tantric one – which existed long before
Western feminism. Shiva's "tree hugging" ritual, however, is another
matter. That really is new.

80 Catherine Keller, *From a Broken Web: Separation, Sexism, and Self*
(Boston: Beacon Press, 1986).

81 Catherine Keller teaches theology at Drew University. Relying on process
philosophy, postmodernism, and ecofeminism, she has created a "theology of becoming." According to the Drew website, that is a "work of
complicated lineage and open future ... [which] interweaves a postmodern biblical hermeneutic with process cosmology, poststructuralist
philosophy and an evolving feminist cosmopolitics. At once constructive
and deconstructive in approach, such theology engages questions of ecological, social, and spiritual interdependence amidst an irreducible inde-
terminacy." In *From a Broken Web*, Keller discusses the innate ethical
"interconnectedness" of women in terms of its theological counterpart
(immanence) and its philosophical counterpart (process theology). Her
book has been very influential.

Keller sees the inferiority of men in ontological terms, unlike Ruether,
tracing it to a way of perceiving and thinking that begins in infancy.
Lurking underneath this male self-concept, moreover, is a "profound fear
of women" (3). Using the metaphor of a spider web, she maintains that this

male orientation is like a broken web (hence the title of the book) or the divided world of Cartesian dualism: spirit or mind versus body, one person versus another, one group against others. Keller extracts from the psycho-analytic theory of Nancy Chodorow (leaving behind the subtlety of Chodorow's thought) what she needs to claim the origin of female intercon-nectedness in child development. Girls have a longer pre-Oedipal period than boys, she argues, and this allows girls more time to experience conti-nuity with the world. Not only do boys represent the sexual "other" to their mothers, she adds, but they experience this negatively as an otherness heightened all too often by absent fathers. Moreover, Keller relies on the process philosophy of Alfred North Whitehead – a man! – for a more immanent and dynamic view of all entities, including selves. These are not only becoming and changing but also interconnected by feeling.

But Keller sees the inferiority of men also in moral terms, tracing it to patriarchal religions – Greek, Jewish, and Christian in the West. That sounds like a contradiction. Men were still free to choose and shape their religions, apparently, and came up with bad ones. At any rate, all of these traditions teach that God is not only absolute but also transcendent and therefore separate from creation: a hero-warrior, a projection of the human male, which reads "like a catalogue of the heroic ego's ideal of himself" (38). This view, claims Keller, maintains patriarchy, exclusion-ary politics, misogyny stemming from strong male ego-boundaries, the sense of a permanent, substantial self, separate individuality, and concern with power, self-control and objectification – the roots, in short, of all suffering and sin. According to Keller, unlike Ruether, these religions are therefore inherently evil. But Keller, like Ruether, has nonetheless devoted her career to the project of rewriting Christian theology.

Either male thinking or masculine religion has had a serious effect on women. If men classify themselves as normative, they must classify women as deviant and therefore dependent (217). As a result, even the female self is split, turned against itself, viewing the world in a fragmented and false way (92). The result of that, in turn, is the loss of self. "But today neither man nor woman nor world can afford the warrior model. Having proved itself an evil deformity, the monster in its demonic sense, it must no more demon-strate its world-destroying weaponry" (92). Consequently, women must claim their real nature by being suspicious of any claims that men make – they must use the "hermeneutics of suspicion" – and thus recover their true nature of "interconnectedness" and "inclusion." This is what we would classify as essentialism ("we" are good), the necessary accompaniment of dualism ("they" are evil or inadequate).

One anecdote tells us something interesting about Keller. Speaking at a feminist conference, Keller recalled reading a book by William Broyles (*Brothers in Arms: A Journey from War to Peace* [New York: Knopf, 1986]) that discussed his experience of war in Vietnam. He made the point that war could have an aesthetic quality. Moreover, given the intensely emotional experience of camaraderie and the intensely direct experience of life itself in the midst of death, "men love war." Keller reacted to this immediately. She had always suspected as much, but now, well, here it was in print – in their own words. For Keller, this was delightful proof that men are innately warlike.

But this was before 9/11 and even before the Gulf War – the first war that allowed women close to combat. By now, many women would consider her attitude naive at best and self-righteous at worst. Female veterans have learned some things about war that other women (and many men) do not know. For one thing, the characteristic attitude that soldiers bring to war is not necessarily the bravado they display for public consumption. This was clear to Winnie Smith, a nurse who served in Vietnam. "As I work," she writes of her day in a ward filled with wounded and dying soldiers, "I remember that part of my mother's last letter saying that soldiers in the newsreels look so happy" (*American Daughter Gone to War: On the Front Lines with an Army Nurse in Vietnam* [New York: Pocket Books, 1992], 119). Years after the war, Smith had learned the lesson well. "Instead of the war in Vietnam, my boy became the focus of my nighttime horrors ... Before this war in the Middle East, my biggest regret was that I had not had a child when I was much younger. Until it ended, I was deeply grateful that Ken is not old enough to be drafted. Now I dread the day when he will be" (349–51). Many veterans of Vietnam felt the same. Among the many mementos left at the Wall in Washington is a bag of marbles accompanied by a letter that says, in part: "From the innocence of boyhood, filled with springs and summers, playing marbles and baseball, autumns playing football, and winters ice skating we went to the reality of manhood and the horrors of war" (Letter to Larry L. Marsh, *Offerings at the Wall: Artifacts from the Vietnam Veterans Memorial Collection* [Atlanta: Turner Publishing, 1995], 166).

At times during her tour of duty, nevertheless, even Smith failed to assimilate the insight she was gaining: "If I could," she noted on one occasion, "I'd be a man. Then I'd be a chopper pilot and fly every day. Up there are no thoughts, only sensations, the cool air rushing past and the serenity of a blue-green world unfolding far below" (143). It is unnecessary to take this statement at face value. Elsewhere she describes a firefight with the characteristic detachment of soldiers watching a distant battle: "Flares glow brightly when they burst, flicker surrealistically as they dim, now dancing shadows on the hillside as they falter and fall before the next burst. It's enchantingly, disarmingly, beautiful" (147). Many people, both men and women, have noted the irony of finding aesthetic or sensual beauty in the midst of wartime carnage. Doing so does not mean that women would like to be drafted into combat any more than it means that "men love war." It simply means that survival in situations of this kind depends on, apart from anything else, the ability to block out terror, even if only for a few moments.

Both men and women can become free from patriarchal patterns, Keller avers, but the task will be far easier for women because of female child development. Men will have a harder time, by contrast, not only because of male child development but also because of sinful male pride. She goes so far as to say that "for a man to find his own (authentically male) integrity of connection, will at this point in history implicate him in a compensatory gynocentricity, a provisional sense of identification with women that functions as an apprenticeship in relation" (*Broken Web*, 203). Men who try to abdicate their traditional identity will also have to risk mockery by other men. But exactly what would be an authentic voice for men? Keller does not say.

The language of "interconnectedness" and immanence has proven immensely popular among feminists. So has the celebration of female bodies. So has the sacralization of female experiences such as giving birth, nursing, feeding, comforting, and so on. Keller, like Ruether, avoids neopaganism itself. But we have shown that for many like-minded ecofeminists, immanent goddesses have become symbols of all these things. They see healing people, cultures, and the planet itself as uniquely female tasks. What they fail to see is the dualism ironically inherent in a way of thinking that is supposedly anti-dualistic. The dualism is no longer between mind or spirit and body, to be sure, but between men and women. Slowly, however, this dualism is giving way to more nuanced or critical discussions by female scholars.

82 Ruether, *Gaia*, 117–18.
83 Ibid., 99.

CHAPTER FIVE

1 We have searched the web for the basis of her claim to the title of rabbi. Because we have found no mainstream, institutional affiliation, we

assume that she either gave the title to herself or received it from an organization such as the Alliance for Jewish Renewal (ALEPH), which calls itself "transdenominational" and offers private *semikhah* (rabbinic ordination; see "Aleph Bet Midrash," *Aleph: Alliance for Jewish Renewal* (2001): 1, www.alephu.homestead.com/faculty.html (accessed 11 April 2005).

2 "Jewitchery Library," *Jewitchery* (22 July 2004): 1, www.jewitchery.com/library.html (accessed 11 April 2001).

3 Raphael Patai, *The Hebrew Goddess*, 3rd ed. (Detroit: Wayne State University Press, 1990).

4 The kabbalists were theological innovators. Along with reincarnation (*gilgul*) and God's dependence on people to "mend the world" (*tikkun*) by finding sparks of holiness in the midst of everyday life, for instance, they added three female dimensions (*sefirot*) (and seven others) to the notion of God. But for at least two reasons, innovative theology did not translate into innovative rulings on Jewish law (*halkhah*) and therefore affect the role of women. For one thing, kabbalistic theology came to rely heavily on neo-Platonic philosophy with its mind-body, spirit-flesh dualism (which associated women with the material and sensual). The rabbis would almost certainly have declared kabbalistic theology heretical, moreover, if the kabblists themselves had not deliberately found ways for it to support the Jewish legal system so strongly and effectively – following any commandment with the proper attitude (*kavanah*) could liberate a spark of holiness and send it back to God – and thus avoid excommunication. Judaism can tolerate theological variation, within limits, but not legal variation.

5 For an attempt to deify Magdalene, see Lynn Pickett, *Mary Magdalene: Christianity's Hidden Goddess* (New York: Carroll and Graf, 2003). However, most attempts to add a goddess to Christianity involve Sophia.

6 Jonathan Darman, "An Inconvenient Woman," MSNBC (29 May 2006), www.msnbc.msn.com/id/12893635/site/newsweek/ (accessed 21 June 20007). Also published in *Newsweek*, 29 May 2006.

7 Darman, "Inconvenient," 2 of 5.

8 Even though they disapproved of Christianity, the Nazis allowed a loophole for Jesus (and thus for Christian members of the Nazi Party). They claimed that Jesus was an "Aryan," not a Jew, because he came from the "remote" Galilee region.

9 Kenneth L. Woodward, "A Quite Contrary Mary: Like Jesus, Mary Magdalene Is Now the Subject of a Cultural Makeover," *Beliefnet* (2003): 2, www. beliefnet.com?Entertainment/Movies/The-Da-Vinci-Code/A-Quite-

Contrary-Mary (accessed 30 April 2009). Woodward adds another
model to explain the current use of gnostic gospels. Referring to the
syncretism of American popular religion, he says that "the operative
assumption is that all sacred texts are of equal value and the reader [of
any anthology] is free to make sacred those that provide personal appeal
... It is the ultimate in consumer-oriented religion, of course, and has the
added advantage of bypassing the authority of any community as to
which texts count as sacred and which do not" (ibid., 3 of 4).

10 John 20: 27.

11 Luke 24: 39.

12 Later on, though, even the prevailing tradition – that of the church –
became ambivalent about the material world, especially the body and its
sexual urges. On the one hand, God had created all of these things; they
were inherently good and therefore appropriate vehicles for the sacraments. On the other hand, they had "fallen" and required a redemption
that would be fulfilled only with the return of Christ; meanwhile, they
were dangerous without strict control.

13 Jane Schaberg and Melanie Johnson-DuBaufre, "There's Something
about Mary," *Ms* (spring 2006); msmagazine.com/spring2006/mary.asp.
Schaberg, who teaches at the University of Detroit Mercy (a Jesuit insti-
tution), has argued that God "raped" Mary, the mother of Jesus; see Jane
Schaberg, *The Illegitimacy of Jesus: A Feminist Interpretation of the
Infancy Narratives* (San Francisco: Harper and Row, 1987).

14 See Carol Ann Morrow, "*Cracking The Da Vinci Code*: Theologian Elizabeth Johnson on Mary Magdalene," *St Anthony Messenger* (2004),
www.americancatholic.org/Messenger/Jul2004/Feature2.asp (accessed 15
June 2007).

15 Woodward, "Quite Contrary Mary," 4 of 4.

16 See, for instance, Ed Conroy, "Will the Magdalene Go Mainstream?
Controversial as Scholarship, Author Margaret Starbird's Interpretation
of Mary Magdalene Is Gaining Popular Influence," *National Catholic
Reporter* (31 October 2003) – but also Rosemary Radford Ruether, "No
Church Conspiracy against Mary Magdalene," *National Catholic
Reporter* (9 February 2001); Victor Greto, "Churches amid Change:
Roles of Mary Magdalene, Women, Rethought," *Milwaukee Journal Sen-
tinel* (12 September 1999); Chris Herlinger, "Enigma for the Ages:
Exhibit Shows Many Faces of Mary Magdalene: Sinner and Saint, Fallen
Woman and Witness," *Washington Post* (15 June 2002); Stephen Huba,
"Catholics Working to Improve Mary Magdalene's Reputation,"
Cincinnati Post (22 July 2000).

17 Amy Welborn, *Decoding the Da Vinci Code; The Facts behind the Fiction of the Da Vinci Code* (Huntington, Ind.: Our Sunday Visitor, 2004); Steve Kellmeyer, *Fact and Fiction in the Da Vinci Code* (Peoria, Ill.: Bridegroom Press, 2004); Darrell L. Bock, *Breaking the Da Vinci Code: Answers to the Questions Everyone's Asking* (Waterville, Maine.: Thorndike Press, 2004); James L. Garlow and Peter Jones, *Cracking Da Vinci's Code* (Colorado Springs, Colo.: Victor, 2004); Ben Witherington, *The Gospel Code: Novel Claims about Jesus, Mary Magdalene, and Da Vinci* (Downers Grove, Ill.: Inter Varsity Press, 2004); Richard Abanes, *The Truth behind the Da Vinci Code* (Eugene, Oreg.: Harvest House, 2004); Hank Hanegraaff and Paul L. Maier, *The Da Vinci Code: Fact or Fiction* (Carol Stream, Ill.: Tyndale House, 2004); Martin Lunn, *The Da Vinci Code Decoded* (New York: Disinformation; St Paul, Minn.: Consortium Book Sales and Distribution, 2004); Bart D. Ehrman, *Truth and Fiction in The Da Vinci Code: A Historian Reveals What We Really Know about Jesus, Mary Magdalene, and Constantine* (New York: Oxford University Press, 2004).

18 Johnson combines Sophianity with Christianity in the form of liberation theology, a worldview (rejected by the Vatican) that combines Christianity with Marxism. "The mystery of God," writes Johnson, "Holy Wisdom, She who is, is the dark radiance of love in solidarity with the struggle of denigrated persons, including long generations of women, to shuck off their mean estate and lay hold of their genuine human dignity and value ... They are bounded by the livingness of Sophia-God who gives life to the dead" (Elizabeth A. Johnson, *She Who Is: The Mystery of God in Feminist Theological Discourse* [New York: Crossroad, 1992], 244–5. Other books by Johnson include *The Church Women Want: Catholic Women in Dialogue* (New York: Crossroad, 2002); *Women, Earth, and Creator Spirit* (New York: Paulist Press, 1993); and *Friends of God and Prophets: A Feminist Theological Reading of the Communion of Saints* (New York: Continuum, 1998).

19 Quoted in Johnson, *She Who Is*, 76.

20 Ibid., 77.

21 Ibid., 79.

22 Ibid., 86.

23 Ibid., 87.

24 Ibid., 88.

25 Ibid.

26 Ibid., 88–9.

27 Actually, theologians never said that Christ (one of God's three aspects) was male, although they did acknowledge that *Jesus* (Christ's earthly manifestation) had been male.

28 Johnson, "She Who Is," 242–3.

29 Gershom G. Scholem, *On the Kabbalah and Its Symbolism* (New York: Schocken Books, 1969), 104–5. See also Gershom G. Scholem, *Major Trends in Jewish Mysticism* (New York: Schocken Books, 1961), 229.

30 Scholem, *Kabbalah*, 105.

31 Ibid., 100.

32 Ibid., 227.

33 Ibid., 104.

34 Ibid., 107.

35 Ibid., 139.

36 Elliot R. Wolfson, *Through a Speculum That Shines: Vision and Imagination in Medieval Jewish Mysticism* (Princeton: Princeton University Press, 1994), 306–7.

37 Ibid., 316.

38 Mary Aquin O'Neill, review of *She Who Is: The Mystery of God in Feminist Theological Discourse* by Elizabeth A. Johnson, *Religious Studies Review* 21, no. 1 (1995): 19–20.

39 O'Neill, review, 19.

40 Mary McClintock Fulkerson, review of *She Who Is: The Mystery of God in Feminist Theological Discourse* by Elizabeth A. Johnson, *Religious Studies Review* 21, no. 1 (1995): 21–5.

41 In India, for example, female symbolism dramatically increased after the seventh century, when many of the states had stabilized; emphasis was placed on maintenance and harmony, therefore, not on aggression and conquest.

42 By incorporating maternal imagery for God, Susanne Heine observes, the tradition could respond effectively to those who were attracted to local polytheistic traditions that included goddesses. This also supported the claim that God represents wholeness and totality. But this approach, expanded the notions of both fatherhood and motherhood: "If we leave aside birth and breast-feeding, there is nothing against understanding physical care, love ... and mercy as a fatherly attitude towards children. And is not a mother's love also concerned to look strictly at a social life in accordance with the criterion of ethical maxims, fighting with children and for children if need be" (*Christianity and the Goddess: Systematic Criticism of a Feminist Theology* [London: SCM Press, 1988], 29).

43 Tikva Frymer-Kensky, *In the Wake of the Goddesses: Women, Culture and the Biblical Tradition of Pagan Myth* (New York: Free Press, 1992), 85.

44 Frymer-Kensky, *Wake*, 97.

45 Genesis 49: 25.

46 Frymer-Kensky, *Wake*, 98.

47 Most biblical scholars agree that the Book of Isaiah had not one author but three, assigning some portions to Isaiah, others to deutero-Isaiah and still others to trito-Isaiah.

48 Isaiah 46: 3–4.

49 Isaiah 66: 13.

50 Job 38: 8–9.

51 Job 38: 28–9.

52 Psalms 131: 2.

53 Deuteronomy 32: 18.

54 Scholem, *Kabbalah*, 140–5.

55 Frymer-Kensky, *Wake*, 115.

56 Ibid., 116.

57 Ibid., 120.

58 Ibid., 127.

59 Elizabeth Achtemeier, "Why God Is Not Mother: A Response to Feminist God-Talk in the Church," *Christianity Today* (16 August 1993): 17–23.

60 Achtemeier, "Why God," 17.

61 Hosea 11:9.

62 Isaiah 40:18.

63 Virgina Ramey Mollenkott, quoted in Achtemeier, "Why God," 20.

64 Mary Daly, *Beyond God the Father: Toward a Philosophy of Women's Religion* (Boston: Beacon Press, 1973), 19.

65 Achtemeier, "Why God," 20.

66 Ibid., 23.

67 Achtemeier notes also that time has become circular once more instead of linear. In this she is mistaken. Biblical (or traditional Jewish and Christian) time has never been linear. It has never been cyclical, it is true, and is thus unlike the notion of time that prevails in Hinduism, say, or Buddhism. But the notion of linear time (a series of unrepeatable events moving relentlessly toward an unknown future) is modern and thus secular. Western religion is based on the idea that we can reverse time, that we can re-experience sacred events periodically through ritual. History is *not* a series of random events, moreover, moving toward an unknown future. On the contrary, history has a beginning and an ending. And the

beginning, in fact, is identical to the end. History is a parenthetical experience marked by an ultimate return to paradise in one form or another. The traditional Western notion of time is neither linear nor cyclical, therefore, but *circular*.

68 Ibid., 23.

69 Hindu gurus often claimed to be incarnations of deities with only the appearance of being human, but checks and balances prevented their claims from becoming megalomaniacal ones that would have had destructive effects on society. Hindus balanced the radical freedom of religious claims with the conservative caste structure, for instance, which ostensibly permitted little change and maintained continuity. The ideas contained in scripture (*shruti* and *smriti*) mitigated the effects of entrepreneurial saints, moreover, as did the two types of ethical norm that governed society: common duties (*samanya-dharma*) and duties defined by caste and stage of life (*varna-ashrama-dharma*).

70 Thomas Oden, "Encountering the Goddess at Church," *Christianity Today*, 16 August 1993, 18.

71 Dale Youngs, "What's So Good about the Goddess?," *Christianity Today*, 16 August 1993, 21.

72 "PCUSA Funds Effort to Re-Create God," *Presbyterian Layman*, January 1994, 1.

73 Ibid., 10.

74 "Despised and Rejected," *Presbyterian Layman*, January 1994, 2.

75 PCUSA Funds," 11.

76 See Pui-lan Kwok, *Postcolonial Imagination and Feminist Theology* (Louisville, Ky.: Westminster John Knox Press, 2005). See also *Postcolonialism, Feminism, and Religious Discourse*, edited by Pui-lan Kwok and Laura E. Donaldson (New York: Routledge, 2002). The essays in this book attack not only the men responsible for colonial conquests and the consequences of those conquests but also a few feminists, including those who "misappropriate" the traditions of non-Western women. Kwok has become a leading advocate of gay rights, however, emphasizing the contributions of Asian-Americans ("Gay Activism in Asian and Asian-American Churches," *Witness Magazine* (undated), www.thewitness.org/agw/kwok051904.html (accessed 14 June 2007).

77 "PCUSA Funds," 10.

78 Ibid., 10.

79 *Presbyterian Layman*, January 1994. After their morning baths or on ceremonial occasions, both unmarried and married women paint on these dots (called the *tilaka*, *bindu*, or *pottu*, depending on the region).

Although maidens may choose from a variety of colours, married women traditionally wear some shade of red. They associate these dots indirectly with goddesses. Even male goddess worshippers wear them. For women, though, the dots symbolize in addition their auspicious marital status and fertility. Widows, by contrast, may not wear dots. These definitions of status have become much more flexible in modern India. See Katherine K. Young, "The Beguiling Simplicity of a Dot," in *New Approaches to Women and Hinduism* (forthcoming).

80 "PCUSA Funds," 4.

81 Ibid., 10.

82 Ibid.

83 Ibid.

84 Eastern Orthodox Christians do refer to *theosis*, a word that clearly has the same origin as "apotheosis" in English. God became human, they say, so that humans could become God – that is, God-like. Orthodox Christians trace this notion back to scripture, according to which people can become "as gods." They can do so, in Eastern Orthodoxy, by meditating on the Jesus Prayer.

85 See Hyun Kyung Chung, *Struggle to Be the Sun Again: Introduction to Asian Women's Theology* (Maryknoll, NY: Orbis, 1990). In this book she argues for what some people would identify as a secular religion. "Doing theology," she writes, "is a personal and political activity" (1). And by "political," she refers to feminism and postcolonialism. This made her an ideal delegate to the Re-Imagining conference. She identifies herself as not only a Christian but also as a Buddhist, a shamanist, an eco-feminist, and so on (all of equal importance to her sense of identity). Accused of syncretism by Christian critics at a 1991 conference in Australia, she retorted: "You are right, I am a syncretist, but so are you. My response is that I know I am a syncretist, but you don't know you are a syncretist because you have hegemonic power" ("Chung Hyun Kyung," *Wikipedia* (4 June 2007), www.en.wikipedia.org/wiki/Chung_Hyun_Kyng (accessed 14 June 2007).

86 "PCUSA Funds," 1.

87 Ibid.

88 Ibid., 10.

89 "Get Set for the Spin," *Presbyterian Layman*, January 1994, 3.

90 David Helm, "Sophia's Choice," *Christian Century*, 6 April 1994, 339–40.

91 Ibid., 339.

92 Catherine Keller, "Inventing the Goddess," *Christian Century*, 6 April 1994, 340–2.

93 See, for instance, Catherine Keller, *From a Broken Web: Separation, Sexism and Self* (Boston: Beacon Press, 1986); *Apocalypse Now and Then: A Feminist Guide to the End of the World* (Boston: Beacon Press, 1999); *Face of the Deep: A Theology of Becoming* (London: Routledge, 2003); *God and Power: Counter-Apocalyptic Journeys* (Minneapolis: Fortress Press, 2005). In the first book, Keller claimed that men are innately inferior to women by virtue of their need to "separate" from others and see themselves in opposition to others, which is why they "love war" (even though her profoundly dualistic point of view is itself a sign of exactly the same problem). In *Beyond Power: Women, Men, and Morals* (New York: Summit Books, 1985), Marilyn French popularized much of what Keller and what many other feminist ideologues have said.

94 Keller, "Inventing," 341.

95 "PCUSA Funds," 1.

96 Keller, "Inventing," 341.

97 Ibid.

98 Ibid.

99 Ibid., 342.

100 Joseph D. Small and John P. Burgess, "Evaluating 'Re-Imagining,'" *Christian Century*, 6 April 1994, 342–3.

101 On the surface, it would seem obvious that failing to make this distinction would mean failing to make a distinction between Judaism and Christianity (not that anyone at the conference had the slightest urge to adopt Judaism). In fact, it would mean failing to understand not only Christianity but Judaism as well. Like Christians, Jews rejected the idea, even the implication, that wisdom or any other divine attribute can exist apart from God.

102 Small and Burgess, "Evaluating," 343 (emphasis added).

103 Ibid., 343.

104 Presbyterian Church (USA), General Assembly, *Minutes,* part 1, 1994, 83–6.

105 Ibid., 82–8.

106 Ibid., 82.

107 Ibid., 87.

108 Ibid., 90.

109 Ibid.

110 Ibid., 87.

111 Nancy J. Berneking and Pamela Carter Joern, eds., *Re-Membering and Re-Imagining* (Cleveland: Pilgrilm Press, 1995).

112 Berneking, in Berneking and Joern, *Re-Membering*, xiii.

113 David W. Cloud, "Apostasy[: Presbyterian Church]," *BibleBelievers.Net* (undated) www.biblebelievers.net/Apostasy/kjcprsby.htm (accessed 14 June 2007); the material originated in *Cloud's Way of Life Encyclopedia*.

114 David W. Cloud, "WCC Conference Honors Sophia Goddess, Gives Ovation to Lesbians," *Way of Life* (2001) www.wayoflife.org/fbns/sophia.htm (accessed 14 June 2007).

CHAPTER SIX

1 Daly is by no means the only one to adopt this policy. A feminist periodical based in Halifax, *Pandora,* made the headlines for refusing to print letters from male readers. In 1990, an editorial said that the courts should never give custody to divorced fathers; in fact, it said, even access to their children should be denied to these fathers. When a divorced father wrote in to argue the point, the periodical duly silenced him according to its policy. He took the case to court. In 1992, *Pandora* won by claiming freedom of the press. Legally, that was the correct decision. As Robert Walker points out ("Tiny Periodical Illuminated Two Principles of Press Freedom," *Montreal Gazette,* 20 June 1994, B3), the law may not prevent newspapers and periodicals from printing anything (except what is considered obscene, hateful, or defamatory), nor force them to print anything (except for retractions in cases of libel). But morally, as women know, being silenced is more complicated than any debate over legal rights.

2 Mary Daly, *Beyond God the Father: Toward a Philosophy of Women's Religion* (Boston: Beacon Press, 1973), 19. Among her more recent diatribes are the following: *Outercourse: The Be-Dazzling Voyage: Containing Recollections from My Logbook of a Radical Feminist Philosopher (Be-ing an Account of My Time/Space Travels and Ideas – Then, Again, Now, and How* (San Francisco: HarperSanFrancisco, 1992); *Websters' First New Intergalactic Wickedary of the English Language (Conjured by Mary Daly in Cahoots with Jane Caputi)* (San Francisco: HarperSanFrancisco, 1994); *Quintessence – Realizing the Archaic Future: A Radical Elemental Feminist Manifesto* (Boston: Beacon Press, 1998); and *Amazon Grace: Re-Calling the Courage to Sin Big* (New York: Palgrave Macmillan, 2006).

3 Daly, quoted in David Sexton, "Nags, Shrews and Snools," review of *Pure Lust* by Mary Daly, *Spectator,* 23 February 1985, 23.

4 When asked about Buddhism and other religions, Daly's words are brief but to the point: "Misogynists! Hateful! All of them!" (quoted in Susan Bridle, "No Man's Land: An Interview with Mary Daly," *What Is*

Enlightenment Magazine Online [1999]: 8, www.wie.org/j8/daly. asp?pf+1 [accessed 12 December 2004].

5 Northrop Frye, *The Great Code: The Bible and Literature* (New York: Harcourt Brace Jovanovich, 1982).

6 See Paul Nathanson, *Over the Rainbow: The Wizard of Oz as a Secular Myth of America* (Albany: State University of New York Press, 1989).

7 Daly, *The Church and the Second Sex* (New York: Harper and Row, 1968).

8 Simone de Beauvoir, *The Second Sex*, translated by H.M. Parshley (New York: Knopf, 1953).

9 Daly, *Church*, 9.

10 Paul Tillich, *The Courage to Be* (New Haven: Yale University Press, 1952).

11 Daly, *God the Father*.

12 Daly, *The Church and the Second Sex*, 5; this passage comes from her "feminist postChristian introduction and new archaic afterwords."

13 Daly, *God the Father*, 35–6.

14 Ibid., 43.

15 Daly, *Gyn/Ecology: The Metaethics of Radical Feminism* (London: Women's Press, 1984).

16 Daly, *Beyond*, 6.

17 Even though Western theologians do not characteristically refer to life as a journey from "ignorance" to "enlightenment" and therefore "liberation," they do refer to it as a pilgrimage from "sin" to "holiness" or "grace" and therefore "salvation." And these words are functional equivalents in some ways. For many generations, at any rate, Christian parents made sure that their children read John Bunyan's allegorical classic about Christian life, *The Pilgrim's Progress* (first published in 1678). The idea that life in the familiar world is a journey between life in prenatal and postmortem worlds, in fact, has been very common throughout the world. This theme, as we say, reveals a significant difference, of course, between Eastern and Western religions. Eastern religions see the journey as a cyclical one, and Western religions see it as a circular one (but not a linear one, which is secular).

18 Diane Rae Schulz, "Spiraling in to the Center and out to the Future: Reading Mary Daly," *Awakened Woman* (undated), www.awakened woman.com/daly.htm (accessed 17 October 2006).

19 Daly, *Pure Lust: Elemental Feminist Philosophy* (Boston: Beacon Press, 1984).

20 Daly with Jane Caputi, *Websters' First New Intergalactic Wickedary of the English Language*.

21 Schulz, "Spiraling," 3.

22 Daly, *Beyond*, 4.

23 Daly, *Wickedary*.

24 One obvious example, at least to Westerners, would be Jesus. Over and over again in the New Testament, he tells followers to rethink traditional assumptions, sometimes by going one step further and sometimes by affirming the very opposite: "You have heard that it was said, 'An eye for an eye and a tooth for a tooth.' But I say to you, Do not resist one who is evil" (Matthew 5: 38–39). Other leaders go much further. Instead of claiming merely that disciples should reform traditional ways, which had been inadequate, they claim that disciples should repudiate traditional ways even though they had indeed been adequate and even holy. The act of doing so, of reversing the moral order, becomes a religious end in itself. This was characteristic of a Jewish messianic movement of the eighteenth century. Jacob Frank required followers to accept the doctrine of purification through transgression. People did not repent, he believed, because they did not feel guilty enough. And they did not feel guilty enough, because they had not sinned often enough. To solve that problem, people would have to embrace sin by actively disobeying every one of the commandments – including the ones that prohibited fornication, say, or incest. The orthodox rabbis were appalled, of course, and excommunicated all Frankists (who found refuge, if they agreed to abandon Frankist antinomianism, in the Catholic Church).

25 Daly, *Outercourse*.

26 Daly's first confrontation occurred after publication of *The Church and the Second Sex*. Some people were wildly enthusiastic; others were less than amused. Boston College announced that it would not renew her contract. It was paying her to teach Catholic theology, after all, not to attack it. But popular support along with a protest by the students (all of whom were male) convinced the college to relent. Daly became a tenured professor. Twenty-five years later, she faced a similar problem, this time due to her policy of not admitting male students to her classes. Eventually one threatened to sue the college. According to the administration, Daly agreed to retire. According to Daly, she agreed to no such thing. They settled the case out of court, and Daly left the college. We consider it worth noting here that Daly's policy has found supporters among mainstream academics. Consider the following statement from Harvey Cox of Harvard Divinity School, author of *The Secular City*: "I cannot believe that the real issue here is about a few classes that are open only to women ... After two decades of relentless gender leveling in higher

education, everyone now recognizes that some women (and men) learn
certain things better in gender-specific situations" (Brian Carnell,
"Regardless of Sex: Mary Daly and the Return of 'Separate but Equal,'"
Equity Feminism (21 September 1999): 2, www.equityfeminism.com/
print/mary_ daly_001.html [accessed 7 January 2007]). Has anyone
tested Cox's principle? When male professors bar women from classes on
male psychology, say, then Cox would have a point about "gender-level-
ing." So far, we are aware of no one who has tried to do that.

27 Paul Tillich, *Systematic Theology*, vol. 1 (Chicago: University of Chicago
   Press, 1951), 155. For the direct link between Daly and Tillich, see Lois
   Gehr Livezey, review of *Beyond God the Father* by Mary Daly, *Journal
   of Religion* 55, no. 4 (October 1975): 478.

28 Published in 1998.

29 Published in 2006.

30 Daly, *Lust*, ix.

31 Daly, quoted in Bridle, "No Man's Land," 5.

32 Again: "As Valerie Solanas lucidly points out: 'The male likes death – it
   excites him sexually and, already dead inside, he wants to die'" (Daly,
   Gyn/Ecology, 352). In that case, apparently, Solanas had a perfectly
   good reason for trying to murder Andy Warhol. He wanted to die anyway. In that case, moreover, Daly has a perfectly good reason for wanting to decimate the male population. They want to die anyway. The
   implication, of course, is that they had it coming. This is surely the
   "logic" of many murderers and mass murderers.

33 Valerie Solanas, SCUM *Manifesto*, with an introduction by Vivian Gornick
   (London: Olympia Press, 1971).

34 Daly, quoted in Bridle, "No Man's Land," 3.

35 Ibid., 6.

36 Ibid., 7.

37 Ibid., 4.

38 Ibid., 9.

39 Ibid. Wittig was a French radical lesbian philosopher; Daly paraphrased
   the English translation, "There was a time when you were not a slave,
   remember that. You walked alone, full of laughter, you bathed bare-
   bellied. You say you have lost all recollection of it, remember ... you say
   there are no words to describe it, you say it does not exist. But remember.
   Make an effort to remember. Or, failing that, invent" (*Les Guerilleres*,
   translated by David Le Vay [New York: Avon, 1971], 89). Interestingly,
   many goddess ideologues have quoted this passage. See Carol P. Christ,
   "Why Women Need the Goddess: Phenomenological, Psychological, and

Political Reflections," in *The Politics of Women's Spirituality*, edited by
Charlene Spretnak (Garden City, NY: Anchor Books, 1982); Margot
Adler, "New Traditions," *Beliefnet* (2006), www.beliefnet.com/story/29/
story_2909.html (accessed 12 December 2006).

40 Daly, *Quintessence*, 180.

41 Ibid., 88–9.

42 Ibid., 3.

43 Ibid., 66.

44 Daly, *Lust*, xii.

45 Ibid., xi.

46 Ibid., x–xii.

47 Ibid., 87.

48 Daly, *Quintessence*, 11.

49 Ibid., 185,

50 Ibid., 11.

51 Daly; quoted in Bridle, "No Man's Land," 3.

52 Ibid., 4.

53 Perennial philosophy posits the existence of universal truths that all people at all times have recognized. First used during the Renaissance, the
term was taken up again by Gottfried Leibniz in the eighteenth century,
and Aldous Huxley popularized it in the twentieth. It remains popular,
appearing directly or indirectly in the works of authors such as Huston
Smith and Karen Armstrong. Here are some basic principles: (1) The
material world is a shadow of some higher spiritual one; (2) the material
body is likewise the shadow of a higher spiritual one – that is, the soul,
spirit, or intellect; and (3) all people are capable of intuiting these truths,
and the goal of all religions is to help them do so.

54 Daly, *Quintessence*, 182.

55 Ibid., 230.

56 Ibid., 6.

57 Ibid., 183.

58 Ibid., 181.

59 The *merkhavah* tradition of Judaism might have originated during the
Greco-Roman period, but we have records of it only from the period following Rome's destruction of the temple in Jerusalem. Because Jews
could no longer make physical pilgrimages to a terrestrial structure (at
least not in connection with an active cult), some began to make spiritual
journeys to cosmic structures. These mystics meditated in order to experience the closeness of God (but not necessarily to unite with God) and
draw divine powers back to earth. At first, they meditated on a visionary

passage, Ezekiel 1: 4–26, in which the prophet sees cherubim drawing the four-wheeled divine "chariot" (*merkhavah*); later mystics have meditated on Hebrew letters in various combinations. By doing so, in any case, they pass in altered states of consciousness through a mystical landscape of various (usually seven) heavens. Guarding each are angels, seraphim, or other supernal beings; encircling each are flames and lightning. After reaching the final heaven, mystics pass through various (usually seven) supernal palaces and eventually, in the final palace, reach a divine image (God's glory, say, or an archangel) seated on the throne of God and surrounded by angelic hosts singing God's praise.

60 Lindsay Van Gelder, "A Yahoo's Guide to Mary Daly," review of *Gyn/Ecology* by Mary Daly, *Ms*, February 1979, 40.

61 Virginia R. Mollenkott, "Against Patriarchy," review of *Gyn/Ecology* by Mary Daly, *Christian Century*, 11 April 1979, 417.

62 Sexton, "Nags," 23.

63 Bridle, "No Man's Land," 8.

64 An observation by Katherine K. Young, who was there.

65 Manfred Hauke, *God or Goddess?: Feminist Theology: What Is It? Where Does It Lead?* (San Francisco: Ignatius Press, 1995); he refers to the dictionary on page 78.

66 Catherine Madsen, "The Thin Thread of Conversation: An Interview with Mary Daly," *Cross Currents* (2000): 2, www.crosscurrents.org/madsenfoo.htm (accessed 15 August 2007); originally published in *Cross Currents* 50, no. 3 (fall 2000).

67 The Daly event was so exuberant that it ended late, which meant inconvenience to those involved in the next event. Participants in that event, black womanists, complained that Daly and her entourage were using their racial privilege as white women – Daly and her colleagues were all white – to upstage black women.

68 Carol S. Anderson and Jennifer Rycenga, "Mary Daly: Grand Agitator and Revolting Hag," introduction to *Feminist Theology* 24 (May 2000): 9–10.

69 Ibid., 10.

70 Mary E. Hunt, "Future Visions: Response to Mary Daly," *Feminist Theology* 24 (May 2000): 23.

71 Jennifer Rycenga, "Passionate Struggle Is Not an Intuition: An Argument and Appreciation for Mary Daly," *Feminist Theology* 24 (May 2000): 31.

72 Schulz, "Spiraling," 4–5.

73 Ibid., 1.

74 Carter Heyward, "Rubyfruit Tangles: Response to Mary Daly," *Feminist Theology* 24 (May 2000): 20.

75 Schulz, "Spiraling," 4.
76 Van Gelder, "Yahoo's Guide," 42.
77 Ibid., 42.
78 Daly discusses the horrors that men have inflicted on women, what she
    calls collectively the "sado-ritual syndrome": Indian suttee, Chinese
    foot-binding, African female-genital mutilation, European witch-burning,
    and American gynecology (Daly, *Gyn/Ecology*, 28). By the 1990s, Hindu
    scholars were criticizing her views of India women in general and of sut-
    tee in particular (Sharada Sugirtharajah, "Hinduism and Feminism,"
    Journal of Feminist Studies in Religion 18, no. 2 [fall 2002] and Renuka
    Sharma and Purushottama Bilimoria, "Where Silence Burns: Sati (Suttee)
    in India: Mary Daly's Gynocritique, and Resistant Spirituality," in *Femi-
    nist Interpretations of Mary Daly*, edited by Sarah Lucia Hoagland and
    Marilyn Frye [University Park: Pennsylvania State University Press,
    2000], 322–48). They have criticized Daly's reliance on Katherine
    Mayo's ahistorical writings in *Mother India* (1927; reprint, New York:
    Greenwood Press, 1969), her essentialism, her over-determinism, her
    polemicism, and her globalizing ethical critique that avoided the context
    – especially the economic, political, social, and cultural factors that have
    contributed to the phenomenon. They were especially annoyed that Daly
    had ignored not only major improvements for the women of modern
    India but also the virtual disappearance of suttee.
79 Anne Doherty, review of *Gyn/Ecology* by Mary Daly, *America*, 31 May
    1980, 466.
80 Mollenkott, "Against Patriarchy," 417.
81 Helen McNeil, "Hag-ography," review of *Gyn/Ecology* by Mary Daly,
    New Statesman, 4 April 1980, 514.
82 S.G. Daveney, "Problems with Feminist Theory: Historicity and the
    Search for Sure Foundations," in *Embodied Love: Sensuality and Rela-
    tionship as Feminist Values*, ed. P.M. Cooey, S.A. Farmer, and M.E. Ross
    (San Francisco: Harper and Row, 1987), 90.
83 Marsha A. Hewitt, *Critical Theory of Religion: A Feminist Analysis*
    (Minneapolis: Fortress Press, 1995), 140.
84 Daly, *Lust*, ix.
85 David Kirp, Mark Yudof, and Marlene Strong Franks, *Gender Justice*
    (Chicago: University of Chicago Press, 1985), 49.
86 Gearhart says that "we" must do several things to create and preserve a
    less violent world than the one that we have. Among them, number three,
    is that "the proportion of men must be reduced to and maintained at
    approximately ten percent of the human race." In other words, women
    must "decimate" men in the most literal sense of that word (Sally Miller

Gearhart, "The Future – If There Is One – Is Female," in *Reweaving the Web of Life: Feminism and Nonviolence*, ed. Pam McAllister (Philadelphia: New Society, 1982), 266. Here is Daly's response: "I think it's not a bad idea at all. If life is to survive on this planet, there must be a decontamination of the Earth. I think this will be accompanied by an evolutionary process that will result in a drastic reduction of the population of males. People are afraid to say that kind of stuff anymore" (Daly; quoted in Bridle, "No Man's Land," 11). Taking a cue from the Nazis, who used the same language in connection with Jews, Gearhart views men as germs or vermin. In that case, the final solution would be to exterminate all or most them. Daly is somewhat more refined, as it were, urging women merely to stand by and watch as "nature" does the dirty work.

87 Daly, *Lust*, x.
88 Daly, quoted in Bridle, "No Man's Land," 10.
89 Margaret Atwood, *Cat's Eye* (Toronto: McClelland and Stewart, 1988).
90 Atwood, quoted in Judith Timson, "Atwood's Triumph," *Maclean's*, 3 October 1988, 58.
91 Daly attacks *men*, all men, not merely patriarchy. "The courage to be logical – the courage to name – would require that we admit to ourselves that males and males only are the originators, planners, controllers, and legitimators of patriarchy. Patriarchy is the homeland of males; it is Father Land; and men are its agents ... The fact is that we live in a profoundly anti-female society, a misogynistic 'civilization' in which men collectively victimize women, attacking us as personifications of their own paranoid fears, as The Enemy. Within this society it is men who rape, who sap women's energy, who deny women economic and political power ... As a creative crystallizing of the movement beyond the State of Patriarchal Paralysis, this book is an act of Dispossession; and hence, in a sense beyond the limitations of the label anti-male, it is absolutely Anti-androcrat, A-mazingly Anti-male, Furiously and Finally Female" (Daly, *Gyn/Ecology*, 28).
92 Paul Nathanson and Katherine K. Young, *Spreading Misandry: The Teaching of Contempt for Men in Popular Culture* (Montreal: McGill-Queen's University Press, 2001), 247.
93 Nathanson and Young, *Spreading*, 20–48.
94 We discuss all this in both *Spreading Misandry* and *Legalizing Misandry: From Public Shame to Systemic Discrimination against Men* (Montreal: McGill-Queen's University Press, 2006).
95 Madsen, "Thin Thread," 2 of 12.

96 We discuss the difference between hatred and anger in *Spreading Misandry*, 229–31.

97 Directed by Arthur Hiller, 1975, based on the play by Robert Shaw, *The Man in the Glass Booth* (London: Chatto and Windus, 1967).

98 For two thousand years, Jews had no state and therefore no army. They reinterpreted their ancient military heroes accordingly. King David, for instance, became a poet. Even the Lord of Hosts became a celestial rabbi. Not all Jews avoided violence during those centuries. During the early twentieth century, for instance, some American Jews – Bugsy Siegel, Meyer Lansky, and a few others – turned to organized crime. But they were anomalies. Fear of anti-Semitism, apart from anything else, prompted most Jews to avoid anything that would bring the community into disrepute.

99 Hunt, "Future Visions," 28.

100 No Jewish feminist to our knowledge has called for the decimation or elimination of men, although some might well like the idea of a world without men. Blu Greenberg was among the first to argue on legal – that is, halakhic – grounds for reforms within Orthodoxy that would foster greater participation by women in Jewish life; see *On Women and Judaism: A View from Tradition* (Philadelphia: Jewish Publication Society of America, 1981). Judith Plaskow, on the other hand, sees no point in reform and urges Jewish women to reject Judaism; see *Standing again at Sinai: Judaism from a Feminist Perspective* (New York: Harper and Row, 1990). Because most feminist ideologues leave Judaism, of course, they are unlikely to have any direct influence on Jewish women who remain loyal to Judaism (much less to instigate a religious revolution within Judaism). But other feminists have already made important contributions to Judaism – which is to say, non-Orthodox forms of Judaism in which secular arguments make sense. The Reform, Conservative, and Reconstructionist movements all ordain women to the rabbinate. Modern Orthodox communities have acknowledged the need to use *halakhah* as flexibly as possible – that is, without denying its traditional authority – to promote the active participation of women. Even "ultra-orthodox" (Hassidic and Heredi) communities now make sure that girls study Torah and Talmud in day-schools for girls such as Bais Yaakov (Sarah Schenirer, a seamstress in Crakow, began these schools in 1917).

101 Lois Gehr Livezey, review of *Beyond God the Father* by Mary Daly, *Journal of Religion*, 55, no. 4 (October 1975): 479.

102 Daly herself sometimes indicates that her religious terminology is more rhetorical than experiential. Like a good liberal, for instance, she argues

that the goddess is "a great metaphor for the unseen fabric of
connectedness" (cited by Doug King in "The Burning Time Revisited:
Rekindling the Fires of Radical Feminism," *Witherspoon* [1 November
2000]: 3, www.witherspoonsociety.org/mary_daly.htm [accessed 7 January 2007]).

103 The Roman Catholic Church has found it necessary to make public statements about subversion from within, a strategy that is more popular
among former Catholic feminists than former Protestant ones. This is
probably due partly to public perception. The Catholic Church, unlike
any Protestant one, has come to represent not only the most powerful
form of Christianity but also the most traditional and most historically
authentic one to both its supporters *and* its detractors. As a result, it is
the setting for almost every movie or television production that deals
with the supernatural. (It is no accident that books and movies such as
The Exorcist take place in Catholic contexts and appeal to millions of
non-Catholics and even non-religious people for precisely that reason.
Other Christian communities believe in, or at least do not deny, the possibility of demon possession. But would a comparable story set within the
context of a Methodist community, say, have the same impact? Hardly.)
With the highest symbolic profile by far, a vanquished or humiliated
Catholic Church would be the biggest victory for goddess ideologues or
even for other ideological feminists (let alone secularists). Many Christians who want to attack religion in general, therefore, zero in on Catholicism in particular.

Many Catholics who might otherwise leave in frustration, as Daly did,
stay on as "dissidents" in order to maximize the impact of *subverting*
such a powerful adversary from within. And the church is by no means
unaware of this strategy. The Catholic Resource Network, for instance,
makes a point of denying Catholic legitimacy to "Catholics" such as
Rosemary Ruether – which is to say, those who explicitly deny official
and basic teachings of the church. Ruether denies, among many other
things, that the eucharist mediates the body and blood of Christ (as distinct from symbols of them, which is a Protestant teaching) and that the
Bible is a repository of divine truth (as distinct from a collection of stories that Christians must "demythologize," which is a secular notion that
underlies all of liberal Protestantism). This website quotes Ruether in the
very act of subverting the church: "unless we manage to insert what we
are doing ... back into ... main institutional vehicles of ministry and community ... it will have no lasting impact ... [Feminist revolutionaries must]
stay in the Church and use whatever parts of it they can get their hands

on ... [In that way, they] will have far more impact, both on the Church and on the world ... than they could possibly gain if they separated from it" (Ruether, "Crises and Challenges of Catholicism Today," *America*, 1 March 1986, 152; quoted in Donna Steichen, *Ungodly Rage: The Hidden Face of Catholic Feminism* [San Francisco: Ignatius Press, 1991], 304); "Rosemary Radford Ruether Unmasked," EWTN Global Catholic Network [1994], www.ewtn.com/library/issues/ruether.txt [accessed 11 December 2006]). In other words, "reform" is a code word for revolution.

CHAPTER SEVEN

1 R.G. Edwards, "Chromosomal Abnormalities in Human Embryos," *Nature* 303, no. 5915 (1983): 283.
2 See, for example, Jeremy Cherfas and John Gribbin, *The Redundant Male: Is Sex Irrelevant in the Modern World* (New York: Pantheon Books, 1984); Cherfas was a guest on *Donahue* on 24 May 1985.
3 Marilyn French, *Beyond Power: On Women, Men, and Morals* (New York: Summit Books, 1985).
4 The word "evil" was for many centuries used in connection with the Devil: transcendent evil personified. Everyone knows what the word "evil" means, but it has come for various reasons to sound archaic in secular circles (though not quite as archaic as "wickedness," a synonym familiar from early translations of the Bible). That is because its original religious usage does not correspond to secular ways of thinking about the human condition.

Christians, for instance, have traditionally understood evil in ontological terms. Among Western Christians, sin is ultimately the result not of a wrong choice but of an ontological state, Original Sin, which each generation since Adam and Eve passed on to the next. (Everyone has periodic access to grace through the sacraments and to ultimate salvation through Christ, of course, but everyone remains a "sinner," nonetheless, and therefore in need of ultimate salvation.) Many Christians have understood evil in anthropomorphic terms too, personifying it as the Devil, Satan, Lucifer, Beelzebub, or whatever. In the past, moreover, many Christians believed that the Devil was represented or even incarnated by his – always his, by the way, never her – earthly agents: infidels (such as Jews or Muslims) or heretics (such as the witches). Christians do believe that they can resist evil effectively but not that they can fully and finally overcome it before the return of Christ and the advent of God's Kingdom. Jews have traditionally believed that all people since Adam and Eve have been sinful but not because of Original Sin. In any situation, people are free to choose the good inclination instead of the evil inclination; however, history and experience indicate that everyone makes the wrong choice on at least some occasions. Sin is an existential reality for everybody, in other words, but not an ontological one (although, for practical purposes, the Jewish notion is very similar to the Christian one).

Since the eighteenth century, our society has come to rely increasingly on a belief in what we now call "progress." Many people have replaced the notion of divine providence, for instance, with that of scientific or technological progress. Through education and humanism, utopians believe, intelligent citizens can create a truly and thoroughly (or "systemically") good society. In other words, they can eliminate evil within the present world order of time and space. Consequently, they are uncomfortable with reminders of the fact that social engineering and even political revolution have so far proven *unable* to eliminate evil. Even reading the daily newspaper raises disturbing questions about the continued presence of malice and suffering in our midst. Moreover, people are uncomfortable with the moral implications of calling whole groups of people evil. This is due partly to the philosophical problem of ontological evil. On philosophical grounds, after all, it could be argued that no one can knowingly choose evil; those who do evil things must actually believe that they are doing something good, legitimate, or at least necessary in particular circumstances. The people who do evil things are deluded and dangerous, to be sure, but not innately evil. To be the latter would be to embrace the notion of evil for its own sake. This would be possible only for ontologically evil beings – that is, demonic or satanic ones.

In our time, many people are uncomfortable for additional reasons with the word "evil." This is due partly to the long and lamentable history of religious or ideological prejudice but also to the current political climate. Consider the requirements of international diplomacy. George W. Bush referred to Iran, Iraq, and North Korea as an "axis of evil." Earlier, Ronald Reagan had called the Soviet Union an "evil empire." Neither president said or even implied that all the people in those countries were evil, but the line between what they said and what people both at home and abroad might have understood was very fine. Calling foreign countries "evil" assaults their national pride, at any rate, which generates hostility.

Now consider the requirements of "political correctness." Many believe that calling domestic groups "evil" wounds their self-esteem and prevents their full participation in society. Underlying political correct-

ness, however, are two dubious assumptions. For one thing, forbidding
people to say ugly things is not the same as preventing them from thinking or believing those ugly things; it merely drives the latter underground.
Worse, those who resort to censorship apply it only to some people; they
consider others exempt on political or ideological grounds. Judging from
expressions of public outrage and demands for public apologies or the
firing of offenders, for instance, it is unacceptable to express prejudice
against women but acceptable to express prejudice against men. This
double standard has contaminated whatever benefit "political correctness" might have conferred.

In our time, moreover, people are uncomfortable with the word "evil"
because of pop psychology. They have found ways of persuading themselves that destructive behaviour (let alone the person who indulges in it)
is not really evil at all but something else, some anomaly that can be
fixed or "cured." Those who harm others, for example, might be "deviant" or "sick" people; they behave as they do because of their experiences as "under-achieving," "disadvantaged," or "abused" children. This
point of view might be appropriate in many cases, of course, but it does
not fully account for the experience of suffering due to malice.

People reject the notion of evil (or at least the word), because they
refuse to admit the existence of forces that they cannot explain in terms
of liberal philosophies and the social sciences – forces that they cannot
control, in other words, by means of social engineering and political ideologies. The fact remains that every society has acknowledged the persis-
tence and pervasiveness of evil. Explanations vary, of course, from one
society to another. Buddhists, for instance, believe that evil is the result of
ignorance and the desire for permanence in a world characterized by flux.
Some small-scale societies, on the other hand, believe that evil is the
result of malice on the part of witches or spirits. Our point here is that
evil, whether we like that word or not, is a universally recognized problem of the human condition (although religions teach that people can
either transcend evil or can restore an underlying good).

To the extent that "evil" retains its ontological associations, it is surely
dangerous when applied exclusively to specific individuals or communities. The claim that some person or some group – a country, say, or a
community – is "evil," for instance, is an ontological claim. It is one
thing to say that people or groups sometimes *believe* in evil ideas or *do*
evil things but another thing entirely to say that they *are* evil. In that
case, we would be morally obliged to destroy them root and branch without considering for a moment any complexity or ambiguity.

The obvious test case would involve Adolf Hitler. If anyone seems to deserve a place in some ontologically evil pantheon, it would surely be the original and ultimate Nazi. But we reject the idea that even Hitler was an evil person – that is, *metaphysically* evil. He was a lamentably ordinary person who, for whatever reasons, held evil ideas and did evil things. Because he was neither an automaton nor a transcendent being, in other words, he could make moral choices and thus be a moral agent. Otherwise, we could hardly hold him morally accountable for anything. The same reasoning applies to the Nazi state, which included people who supported its ideology, people who were indifferent to it, people who rejected it, people who passively resisted it, and people who actively fought against it. The supreme irony, in fact, would be to demonize all Germans, either during or after the Nazi period, in the same way that the Nazis demonized all Jews. We can acknowledge the existence of evil as part of the human condition, in short, without claiming or even implying that is *incarnate* as specific people or groups of people.

In this context, Mahatma Gandhi's approach is instructive. Gandhi cautioned his supporters not to demonize the British as either individuals or a class. He blamed the imperial system. At the heart of *ahimsa* was not only non-violent action, after all, but also non-violent thought. This meant avoiding any kind of hostility. Gandhi thus required Indians to oppose colonial rule but also to see the British as "brothers" and "sisters," not alien others. He was so successful in bringing about change without generating hatred or violence that he was honoured, while visiting England, even by those who had lost their jobs due to the Indian boycott of British goods.

5 In connection with this, Susanne Heine raises an interesting question: What if the biblical tradition had focused on a mother goddess instead of a father god? "Let us ... take up the remarks of many women who say that their unhappy experiences with their physical father got in the way of their access to a heavenly father, but they could have trust in a heavenly mother ... In the course of the feminist revolution women have discovered their problems with their physical mothers, which are worked out less in open violence than through subterranean psychological pressure, yet prove just as great a burden in adult life" (Heine, *Christianity and the Goddess: Systematic Criticism of a Feminist Theology* [London: SCM Press, 1988], 30). She refers to such common problems as the manipulation of guilt: "Feminists ... make men and fathers responsible for damaging mothers but which comes first, the chicken or the egg? ... Women with bad experiences of their fathers may be helped by the

mother in heaven; women with bad experiences of their mothers may be helped by the father in heaven. Again, it was in a conversation with women after a lecture that I heard one of them say: 'If God is a mother, I'm scared of the resurrection.' Neither the phenomenological selection of feminine features of the biblical God nor the historical-critical quest for the place where these features arose, nor recourse to human experiences of parents, seem to me to take us further. If one reflects on the terrifying variety of possibilities of violence between parents and children, then the 'disembodied' and transcendent conception of God as 'wholly other' which is so reviled by feminists takes on power to release us: 'Thank God' that God is different from us human beings!'" (31).

6 One has only to think of what happened during the utopian experiments of France, Russia, and (Nazi) Germany.

7 For example, see Judy Rebick, *Ten Thousand Roses: The Making of the Feminist Revolution* (Toronto: Penguin Canada, 2005).

8 Katherine K. Young, introduction to *Feminism and World Religions*, edited by Arvind Sharma and Katherine K. Young (Albany: State University of New York Press, 1999), 14.

9 See, for example, Jill Watts, *God, Harlem U.S.A.: The Father Divine Story* (Berkeley: University of California Press, 1992) and Robert Weisbrot, *Father Divine* (New York: Chelsea House, 1992).

10 Young, "Postscript," *Feminism and World Religions*, 295.

11 See Paul Nathanson and Katherine K. Young, *Spreading Misandry: The Teaching of Contempt for Men in Popular Culture* (Montreal: McGill-Queen's University Press, 2001) and Paul Nathanson and Katherine K. Young, *Legalizing Misandry: From Public Same to Systemic Discrimination against Men* (Montreal: McGill-Queen's University Press, 2006).

12 See Mary Daly, *Beyond God the Father: Toward a Philosophy of Women's Liberation* (Boston: Beacon Press, 1973), 19. See also Patricia Lynn Reilly, *A God Who Looks Like Me: Rediscovering a Woman-Affirming Spirituality* (New York: Ballantine Books, 1995).

13 Secularity is a characteristic feature, a defining feature, of both modernity and postmodernity. Feminists who join the goddess movement, however, base their whole way of thinking on a peculiar mix of modernism and postmodernism. These women are modern in the sense of relying on critical scholarship (when the latter serves their own purposes). But modernists reject religion, because they cannot verify the sacred in scientific terms. These women are postmodern, on the other hand, in the sense of rejecting the conclusions of modernism. But postmodernists reject

religion, because the sacred is by definition a "privileged" category, and
the whole point of postmodernism is to reject any kind of "privileged discourse." Goddess ideologues are probably involved for secular (political)
reasons rather than religious ones. They might be religious, because
compartmentalization is one way of adjusting religion to modernity (and
postmodernity); some people do manage to isolate the experience of religion from every other aspect of life. But even that is unlikely in the goddess movement, which claims that the goddess is an *integrating* factor.

14 One front for ideology is civil religion. This consists of symbolic acts and
words, sanctioned by the state, that give public expression to national or
communal identity. One feature of the civil religion in our society is the
current prevalence of "political correctness" in general and its official
endorsement of "diversity" or "pluralism" in particular. Given this atmosphere, even the most radical claims or plans acquire both credibility with
the public and support from the state. After all, who would (dare to)
deny anyone the right to make any demand on behalf of any group that
defines itself as oppressed? In theory, that sounds fine. Why not expand
democracy to include all groups? In practice, it presents a very important
problem. We suggest that both feminist ideologues and goddess
ideologues exploit the rhetoric of civil religion – expressed in our time,
once again, by words such as "diversity" and "pluralism" – as a publicly
and officially respectable front for their own purposes. This rhetoric
undermines the ability or willingness to think critically – that is, to subject the claims or plans of political groups to moral or intellectual scrutiny on the same basis. Society thus allows or even encourages these
feminists, for instance, to say what people would otherwise consider preposterous or outrageous; they ridicule anyone who disagrees. With opponents silenced not by secret police but by public opinion and sometimes
by legal action, feminist ideologues are free to enter and eventually dominate the public square. Ironically, this double standard defeats the very
"diversity," or "pluralism," that civil religion enshrines.

The academic community's very own civil religion – postmodernism –
provides another front for ideology. (See Nathanson and Young, *Spreading*, 194–233.) Postmodernism, ironically, denies the ability of thought to
describe the world with any significant level of objectivity. Instead, this
ideology presents us with subjective – and politically motivated – "discourses." But is some objectivity not better than no objectivity at all?
Postmodernists insist that openly embracing radical subjectivity is prefer-
able to "hiding" behind the illusion of perfect objectivity (even though no
modern scholar would claim the attainment of perfect objectivity). And

academic ideologues agree. Why? Because of a tacit agreement that postmodernists will refrain from taking postmodernism to its logical conclusion of "deconstructing" their own ideologies along with all other "discourses." Not surprisingly, many postmodernists are among the most ardent ideologues. If we could rely on academic leadership in the struggle against ideology, political correctness might not matter so much. Unfortunately, many academics are among those who most vigorously demand political correctness – not only in the university but also in the public square.

15 Can we assume that the goddess movement is a specifically religious movement? No one can get into anyone else's mind, so no one can say with absolute certainty that these women are not having religious experiences. But goddess ideologues either say or imply that their goal is the empowerment of women (discussed in chapter 3). This suggests that the orientation is framed in secular, not religious terms. For the word "religion" to have any meaning for scholars in religious studies, however, it must have at least one defining feature. People associate many things, both historically and cross-culturally, with religion: rituals, myths, ethics, laws, and so on. But one characteristic is the *sine qua non* of religion, what all religions have in common, no matter how different they are in other respects. This is what Mircea Eliade and many others have called "the sacred," or "holiness." To experience the sacred is to experience some other level of reality. This experience has *no purely psychological or other counterpart*. It is not reducible to an experience that could be described in purely emotional or cognitive terms. It is *sui generis*, says Eliade, and thus ineffable. Therefore, it is an experience that no one can legitimate or even describe adequately in secular terms.

By saying that, we are rejecting reductive definitions of religion. For Emile Durkheim, the sacred was really nothing more than the worship of our own societies, the glorification of our own values expressed in cosmic terms. For Freud, on the other hand, it was the propitiation of our own darker selves, the projection of our own fears onto a cosmic plane. And for Marx, it was a way to legitimate our own greed (or, at any rate, that of the ruling classes).

16 By allying themselves politically with oppressed minority groups, they must take these other needs and problems seriously. Ideologically, however, they are committed to the idea that women are the *original* and *archetypal* oppressed group; other manifestations of oppression are derivatives of sexism – by which they refer specifically to misogyny, not misandry. They support more general causes too. But these are human or

planetary problems, not women's problems and therefore have ideological value only to the extent that they demonstrate some innate moral sensitivity of women.

17 See this chapter, note 12.

18 Sexism, like racism, is hatred for a biologically defined group of people.

19 We have discussed these problems – trying to condone, justify, and trivialize misandry – at great length elsewhere; see Nathanson and Young, *Legalizing Misandry*, 215–17; 330–9.

20 By definition, monotheism allows only one god or goddess. At the elite level in Western religion, this deity ultimately transcends both maleness and femaleness. At the popular level, that is not always the case. The dominant imagery, at any rate, has been male. Those who would prefer the dominance of female imagery, therefore, must turn to a goddess. *When they do so in connection with the dualistic sub-tradition* that has crept into Western religion – it has surfaced in Manichaeism, Marxism, Romanticism, and most recently feminism – the result is misandry.

21 Included in "culture" is religion. This is not a theological statement, which would be beyond our competence as academics, but an empirical statement that relies on historical evidence. Our point is not that God created all people in the divine image and thus as equals, for instance, but rather that this is what millions of Christians, Jews, and Muslims believe.

22 You could argue, as many have under the rubric of "complementarity," that men and women are different but equal – that both sexes make distinct contributions to society and are therefore of equal value to society. Our point here is that this argument is a cultural mechanism; it is not self-evident. In fact, many people would now deny it or even denounce it as a way of reasserting traditional gender roles.

23 Betty Friedan, *The Feminine Mystique* (New York: Norton, 1963).

24 For a discussion of some problematic aspects of goddess worship, see Mary Jo Weaver, "Who Is the Goddess and Where Does She Get Us?" *Journal of Feminist Studies in Religion* 5, no. 1 (1989): 58–9.

25 Natalie K. Watson makes the same point: "Daly denies the church all empowering potential for women," she writes, "and views the church mainly as an institution, the primary purpose of which is to destroy women and to jeopardize women's liberation. This essentially denies centuries of women's history within the church and attempts to replace women's existing traditions within the church with an ideal of women's sisterhood that bears the same potential to be transformed into either destructive anarchy or a restrictive institution like the patriarchal church.

Daly's concept of 'sisterhood' remains essentially disembodied and obsessed with the destructive forces of patriarchy which attack women's bodies, so that it overlooks the transformative presence of women's bodies embodying the body of Christ" (*Introducing Feminist Ecclesiology* [Cleveland: Pilgrim Press, 2002], 103).

26 Nathanson and Katherine, *Spreading*, 61.

27 We already have sperm and egg banks. On the research horizon, moreover, are not only technologies that would enable women to reproduce without men (such as parthenogenesis) but also those that would enable men to reproduce without much participation by women (by means of artificial wombs, for instance, or having fetuses implanted in their abdomens).

28 Agricultural surpluses led not only to urbanization but also to social stratification according to literacy and other forms of specialization. The few elite men who used their minds to govern or to plan and administer massive building or irrigation projects – kings, court officials, high priests and scribes, temple managers – now had much higher status than the masses of men who merely used their bodies to plough the fields. The male body as such, in other words, no longer conferred on elite men any status in daily life. It still mattered – and would continue to matter from then on – in only one context: war. A few elite men led the others on raids or in battles; the masses of men, though, became the ancient equivalent of cannon fodder. Meanwhile, to support the legitimacy of their new intellectual functions, elite men found ways of reinforcing the social gap between themselves and others. One of these was to prevent women (and low-status men) from doing what high-status men did. High-status women were now precisely those who did not have to work in the fields and could therefore live primarily within the private sphere of home. (This did not make them housewives in the modern sense, though, because their tasks included, as well as the tending of their own children, the administration of households that were very large by modern standards.)

29 For an excellent summary of recent scientific studies on the distinctive and necessary features of fatherhood, ones that should (but seldom do) command public respect and therefore legal incentives, see W. Bradford Wilcox, "Reconcilable Differences: What Social Sciences Show about the Complementarity of the Sexes and Parenting," *Touchstone* 18, no. 9 (November 2005), www.toucstonemag.com/archives/article.php?id= 18-09-032-f (accessed 21 December 2006).

1 This would apply in most ways to Jews no less than Christians, even
   though Jews never used the biblical text to articulate doctrines such as
   Original Sin or the Fall. Jews have never believed that all people are
   innately contaminated by the disobedience of their primeval ancestors,
   whether that of both Adam and Eve (as the biblical story clearly states)
   or primarily that of Eve (as some post-biblical traditions had interpreted
   it). For Jews, in other words, the story has always been descriptive (all
   people disobey God from time to time by freely choosing evil over good)
   and not prescriptive (all people must be cleansed from an ontological
   stain that Adam and Eve transmitted to all succeeding generations,
   according to Christians such as St Augustine, by placing their faith in
   Christ as the New Adam).

2 As we have already pointed out, dualism entered Western religion during
   the biblical period in connection with a historical struggle between "us"
   (represented by the monotheistic Hebrew, or Israelite, community) and
   "them" (represented by polytheistic communities such as the Egyptians,
   Canaanites, Babylonians, Assyrians, and so on). But this mentality
   became much more pervasive and deeply embedded during the post-biblical period. Persian Zoroastrianism exerted a heavy influence on the
   Greco-Roman world, which was where Jews and Christians lived, in connection with a cosmic, or metaphysical, struggle between holiness (especially closely regulated sexual activity or sexual abstinence) and sin
   (especially succumbing to illicit sexual activities). This dualistic mentality
   fostered explicit suspicion of or hostility toward not only women but also
   femaleness. (It fostered implicit contempt for men too for succumbing so
   easily to sexual temptation.) The same dualistic mentality is pervasive
   even now among those like the goddess ideologues who glorify femaleness and demonize maleness.

3 Reform in this sense would by no means be a modern (and therefore secular) innovation. Anyone can see precedents; the Bible records not one
   but several reform movements. One of these was the deuteronomic one
   (in which Josiah, king of ancient Judah, used a newly discovered scroll,
   now called Deuteronomy, to legitimate many religious changes), but the
   prophetic one is of most interest here. The biblical prophets explicitly
   rejected the dualistic premise that evil is something "out there" and characteristic only of "those others." On the contrary, they promoted the
   un-dualistic premise that evil is often "in here" and therefore just as characteristic of "us" as it is of "them." With precisely this premise in mind,

they challenged their own kings to acknowledge the moral standard that God had revealed.

4 Riane Eisler, *The Chalice and the Blade: Our History, Our Future* (San Francisco: HarperSanFrancisco, 1995), xviii.

5 Eisler, *Chalice*, xix.

6 Ibid., 66.

7 Ibid., xxiii, 149.

8 We discuss "honorary women" in both *Spreading Misandry* (8 and 247) and *Legalizing Misandry* (214, 217, and 472–3).

9 Cynthia Eller, *The Myth of Matriarchal Prehistory: Why an Invented Past Won't Give Women a Future* (Boston: Beacon Press, 2000), 181–2.

10 Ibid., 187.

11 Ibid.

12 Ibid., 182.

13 Ibid., 188.

14 Rosemary Radford Ruether, *Goddesses and the Divine Feminism: A Western Religious History* (Berkeley: University of California Press, 2005), 308.

15 Ibid.

16 Both theologians and academics have always found it hard to distinguish religious reform from religious revolution. The Protestant Reformation, for instance, actually amounted to a revolution. But the Catholic response, the Counter-Reformation, did not. "History is filled with examples in which reform has resulted in revolution, which often means the formation of new religious communities. In the West today, many Protestant groups have made major reforms to improve the status of women ... Some Catholics believe that their own church has not and probably will not go far enough. Several solutions are possible: to forget about religion altogether; to try and force the church to adopt their point of view; and to do what Christian dissenters have always done: form their own churches. Religious affiliation is no longer dictated by the state. People are free to choose not only non-Catholic forms of Christianity, moreover, but any other religion. This can be very difficult, because of family or community loyalties. But those Christians who no longer agree with their religious community have always made choices of this kind" (Katherine K. Young, "Postscript," in *Feminism and World Religions*, edited by Arvind Sharma and Katherine K. Young [Albany: State University of New York, 1999], 294).

But not everyone is radical enough to adopt any variant of that all-or-nothing position. Many religious people, possibly most, are willing

to advocate reforms within the contexts of both theological and cultural
continuity. They could examine "the merits of change in light not only of
their own traditions but also of scholarship (based on science, cross-cultural studies, or whatever else might be academically relevant). With
these things in mind, the need for change could be reassessed from
within. If the demand for change has merit, insiders would have to deter-
mine what kinds of change could be instituted without destroying their
tradition's identity ... At the end of the day, any community might
decide, even if the ethical merit of change is clear, that the degree of
change required could not be incorporated; as in all ethical dilemmas,
choices must be made. Some people might leave the community, seeking
justice elsewhere. Others might reaffirm the priority of group solidarity"
(ibid., 296).

17 In some cases, the proposed changes are profound but not alienating to
most people. Consider the seamless transition from biblical religion to
rabbinic Judaism, for example, or from Vedic religion to *bhakti* Hinduism. In other cases, the proposed changes are not only profound but also
alienating to most people in the larger community. Thus the community
expels the dissenters as heretics. Examples would include the expulsion of
Karaites from Judaism, say, or Bahais from Islam. In still other cases, the
proposed changes are not only alienating to the larger community but
also liberating to the dissenters. Both groups agree that they cannot rec-
oncile their differences and should not even try to do so. This leads to a
mutually acceptable but nonetheless unpleasant parting of the ways. One
obvious example would be what happened when the early Jewish Christians separated from the larger Jewish community. The fact is that some
reforms are so radical, so out of keeping with tradition (no matter how
flawed it might be), that most people cannot accept them without
destroying their own identities. In any case, dissenters within the larger
community become sects on their own. After a while, sects can become
large or influential enough to be considered distinct religions (see Young,
"Postscript," 294).

Because radical change in the name of reform has provoked major conflicts in the past, it should come as no surprise to find the same thing
happening today. This occurs when radical reforms threaten personal or
collective religious identities. As a result, we occasionally read of heresy
trials and excommunications – though not, fortunately, of hangings or
burnings.

18 We say this because religion, unlike citizenship, is now a voluntary matter. No one has to belong to this or that religious community. Anyone

can leave to join another community or not to join any. Those who take pride in their celebration of "diversity," moreover, have no obvious reason to insist that every religious community organize itself in precisely the same way. Leaving one community for another is never easy, and yet many people have done precisely that throughout history (especially Christian history) (see Young, "Postscript," 294–5).

19 The Hebrews did not necessarily invent monotheism. Either a little earlier or a little later, the Egyptians produced their own monotheistic revolution under Pharaoh Amenhotep IV. Under his new name, Akhenaton, he repudiated the traditional gods and goddesses with a single god: Aten. This meant, apart from anything else, the disestablishment of Egypt's many temples and therefore the emnity of its many priests. Akhenaton's successor revived the old religion and thus ended this experiment in monotheism.

20 We are referring to the fulfillment of a process, not an overnight change. At an early stage, the Hebrews probably acknowledged the existence of other gods but worshipped only one of them.

21 Jewish and Christian feminists agree with traditional theologians that gender attributes are ultimately inconsistent with divine ones – otherwise, they would not remain Jews or Christians – even though theologians have always tolerated these attributes as concessions to popular anthropomorphism. One solution has been to emphasize the few feminine attributes along with the masculine ones. Another solution, however, would be to eliminate all gender attributes, including the masculine ones. But this would mean rewriting liturgies and (among Christians) avoiding centuries of art and censoring scripture.

22 See, for example, David C. Geary, "Evolution of Fatherhood," in *Family Relationships: An Evolutionary Perspective*, ed. C. Salmon and T. Shackelford, 115–44 (New York: Oxford University Press, 2007). Geary includes an extensive list of references.

23 See E. Anthony Rotundo, *American Manhood: Transformations in Masculinity from the Revolution to the Modern Era* (New York: Basic Books, 1993).

24 Strictly speaking, the term "male monotheism" is inaccurate. And yet, modern and liberal theologians notwithstanding, the stubborn fact remains that many of the faithful – Jews, Christians, and Muslims – keep thinking of God as a masculine being (though not, at least not technically, as a male being). Is their embarrassing recalcitrance due entirely or even primarily to the familiar words of scripture and prayer (most of which, though not all, do indeed describe someone who acts more like a

father than a mother)? Or do those words themselves suggest a need – a legitimate need – that the ancients recognized in the transition from polytheism to monotheism?

APPENDIX

1 Religious worldviews include not only those of large-scale societies but also those of small-scale ones (such as the aboriginal peoples of Canada). The former, known as "world religions," include Zoroastrianism, Buddhism, Jainism, Hinduism, Sikhism, Confucianism, Taoism, Shinto, Judaism, Christianity, Islam, and Bahai.

2 The word "supernatural" refers to something beyond the natural order. It might refer to deities, ancestors, ghosts, and other beings, the true self, "non-duality," omnipresent vitality, a power, "emptiness," or simply the "unnamable." We can distinguish the supernatural from the natural in various ways (such as immanence within it) or deny its existence (if the material realm is an illusion). The pre-modern Chinese placed so much emphasis on family and daily life, for instance, that the supernatural – Heaven, Tao, or the ancestors – fell into the background (but did not completely disappear).

3 People can experience ineffable or transcendent experiences as eruptions into the everyday realm, or they can induce these by means of religious techniques.

4 There is a profound *difference* between the secular and the profane, which we will discuss below. For the time being, it is enough to say that the profane is the other side of the sacred; neither can exist without the other. The secular, on the other hand, is characteristic of modernity and recognizes neither the sacred nor the profane.

5 In common parlance, the word "myth" refers to propositions that are errors, lies, primitive scientific theories, or childish fantasies. In scholarly parlance, however, myths are symbolic stories – not propositions – about the human condition and its existential problems. Some are about ultimate origin and destiny (divine creators of the cosmos, primeval founders of the community, and so on). Others provide exemplary figures, human or animal, as guides to proper conduct. At first, people transmit them orally. Eventually, some societies transmit them in written form and even incorporate them into scripture.

6 Theologians produce doctrines, or beliefs, and sometimes organize these (often for liturgical purposes) as creeds. But religion itself *is not* synonymous with these secondary expressions of religion. Neither is "faith."

Christians, especially Protestants, do emphasize faith, by which they refer
not primarily to beliefs but to trust in God. But even their religion
involves a lot more than either personal faith or personal beliefs.

7 It would be hard to imagine any religion that has not expressed itself
through the arts. Even religions such as Judaism and Islam, which
explicitly oppose visual representations, have produced visual art. In fact,
we know about many religions mainly because of the artifacts that they
left behind. Art has now gone its own way, just as science and many
other cultural enterprises have, but it was once intimately linked with
religion.

Like "religion," "culture," and several other universal features of
human experience, experts have found it hard to define "art." It covers a
lot of territory. Complicating matters has been the avant-garde notion of
art that emerged in the late nineteenth century among radical painters –
those who rejected conventional styles (which meant rejection by those
who promoted them) – and has since become the standard definition in
the elite cultures of modern or modernizing societies. A work of visual
art, for instance, must (1) be *innovative* in some way; (2) clearly represent the *personal* vision of one individual and thus exemplify self-expres-
sion; and (3) involve either a *critique* of society or an *experiment* in
visual perception (art for art's sake). But this definition of art has several
serious disadvantages. For one thing, it has tended to make art esoteric
and therefore inaccessible to most people. Moreover, it excludes almost
all of Western art before the twentieth century and almost all non-Western art. Even though earlier periods in the history of both Western and
other cultures valued innovative works, for instance, they did not value
innovation as an *end in itself*; they merely valued superior realizations of
traditional goals (in the West, more effective access to the saints on icons,
or more effective imitations of natural forms). These traditional goals,
varying considerably from one culture to another, have included trans-
mitting information in symbolic form about the environment, glorifying
regimes or elite lineages, edifying viewers by encouraging them to con-
template moral, theological, or philosophical traditions, adding beauty to
everyday life, and so on. Finally, the avant-garde definition of art
excludes popular culture even in modern Western societies. From that
point of view, most movies and television shows are either "bad art" or
something other (and less worthy) than art. Even though the boundary
between "good art" and "bad art" is notoriously subjective, it is prefera-
ble to overly broad definitions (such as the one that would define the arts
simply as visual, literary, or musical forms of communication). From our

point of view, "good art" has (at the very least) a powerful effect on people; "bad art" has (at most) a weak effect.

8 Sources of authority include ancestors, religious leaders, scriptures, laws, custom, consensus, perception, inference, and so forth. When examining the source of religious authority, it is important not to remain at the most general level such as Christianity. Sub-traditions such as Roman Catholicism make their own adjustments. Roman Catholics acknowledge three sources of authority: scripture, tradition (teachings handed down by successors of the Apostles), and the church's *magisterium* (papal interpretation of scripture and tradition). For Quakers, on the other hand, the *meeting* has authority because of guidance from individual experience and scripture (and thus from the Holy Spirit), although some meetings place more emphasis on scripture than experience.

9 A group with strong boundaries might require formal conversion and expulsion. One with weak boundaries might offer informal affiliation, thus allowing several identities. The Chinese say, "A Confucian by day, a Taoist by night," for instance.

10 "New religions" are border phenomena, some falling into the religious category and others into the hybrid one. New Age religion is an eclectic movement. It originated in the late 1960s, although it had some antecedents: Western forms of esoteric religion such as gnosticism, kabbala, and theosophy; Hindu, Buddhist, Islamic and other mystical traditions; and aboriginal worldviews. Emphasizing personal experience under the rubric of "spirituality," advocates oppose conventional religious institutions, aligning themselves instead with Jungian or transpersonal psychology, environmentalism, alternative medicine, and feminism (including goddess ideology and other forms of neopaganism).

11 The word "secular" has a long history. In Latin, *saeculum* refers simply to the "world" of everyday life. For Roman Catholics, therefore, the "secular clergy" are neither indifferent nor hostile to religion; they simply live and work – as bishops, priests, and deacons – among laypeople in the parishes. The "regular clergy," by contrast, live according to a monastic rule (from the Latin *regulum*); they live and work in monasteries or convents and thus (at least to some extent) apart from laypeople. In popular parlance today, however, "secular" has taken on the connotation of "worldly" (as distinct from "otherworldly"); by extension, it has come to mean "indifferent or hostile to religion."

12 Nature includes human nature, of course, which is genetically programmed to produce culture.

13 Ninian Smart, *Worldviews: Cross-cultural Explorations of Human Beliefs* (New York: Scribner's, 1983) 53.

14 Charles Taylor, plenary address "Multiculturalism and Spirituality in a Secular Age" (Montreal, 23–26 September 2008).

15 Taylor defines modernization in connection with the rise of science and technology, industrialization, social and geographical mobility, the growth of mega cities, mass communication, economic globalization, and either the decline of rural culture or its transformation into something akin to urban culture.

16 Taylor, "Multiculturalism and Spirituality in a Secular Age."

17 One form of interaction between religion and politics produces "civil religion," a publicly affirmed symbolic system that celebrates the nation and therefore legitimates the nation-state. It might or might not coincide with specific traditional religions. The British civil religion clearly does. Presiding over it, after all, is an established religion: the Church of England. Its original political function, legitimating the monarchy and its political power, lapsed long ago due to the development of parliament. Its current function is not only to celebrate national continuity but also to legitimate religious tolerance. The American civil religion coincides with a specific religious tradition too, though not as explicitly as the British one. It originated in Europe as an intentionally vague form of Protestantism known as Deism. Most Americans found Deism acceptable as a unifying force in public life because it was compatible with more specifically Protestant (and even Catholic or Jewish) doctrines. Demographic changes due to massive immigration and secularization, however, now often require the abolition of even the vaguest references to God, the Bible, the Ten Commandments, and so on. The American civil religion's function is still to celebrate national unity but to do so more thoroughly than ever before, which explains the recent addition of Martin Luther King Day. The Canadian civil religion, which originated as a version of the British one (adapted to play, as it were, in Quebec), now relies not on an implicitly religious worldview but on an explicitly secular one known as "multiculturalism" (although it occasionally allows symbolic expressions of religions in the name of "diversity"). But civil religion occurs not only in the West (much less the modern West). In the past, Hindus, Buddhists, and Confucians ritually legitimated rulers and expected them to uphold those religious worldviews or more general symbol systems that legitimated religious tolerance.

18 Consider the civil religion of Nazi Germany. Every year in Nuremberg, the state celebrated Parteitag (Party Day). This took the form of a

religious festival (and pilgrimage for out-of-towners) with elaborate liturgical processions, bloodstained relics for use in consecrating new flags,
hymns such as the "Horst Wessel Lied," and the presence of Germany's
charismatic leader. Another civil religion emerged in communist countries
such as the Soviet Union and China. The Chinese version relied on elaborate liturgical processions, Mao's "little red book" as the functional
equivalent of scripture, and something like the charismatic leader's
apotheosis after death. Both civil religions used implicitly religious forms
(such as rituals) for explicitly secular functions (promoting political
ideologies).

19 Like states, ethnic communities often develop "civil religions." These too
might or might not coincide with traditional religions. One example
would be the hybrid Jewish "civil religion," which is explicitly secular
(associating Jewish identity not with the Torah but with the Nazi Holocaust and the State of Israel) but implicitly religious (with rabbis among
the communal leaders who preside over public ceremonies, often in synagogues, to commemorate the Holocaust and celebrate the State of Israel).
In itself, this is not rabbinic Judaism. Some participants are religious
Jews, but most are secular Jews.

20 Secularizing religious communities often maintain traditional symbols at
the explicit level, at least to some extent, but they may either reinterpret
or modify them in connection with modernity (or "relevance") at the
implicit level. Some liberal churches, for instance, focus very heavily
on secular activities such as social activism, community building, group
therapy, and so on (all of which are compatible with Christianity but
not religious per se). Some evangelical churches, on the other hand,
focus very heavily on self-realization or even prosperity. Non-Orthodox
Jews often focus on ethnicity (known as "Jewishness" or "Jewish
peoplehood").

21 Some secular feminists draw from their political movement both personal
and communal meaning, purpose, and identity. The result is a feminist
civil religion that combines explicit secularity (books, for instance, that
are either indifferent or hostile to religion as a "patriarchal" conspiracy
against women) and implicit religiosity (books that have taken on
quasi-canonical status, such as Betty Friedan's *The Feminine Mystique*,
or Simone de Beauvoir's *The Second Sex*). Some days have become the
functional equivalents of holy days (for example, 6 December in Canada,
commemorating Marc Lépine's murder of fourteen "feminists" in Montreal). Some events, moreover, have become the functional equivalents of
liturgies (such as memorial services on 6 December, which often rely on

fourteen candles in imitation of the six candles that Jews use to commemorate the Nazi Holocaust, and the distribution of pink ribbons as if they were communion wafers). And some places become the functional equivalents of pilgrimage sites (such as the park in Vancouver that honours Lépine's fourteen victims). The feminist civil religion overlaps with some national ones. Canada, for instance, gives official recognition to 6 December, often sending political leaders to its memorial services. By contrast, some forms of Wicca and "goddess religion" are explicitly religious (full-moon rituals or visits to ancient goddess shrines) but are implicitly secular (women's "empowerment").

22 Popular culture is a very broad category. One aspect of it is entertainment: productions such as movies and television shows. Under analysis, these reveal underlying patterns of thought and perception that have emerged directly from religious traditions. In the West, for instance, these productions are often about topics such as origin and destiny, good and evil, guilt and healing, coming of age, and the self-sacrifice of "Christ figures." Popular culture provides one way of bringing these topics into the public square, therefore, without breaking down the separation of church and state. To the extent that they express widespread worldviews – and they do – movies and television shows reflect hybrid worldviews. In many (but not all) ways, they do for secular societies, or ostensibly secular societies, what traditional stories do for religious ones.

Nathanson has discussed hybrid worldviews in connection with two case studies in the context of popular culture. One of them, *The Wizard of Oz* (Victor Fleming, 1939), is explicitly secular (containing no references at all, for instance, to God) but implicitly religious (recapitulating basic patterns of thought that originated in biblical religion). Nathanson refers specifically to Dorothy's "going home" and "growing up" in connection with the Jewish and Christian notion of returning to paradise. Not surprisingly, this movie has become deeply embedded in American culture; it is a "classic," not merely a "cult" movie. See Paul Nathanson, *Over the Rainbow: The Wizard of Oz as a Secular Myth of America* (Albany: State University of New York Press, 1991).

Another hybrid worldview, Nathanson argues elsewhere, spontaneously revealed itself dramatically after the death of Princess Diana. This phenomenon intertwined religious and secular features so closely that it is difficult to separate them. The funeral itself took place in St Paul's Cathedral and was therefore explicitly Christian. Other events were religious in a derived or historical sense. These included prayers addressed to Diana as if she were an established saint or even the Virgin Mary, setting up memorial shrines with flowers and candles, and making pilgrimages to her tomb at Althorp. On the secular side, however, was Diana's worldly life as a fashionable celebrity (albeit a charitable one). More important was (and is) the underlying content of this worldview: neo-Romanticism (the celebration of emotion as an end in itself), which remains prevalent due to the efforts of Oprah Winfrey and similar cultural authorities in connection with personal growth and New Age spirituality. See Paul Nathanson, "I Feel, Therefore I Am: The Princess of Passion and the Implicit Religion of Our Time," *Implicit Religion* 2, no. 2 (1999): 59–87.

Celia Rabinovitch, on the other hand, has studied hybrid worldviews in the context of elite culture. She shows how surrealism, an art movement that reached its height during the 1930s, focused attention on a state of mind that represses the rational; replacing it is the mysterious, the uncanny, the weird, the dreamlike – all of which are characteristic features of the sacred in some cultures. See Celia Rabinovitch, *Surrealism and the Sacred: Power, Eros, and the Occult in Modern Art* (Boulder, Col.: Westview Press, 2002).

23 Transient or virtual communities distinguish themselves from those of "organized" or "institutional" religions. The latter have always produced spirituality – private acts of piety or contemplation (as distinct from public ones) – and, in a more general sense, the search for meaning (both personal and communal). Many people today use the word "spirituality" to describe vaguely similar but ultimately secular activities (such as self-actualization in a purely psychological sense or ecological preservation in a purely material sense). These activities have become detached from (organized) religion, in other words, and re-attached, no matter how vaguely, to therapeutic or environmental movements – often via online chat groups. The resulting informal or virtual communities are explicitly secular in connection with psychological health or planetary rescue but implicitly religious in connection with peak experiences and finding the true self or recreating paradise on earth. The Transhumanists, for example, are explicitly secular (as neo-rationalists who glorify science as distinct from neo-romantics who glorify feeling) but implicitly religious (with their goal of eliminating death and thus achieving immortality).

Index

Abanes, Richard, 12
Abel, 195
abortion, 114–15, 306n72,
  314n175
Achtemeier, Elizabeth, 196–8,
  343n67
Adam. *See* Fall of Man; paradise
Adler, Margo, 99
Afrekete, 127
African religions, 66, 127
Africans, 291n79, 294n97
agriculture: and demography,
  300n28; and fertility, 193; and
  happiness, 49–50; and horticulture, 50, 74–7, 181; and iron
  plough, 38, 291–3n81; and literacy, 365n28; and natural environment, 49–50; and patriarchy,
  67; and religion, 183, 193; and
  sex, 291–3n81; and social stratification, 10, 74, 365n28; and
  specialization, 365n28; and state
  formation, 48–9, 75–7. *See also*
  pastoralism
Albigensians. *See* Cathars
Allende, Isabel, 5

Amerindian religions, 32–3, 126.
  See also Hopi religion; Zuni religion
Amish, 308n98
analytical psychology. *See* Jungian
  analysis
Anath: as fertility goddess, 193,
  289n52; and Jewish feminism,
  183; as local goddess, 56; as
  martial goddess, 70
Anatolia, 303–4n59
Anderson, Carol, 231
androcentrism, 76, 82–3, 249–56,
  264. *See also* essentialism;
  gynocentrism; men; misogyny
anger, 236. *See also* hatred
animal husbandry. *See* pastoralism
animals. *See* domestication of animals; hunting and gathering;
  neolithic art; paleolithic art;
  sexual imagery
anti-Catholicism, 6, 8
anti-Christ, 313n161
anti-Judaism. *See* Christian
  theology
anti-Semitism. *See* Jews

Durga, 70–1, 295n98
Durkheim, Emile, 363n15

Eastern Orthodoxy, 113, 184,
327n41, 345n84: and icono-
clasm, 9. *See also* Catholicism;
Protestantism
Ecclesiasticus, 188–9
ecofeminism: and authority, 172;
Chung on, 203; and dualism,
174; and essentialism, 174; and
goddess ideology, 149, 170,
174; and infiltration, 174; on
science and technology,
332–4n77; as word, 324n1. *See
also* environmentalism; Gaia;
goddess ideology; ideological
feminism; Sophianity
ecology. *See* ecofeminism; environmentalism
economic systems. *See* food production
Eden. *See* paradise
egalitarian feminism: and
environmentalism, 170; and
ideological feminism, 14, 15, 16,
56–9, 230–40, 268; and New
Age, 149. *See also* ideological
feminism; sexual equality
Egyptian religion, 369n19
Egyptians, 23, 56, 79–80, 303n55
Ehrenreich, Barbara, 38,
285–7n39, 288n45, 291n73,
294–5n98
Eisler, Riane: on antiquity, 25; and
dualism, 73; on Gimbutas, 73;
and goddess ideology, 3–4, 5,
233; on "gylanic" golden age, 3,
72; on matrilineality, 40; on
men, 36; and misandry, 36; on

patriarchal invaders, 73; and
scholarship, 262; on sex differences, 36
Eliade, Mircea, 22, 33, 28 1n1,
363n15
Elkins, Heather Murray, 212
Eller, Cynthia, 16, 55, 131–6,
316n189
ends and means. *See*
consequentialism; ideological
feminism
Engels, Friedrich, 25
Enlightenment, 163, 316n187
environmentalism, 149. *See also*
ecofeminism
envy. *See* sexual equality
equality. *See* Christian theology;
egalitarian feminism; hierarchy;
ideological feminism; Jewish theology; sexual equality
eschatology. *See* Christian theology; Jewish theology
essentialism, 51, 237–8
EST, 322n48
eternal return. *See* myth; paradise
eternity. *See* Christian theology;
history; Jewish theology; sacred
time
Eucharist, 113–14, 115, 165,
314n175. *See also* Renaissance
art
euthanasia, 314–315n178
Eve. *See* Fall of Man; paradise
evil, 4, 11, 357–60n4. *See also*
Christian theology; Fall of Man;
goddess ideology; goddess religion; Jewish theology; maleness;
men; witches
evolution: and harems, 35; and
infanticide, 290n66; and pair